FRONTIERS IN SOCIAL THOUGHT

FRONTIERS IN SOCIAL THOUGHT

Essays in Honor of Kenneth E. Boulding

Edited by

MARTIN PFAFF

International Institute for Empirical
Social Economics, Augsburg
and
University of Augsburg

1976

NORTH-HOLLAND PUBLISHING COMPANY
AMSTERDAM · NEW YORK · OXFORD

© NORTH-HOLLAND PUBLISHING COMPANY—1976

Library of Congress Catalog Card Number 75-23207
ISBN North-Holland 0 7204 3807 1
ISBN American Elsevier 0 444 10969 2

Publishers:
NORTH-HOLLAND PUBLISHING COMPANY
AMSTERDAM · NEW YORK · OXFORD

Sole distributors for the U.S.A. and Canada:
AMERICAN ELSEVIER PUBLISHING COMPANY, INC.
52 Vanderbilt Avenue
New York, N.Y. 10017

The contribution toward printing costs by Stifterverband für die Deutsche Wissenschaft is gratefully acknowledged

Library of Congress Cataloging in Publication Data
Main entry under title:

Frontiers in social thought.

At head of title: Festschrift.
1. Economics—Addresses, essays, lectures.
2. Boulding, Kenneth Ewart, 1910–   I. Pfaff,
Martin. II. Boulding, Kenneth Ewart, 1910–
HB171.F78   330   75-23207
ISBN 0-444-10969-2 (American Elsevier)

PRINTED IN THE NETHERLANDS

Acknowledgment

The editor wishes to acknowledge gratefully the advice and assistance of Professor Donald J. Montgomery (Michigan State University) who served as consulting editor on the Festschrift during his period as Guest Professor at the University of Augsburg and Guest Scholar at the International Institute for Empirical Social Economics.

Contents

Introduction
A tribute to Kenneth E. Boulding

A personal dedication

MARTIN PFAFF

To me Kenneth E. Boulding appears like a gem with many facets. It is indeed very hard to point to any one of these which adds greater lustre or by itself makes for his overall brilliance.

Above all I see in him a prototype of the man of the future, a true citizen of the world, an internationalist who moves freely from one part of the world to the other, being welcomed in each and making his imprint on all. He is also a prototype of the combination of the thinker and the actor, a thinker who by perceiving the shape of things changes himself, an actor who by acting out his own nature changes others.

Born on January 18, 1910 in Liverpool he pursued diligently the early career of a bright lad coming from lower socio-economic circumstances. The Earl of Sefton Scholarship at Liverpool Collegiate School (1923–1928) was followed by the Open Major Scholarship in Natural Sciences at New College, Oxford (1928–1932). This, in turn, led to a Bachelor of Arts (first-class honors, School of Philosophy, Politics and Economics) at Oxford University in 1931, and to a Masters degree at Oxford in 1939. As early as 1932, however, the international factor in his life came to the fore in the form of a Commonwealth Fellowship at the University of Chicago (1932–1934) which proved to be a major force in his own choice of geographic location and base of operations. Thereafter, his own professional career at the University of Edinburgh, at Colgate University, Fisk University, Iowa State College, McGill University, University of Michigan, University of Colorado, as well as many visiting assignments at the Center for Advanced Study in the Behavioral Sciences, Stanford, California; the University College of the West Indies, Jamaica; the International Christian University, Tokyo, Japan; the University of Natal, Durban, South Africa; the Japanese Broadcasting Company, Tokyo; and the University of Edinborough, show the complete circle of international exposure and activity which has taken him well-nigh to all parts of the world.

It is striking indeed to observe how the visions and impressions or the images (to use his own term) that he collects in being a "migrant scholar" are fashioned into a pattern and sharpened into a train of thought which takes expression in some form of publication or other. Indeed his publications are too numerous to elaborate on. Twenty-five books and hundreds of articles ranging across all layers of the social sciences, reflect the prolific activities that he has engaged in. It is for these reasons that I view him both as a thinker and as an actor.

The second most striking aspect of Kenneth Boulding to me is that he is a liberated man, in the sense that he has risen above his own handicaps and turned his own weaknesses into strengths. An example of this is his extreme shyness and a speech handicap which presumably has given him quite a difficult time throughout his career. Anyone who has seen Kenneth perform on the public stage, however, realizes that he has truly overcome his shyness, and that he has also learned to use his handicap as an instrument of communication. He can move the audience to the edge of their seats, make them weep or cry at will, share in his joys and sorrows, and appreciate the faculties of intellectual argument. This is no mean accomplishment for a man who had considerable difficulties with public speaking at an early age.

Thirdly I see in Kenneth a moral teacher, an individual who, having perceived the relativity of values, nonetheless chose a particular path for himself. This part combines thinking and action in a view of the world which is perhaps strikingly modern and yet at the same time traditional. His role as a moral teacher is reflected best through his participation in the Religious Society of Friends; in the international travels to the Soviet Union and other parts of the world in order to open new frontiers of communication between different subcultures vying for supremacy. Perhaps he has drawn therefrom the inspiration in trying to synthesize, and to move on to a higher level of discourse, in the ethical as well as in the social and political spheres. The role of Kenneth as the moral philosopher and teacher is reflected, for example, in *The Prospering of Truth.*[1] It also appears in his concern with the role of ethical values, the social sciences, and particularly in economic choices.

The fourth facet adding to his moral and intellectual brilliance consists in his role as a social reformer: He has provided impetus to the student movement (some progressive student movements were started in his basement in Ann Arbor); to the Women's Liberation movement to which he has given a lot of time and effort, particularly in the context of the formal setting of the American Economic Association's Committee for Women's Status in the Profession. His concern for the black struggle for

[1]Swarthmore Lecture 1970 (Friends Home Service Committee, London, 1970).

equality in the American system is reflected in his position at Fisk University during the period 1942/43 and in a variety of activities undertaken to further the advancement of minority groups. This concern for the place of the disadvantaged is shown also by his scholarly interest in eliminating poverty.

The fifth, and one of the most enchanting facets, is that of Kenneth, the poet, the visionary, the dreamer, the formulator of sonnets and songs.[2]

From the poet to the singer is seemingly a small step. It takes little effort for Kenneth to play a rather enthusiastic role in any group's expression of its joys and sorrows (both in the context of more serious religious meetings as well as in the more relaxed and reckless mood of social gatherings).

The sixth facet, which shines most brightly to me, and with which I have the closest aquaintance, is that of Kenneth as scholar, the writer of books, treatises, pamphlets; the perfector or maintainer of an ongoing intellectual system; the visionary and prophet of new developments; the builder of institutions; and the source of inspiration for others. Indeed, it is hard for anyone who has not moved so freely and so naturally across the whole realm of the social sciences, and who has not had some glimpses into the land of the physical sciences, to appreciate the totality of his vision of man and society and of the ultimate destiny of mankind. Nonetheless, I see his own evolution as a thinker and as a scholar along a continuum, ranging from the more formal knowledge of established economics; transcending the approach of neoclassical or Keynesian economics and rediscovering the relevance of the political economy in which cultural, social, and political forces are paramount in explaining economic allocations, quite apart from the forces which economists have associated with the behavior of markets. The major expression of his view of the political economy, in turn, led him to the view of the "grants economy" as contrasted with the traditional view of "exchange systems" as the organizing force in economic society.

These three strata of economic thinking can be viewed, as it were, as the steps on an ever ascending staircase of intellectual development. The next major platform reached in this development consists in the transcending of economics, his going "beyond economics", and "towards a general social science", embracing all disciplines as strands of a pattern of understanding of man and society.

Yet another platform on this staircase of intellectual evolution appears in his concern with matters quite clearly beyond economics, that is with

---

[2]*There is a Spirit, The Naylor Sonnets* (Fellowship Press, 1945).

international systems, peace, conflict resolution, and politics in general. Finally, a major platform is found in his view of the totality of existence of the social system as embedded in the physical or ecological environment; for instance, his concept of the "cowboy economy" as giving way to the "spaceship earth" clearly closes the circle from the social to the physical sciences.

His role as a maintainer and perfector of an ongoing intellectual system is most clearly demonstrated in his early years: Having been exposed to the "prevailing dogma", he proceeded to refine and perfect it. This is reflected in his early articles[3]:

From the displacement-cost concept, to the pure theory of population and capital, to the consumption function, to time and investment, we find a logical progression of traditional reasoning which culminated in his very influential book entitled *Economic Analysis.*[4] Indeed, this book set the tone for a whole generation of teaching in economics. It was followed by another book of similar import, written by Paul Samuelson.

In the general area of economics Kenneth was substantially concerned with the theory of the firm and with human organization.[5] This is also expressed, among other things, in his interest in price theory[6] and in the role of linear programming in the theory of the firm.[7] There followed among other things, and partly influenced by his activities at Iowa State College and at the League of Nations, a preoccupation with agricultural policy, and with other areas of the application of the apparatus of economic policy.

The widespread recognition of his role as maintainer and perfector of an intellectual system is evidenced by his being awarded the John Bates Clark medal of the American Economic Association in 1949, the Distinguished Fellowship (1969), the American Council of Learned Society's Prize for Distinguished Scholarship in the Humanities (1962), Fellowship in the American Academy of Arts and Sciences (since 1958), and Fellowship in the Philosophical Society (since 1960). This accomplishment is also reflected in the formal recognition of his professional role:

---

[3]In 1932, for example, he published 'The Place of the "Displacement Cost" Concept in Economic Theory', *Economic Journal 42*, 165 (March 1932) 137–141; or his article on 'The Application of the Pure Theory of Population Change to the Theory of Capital', *Quarterly Journal of Economics 48* (August 1934) 645–666.

[4]*Economic Analysis* (Harper, New York, 1941).

[5]The latter in fact lead him to his book *The Organizational Revolution* (Harper, 1963; Quadrangle Paperback, 1968).

[6]*Readings in Price Theory*, edited with W. G. Stigler, Homewood, Ill. Richard Irwin (1952).

[7]*Linear Programming in the Theory of the Firm*, edited with W. A. Spivey (McMillan, 1960).

He was elected Vice President of the American Economic Association in 1958, and President in 1968.

His interest in economic policy is demonstrated, for example, in his book *Principles of Economic Policy*[8], and in *The Skills of the Economist.*[9]

Kenneth, the visionary scholar, the reformer of the existing system, is reflected in a myriad of papers and in a sequence of major books. The first book, entitled *A Reconstruction of Economics*[10], already criticizes the underlying paradigm of exchange economics (as he would call it later). He challenges the prevailing view that economics should be concerned mainly with behavior of markets; and he directs his sight towards the behavior of man. Thus by necessity he encloses a much broader frame of vision within the purview of economic concerns. Indeed, within the area of changes in economic theory and policy analysis he has made several major impacts: For one, his emphasis on transfer-payments concepts in national accounts, and on the problem of poverty and income maintenance culminated in the University of Michigan Faculty Seminar on Income Maintenance. This has given rise to a whole school of thought.[11]

In attempting to "reconstruct" economics, Kenneth broke with the cake of custom. Indeed, the fifties, and particularly the second half of the fifties, appear as a period of change, being characterized by a searching for new vistas or for a new "Weltanschauung". Many of his explorations into the social sciences made it possible for him to return in the late sixties and early seventies *again* to attempt to reconstruct or extend economics, in a way that it would reflect both its traditional preoccupation and a wider vision based on the social, political, and cultural forces in economic affairs. This synthesis of traditional economics with the newer vision of the social sciences, or of a general social science, led him also to propagate the concept of the "grants economy". He recognized quite clearly that, contrary to popular ideology, all real-world economic systems are shaped by the interaction of both exchange and grants forces. This visionary image differs markedly from the political ideology which emphasizes as coordinating mechanisms markets in capitalist systems and planning in socialist systems. In so doing he moreover

---

[8]Prentice Hall, 1958.
[9]Howard Allen, 1958.
[10]Wiley, 1950 (Science Editions, 1962).
[11]See, for example, James Morgan, Martin David, Wilbur Cohen and Harvey Brazer, *Income and Welfare in the United States* (McGraw-Hill, New York, 1962). The authors acknowledge the seminal role which he played in the context of the seminar, and in getting them started on a whole sequence of studies of human welfare and poverty.

challenges and questions the prevailing axioms of political discourse all round the world.[12]

His "withdrawal" from economics and his "return" to shape a new type of economics is reflected in his books *Beyond Economics*[13] and also in *Economics as a Science*.[14]

Which, then, were the pastures that he had to transgress, and the areas that he had to master, before he completed his withdrawal and until he returned to the reformulation of economics? Only three resting places, as it were, of this intellectual journey need be identified here. His concern with general social science of which the existing disciplines were at best special cases and components, is revealed in a variety of papers.[15]

Of particular import to Kenneth appears the role of knowledge and learning both in the individual and in society, and the role that this knowledge has in shaping images[16] and attitudes, and in leading to the acquisition of preferences. His concern with the role of social sciences in general is reflected in several books.[17] From a preoccupation with the concepts of general social science, Kenneth proceeded to a concern with the general social dynamics that shape human institutions and affect man's destiny on earth. (His concern with the methodological and ontological questions is demonstrated in a variety of papers with a methodological bent; these compare, for example, the static vision with the dynamic vision; its implications for growth, development, and the stationary state; and so on.)

"Kenneth the scholar", in cooperation with "Kenneth the moral philosopher and thinker", is best reflected in his papers and books in the area of war, peace, conflict resolution, and international systems. As early as 1945 he made a major contribution in his book *Economics of*

---

[12]*The Economy of Love and Fear*, A Preface to Grants Economics (Wadsworth, 1973); *Redistribution to the Rich and the Poor*, ed. by Kenneth E. Boulding and Martin Pfaff (Wadsworth, 1972); *Transfers in an Urbanized Economy*, ed. by Kenneth Boulding and Martin and Anita Pfaff (Wadsworth, 1973).

[13]Michigan Press, 1968 (Ann Arbor, Paperback, 1970, nominated for a National Book Award, 1970).

[14]McGraw-Hill, 1970 (McGraw-Hill Paperback, 1970).

[15]Among these, perhaps the most celebrated and most often reprinted, in a variety of books and journals, is 'General Systems' Theory: The Skeleton of Science', *Management Science* 2, 3 (April 1966) 197–208.

[16]*The Image* (University of Michigan Press, 1956; University of Michigan Paperback, 1961).

[17]*The Impact of the Social Sciences* (Rutgers University Press, 1966); *A Primer of Social Dynamics* (The Free Press, 1970; Free Press Paperback, 1970); and *The Appraisal of Change* (in Japanese), (Japan Broadcast Publ. Co. [Nippon Hoso Shuppan Kyokai], Tokyo, 1972).

Peace.[18] In *Conflict and Defence*[19] he attempted to formulate the general theory of conflict behavior, thus making a major contribution to the theory of political systems. This work was followed (edited with Emile Benoit) by *Disarmament and the Economy*[20], and by *Peace and the War Industry*[21].

These books show clearly the interface of Kenneth the scholar with Kenneth the moral philosopher, who sees in the resolution of conflict and the attainment of peace one of the major values worthy of adoption at the present juncture of human evolution.

The fusion of Kenneth's concern with political science and his tradition as a scholar trained in economics (whose concerns culminate in his vision of the grants economy) is also shown in his concern with economic imperialism, the problem of exploitation, of power, and its ramifications in the economic sphere.[22]

At a time when well-nigh all economists (in any case, all major economists) focused on the desirability of growth and development, Kenneth's voice was raised not unlike that of a prophet in the wilderness, pointing to the dangers of excessive growth, the ecological depletion, and the problems of the space-ship earth. Indeed, in his Reconstruction he already emphasizes an ecological vision of man and society as an important concept that should guide contemporary economic and social policy.[23]

Kenneth's transition from the perfector of a system to a visionary prophet or heretic should not distract one from his third major role as a scholar, namely that of a builder. The University of Michigan's Faculty

---

[18]Prentice Hall, 1945 (reissued Books for Libraries Press, 1972).

[19]Harper, 1962 (Harper Torch Book, 1963).

[20]Harper, 1962 (Harper Torch Book, 1963).

[20]Harper and Row, 1963.

[21]Edited and with an introduction by K. E. Boulding (Aldine [Trans-action Book 11], 1970).

[22]*Economic Imperialism*, edited with Tapan Mukerjee (University of Michigan Press, 1972; University of Michigan Paperback, 1972).

[23]See for example 'Economic Progress as a Goal in Economic Life', in: Dudley Ward (ed.), *Goals of Economic Life* (Harper & Row, New York, 1953) 62–83; and also 'The Fruits of Progress and the Dynamics of Distribution', *American Economic Review 43*, 2 (May 1953), 473–483; and 'The Economist and the Engineer: Economic Dynamics of Water Resources Development', in: Steven C. Smith and Emery M. Castle (eds.), *Economic and Public Policy in Water Resource Development* (Iowa State University Press, Ames, Iowa, 1964) 82–92; 'The Economics of the Coming Space-Ship Earth', in: Henry Garrett (ed.), *Environmental Quality in a Growing Economy*, Essays from the 6th RFF Forum, (Johns Hopkins Press for Resources for the Future Inc., Baltimore, 1966) 3–14; and 'Environment in Economics', in: William W. Murdoch (ed.), *Environment, Resources, Pollution and Society*, (Sinauer Assoc. Inc., Stamford, Conn., 1971) 359–367.

seminar which led to a series of studies embedded within the confines of the Survey Research Center, University of Michigan; his founding— together with others—of the Society for General Systems Research; the Society for the Study of Conflict Resolution, including the Center for the Study of Conflict Resolution at the University of Michigan; and of the Association for the Study of the Grants Economy, indicates the role that he plays in the field of action. If he is a heretic, then indeed he is one who gives rise to movements of heretics in the particular fields that we may hope will influence the dialogue of the social sciences in the years to come.

Kenneth's role as a builder of institutions, seemingly at the fringe of his training as an economist, has also been recognized through the many offices that he has held—for example, President of the Society for General Systems Research (1952–59); Vice-President and Chairman of Section K, American Association for the Advancement of Science (1966–67); Vice-President, International Studies Association (1969–70), (President-Elect 1973–74); President, Peace Research Society (International) (1970); President, Association for the Study of the Grants Economy (1970 onwards); Member, Scientific Council, Stockholm International Peace Research Institute, (1970 onwards).

From the role of scholar who directs his sight at the future and who studies the present evolution of social systems, it is but a small step to the role of the social philosopher.[24]

When one surveys the vast field of his interests, a few themes appear as most striking. Among these we find his concern with social justice and equity, legitimacy, and the taming of power; with the role of knowledge in the evolution of society; and with the role of moral choices in social institutions (including economic analysis and theory).

Yet another image appears to many scholars as Kenneth the critic: As someone has characterized him, he is "a man with an iron fist in a velvet glove". These activities are reflected in nearly 150 reviews of books, papers and articles, ranging across the entire sphere of the social and physical sciences. To paraphrase Kenneth himself: "one learns only from failure, success only confirms existing images". This implies that he certainly has made a contribution to the learning experience of others, by pointing out their strengths and weaknesses, and by providing a sense of direction.

With all of this prolific activity it is very hard indeed to see the forest

[24]*The Meaning of the 20th Century* (Harper and Row, 1964; Harper Colophon Book, 1965); and *Toward the Year 2000* (Social Science Education Consortium, Boulder, Colorado) Publication No. 132, Monograph Series 1971, pp. 14.

for the trees. Kenneth Boulding's brilliance and manyfold activity in diverse fields have earned him a reputation as one of the outstanding social scientists of our age. The many areas in which he has played a seminal role tend perhaps to distract from the overall impact that he has had on the social sciences and on many individual scholars. Perhaps his greatest contribution to human evolution will be found in the effect that his vision of man and society has in raising the level of discourse out of the existing tracks, and in producing a new consciousness on the part of man about his role and ultimate destiny.

Three facets of Boulding

CYNTHIA EARL KERMAN

Sometimes an impression of a personality can be gained by looking at the individual's pro's and anti's: what is he for, and what is he against? We commonly use this method in assessing political candiates, but I think intuitively we use it also in deciding our congeniality with friends, our mode of approach to colleagues, and our strategy with adversaries. Combined with a look at a person's effectiveness in bringing his values into fruition, this method may lead us into an evaluation of life and significance.

Those who know Kenneth Boulding will probably have multiple impressions of him. He is a person who has broken many established patterns, and created new ones. He has built systems to organize thought, but sometimes his thinking seems totally disorganized in a presentation in which one idea leads randomly to another. He is against violence, deception, coercion (in learning as well as in government), rigidity, unexamined ruts, and all fixed-choice situations. He is for love, joy, and laughter, the fullness of life, investigation of all sorts of phenomena, the expansion of thinking, multiple perspectives, integrity in means and ends, and the discipline that creates an ordered beauty.

Values grow out of lives, and Boulding, though a thoroughly unique individual, is probably no exception to this rule. It may be useful, then, to look at his life and values in relation to his contributions to society.

Kenneth Boulding was born in January, 1910 in Liverpool, England. His mother and father were both devout Methodists at a time and place when Methodism was a nonconformist sect attracting mostly the working-class population. His father, though never a professional in the church, was a lay minister. He had worked in a city mission with the poor and outcast, preached occasionally, and all his life served in the Sunday School and in charities for poor and crippled children. Following his father's and step-father's trade, Will Boulding was a plumbing and heating man, much of whose business was the installation of central heating systems in homes, churches, and public buildings. His wife, trained as a seamstress and household helper and sent out from her small-town background "to service" in the city until her marriage, had prayed eight years for a son before she was rewarded with Kenneth, her only child. Her two sisters, Flossie and Ada, had no children, so he was the only child in a circle of adoring adults, who expected a great deal of him.

The Boulding home and business were located in one of a series of identical brick-faced, chimney-pot-topped narrow row houses on Seymour Street in Liverpool, close to some of the city's most poverty-stricken areas. For a few years after Kenneth's birth, the business prospered and Will hired several employees and was even able to take a house in the suburbs; but World War I brought to the country and the family a depression from which it took a generation to recover, and the financial situation for the Bouldings was touch and go from then on. They moved back to the business location on Seymour Street and tried to scrape up the small fees necessary to enter their son in one of the neighborhood elementary schools.

A succession of schools and a struggle to control the extreme problem of stuttering that handicapped him brought young Kenneth eventually to some teachers who recognized his tremendous intellectual gifts. With their help he was able to qualify in a city-wide scholarship competition and to win a scholarship to the best high school in Liverpool. From there, regularly placing among the highest in his classes, he went on with a scholarship to Oxford, shifting from a scientific interest to the social sciences and humanities. After graduation with a "first" in his field of Politics, Philosophy, and Economics, and a year's graduate study at Oxford, he was awarded a Commonwealth Fellowship for study in the United States. He spent two years at the University of Chicago and Harvard, working with Frank Knight, Jacob Viner, and Joseph Schumpeter.

During his high school and college years, he had continued his family's interest in religion. Participating actively in Methodist study-camps and evangelistic retreats conducted by groups of young people, he found a new depth and certainty in his Christianity. At the same time he discovered a freshness and authenticity in the silent worship of the Quakers, and a support there for the utter rejection of war and fighting that he felt he must make; so during his Oxford years he joined the Society of Friends. His early published writings were an alternation between scholarly articles in economic journals and writings on various facets of pacifism, published by the Friends.

His father's death in a state of bankruptcy in 1933 during Boulding's U.S. study left his mother completely dependent on him. For the next seven years, his task was job-finding and career-building in the midst of the depression, to make some kind of a life and reputation for the sake of himself and his mother. Three constricted, difficult years teaching at the University of Edinburgh were followed by four underpaid but environmentally exhilarating years at Colgate University in upstate New York, which he felt was almost a pastoral Eden. His taking a job in the United States, which turned out to be a permanent move, was facilitated by his serving as a delegate to a Quaker conference in Philadelphia in the summer of 1937. His eagerness to make the shift grew out of his enthusiastic appreciation of the vastness, openness, and wondrous jumble of alternatives (both in scenery and in intellectual positions) that he had found in America during his graduate days.

The year of 1941 brought four major changes. His first book, a text-book in economics, was published. He met and married Elise Biorn-Hansen, shifting the focus of his homelife from mother to wife. He switched jobs, beginning a year's work with the League of Nations in Princeton, New Jersey. And the U.S. entered the war, making even more incisive the dilemma that he had felt in the contrast between his warm, secure situation and that of the Jews in Hitler's concentration camps and of his friends and relatives in England under bombs.

His involvement in the Society of Friends and his struggle to witness in wartime to his pacifist position were shared by his wife Elise. They fostered and nourished Friends Meetings wherever they went, counseled young men faced with the draft, and set up projects for young people where they could find service, fellowship, and opportunities for study and worship. Boulding produced out of these years a series of sensitive devotional sonnets, his only book of published poetry[1]; he was prepared, but not required, to go to jail as a conscientious objector rather than serve in a CPS camp or the army; he fought through an application for U.S. citizenship without making the usual promise to bear arms.

At the same time, leaving the League of Nations in 1942, he was carrying forward his teaching career in economics, at Fisk University, Iowa State College, and McGill University. In his Oxford days, he had dabbled in Socialism, then become very excited about Keynes. The justice implied in socialist ideals attracted him, but the necessary coercion did not; and he opted for the mixture of large-scale planning and small-scale free choice laid out in Keynes' theories of economics. As Keynes continued to write and develop his thinking, Boulding became one of the interpreters and teachers of Keynesian economics—but never a slavish follower, he has added his own original contributions to economic theory.

---

[1] *There Is a Spirit: The Nayler Sonnets* (Fellowship Publications, Nyack, N.Y., 1945).

By the time he went to the University of Michigan in 1949, he had become very interested in the integration of the social sciences, in going beyond economics to see what insights could be gained by using the tools of one discipline on the problems of another. The nineteen years at Michigan were productive in the cross-fertilization of knowledge. His prolific writings had already overflowed the banks of their first two streams, economics and religious pacifism, and were moving into the areas of general social science. Increasingly his interests took in learning theory, ecology, history and its lessons for the future, systems theory, conflict resolution, ethics, and combinations such as ethics and social science, or conflict resolution and economics. Still teaching economics, he bargained for time to work in interdisciplinary exploration, and was a major force in building organizations (with their concomitant journals) in the new fields of General Systems and Conflict Resolution. He has continued these broad interests in his present appointment at the University of Colorado, where he has taught since 1967.

How does a person who grew up in the poverty-stricken "inner city" of Liverpool, broke through the class system to achieve an excellent education, had both scientific and literary leanings, became a well-known American economist, then snapped the bonds of economics to extend his thinking into wide-ranging fields—a person who is a religious mystic and a poet as well as a social scientist—how does he put this all together?

My personal assessment of Boulding's significance can be divided into three areas, which roughly correspond to three somewhat conflicting elements in his personality: his attractions to science, to the literary-artistic world, and to religion. First, he is an *organizer of ideas*, a creator of rational, well-built edifices of thought. This function incorporates his leanings toward discipline and order. Second, he is a *stimulator of ideas*, a radical innovator role which relies on his ebullience, spontaneity, and fluidity. And third, he is a carrier and *preserver of values*, a basic, unyielding conservative in clinging to the good things that he holds most essential.

Boulding as an organizer of ideas

Boulding's skill at organizing ideas has been shown in many ways. We may say that this represents the "science" side of his personality. His first book, *Economic Analysis*, the text on which economics students all over the world have cut their teeth since 1941, was mainly a reorganization of familiar economic principles to present them in what seemed to Boulding more rational connections and learnable forms. His *Reconstruction of Economics*, in 1958, was a radical rearrangement of traditional ways of conceiving, recording, and relating various factors in the economy. *The Image* (1956) is a magnificent example of multi-dimensional organization of a wealth of ideas to form a consistent structure.

Every writer, of course, organizes ideas, but the uniqueness of Boulding in this area is in the larger grasp, broader range, and entirely fresh perspectives that he takes on with respect to a mass of material. It is as if he slices his loaf of bread horizontally, or from corner to corner diagonally, instead of in the standard identical vertical slabs. For instance, we can pull a number of examples from just one book, *Conflict and Defense* (1962). At one point he examines conflict as a game, then as an ecological interaction, then as an epidemic, and draws new learnings from each model. But the main thrust of this organizational bent is to arrange what we know in a pattern that makes sense, that has rational form and balance, that fits with other things we know. In his preface to this volume he describes such an aim:

Whatever originality this book may possess is a matter of building rather than of brickmaking; most of the bricks were made by others and my main task has been to fit them together into a reasonably coherent structure. (p. viii)

Building thought into patterns, carefully thinking through and developing a theory, sometimes in minute detail, has occupied him from his student days. To ask himself a question and follow through all its ramifications has always been a delight to him. His early journal articles dealt with such explorations, and his letters to friends often followed this model, when he was thinking through his views on social and moral issues. In addition, there are a number of specific directions in which his theory development has made a special contribution to society's thought.

One of his specialties is explaining non-material forces in physical or social-scientific terms. "Grants economy" and "integrative system" are terms that he invented to classify and measure the effects of love and duty in the interactions of society. We all know that parents usually consider themselves responsible for the support of their children, and often for their aging parents as well; but this sense of family caring is put by Boulding in terms of a bargain or economic exchange made in two steps:

The middle-aged support the young now in return for an implicit bargain that in twenty-five or thirty years the young, who will then be middle-aged, will support the middle-aged, who will then be old. (p. 201)

Or again, biological terms are made to describe religious allegiances: "A child brought up in a heavily religious atmosphere ... seems often immune to the infection of currently fashionable religious movements." (p. 134). And intellectual history is put into the frame of geologic changes: "Ponds and even seas fill up with mud and plant deposit, . . . things get debunked on which great social systems depend, and cannot be rebunked." (p. 121).

Just such interplay as this between disparate fields of knowledge has made Boulding one of the founders and leaders in the kind of thinking known as General Systems. System theory as such involves the recognition of the interaction of a number of factors within a segment of experience (such as the appearance of a cold front, or the planning of a mass-transit system) and the development of a model which can measure and predict the effects of certain inputs. General Systems is the development of theoretical models which can be applied to several kinds of segments of experience, such as physical, biological, and social systems. For instance, the concepts of birth and death can be used (as Boulding has used them) to apply to molecules of water flowing into and out of a lake, and to students being "born" into and "dying" out of a university as they register and eventually graduate. This kind of thinking is conceptually elaborate, with a horizontal dimension (the model of behavior) and a vertical dimension (the hierarchy of systems to which it can be applied). Boulding, in fact, has used the image of a hotel with many stories to represent General Systems theory. This sort of theory is therefore appealing to someone like Boulding who is fascinated by the organization of chaos into aesthetically pleasing structures.

Among Boulding's social-system creations which will be familiar to readers of his articles are the Threat System, the Exchange System, and the Integrative System. Within these terms he classifies benevolence, malevolence, and neutrality, the variously motivated exchanges that people make with each other, and the various kinds of glue that hold society together.

There is another strand to Boulding's interweaving or organizing of thought. Beyond the connections of the territories of physical and social science which we have mentioned, he has been able to ally the often antagonistic kingdoms of science, religion, and literature. He has accomplished this, not without struggle, by committing himself to all three and combining them within himself—lending science to religion, and applying religion to science; illustrating scientific principles with literary examples, and shaping them in literary form; letting religious inspiration flow out in poetry and social criticism in verse.

We can identify, I think, some of the sources in Boulding's life which could have built and strengthened this bent for organization, for neatening up the picture of the world.

As we have observed, his family had an undependable income which never rose above the lower-middle level. Living in row housing in a semi-slum neighborhood, he was familiar with squalor and dissipation, though his family was squarely on the side of charity, morality, respectability and neatness. His Aunt Flossie particularly embodied a tense adoption of middle-class standards in housekeeping and behavior. The impact of World War I in his early childhood was extremely dislocating, and from the time he started school young Kenneth was troubled with a stuttering problem so severe that one school refused to accept him as a pupil.

It was discipline, plus his own high-powered intellect, that paved the road out of this somewhat uncertain situation. Working evenings and week-ends with special assignments from teachers who took a particular interest in him, and taking advantage of newly-provided government support for disadvantaged students, Boulding earned a series of scholarships so he could attend the best city schools and eventually Oxford University. He learned through this that hard work and disciplined pursuit of a goal brought success. At the same time he received a thorough training in both literature and science, since his interests lay in both fields. In fact, his first year at Oxford was on a scholarship in chemistry; at the end of that year he shifted to the study of politics, philosophy, and economics. He had the basis, then, for broad connections of thought and rigorous models for organizing it.

The usefulness of order and discipline was thus proved. The delights of order, in addition, were embodied in the many trips that he and his family made about the English countryside, "collecting cathedrals." It was always a joy to him and his mother to marvel before a perfectly-formed tower or an elegant stained-glass window, or laugh at an architectural anomaly, or identify the embodiment of some abstruse technical term in the stones of a decorative entrance. Boulding sometimes speaks of himself as a "frustrated architect," and it is not accidental that so many of his images and concepts take an architectural form.

These may supply a few of the clues to Boulding's bent for the organizing of thought: the need, the means, and the enjoyment and "payoffs" for this kind of activity.

Boulding as a stimulator of ideas

There is a contrary facet, however, to Boulding's thinking, under which we might loosely place the "literary-artistic" side of his personality. When we look at Boulding in his role as *stimulator* of ideas, we see fluidity, spontaneity, and sometimes shockingly unexpected statements. This amounts to chaos juxtaposed to the order that we have just described. We see a questioner of categorical assumptions, a breaker of idols, a rejector of encapsulated ideas. *Business Week's* sketch of him in 1969 was headed "Heretic Among Economists."[2] At various times Boulding has described economics as "the theory of the no-person group" and econometrics as "the attempt to find the celestial mechanics of a nonexistent universe." In speaking of the armies of planners predicting what is to come, he decried the "perception of order where there isn't any: the awful truth is that there is a lot less order than you and I think; we need an Institute for the Study of Clouded Crystal Balls." A man whose constant dedication has been to the increase of knowledge, he has made the statement, "Humble honest ignorance is one of the finest flowers of the human spirit." A university teacher all his life, he has given a public lecture on the topic, "The University as a Subversive Institution." To a society which has struggled for three and a half centuries to forge civilization out of a wilderness, he has declared that civilization is a bad state and we should try to move into an era of "Post-Civilization."

It is a real truth that creativity requires surprise. It needs the rubbing together of unlike objects or ideas to form a new one. So a man who serves this function, who takes the usual expectations apart and puts them together upside down, is a channel of creativity which flows within himself and spills over to those around him.

As Boulding has said, "Necessity is the mother of invention; playfulness is its father." His playfulness, in turn, has stimulated others to new ideas and to restructuring of their thinking. Many thinkers at the cutting edge of theory development have shared the mutual benefit of close interchange of ideas with Boulding. There is such a group in peace research, including sociologist Robert Angell, psychologists Daniel Katz and Herbert Kelman, political scientists Robert C. North and David Singer, and mathematical biologist Anatol Rapoport. Another group, in General Systems, includes biophysicist John Platt, physiologist Ralph Gerard, biologist Ludwig von Bertalanffy, and systems analysts Milton Rubin and Mihajlo Mesarovich. Among those acknowledging his stimulation of their thinking on social philosophy are sociologist Alvin Toffler and economist-management-specialist Peter Drucker. The sudden light that comes in bringing together nuggets of unlike thought sometimes illuminates unexpected corners.

What can we say, as we look at Boulding's life, as to the sources for such iconoclasm? Sociologically, it has been shown that people who are on the borderline between two cultural groups are likely to be the instigators of change in society—the misfits or "marginal men." In many ways, Boulding was a marginal man. He was an intellectual in a non-intellectual segment of the population. He was set apart in school by

---

[2]*Business Week* (January 4, 1969) 80–82.

his stuttering. He was from a community, Liverpool, which represented to many in England the dregs of society. In cultured circles a Liverpool accent was a crippling disadvantage. So that economically, socially, and physically, Boulding had to break through barriers in order to become what he knew he could become. It is not surprising that the breaking of barriers in the field of thought—the shifting of expectations—became an active mode for him. The spaces, the cracks that let him out of a tight socio-economic box, became symbolic of the looseness and playfulness of thinking that makes room for new ideas to emerge from the cracks.

He was not the first in his family to feel a need to break out of a box. His mother was restive in her housewife role, and tried her hand at poetry and bookselling. She really wanted to do something glorious and become famous, but ended up pouring most of her dreams into her son. His mother's sister, Aunt Ada, had an impish personality that persisted into maturity; she liked to play jokes on people and had a way of turning even difficulties into witty reports. Though her venture to Australia to make her fortune brought hard work and loneliness instead, she retained her high spirits through it all, and to the end of her life was a gay companion and a playful visitor with the Boulding children.

It was a household full of fun that Kenneth Boulding grew up in, though it had its share of interpersonal tensions. As its only child he became the entertainer, the one who was expected to provide much of the fun, especially when adults were caught in problems. Again, this pattern persisted and has brought its payoffs in the fun of playing with ideas and in the role of entertainer on the lecture platform.

Boulding as a preserver of values

It is something of a shock when a presumed sober economist, at a sober conference on the utilization of manpower, comes out with a statement like:

There is no such thing as manpower, save as a hot abstraction to be handled with long tongs. Not Manpower, but Men . . . .: men in their infinite variety and sacredness, in their complex personalities and unfolding desires.[3]

Speaking as an economist on the allocation of resources, Boulding noted,

After spending four billion dollars on flood control in this country, we are more in danger of major disasters than before, because we have treated floods as a problem of the river, not as a problem of people.[4]

[3]'An Economist's View of the Manpower Concept', in: Boulding, *Beyond Economics* (University of Michigan Press, Ann Arbor, 1968)15.
[4]'The Misallocation of Intellectual Resources', in: *Beyond Economics*, p. 155.

And as a major speaker at a conference on ecology, he declared, "The end is nonviolence, benevolence, the love relationship; [these are] means which *are* ends.... I will confess I am a Christian—that's not a hopelessly bad thing to be."

Boulding has never been afraid to put his values out in the open. With other humanistic social scientists, he holds that it is better to make your biases clear than to let them warp your position unseen. His biases, for life in its complicated interactions, for people with their sometimes untapped potential, for individual choices and the power and resources to make them, for beauty in all its natural or man-made manifestations, and for the increase and dissemination of knowledge, shine through all his writing, lecturing and personal contacts. The centrality of love as a potent constructive force in society, the "phylum" of Christianity as a spiritual-ethical heritage, the mystical sense of a divine force acting in the world in unexpected ways, are all elements of the values of which Boulding is a preserver and persuader.

In his political philosophy, the values of Progress, Justice, and Freedom form the foundation of the ideal human society: material goods sufficient to sustain life, a fair chance for all, and open alternatives for people to make individual choices. As he thinks of society's goals, he would have it move toward the learning of community: managing and restraining conflict, and growing toward a widespread love-relationship. Essential for both foundation and goal are the growth, development, and utilization of knowledge, for only as we have realistic images of what exists and what is possible—only as we develop ideas and try them out—can we have the technology to progress, the information on which to base justice, and the experience to move from where we are to where we want to be.

Boulding has demonstrated his value-preserving function in his exploration of value-areas that others ignore. For example, he has spearheaded the investigation of one-way transfers, or grants, noting that such exchanges are paid for in good will, good feeling, or sense of identity rather than in material goods. In his analysis of social systems, the benevolence of the Integrative System (in part represented by the religious dimension of society) is set up against the malevolence of the Threat System (the military) and the neutrality or selfishness of the Exchange System (economics) as motivational factors—a contrast to those who hold that personal advantage is the only force that moves people. In this scheme, the building of one's identity or sense of self is as much to be reckoned with, as strong a value (even when bought with "negative payoffs"), as is material benefit.

Boulding's central belief in the value of persons is not an empty intellectual exercise. His view of the teacher as a guide to what the student can discover himself, rather than as the pourer of knowledge into empty jugs, is symbolic of his respect for individual choice and individual integrity, as well as for the potential within each human being. When a visitor calls at Boulding's office, he or she receives equally courteous treatment, regardless of rank or status; and even someone others regard as a "crank" will get a hearing at least once—for Boulding has a secret suspicion that prophets often come in disguise, God moves in unexpected ways, and the people who do not fit the expected mold are sometimes those who hold the future in their hands.

His life witness for pacifism has been another demonstration of his preservation of values. He came to this conviction as a boy, without much support from anyone he knew, and largely from the traumatic impact of World War I. He maintained it through the torment of World War II when his friends felt such a stand was a betrayal of all they stood and fought for, and when he himself was torn by the need to demonstrate against Hitler's evil but the greater need to demonstrate *for* the love of Christ. His second published book in economics was *The Economics of Peace*, at a time when other economists were concentrating on the economics of war. A public statement that he made, calling for the use of spiritual rather than physical weapons, cost him his League of Nations job. The determination to declare himself a pacifist while becoming a U.S. citizen turned a relatively simple routine into a lengthy legal battle. Other public witnesses, both by lecturing and by standing silent in visible places, continued to make his position plain through the long Cold War and the Vietnam conflict. But the most clearly evident fruit of this long dedication is its translation into a new discipline or branch of knowledge, peace research.

Through his idea-stimulating and enthusiasm-inducing among other academic people who shared his concern about the priority of peacemaking, Boulding was instrumental in the foundation of the *Journal of Conflict Resolution* at the University of Michigan in 1957, and soon after, the formation of the Center for Research on Conflict Resolution. Though the Center was closed in 1971, these two organs helped to establish the legitimacy of the study of conflict processes in all areas of social relations, together with their management in constructive ways. Other similar centers have been established, and other journals have followed, to expand the impact of this intellectual, value-based exploration.

Here, in his role as preserver of values, is the application of the religious dimension that has been so important all through Boulding's life. The sources of these firmly-held and widely-disseminated values are clearly in his Methodist-Quaker background and convictions. The devotion of his mother and father to the church and its teachings was a part of the fabric of his early life. They were people who took in aging parents for the later years of their lives; who nourished and comforted neighbors in times of trouble; who spent countless weekends providing outings for poor and crippled children; who made sacrificial gifts to the church in money, time, and talent. To this pattern of devotion was added, for Kenneth as he was growing up, an acquaintance with Methodist clerics who had an intellectually respectable theology, and an exposure to the mystical experience of Quaker worship. Among the Quakers he also found people who had already given their allegiance to the conviction of pacifism to which he had found his own way.

Love, nonviolence, beauty, joy, the sacredness of the human being: all revolve around the central Christian concept of God's gift of his son for the salvation of man, and the central Quaker concept of the Inward Light, or the indwelling divinity in each person. The fields in which Boulding has been active—economics, ecology, peace research, creativity in learning and teaching, social criticism and philosophy of history—all come together within this scheme. They deal with the enjoyment, promotion, and preservation of the potential for life and growth within each person; the stewardship of the resources on earth for supporting, not for destroying, life; the building of community across the artificial boundaries of race and nation and class; the boundless adventure and the desperate necessity of the unfolding of knowledge; the tying together of fragmented man, head and heart and soul. In his role as preserver and persuader of values, these are what Kenneth Boulding is committed to.

Preserver of Values, Organizer of Ideas, Stimulator of Ideas—triple threat or Renaissance Man—whatever grand titles we give him, however we analyze his complexities and his gifts, something always escapes. Exposure to the man himself upsets the neat schemes. What we really see in Kenneth Boulding, beyond whatever regularities or truths we may think we discover, is a tremendous unpredictable flow of creative energy that bloweth where it listeth; and most of the time I suspect he does whatever he does just for fun. Fortunately, what is fun for him often turns out to be education, illumination, entertainment or benefit for the rest of us.

A. *Economics as a Social Science*
and
The Philosophy of Science

A.1.   Economics as a behavioral science

GEORGE KATONA

Interchange of ideas with others represents, I believe, the most important way of acquiring new insights. Yet usually we think that our ideas have originated entirely in ourselves and rarely do we attribute them to other persons. I am in the fortunate position to be well aware of certain ideas which I learned from discussions with Kenneth Boulding in Ann Arbor in the early 1950s.

When I wrote my *Psychological Analysis of Economic Behavior* (New York, 1951), I was critical of many tenets of economic theory. Boulding warned me not to attribute my own aims to economic theory. Economists are interested in the behavior of the market, not in the behavior of men, he said. Somewhat later he wrote that the economist "studies the behavior of prices ... He is not really interested in the behavior of men".[1] In this way economic theory is simplified because commodities are "simple-minded creatures". The behavior of men and even of economic men is much more complex. Boulding proceeded to clarify the role of the human factor in economic behavior by introducing some felicitous expressions. The stimulus to which we respond is information because the messages that reach us consist of information. "The meaning of a message is the change which it produces in the image" (*op. cit.*, p. 7) and "Behavior depends on the image" (p. 6). In these formulations the influence of perceptions and attitudes on behavior as well as the plasticity of behavior is acknowledged. Some years later he wrote of the functions of learning and concluded that "Once we admit that utility or betterment functions are learned, neo-classical economics, especially welfare economics, falls apart at an alarming rate".[2] Our response to information received then depends not only on our image but also on its

---

[1] Kenneth E. Boulding, *The Image* (The University of Michigan Press, Ann Arbor, 1956) 82.
[2] Kenneth E. Boulding, 'Human Betterment and the Quality of Life', in: B. Strumpel, J. N. Morgan and E. Zahn (eds.), *Human Behavior in Economic Affairs* (Elsevier, Amsterdam and Jossey-Bass, San Francisco, 1972) 461.

transformation over time and, to use the formulation of Gestalt theory, it depends on the greater context in which the information is placed by its recipient.

The crucial question is: What difference does it make if we study the economic behavior of men rather than the behavior of the market? A few examples that have emerged from 25 years of research in psychological economics[3] should illustrate that it matters greatly how we proceed. We shall try to show that traditional assumptions about inflexible relations between economic variables are inconsistent with the sometimes greatly changing images. The introduction of the human factor provides a better understanding of economic processes, for which, however, we have to pay a price. We must give up the notion of establishing laws that are generally valid—at all times and in all places. Some principles that we establish may have the following form: In the context X the response to A is B, whereas in the context Y the response to the same A is C. In the light of the first example presented below, within the context of fear of shortages and rapid inflation we respond to price increases by stepping up our expenditures, whereas within the context of uncertainty about creeping inflation we respond to price increases by postponing some of our discretionary expenditures and saving more.

1. Inflation and consumer spending

For traditional economic theory, the relationship is clear beyond any doubt: Inflationary price increases are associated with an increase in consumer expenditures. This is true (a) because excessive demand brings about and sustains inflation, and (b) because the expectation of higher prices induces the rational man to buy goods and services in advance and in excess of his needs so as to acquire them at lower prices than would prevail later. Stepping up expenditures implies reducing the amounts saved, which is likewise thought to be rational: Most savings are not protected against inflation and therefore in a period of rising prices it appears more appropriate to reduce savings than to add to them.

Psychological considerations and observations made in the years following World War II indicate a reverse relationship. The better off people feel, the more they spend, and the worse off they feel, the less they spend. Inflation makes people feel worse off; when prices increase, living standards worsen, or improve to a lesser extent than a person feels

---

[3]The examples will be discussed very briefly in this essay. For a much more extensive discussion, see the author's book, *Psychological Economics*, Elsevier, New York, 1975.

entitled to in view of his rising income. (Income increases were found to be commonly attributed to one's own work and not to inflation.) Therefore inflation is felt to detract from the enjoyment of the well-deserved fruits of one's labor. Furthermore, inflation creates uncertainty, which is always an unpleasant state and increases the need for savings. The expectation of inflation is associated with the belief that more money will be needed to pay for necessities and therefore less money will be available for discretionary purchases.

We conclude that inflation means bad times and therefore when it accelerates, as well as when it is expected to accelerate, people spend less and save more than before.[4] This was observed repeatedly in the 1950s and 1960s. Increased saving as a reaction to inflation and to anticipated inflation contributed to bring about the recesion of 1970. At that time, survey respondents who expected rapidly rising prices denied that they had bought anything in advance of their needs in order to beat inflation.

Nevertheless, twice during the last 25 years, in 1950 and in 1973, the American people behaved differently. To the outbreak of the Korean war and especially to news of military reverses in Korea, people responded by stocking up and hoarding. Again in 1973, unprecedented large increases in food prices led to increased purchases of a great variety of goods. At that time the proportion of survey respondents who reported that they had bought automobiles before their price went up any further was particularly large.

Does it follow that no generalization can be made about the relation of inflation and the direction of change in consumer spending? Even if this were true, little damage would be done. It is possible to determine through sample interview surveys whether situation 1 or situation 2 prevails, i.e. whether people feel uncertain and dismayed because of their "image" of creeping inflation, or whether they react to sudden heavy blows. These observations permit, however, the following tentative generalization: Uncertainty and doubt tend to paralyze, i.e. lead to spending less, whereas fear of such specific developments as shortages and runaway prices energizes people to act, i.e. leads to spending more.

During the recession of 1970, a period of rising unemployment, the American people saved record amounts. This did not come as a surprise to behavioral economists. The lesser rate of buying of durable goods reduced borrowing and therefore brought about a higher rate of net saving than a year or two earlier. At the same time the expectation of

---

[4]See George Katcna, *The Powerful Consumer* (1960) Ch. 12 and *The Mass-Consumption Society* (1964) Ch. 14 (both McGraw-Hill, New York).

inflation and of bad times induced people to save a larger share of their money income which did not decline. Most of the money saved went into banks (including savings and loan associations and certificates of deposit). Americans were aware both of the rapidly rising prices and the fact that money in banks was not protected against inflation. but banks provided safety for their savings, which they valued highly, while investments in common stocks were thought to be risky. Many people also felt compensated for the expected slow and gradual decline in the purchasing power of money by the high interest rates paid by banks.

Inflation cannot be understood without consideration of the human factor. In the last 25 years new attitudes toward inflation developed and many people acquired new patterns of reaction to different kinds of information and experience. The learning process will no doubt continue and may bring about further changes in the response to inflation— perhaps making moderate inflation more tolerable than it has been.

2. The predictive value of attitudes and expectations

Consumers' discretionary expenditures on homes, durable goods, travel, hobbies, and the like became the most sharply fluctuating element of GNP in the 25 years following World War II. They depend not only on consumers' ability to buy, but also on their willingness to buy. Changes in the manner in which people perceive their situation—whether they are satisfied with its recent changes, and whether they are optimistic or pessimistic about forthcoming changes—make for greater or lesser willingness to buy. In addition, consumer expectations about general economic trends and prices emerged as variables of crucial importance in bringing about an increase or decrease in the willingness to make discretionary expenditures.

This brief summary of many years of research has implications for the theory and the methods of forecasting economic trends. Extrapolations or projections of past trends and of past relationships have been and still are the major basis for predictions. What is often called the standard forecast, resulting from solving simultaneously numerous equations on the relation between economic variables (between consumption and income, or investments and profits, for example), yields information on the effect of changes in certain parts of the economy on other parts, provided the relations persist under different conditions. But if people are capable of learning and therefore do not always respond in the same way to the same situation, forecasting methods are needed that are different from extrapolations.

There exist data which reflect past happenings and at the same time foreshadow future developments. Building permits issued for one-family homes may serve as an example for such anticipatory data. Even though the permits relate to what has happened in the past—decisions to build and applying for a permit—they also indicate what will happen in the future. Although the correspondence between the rate of future residential construction and the earlier issuance of building permits is not perfect, changes in the latter foreshadow trends in the former. The same is true of unfilled orders, or of appropriations as well as expectations and estimates of investment outlays by decision makers in business firms. Therefore, shortly after World War II governmental as well as private agencies began to measure business investment plans through surveys of top management. Even earlier, the Survey Research Center of The University of Michigan (and its predecessor agency in the federal government) instituted surveys of households with questions on buying intentions and consumer sentiment. The rationale of these studies has been that attitudes and expectations reflecting willingness to buy change earlier than behavior (purchases of consumer durables). Findings about subjective variables, together with trends in such objective variables as income that indicate ability to buy, are expected to foreshadow trends in the discretionary expenditures of consumers.

Anticipatory variables are most useful at the time of turning points when past trends fail to continue. They need to be used, however, at other times as well to indicate that extrapolations are permissible because turning points are not in the offing.

Three major problems must be considered before the predictive value of anticipatory data can be evaluated. The first problem is the relation of microeconomic to macroeconomic changes. Attitudes and expectations, sentiment and mood, hopes and fears reside in the individual. They may change because of personal or even idiosyncratic happenings. What happens to one individual may differ greatly from what happens to his neighbor. But other factors as well influence individual attitudes, and at certain times they exert a most powerful influence in the same direction among millions of people. Similar information is transmitted by the mass media to thousands and thousands of individuals and is reinforced by word of mouth. Then a message may come through, and people's images, for instance about the trend of the economy or of inflation, change in the same direction at the same time. When individual experiences alone determine the change of attitudes, there may be little change on the aggregate level and neither an increase nor a decrease in willingness to buy may be predicted. But the situation is different when macrodevelopments dominate very many people's feeling and thinking. Thus, to point to some crucial instances, in 1957 and again in 1973 economic attitudes and expectations of most people deteriorated sharply. This was true even of those with rising incomes and favorable personal experiences. The reduction in consumers' discretionary expenditures and the onset of recessions came several months later.

The time span between the change in attitudes and the change in behavior constitutes the second major problem. If the two were to occur at practically the same time, attitudes could not be used for purposes of prediction. If the lag in behavior were very long, attitudes would likewise lose much of their predictive value because new and unexpected developments might interfere with their effectiveness. Between 1952 and 1972, however, a lag of six to nine months was indicated between the onset of the two types of changes. It was reasonable to assume that social learning, the acquisition of new information by millions of people resulting in a change in their behavior, would be slow and gradual. Normally it takes time until all kinds of people learn of new developments, trust them, and act accordingly.

Yet again the variability of the learning process must be acknowledged. In 1973 in two instances masses of consumers learned of new developments very fast and changed their behavior almost immediately. In the summer of that year when food prices rose sharply, housewives had shocking experiences when they were unable to purchase all the food that they planned to buy and considered necessary. Again in the winter of 1973–74, shortages and the threat of shortages in gasoline and fuel oil, as well as rapid increases in the prices of energy, became immediately known to practically everybody. The deterioration of consumer sentiment was very sharp under these circumstances and reflected immediate rather than forthcoming distress. But the worsening of consumer attitudes and expectations continued in 1974 and again indicated the onset of a recession far in advance.

The third major problem concerns the question as to whether it is possible to forecast forthcoming changes in the attitudes themselves. A lengthening of the forecasting period and possibly an improvement of the forecasts would result if objective changes in the environment, which trigger the change in attitudes, could be substituted for the subjective variables. Repeated attempts have been made to substitute, for instance, changes in unemployment or on the stock market for changes in consumer sentiment, assuming that the former gave rise to the latter. It appears, however, that the considerations responsible for a change in attitudes vary from time to time. After the fact it is possible to find out what was responsible at a given time for an improvement or a deterioration of consumer sentiment. But attempts to designate universal causes of attitude change are bound to fail in view of the flexibility of human behavior. Therefore it is not possible to dispense with periodic measures of consumer sentiment and it is necessary to rely on the contribution of anticipatory variables to forecasting.

3. Will the consumer economy persist?

The essence of the consumer economy which developed after World War II may be expressed by stating that the consumer is no longer an unimportant transmitter of income generated by business or government. Nor is the consumer a puppet manipulated by salesmanship and advertising of big business. Individual consumers, to be sure, have great difficulty in obtaining redress for inferior merchandise purchased. But in the aggregate the consumer sector is powerful. Business is much more successful when it caters to consumer tastes than when it attempts to persuade consumers to buy what it itself would like to manufacture and sell.[5]

Clearly, the consumer is not yet sovereign. Neither is business (notwithstanding J. K. Galbraith's books). The learning process, and the persuasion process as well, consist of two-way communication: from the teacher (or big business and the advertiser) to the learner (or the consumer) on the one hand, and from the learner to the teacher on the other. As Boulding put it, "There is nothing illegitimate or evil about persuasion" (op. cit., 1969, p. 462). The principal question is not even whether the object of persuasion is good or bad, but whether those who are to be persuaded have any choice; or more precisely, whether they are in a position to resist. No doubt, in many instances we easily succumb to advertisements. This happens primarily when we believe that it does not matter which choice we make (which brand we purchase). In matters that we consider important, however, advertisements are rarely influential or, at best, represent one item of input.

During the 25 years following World War II, consumer thinking and feeling drove the economy ahead. This period was characterized by optimistic attitudes and expectations. At all times substantially more people felt better off than worse off, expected good rather than bad times, and were satisfied rather than dissatisfied with their income and

---

[5]In 1973–74 the largest automobile manufacturers spent much money in vain to persuade American consumers to buy big cars. Survey findings indicated long before the onset of gas shortages that with respect to necessities such as a car, Americans require a functional product and tend to economize. Manufacturers who relied on survey findings on the growing preference for small cars were much more successful than those who tried to impose their own will on the people.

standard of living. Optimism and confidence contributed to rising levels of aspiration and striving for further gains.

In the early 1970s social critics frequently asserted that the optimistic era had come to an end. The recessions of 1970 and 1974, rapid inflation, and the energy crisis with a threat of shortages in a variety of resources may be mentioned as economic factors allegedly producing a fundamental change. On the social scene, the spread of violence, urban decay, as well as the pollution of air and water, indicated that economic growth and an increasing GNP were far from identical with better quality of life or happiness.

No doubt, GNP is not a reliable yardstick for socioeconomic or noneconomic trends. As Boulding often said, it is necessary to measure the bads and to deduct them from the value of the goods. In addition to economic indicators, we also need social indicators. In either case both objective and subjective measures are required. The objective economic indicators, mostly measures of GNP and its parts, are to be supplemented by such subjective indicators as changes in the proportion of families being and expecting to be better off. The objective social indicators—number of physicians per capita, educational achievements, crime statistics, etc.—fail to reflect people's satisfaction with their health, education, family life, or the local and national government. Such satisfactions need to be measured. Changes in the measures provide an indication of an improvement or a deterioration in the quality of life.

It has been said that economic and social indicators differ greatly from each other. There is little truth in this statement when subjective economic and subjective social indicators are compared. Measures of the feeling of well-offness and of satisfaction with various life domains are inter-related.

Changes in life styles are taking place all the time. The trend toward informal living and the very large increases in the importance attached to leisure-time pursuits may be recalled. These changes altered the assortment of consumer goods and services required, but did not reduce their total quantity; the importance attached to consumption aspirations was increased rather than decreased by the new life styles. What remained constant over several decades was the high value attributed to progress and improvement, while what was meant by progress changed.

In 1973–74 many Americans lost faith in the economy and the government, yet maintained confidence in their own ability to advance. In order that prosperity be restored it is necessary that progress should retain its incentive value. But a redefinition of what is seen as progress may be required in order to conserve resources and improve the environment. It is possible to sketch a scenario which would go far toward accomplishing both goals.

It is not what I myself possess and enjoy which alone constitutes my standard of living. Since earliest times the family has been the subject of needs and wants. A further extension of the ego also has occurred frequently. In order for my children to be healthy, well-educated, and able to live in peace I must be concerned with my neighbors, with all people in my community and country, and even the world. Recognizing that the behavior of other people affects my fate, my concern about the health, the education, and the welfare of others should grow. It is possible that in the future personal well-being will be seen to depend to an increasing extent on services and public goods available to very many people. Increased expenditures on services and public goods make use of fewer natural resources and contribute less to pollution than an increase in the quantity of consumer goods purchased. Thus the proved adaptability of human motives and wants to changing conditions offers the best hope for reconciling the incentives derived from the prospect of progress with the requirement of improving the environment and conserving resources.

4. Behavioral economics

This essay should serve to illustrate that economics as a behavioral science has already made some progress and has added to our understanding of economic processes. But very much remains to be done because, as Boulding has emphasized, men are much more complex than commodities. Behavioral science, consisting of the study of man and of groups of men by means of the scientific method of controlled observation, must be recognized to differ from social science. The valuable report on *The Behavioral and Social Sciences*[6] erred in using the two terms behavioral science and social science interchangeably. The difference is not, as the report suggests and with some justification disregards, that the former is concerned with the individual as the unit of analysis whereas the latter takes social or institutional aspects as the focus of analysis. The difference may be better understood by noting that all of economics is a social science, whereas economics as a behavioral science encompasses only parts of the discipline, and also extends beyond the

[6]A report issued under the auspices of the National Academy of Sciences and the Social Science Research Council, prepared under the chairmanship of Ernest R. Hilgard and Henry W. Riecken (Prentice-Hall, Englewood Cliffs, 1969). See especially p. 20.

traditional limits of economics by not restricting its scope to the analysis of markets. We are engaged in behavioral economics when we analyze processes of spending, saving, investing, price setting, etc., rather than study the relations between amounts spent, saved, or invested and prices. In the latter case reliance on allegedly inflexible traits of human nature enables us to shove the human actor off the stage. In behavioral economics, however, we study the behavior of human beings, including the behavior of small and large groups of people, as it changes under different circumstances due to the acquisition of new information and experience.

A.2. Boulding and structuralism

ROBERT A. SOLO

To allay the impatience of the hasty readers who at the signal of a word like "structuralism", are ready to flip the pages in the belief that they have heard all this before, we must insist that the term "structuralism" as we use it here has absolutely nothing to do with a focus on institutional structures in social affairs or economic organization, nor with behaviorist psychology. Indeed, what is meant here by the word is quite the opposite of what it seems to connote to most American academics.

We will use the term to refer to two very different sorts of things; first, an organized or, at least, a self-conscious intellectual movement that seeks to establish a quasi discipline in academia with recognized masters and admitted disciples to be expressed in university studies, research centers and the effort to create a new research paradigm; secondly, a set of theories and bodies of thought that have evolved in different sciences but that share in (and hence can be identified by) a characteristic analytic approach or outlook. Thus we will view structuralism as a diverse set of theories and bodies of thought sharing a common analytic outlook, and also as a willed association and an organized movement. The movement claims to take cognizance of, to generalize upon, to develop, and to propagate the structuralist outlook. In fact it is not clear at all that the movement comprehends or diffuses the essentials of structuralist thought, and moreover the value of the movement is quite independent of the structuralist outlook that it claims to convey. On the other hand, structuralist thought erupts and develops independently of any connection (or even awareness) of the movement. Thus we will hold that some of Boulding's finest work is a brilliant realization of the structuralist analytic, yet I doubt that Kenneth Boulding is himself aware of the common strand that links his own thinking to corollary developments across the scientific and philosophical spectrum sharing the characteristics of structuralism or that he is even aware of the philosophical school and consciously-willed movement called "structuralism".

1. Piaget and the demand for a new epistemology: The structuralist movement

The founder, organizer, propagator, indeed the prophet of the structuralist movement is Jean Piaget.

Between the purpose and vision of the founder and the practice and thought of the followers there is in this instance (and nearly always) a world of difference. This essay has to do with the founder's purpose. It is, so to speak, biblical exegesis, not a sociology of church practice. In interpreting the structuralist movement, we will confine ourselves to Piaget's message and intent.

Jean Piaget, now in his eighties, began a professional career as a prodigy studying the marine life of the Swiss lakes. While still in his early teens, his publications had earned for him an international reputation as a marine biologist. He went on to become a professor of philosophy, a professor of the history of science, and an experimental psychologist. Following upon his studies of child learning, he has been widely recognized as the greatest living psychologist. In his roles of experimental psychologist and of professional philosopher, he was faced with a contradiction in outlooks. What he found to be true as an experimental scientist was flatly contradicted by the Truth of the academic philosopher; specifically the confrontation was in the realm of epistemology, that "science of knowledge", which has become the domain of academic philosophers and the main fare of Anglo-American philosophy in recent decades. Piaget took the position not simply that the philosophers were wrong, but that it was wrong to leave the problems of epistemology to philosophers whose thought and doctrines were outside the reach of experimental test, and cut off from the nutritive force of experience.

The separation of epistemology from empirical science is relatively recent. It was one with the modern fragmentation of thought into areas of professional specialization.

For Piaget this separation distorted the subsequent development of thought. He points out that those great philosophers who did significantly advance the science of knowledge, like Aristotle and Descartes, were also great scientists. They acquired their understanding of the character of knowledge and the conditions of coherence and logical inference, and the criteria of verity through and as a necessary part of their formidable effort to comprehend empirical phenomena. Epistemology and science were, for them, two sides of the same coin, interdependent and mutually re-enforcing. The splitting off of the science or knowledge from the knowledge of science was, in Piaget's view, a pernicious historical aberration whose product has been sterility and obscuranticism.

Epistemology, Piaget holds, has three constituent subject areas. It has been concerned with the conditions of coherence and consistency in statement and with the development of coherent and consistent systems of inference. This is the subject matter of "logic". In its symbolic form, logic merges into and becomes mathematics and in Piaget's view, after Aristotle, it has not been the logicians but the mathematicians that significantly advanced the development of these systems of inference.

The science of knowledge is further concerned with the sources of information, the character and the organization of statement, and the methods and the criteria for determining verity or credibility of statement. But this, Piaget holds, is the very stuff of the empirical science. Only in the endeavor of the empirical sciences can conceptualization and theory concerning this aspect of the science of knowledge conceivably be related to experience, or be obliged to withstand the test of experience, and in that way evolve through a process of meaningful learning. And here also, Piaget maintains, though the academic philosophers claim domain, it has not been they but empirical scientists who, seeking to understand phenomena incomprehensible in handed-down conceptual forms, e.g. subatomic phenomena, have significantly advanced this phase of the "science of knowledge" as well—while, as Georgescu-Roegen[1] has so brilliantly shown, the role of professional epistemologists and philosophers of science, emeshed in a dogma and tradition of classical mechanics, has been obscurantist and quite blindly resistant to innovation in thought.

And finally, the science of knowledge is concerned with the condition of awareness, the character of the capacity for knowing, and the process of learning, i.e. with the theory of the mind. It is here in the confrontation of the philosopher's dogma and the experimentalist's finding, that Piaget's demand for a new epistemology takes structuralism as its banner. Logical positivism and its precursors and variants have for generations, nay for centuries, dominated the philosopher-epistemologist conception of knowledge and the mind. It is a theory that equates awareness to impression, learning and knowledge to the accumulation of impression, and thought to the logical ordering and manipulation of impression. The mind is understood as a cross between a sponge and a calculating machine, helter-skelter absorbing and manipulating impres-

[1] N. Georgescu-Roegen, *The Entropy Law and Economics* (Harvard University Press, Cambridge, 1971).

sion, sensation, image or, in the up-to-date and sophisticated models, as an analogy to a self-programming computer. That such *a priori* theory, with no more link to experimental verification than the philosopher's armchair introspection, should be imposed from on high by those who claim authority in the science of knowledge without a sideward glance at experimental psychology is itself an affront to the canons of science. More, it is a theory of the mind and of learning that was in total contradiction to Piaget's discoveries. For in his studies of child learning Piaget has found a systematic unfolding of a genetic capability for observation and problem-solving. The child develops, in a predictable sequence, a series of *cognitive structures.* These determine the capabilities for observation and learning, and fix the boundaries for thought.[2]

Piaget's point of view is certainly precedented. Hume noted the impossibility of explaining cognitive functions such as the deduction of cause and consequence through the accumulation and logic ordering of impression. Kant postulated a complex cognitive structure as the *a priori* prerequisite of observation and awareness. But the force of Piaget's attack rests on something other than the claim that his is a superior conceptualization of thought and learning. It rests rather on the demonstration that the phenomena at issue are subject to systematic observation with hypotheses put to experimental test, i.e. that they fall within the scope of science. It is through scientific inquiry and not through a contest of untestable intuitions and arm-chair speculations that the truth should be pursued. Hence it is not in the philosopher's domain that the conceptualizations and theories of learning and the mind (Piaget's or another's) should be challenged, refuted, or further developed.

If then logic and the systems of inference belong to mathematics, and the mathematical capability must be built into each one of the empirical sciences; and if the conceptualization of knowledge and the determination of verity can develop only through and as part of the systematic struggle to comprehend event and phenomena as a function of empirical

---

[2]Jean Piaget, *La construction du réel chez l'enfant*, 3rd Ed. (Delachaux et Niestle, Neuchatel, 1963). *Ibid., Etudes sur la logique de l'enfant* (Delachaux et Niestle, Neuchatel, 1962). *Ibid., La Formation du symbole chez l'enfant* (Delachaux et Niestle, Neuchatel, 1962). *Ibid., La Psychologie de l'intelligence* (A. Colin, Paris, 1967). J. Piaget and B. Inhelder, *Le development des quantités physique chez l'enfant* (Delachaux et Niestle, Neuchatel, 1962). *Ibid., La Genèse de l'idee d'hasard chez l'enfant* (P.U.F., Paris, 1951). *Ibid., L'Image mentale chez l'enfant* (P. U. F., Paris, 1966). B. Inhelder and J. Piaget, *De la logique de l'enfant à la logique de l'adolescent* (P.U.F., Paris, 1970). J. Piaget and A. Szeminska, *La Genèse du nombre chez l'enfant* (P.U.F., Paris, 1964). J. Piaget, B. Inhelder and A. Szeminska, *La geometrie spontanée de l'enfant* (P.U.F., Paris, 1948).

science; and if the theory of thought and learning can only develop through the systematic study of these as empirical phenomena in the domain of the experimental psychologist or others so concerned, then nothing of epistemology remains for the academic philosophers speaking *ex cathedra* on the theory of the mind, and pontificating on that which is properly "scientific" without being engaged in the experience of science or faced with its crises.

It is on these grounds that Piaget urges the re-integration of the elements of epistemology back into each of the practicing sciences. Structuralism is most meaningful and can be best understood as a movement to re-unite the science of knowledge with the knowledge of science. Deliberately and systematically it would build a trained capability for the sophisticated and disciplined study of the character of its knowledge, of the boundaries of its search, of the form of its statements and of the basis of credibility of statement, into each of the practicing sciences.

The case for the *structuralist movement* is the case for building a new epistemological focus and capability into each of the practicing sciences.It is an argument that does not depend on a commitment to the structuralist or any other particular outlook or orientation.

About Piaget's disciples, real or nominal, calling themselves structuralists and giving courses and writing books on structuralism, I have little to say. To comprehend and assess adequately the actual state of the movement would require a study far broader and more detailed than I have been able to devote to the matter. It is my impression that the structuralist movement is diversified, vigorous, and inchoate, long grown beyond Piaget's tutelage. Lodged in numerous university departments, its practitioners see structures, structures, systems and structures everywhere: operational structures, psychological structures, ideological structures, logico-mathematical structures, analytic structures whose relationship to Piaget's central idea may be tenuous and equivocal or non-existent. One cannot be sure as to how much of all this is but a belated awakening to the elementary fact that any organization of thought or behavior can be understood as a system, and that every system can be seen as having a structure. Surely much old luggage has been given this as its new handle, and the structuralist label has been glued on bottles that contain the same wine or vinegar as before. In the department of economics in one French university that I know, the course given in systems and structures was a familiar melange of mathematical models topped off with a new bit of philosophical dressing. In another it was a solid and traditional offering in comparative economic systems. In the accepted French fashion the movement has been politicized, dividing into antagonistic camps along habituated ideological lines, Marxist vs. non-Marxist vs anti-Marxist.

2. C'est comme ca.

Whatever its qualities or defects, the movement has built a research base and a forum for discourse concerning the character of knowledge, inquiry, statement, and verity into a number of practicing sciences and disciplines.

3. Structuralist Thought[3]

Aside from the structuralist movement, and indeed for the most part quite without any conscious linkage to it, there are recently-emerged bodies of thought that can, because they share a common characteristic(s), be identified as *structuralist*. Indeed I would hypothesize that what can be called "frontier" or "revolutionary" thought in psychology, anthropology, linguistics, the history and philosophy of science, and (with Boulding) economics, and probably in other disciplines as well, is essentially *structuralist* in character.

What then are the identifying elements of *structuralist* thought? Taking Piaget's work as the initial model, structuralism can be understood as an approach that:

(1) postulates a distinctive cognitive structure as underlying, determining, and setting boundaries upon observation, behavior, thought;

(2) seeks to identify the constituent elements and integral form of cognitive structures;

(3) conceives of learning or development as a sequential change in cognitive structures.

Piaget's structuralist outlook opposed itself to the logical-positivist sponge-and-calculating theory of the mind and the conception of learning as a unilinear process of imitation, behaviorist conditioning, or the accumulation of impression.

Structuralist also is the thought of Erik Erikson, psychiatrist and social psychologist, who has profoundly affected American thought in such works as *Identity: Youth and Crisis* and *Young Man Luther*. He departs from Freud's conception of neurotic deviations from the normative equilibrium to posit a theory of "epigenesis" wherein development or basic learning takes the form of a systematic unfolding of a series of

[3]See Bibliographical References on structuralist thought.

distinctive, genetically-rooted cognitive structures. Each of these cognitive structures has a behavioral pattern, a character of thought, critical psychic needs and corresponding dangers of conflict and derangement specific to itself. Erikson links the dominant ideology; i.e. that cognitive structure shared and underlying the thought and behavior of a whole society or social group, to the psychic condition and formation of the cognitive understructure of individual thought, and he locates the energy source for fundamental ideological and, hence, institutional and behavioral change, in the contradiction between that ideology that society offers and the cognitive understructure that the individual psyche requires.

Claude Levi-Strauss, who is at the forefront and frontier of anthropology, is both structuralist in the character of his thought, as well as in his self-identification with the movement. He rejects that form of logical positivism which has long dominated anthropology and sociological theorists of social change that conceives of "primitive man" as an early phase in a unilinear emergence into rationality and modernity, where this emergence is achieved through experience and the consequent accumulation of knowledge. Instead of this theory of the mind as sponge and calculating machine projected from the individual to the social entity, Levi-Strauss asserts that a distinctive, identifiable and integral cognitive structure underlies and explains thought and behavior in all primitive societies, and that that structure has a rationality proper to itself. He has produced overwhelming evidence in support of this theory. Hence, the variation as between "primitive" and "modern" is not a difference in the degree of rationality or in the accumulation of information, but in the structure of cognition which determines the character and the limits of observation, thought, and behavior.

So also in the history and philosophy of science. In the *Origins of Modern Science* Butterfield demonstrates with beautiful lucidity that the transition from Aristotelian to Newtonian science cannot be understood as emerging knowledgeability produced through a sequence of discoveries or the accumulation of information and its logical manipulation, but that it came about rather through a slowly wrought change in men's "thinking cap".

Few books have so deeply affected the thought of present generations as *The Structure of Scientific Revolutions* by Thomas Kuhn. In it he confronts ideas long dominant among the academic philosophers of science, exemplified by, say, Karl Popper, currently the great man of the old tradition. In Popper's conception, the advance of science is unilinear and indefatigable, proceeding through the accumulation of information acquired through the universal and unceasing experimental efforts to test established theory. When the theory meets its limits, when it fails the test, it is thence refuted, rejected, discarded, and in its place a new theory is installed that cannot be refuted within the range of present information, until again information grows beyond the range of its powers to explain and predict, and in turn it is refuted, abandoned, replaced by another more adequate theory, and so on and on in the eternal construction of a more and more perfect edifice of scientific law. Thomas Kuhn rejects all that and disproves it. He demonstrates that the sciences operate in, so to speak, a sea of anomalies. The scientific disciplines are not to be understood as a set of unrefuted and currently irrefutable laws, but rather as a pattern of thought, called by Kuhn a "paradigm", consisting of model experiments, an outlook on selected phenomena that is at once positive and negative, a cluster of commensurable theories, coexisting with and untouched by contradictions and lacunae, known and ignored. It is this cognitive structure that determines and sets boundaries upon the questions that are asked, and the problems that are ignored, the direction and the limits of inquiry, the form of experiment and, hence, the character of the information forthcoming. In the frame of this given cognitive structure, *normal* science produces, accumulates, and manipulates information according to implicit rules. But fundamental advance occasionally occurs at an entirely different dimension. Proceeding neither through the accumulation and logical manipulation of information, nor the discovery of fact, nor the refutation of law, revolutionary science has the aspect of a psychological transformation, disintegrating and replacing the understructure of thought, stepping from one paradigm into another.

Michel Foucault, widely considered to be the most important European philosopher, also writes on historical change in scientific thought. In *The Order of Things*, his massive chef-d'oeuvre, Foucault covers in detail, development in natural history–biology, general grammar–linguistics, and political economy–economics, and philosophy, from the sixteenth through the twentieth centuries. There he analyzes the revolutionary changes that have occurred over the centuries in these very different bodies of thought. He finds, and with great force demonstrates, that the revolutionary changes that occurred in each of these areas of inquiry, occurred more or less simultaneously and, moreover, though there was no research overlap, that in every instance change had the same essential character. Such changes were as variations upon the same theme. Century after century, revolutionary changes in diverse bodies of science and art, thought and behavior, reflect and express the coming into being of a new and underlying structure of cognition called by Foucault the "episteme". Foucault disdains to identify himself with the movement, but the structuralist movement as well as the wide coincidence of emergent thought having the same character as his own, confirms his hypothesis and suggests the structuralist character of the oncoming episteme.

Noam Chomsky is credited with achieving a revolution in linguistics. He has been a devastating critique of logical positivists, radical empiricists, or behaviorists with a non-theory of the mind. Taking language as the universal example of the mind's function, he finds that the learning of language proceeds through the genetic unfolding of cognitive structure, and that the form and character of language itself reflects and may reveal the deep structure that determines the base and boundaries of thought.

4. Boulding and structuralism

I have no reason to suppose that Kenneth Boulding identifies himself as a structuralist, or that he is aware of structuralism as a movement, or that he is aware of the structuralist character of thought in other disciplines. Yet in economics, in a remarkable way, Boulding has been the progenitor of a structuralist movement (as we have defined the movement), and the great champion of structuralism (as we have characterized structuralist thought) in its confrontation with the long dominant logical-positivist conception of the mind.

As a movement structuralism has been above all an effort to build epistemology back into the empirical sciences. In economics, Boulding has pursued this end with unflagging zeal. His Presidential address to the American Economic Association, his book on *Economics as a Science*, most of the essays in *Beyond Economics*, indeed I venture that most of the Boulding's writing in recent years have been epistemological in character, analyzing the processes of learning and the nature of knowledge, bringing to the surface of awareness the paradigm that structures the economist's observation and thinking, studying it carefully and constructively, pointing out its lacunae, and attempting always to overcome its boundaries and to extend its scope. His conceptualization of the grants economy and his introduction of general systems theory and of ecological models into economic analysis were essentially epistemological innovations.

Not only has Kenneth Boulding been pre-eminent as the epistemologist of the discipline, and, in that sense, of the structuralist movement— his thought is also in the structuralist mode, and his challenge to the neoclassical economists' theory of the mind is precisely the confrontation between the structuralist and the logical positivist analytic. The sponge-and-calculating-machine theory of the mind is built into the foundation of economics. The mind absorbs and learns the sensations of work and consumption, arranges these in a hierarchy of preferences and as a table of equivalents, and thenceforth dictates a pattern of choice and behavior calculated to maximize net gain. Boulding's different conception is perhaps related to his leadership in another innovationary lines of thought. For, aside from any question of intrinsic verity, the neo-classical idea of the mind was operational as a cog in a plausible theory for explaining the behavior of individuals and of firms that expressed the will of entrepreneurial individuals in competitive markets. But that conception of mind won't work at all in explaining the behavior of large organizations and of the individuals whose activities mesh together as the constituent elements of large organization. And it was Kenneth Boulding who announced the "organizational revolution".

Boulding's *The Image* is an act of introspection that leads the reader to the act of self-discovery. Without a touch of pedantry or academic pretension, the self-analysis unfolds with spontaneity, ease, and purity of expression. Like all great works of art, it follows a line of inner necessity where every word is required, and the whole could have no other form. It displays before us the working of a mind, as it moves out under the impulsion of whim or will, uncovering a topography of thought in diverse regions of concern that constitute the terrain and the structure of anticipation, expectation and behavior. There was never so splendid and convincing a statement or analysis of cognitive structure as this.

Yet, having stated his conception of cognitive structure, Boulding left it at that. He did not attempt to explain the process of its formation and transformation. Neither for that matter, did Piaget, Kuhn, Levi-Strauss, Chomsky or Foucault. Boulding has never forced a confrontation with the neo-classical theory of the mind as calculating device programmed to a preference map, no matter that it is incongruous and incommensurable with his own conceptualization, nor has he attempted to develop its implication for or application in the analysis of phenomena. Nor have the lazy minds of the profession, inert in traditional grooves, taken up the implicit challenge. So *The Image* remains, a solitary monument outside the boundaries of the social sciences, admired by some economists without affecting economic thought.

In spite of Boulding's lonely labors, we must still ask these questions. Is there the need to build the epistemological capability systematically into the discipline of economics and the other social sciences? In other words, do we need a structuralist movement here? And is the structuralist outlook on cognition and learning relevant for economic analysis? Are we also due for a revolutionary displacement of that theory of the mind that remains at the base of prevailing economic theory?

5. An epistemology for economics?

For half a century economics has been in a state of epistemological crisis, with no end in sight. It is a crisis in respect to what economics must know of itself, i.e. concerning the conditions of coherence, the criteria of credibility, propriety of statement and boundaries of inquiry, and as to what economics must know about the character of knowing and the process of learning. Consider:

Paul Samuelson's *Foundations of Economics*[4], written in the 1930s, was an epistemological treatise pure and simple. It was itself not *about* the world of phenomena and event. Of itself, it can lay no claim to empirical verity. That is to say that Samuelson took the neo-classical paradigm and what it had to say about the world of event and phenomena as given. He neither challenged and tested the theory, nor did he develop and extend its implications in predicting event or explaining phenomenon. What he did was to give to the accepted theory another form of statement. He did so on grounds that were strictly epistemological, following the proposition that mathematics is the properly "scientific" form of statement. Subsequently the mathematization of statement in economics became a major preoccupation of the generation, followed by parallel movements in other social and behavioral sciences. Nor is the game concluded. A reaction now finds expression in the heart of the establishment. Thus Wassily Leontief, creator of input-output analysis and a mathematical economist of world repute, in his inaugural address as President of the American Economic Association, denounced the sterility of what he called the mathematical model-building factories[5], in which he included virtually the whole apparatus of modern economic endeavor. And the renowned econometrician, Nicholas Georgescu-Roegen, in his recent book[6] attacks the very epistemological foundations that Samuelson laid down for economics, and the logical positivist interpretation of the character of science from which Samuelson's arguments for the mathematizing of statement in economics are ultimately derived.

Also in the 1930's Sir John Hicks led a major change in the neo-classical paradigm[7] through the replacement of the utility calculus with the so-called "indifference analysis". This again was epistemology pure and simple. Certainly the change from the utility calculus to the

---

[4]Paul Samuelson, *The Foundations of Economic Analysis* (Harvard, 1947).
[5]W. Leontief, 'Theoretical Assumptions and Non-Observed Facts', *The American Economic Review* (March 1971).
[6]Georgescu-Roegen, *op. cit.*
[7]John R. Hicks, *Value and Capital* (Oxford, 1939).

indifference analysis was not based on any new discovery nor any new
information concerning phenomena nor on any experimental findings nor
by reference to the explanatory powers of indifference analysis. It had
rather to do with what economists can and cannot say, what questions
they may and may not ask, following a changing epistemological mode in
academic philosophy. It did not change the neo-classical theory of the
mind except to forbid the substantive responses (utilities) registered by
one sponge-calculating-machine from being compared with those registered by any other. Inter-personal comparisons were tabooed, so that
economists were forbidden to say that the rich were better off than the
poor. And in any case "better off"—a value judgment—was likewise
tabooed as "unscientific", hence epistemologically improper. Thus it
became a second major preoccupation of the generation somehow to
fashion an economics that would be viable and relevant to social issues
within those epistemological constraints—an effort, alas, that could not
succeed. Here also a reaction is in train. Economists of the New Left
direct their fury precisely against those "scientific constraints" that in
their eyes abort the very possibility of social relevance.[8]

The epistemological crisis is actual. Epistemological questions are
inescapable. That questions concerning the appropriate form of statement, the basis of credibility, the boundaries of analysis, the objectives
of search in relation to a changing universe of phenomena and need will
perennially arise, is not at issue. What is at issue rather is at what level of
discourse those questions will be answered. Will it be a discourse that is
self-aware and disciplined, designed to expose the whole of a question to
analysis and criticism? Will it be organized to seek for and develop, to
consider and to test ideas, information, theories that relate to the matters
at issue? Consider the aforementioned mathematizing of statement in
economics or the introduction of indifference analysis as a new theory of
cognition and a constraint upon economic inquiry. With due respect to
his considerable abilities, nothing in Sir John Hicks' experience or
achievement qualified him to speak with any authority on the processes
of thought, on the conditions of knowing, on the commensurability of
individual sensation, or on the psychology of choice. Paul Samuelson
was no more qualified to pronounce on the essential character and
preconditions of science than any other very intelligent young man with a
flair for mathematics who has done graduate work in economics at
Harvard. The greatest economist of the preceding generation, Alfred
Marshall, himself a mathematician of considerable force, was absolutely

[8]See for example, 'Symposium: Economics of the New Left', *Quarterly Journal of
Economics* (November 1972).

opposed to the mathematization of statement in economics. Had anything occurred, had any discovery been made, had there been any achievement that more definitively established the value of mathematical statement in economics in the years between Marshall and Samuelson to tip the balance of evidence in favor of the arguments of the latter? I doubt that one economist in a thousand has any notion of the controversy or is aware of the arguments at issue, for what is more alarming than the non-qualification of the leaders in these crucial areas of epistemological change, has been the ignorance of those who followed. Whether on a road to glory or up the garden path, economics followed blindly, without reasoned argument, without true dialogue, without search and selection, without a critical and informed response, and with never an effort to test and to evaluate effects. Epistemologically naive, not understanding the problems at issue, without the competence to judge or challenge or oppose or question, economists followed like sheep in panic, each concerned not to be left behind in the movements of the troupe.

There was no rational discourse on issues of epistemological change and there should have been. In the name of science and common sense there ought to have been a rational discourse, a disciplined learning built into economics and into the training of its practitioners, preparing them to confront those problems that arise from the very roots of the discipline concerning the nature of the discipline, its objectives, its preconceptions, the propriety of its statement, its criteria for credibility and coherence.

For these reasons the epistemological capability should be developed at the heart of the discipline, in economics and in every other practicing science. Piaget's message speaks to us. We too need our structuralist movement.

The model for the organization of a universal epistemology is clearly mathematics. (Indeed mathematics itself is an epistemological technique for logical deduction and for the organization, clarification, and testing of the internal coherence of complex statement). The mathematical capability in recent decades has come to be built systematically into each of the empirical sciences, shaped to its research conditions and needs. At the same time mathematics exists and is developed as an integral discipline, with a webwork of relationships carrying idea and information to practitioners in all of the empirical sciences. In economics, for example, mathematics and the sub-discipline of econometrics are built into the curriculum as intrinsic to the training and as prerequisite to the professional certification of the economist. Econometricians and mathematical economists, econometric journals, and journals of mathematical economics serve as a bridge between the evolving universe of mathematical capabilities and the practice of economics, drawing the relevant advances made in the former into the problem-focus of the latter, and perhaps feeding the experience and creative achievement in the latter back into the learning processes of the former. This relationship between economics and mathematics is not natural or necessary. It is a relatively new development, systematically organized during the post World War II decades. Equally a universal epistemology could be so organized, going beyond the development and propagation of an important epistemological technique (mathematics) to the consideration of the why and wherefor in the use of this and of any other technique for the organization of information and the establishment of coherence and credibility.

The establishment of a universal epistemology does not require an acceptance of the structuralist or of any other particular outlook on learning and thought or theory of the mind, nor does the value and impact of the structuralist outlook depend on the development of a universal epistemology. There remains then this question. What has the structuralist outlook to do with the development of the social sciences generally or of economics in particular?

6. *Economics and the structuralist outlook*

All the sciences rest on an epistemological base, and therefore epistemological capabilities, insights, and innovations are related to control and progress in every one of the sciences. But not all of the sciences require a theory of the mind nor does their inquiry relate to the study of the learning process. Physics, for example, neither rests upon a theory of the mind nor does it inquire into the phenomenon of learning. That aspect of the sciences of knowledge has, therefore, no particular relevance for physics, and neither therefore has structuralist theory, concerned as it is with cognition and learning.

But certainly this is not the case in economics. Neo-classical economics rests foursquare on a theory of mind and motivation, and even those who accept without question the truth and adequacy of that theory would hardly deny that one path in the development of that theory would be through whatever leads to a greater knowledge of what are essentially cognitive functions. Thus if the generality and scope of profit-maximizing rationality could be "scientifically" established, or if the character of anticipation and its effect on entrepreneurial behavior could be determined, or if the effect of an ambiance of risk on thought and behavior could be more fully understood or if the development of consumer values could be explained, all of this would count as a positive development for the neo-classical theorists. Since these are cognitive phenomena, a deepened understanding with respect to them would *ipso facto* not only advance economic theory but would enrich epistemology as well. Conversely such inquiry as deepens the understanding of cognitive functions could be relevant to the development of economic theory. But aside from the neo-classical paradigm, there are problems of great concern to modern economics where a theory of cognition, decision, and learning is crucial, and is entirely lacking. With respect, for example, to the following:

(1) Choice and behavior of large autonomous groups, e.g., the modern corporation and trade union. Neo-classical theory fails to explain such behavior in the "organizational sector" in part at least because that theory is based on the assumption of the self-interested choice of individuals. Individual choice is of quite another order than the decision or policy-producing behavior that underlays the activity of complex groups. Game theory, which conceives of individualized choices operating in the context of variable sets of rules, fails to explain behavior in the organizational sector for quite the same reason.

(2) Economic development and the phenomenon of underdevelopment. Economic development is virtually a process of social learning, and underdevelopment is the consequence of a failure of spontaneous social learning.

(3) Technological advance as the essential constituent of higher productivity and, hence, economic growth. Technological advance is a learning phenomenon, and research and development (R&D) institutionalizes and builds the learning function into the operation of large corporate and public organizations.

Although it rests foursquare upon a theory of the mind, neo-classical economics is not conceptually equipped to examine and re-examine, to challenge and test, to analyze, to investigate, to reconceptualize and transform the theory of thought upon which its analysis depends. That theory of the mind, with cognitive process conceived as an optimizing program geared to an indifference map, is and has for two centuries been posited as axiomatic, self-evident, outside challenge or change. Yet it is wholly incapable of explaining the cohesion, discipline, or policy-formation of the complex organization and groups that are prime entities in the modern economy. It excludes the learning process even for the individual, and hence aborts the analysis of economic development and economic growth as social learning functions.

The virtue of Boulding's demonstration in *The Image* is not only that it unfolds a dynamic of thought in absolute contrast to the sponge-and-calculating-machine theory of the mind. It also opens the way to a search for cognitive structures that can explain the intermeshing of expectations, the integration of purpose, and the coordination of activity in corporate, group, and social policy and behavior, as well as the effort to understand the process of transforming cognitive structures to explain individual, corporate, group and social learning or development.

If economics has no theory of social learning, neither have any of the other social sciences. If economics has not uncovered the cognitive structures underlying the behavior of complex groups, neither has psychology or any of the other social sciences. If economics does develop an adequate theory of social learning, if it could succeed in conceptualizing the cognitive understructure and explaining the behavior of a set of complex groups, in so doing it would make a contribution to epistemology of importance to every other social science. And if it is the others who deepen the understanding of cognitive and learning functions, that would raise the problem-solving, phenomena-elucidating capacity of economics. For it is the quality of epistemology that it relates to the endeavor of every science. It can be advanced through the effort and experience of any single one of them, and the advance in one can be of importance to all. Such is the case for building not only an epistemological capability but also the structuralist inquiry into all of the sciences of society and man. There is yet another reason why the universalization of the structuralist inquiry might serve the common weal.

7. The structuralist outlook and bridges between the disciplines

A bridge has been built between economics and mathematics that permits the systematic cross-flow of ideas and information. No other bridges have been built. No other systematic and mutual inter-penetration links economics to the other sciences, none for example to sociology, psychology, social psychology, political science despite their overlap of interests. And the practitioner who attempts to relate to others across disciplinary lines is left amazed at how difficult it is to do so. If asked why, he will probably respond "Because we think differently". The mathematician also thinks differently, yet each of the social and behavioral sciences can bridge into his discipline and communicate with him. Why not with each other? The reason is perhaps that each of the social and behavioral sciences operates in a cognitive structure that is both very complex and largely hidden from view, a structure that merges into the more encompassing one in the frame of which the practitioner sees the world at large and organizes his ordinary observations and his daily experience. The practitioner absorbs and is himself absorbed into a sub-surface system of thought, the more difficult to comprehend precisely because so much of it has merged with the natural, habitual, self-evident, undifferentiated flow of day-to-day existence. This is less the case with the physical sciences. A greater distance separates them from the swirl of event, opinion, and choice in the common life. They are, so to speak, artificial creations whose cognitive structures are explicitly formulated and objectively visible. Particularly the precise, self-contained and internally coherent cognitive structures that determine the system of mathematical thought, are detached from the murkiness and indissoluble mystery of observed and felt phenomena. Correspondingly as the structure is explicitly articulated and visible, it becomes easier for the outsider to grasp its nature, to know where his own thought stands with respect to it, and to communicate with those who operate from the inside. For this reason, the cross-perception of cognitive structure and cross-disciplinary communication has been easiest with mathematics and most difficult for the social and behavioral sciences. The structuralist approach is pointed towards the analysis of cognitive structure. Insofar as it succeeds in bringing to the surface of awareness that complex structure of cognition that frames the thought of practitioners in the different social and behavioral disciplines (no simple task, and quite removed from the apologia of authorities or the chronologies of historians), a way will have opened to inter-disciplinary cross-perception and communication.

Bibliographical references on structuralist thought

KENNETH E. BOULDING
Beyond Economics (University of Michigan Press, 1968).
The Image: Knowledge in Life and Society (University of Michigan Press, 1968, copyright 1956).
Economics as a Science (McGraw Hill, 1970).
The Impact of the Social Sciences (Rutgers University Press, 1966).
A Primer on Social Dynamics (Free Press, 1970).
The Skills of the Economist (H. Allen, 1958).
HERBERT BUTTERFIELD
The Origins of Modern Science (Free Press, 1968).
NOAM CHOMSKY
Syntactic Structures (Mouton, London, 1965).
'On The Notions of a Rule of Grammar' in: *Structures of Language and Its Mathematical Aspects*, Symposia in Applied Mathematics, Vol. XII, (1961) 6–24.
Current Issues in Linguistic Theory (Mouton, London, 1964).
Language and the Mind (Harcourt, Brace and World, New York, 1968).
and MILLER
'Introduction to the Formal Analysis of Natural Languages', in: *Handbook of Mathematical Psychology*, Vol. II, (Wiley, New York, 1964).

Topics in the Theory of Generative Grammar (Mouton, London, 1969).
Problems of Knowledge and Freedom: The Russell Lectures (Vintage, 1971).

ERIK ERIKSON

Childhood and Society (Norton, 1963).
Identity: Youth and Crisis, (Norton, 1968).
Young Man Luther (Norton, 1962).
Insight and Responsibility (Norton, 1964).
Gandhi's Truth (Norton, 1969).

MICHEL FOUCAULT

The Order of Things (Random House, New York, 1970). Published in France as: *Les mot et les choses* (Gallimard, Paris, 1966).
L'archeologie du savoir (Gallimard, Paris, 1969).

THOMAS S. KUHN

The Structure of Scientific Revolutions (University of Chicago Press, 1962).

CLAUDE LEVI STRAUSS

Anthropologie structurale (Plon, Paris, 1958).
Mythologiques (Plon, Paris, 1964).
La Pensée sauvage (Plon, 1962).
Les structures élémentaires de la parenté (P.U.F., Paris, 1949).
Le totémisme aujourd'hui (P.U.F., Paris, 1962).
Triste tropiques (Plon, Paris, 1955).

JEAN PIAGET

Biologie et connaissance (Gallimard, Paris, 1967).
(and others)
Logique et connaissance scientifique (Gallimard, Paris, 1967).
Histoire et méthode, 2nd Ed. (P.U.F., Paris, 1967).
Les theories de la causalité (P.U.F., Paris, 1971).
Epistémologie des sciènces de l'homme (Gallimard, Paris, 1972).
Epistémologie Mathematique et psychologique (P.U.F., Paris, 1961).
Etudes sociologique (Droz, Geneva, 1965).
Introduction a l'epistémologie génétique (P.U.F., Paris, 1950).
La structuralisme (P.U.F., Paris, 1968).
Biologie et connaissance, (Gallimard, Paris, 1967).

B.   Integrative systems

and

the distribution of human welfare

B.1. On Boulding's conception of integrative systems

MANCUR OLSON*

In a volume of essays issued in honor of a distinguished scholar, it is particularly appropriate to analyze the principal theme of the honored scholar's work. The work of Kenneth Boulding is, however, so rich and variegated that any effort to relate it all to any single theme would probably do violence to some of his ideas and would certainly conceal the unusual breadth of his achievement. Ken Boulding's scholarly achievements cannot even be contained within the traditional boundaries of any single discipline, even though his nurture as an economist shows up in all aspects of his work, and in a way which makes me as an economist prouder of and more hopeful about my discipline. If it is not possible (for me, at least) to do justice to the main body of Boulding's work, I must be content to discuss only part of it. The part about which I hope to have something to say is moreover not in my opinion even the best part of his work: it is his analysis of the "grants economy", and specifically the concept of "integrative systems" that plays such an important role in that analysis. It is a measure of Boulding's singular talent, though, that even his lesser work is characteristically interesting and useful. The notion of the grants economy and the concept of an integrative system in my judgment deserve more serious attention from economists than they have so far received; they raise the most fundamental questions about what Kaldor has called the "stylized facts" on which much of economic theory is built, and the economist should not rest until these questions are satisfactorily answered. Many of Boulding's writings and speeches on the grants economy are I think also among the most engaging and entertaining I have been privileged to read or to hear by any economist. The ennobling sentences, the wry humor, the brilliant asides, and the charming style in Boulding's work on the grants economy would by themselves repay the audience's attention many fold.

*The author thanks the National Science Foundation, Resources for the Future, and the Woodrow Wilson International Center for Scholars for support of his research.

They reveal, too, the exceptional generosity and nobility of spirit of this wonderful man.

Because this articles focuses directly on an aspect of Boulding's work, it must to be self-contained briefly summarize, or at least refer to, the argument that will be criticized, even though that short summary will contain nothing that is new to many of the readers of this volume. After summarizing Boulding's argument, this paper will go on to show that an effort that some economists make to dismiss it is untenable. The paper will then endeavor to argue that most of the monies that Boulding classifies as grants are better described as expenditures on public goods, and that his observation that "integrative systems" degenerate into "threat systems" can be better explained with the deductive methods of the new political economy than through Boulding's hypothesized change in preferences. The suggestive rejoinder that Boulding gave to my criticism when it was first presented is then referred to and summarized. The bulk of the paper is taken up with my reply to Boulding's rejoinder, and my effort to point the way toward a more general theory that could encompass both the insights of Boulding's grants economy and also the orthodox theory of economics and collective choice. As the reader will see, I have taken Boulding's views very seriously indeed. Most of my initial summary and criticism of Boulding's argument—the first third of the paper—was previously published in an anthology intended primarily for a German audience.[1] Though my main concern in this paper is with my reaction to Boulding's rejoinder, that cannot be understood without an understanding of my initial criticism of his argument or of the rudiments of his rejoinder.

The discussion must begin with the trinitarian taxonomy that underlies the notion of the grant's economy, because the concept of an "integrative system" is at least at times defined as the residual category in this exhaustive taxonomy. Boulding's taxonomy allows for the following three types of systems:

(1) *Exchange systems*, in which goals are achieved and activity is organized through the market mechanism. The market sectors of western economies today provide numerous examples of such systems.

(2) *Threat systems*, in which threats of actions that will bring losses in welfare are used to organize and bring about the desired behavior. The slave systems of history, and the existing system of international relations, are examples of threat systems.

[1]Mancur Olson, 'The Economics of Integrative Systems', in: Berhard Külp and Wolfgang Stützel (eds.), *Beiträge zu einer Theorie der Sozial Politik; Festschrift für Elizabeth Liefman-Keil* (Duncker and Humbolt, Berlin, 1973) 31–42; rights to reprint retained exclusively by the author.

(3) *Integrative systems*, or (as Boulding has sometimes called them) "love systems", which presumably are those which feature neither market exchange nor threats, but instead organize and induce behavior through "love", that is, an interdependence of utility functions such that "what you want, I want". The nation-state (especially the "welfare state") and the family are the principal "integrative systems" that he discusses, but churches, and presumably other "voluntary associations" as well, are also in this category.

In this system of classification Boulding gives a leading role to differences in motives. In pure exchange systems, self-interest is, of course, the appropriate and expected motivation. In threat systems and love systems, on the other hand, malevolence and benevolence are, as Boulding sees it, most important. In these two types of systems, the "heroic" ethic, which glorifies passionate behavior, unmindful of costs and alternatives, tends to prevail, and the egotistical calculations of the marketplace are held in contempt. Boulding argues that threat systems tend to breed malevolence and a desire for vengeance, and thus tend to be unstable as well as unappealing. Integrative systems, by contrast, generate benevolence and affection, and Boulding is naturally partial to them.

One extremely interesting observation to which Boulding has been led by his taxonomy is that integrative systems on occasion show a tendency to degenerate into threat systems. Socialism is more nearly in keeping with the ethic of integrative systems than laissez faire, yet it can, as Boulding sees it, all too easily involve or lead to a threat system, as in the totalitarian states of the "socialist bloc". In the family, too, the love system can all too easily degenerate into threats of divorce, withdrawal of affection, or duress. Boulding does not give any detailed explanation of why love systems can tend to become threat systems, but it seems to be the case that some ambiguous "love-hate" emotion is thought to play a decisive role in these cases.

Boulding's focus on differences in motive, and his partiality to integrative systems, shows up in the whole range of his work on the "grants economy". It is also evident in the preoccupations of a whole learned society, the "Association for the Study of the Grants Economy", which has been created to build upon the foundation that Boulding has laid. Both in Boulding's own work and in much of that in the learned society, the extent to which a given country is organized in terms of an integrative system is roughly measured by the percentage of its national income used for grants.

In Boulding's conception, this is by no means a small percentage. He puts it this way: "However we draw the line, the grants economy is becoming a sizeable part of all modern economic systems. In the United States it has risen from something like three percent of the Gross National Product in 1910 to somewhere between 10 and 20 percent today, depending on how we define it. In the socialist countries, the whole investment sector is in the grants economy, as there is really no capital market".[2] The substantial size of the grants economy in Boulding's conception is due to the fact that both the redistributive transfers of the government, as well as its expenditures for such purposes as education and research, are counted in the grants economy.

Though, as this writer will shortly argue, Boulding's conception suffers from a fundamental flaw, it is nonetheless worthy of a great deal of attention and criticism—and far more than leading economists have so far given it. Boulding's classification offers a fresh and useful perspective on some of the most important and intriguing problems in social science. No economist should dismiss it unless he has a better way of explaining all of the phenomena for which Boulding's approach attempts to account.

A few economists are nonetheless inclined to dismiss Boulding's conception out of hand, usually on the grounds that the benevolent behavior to which he attaches such importance does not (and perhaps could not) exist. They argue that the very idea of a one-way, philanthropic transfer is mistaken. If a philanthropist makes a contribution to some individual or institution, he does so because he believes that this will put him on a higher point on his preference ordering than he would have been had he not made the contribution; he expects to receive recognition, preferment, social status, tax deductions, or other things he wants as a result of making the contribution. Those who make this type of criticism are making either or both of the following assertions: (1) that whatever an individual does, he does in the expectation that it will increase his welfare, or (2) that as a matter of fact people choose whatever alternative they think will be in their self-interest, though there will often be alternative courses of action they could have chosen which they would not believe were consistent with their self-interest.

Obviously, the first assertion makes self-interested behavior part of the *definition* of behavior, in the manner of the nineteenth-century utilitarians. It is perfectly possible, and often useful, to define individual utility or welfare in such a way that all behavior must be intended to increase an individual's welfare. This is, as we know, done in most textbooks of economic theory. Such a definition of utility maximization

---

[2]Kenneth Boulding, 'An Invitation to Join a New "Association for the Study of the Grants Economy"', *ASGE Newsletter*, No. 1 (October 15, 1969).

makes economic theory, *as a whole,* untestable, but the usefulness of economic theory has long been evident, so there is no harm in this. And it can allow a more parsimonious statement of many models or arguments. But the statement that all individual choice is intended to increase the welfare of the individual who chooses, is, of course, devoid of content. It is an empty statement which contains no information, but simply states that the word "choice" is arbitrarily defined to mean "an attempt to choose an alternative that increases one's welfare". No such procedure, however useful for other purposes, could cast doubt upon (or support) Boulding's estimate that 10 to 20 percent of the U.S. national income is used for grants.

The second assertion, which makes genuinely selfless behavior logically possible, but asserts that it never happens, is a relevant empirical hypothesis that is, at least to some degree, subject to empirical verification or refutation. It could conceivably be correct, but no one can properly assert with confidence that it is until appropriate empirical investigations show that it is, and no one has yet done empirical research which shows this. It is true that the existence of what is conventionally called philanthropy does not necessarily disprove the hypothesis that all behavior is selfish, since (as Boulding himself emphasizes) there can be significant benefits in the form of favorable publicity, etc., from philanthropy. But just as much philanthropy is probably explained by a desire for favorable recognition and the like, so there is some that almost certainly is not explained in that way. There are evidently some gifts that are given by persons who remain forever anonymous, both to the recipient of the gift and the rest of the world, and in institutional settings such that any tax subsidy to philanthropy is far from enough to cover the cost of the philanthropy. This observation is not offered as a conclusive refutation of the hypothesis of invariable self-interest, since the facts in these cases may not be what they appear to be, or there may be (nonpsychic) benefits to the philanthropist that only more detailed research would reveal. Yet the apparent existence of anonymous philanthropy, as well as a variety of actions of other types (such as giving one's life, in conditions of relative anonymity, to help obtain a state of affairs that the individual won't be around to enjoy), creates a presumption, in the absence of further research, that genuinely selfless behavior, however rare or marginal it might be, does occur.

Among those who appreciate the distinction between language which makes behavior selfish by definition, and the empirical hypotheses that it need not logically be but is in fact so, there is probably a confusion of average and marginal variables and a neglect of "price effects". Let us assume for purposes of argument that no totally, or even

primarily, selfless choices are made. It could very well still
be the case that individual behavior could be considerably influenced by
genuinely self-sacrificing motives. A rich individual, who happened to be
in a strong bargaining position vis-à-vis a poor man, might refuse to
engage in any transaction with the poor man which was not advantageous
to himself, and also insist on getting the lion's share of the benefits of the
transaction. Yet, at least with respect to aspects of the transaction which
were of minor importance to himself, yet of intense value to the poor
man, he might forego a minute gain to himself in order to bring the large
advantage to the poor man, even when his bargaining position was so
strong he did not need to do this to get the poor man to agree to the
transaction.

The force of the contention that selfless behavior must sometimes
have an influence at the margin, especially if it is not very costly, will be
evident if the following type of mental experiment is tried. Imagine a
philanthropy with a production function so efficient that a small amount
given to it would lead to disproportionately large benefits to worthy
recipients. A person might be confronted with a situation in which a
small contribution from him (say, for the purchase of a wondrous drug)
would save the lives of vast numbers of people, who by assumption
would not be his enemies, or a source of overpopulation, or otherwise
affect his costs or welfare except through the charitable contribution at
issue. Would not *some* people in such a situation, even in complete
anonymity, be willing to give a few dollars to save, say, a million people?
And, if not, does anyone believe that *no one*, out of purely selfless
motives, would give even a penny? The defense—of the possibility of a
grants economy—rests.

No proof of the possibility of a grants economy could, of course, be
sufficient to show that as much as 10 to 20 percent of the U.S. national
income is in the grants economy, in the sense that it is primarily
explained by the benevolent motives that Boulding assumes are predominant in integrative systems. How does Boulding get 10 to 20 percent of
the national income into the grants economy, when philanthropic contributions by conventional definition don't add up to anything like that
much?

One way is by including some redistributions of income by government in the grants economy. To a great extent this is appropriate, but it is
also likely to be misleading if the implications of such a procedure are not
spelled out. The practice of putting governmental redistributions in the
grants economy can be misleading because such redistributions obviously can (and sometimes do) take place without any benevolence, love,
or self-sacrifice whatever.

They can (and sometimes do) result from greed in its purest form. Let us take first one of the simplest and most classical types of governmental redistribution, in which a progressive income tax is used to obtain resources, some of which are then used, say, to provide hot lunches for all school children. Though the U.S. income tax is by no means as progressive in practice as a casual glance at rate schedules would suggest (mainly because of disproportionate tax avoidance among those with high incomes), and though a hot-lunch program may also have regressive effects (because poor school districts and poor children may find even this federally subsidized program too expensive), we shall, to put the case for the grants economy at its strongest, assume that the system is understood by all of its supporters to be a program which on balance redistributes income away from the rich. Even on this assumption, however, it need not follow that selfless behavior necessarily plays any role in the process. If income is distributed in the form of a Pareto distribution, with a long tail reflecting a significant minority of people with incomes many times as large as the median income, and if political power is distributed on a one-man, one-vote basis, self-interest will bring about some redistribution of income from rich to poor. Though a model that would do full justice to the institutional complexities of any modern society, and take account of all the logical possibilities, would have to be extremely elaborate, the simplest of plebiscitarian models will capture the essence of the situation at issue. This is that a majority of voters will find that they profit from a redistribution of income from the rich to the most of the population. As Duncan Black has shown, there will be a tendency for the median voter to determine the outcome in a simple ("one-dimensional") struggle over the extent of the redistribution from the rich to the rest, and the median voter has an income that is not only much less than that of those with the highest incomes in society, but even less than an average income. He therefore has an incentive to vote for redistributions from at least the higher and upper middle income people to the rest of the society. Though it is in general important to look at such situations in more detail, the only purpose here is to show how easy it is to get redistribution of income from the rich to the rest with no behavioral assumption other than that of self-interested political behavior. Since that purpose has been already achieved, we need not here develop any detailed model.

There is, however, one further aspect of the situation that needs to be considered, and which probably explains why Boulding (who has long understood the point made above) has tended to put governmental redistributions in the grants economy. That aspect has to do with the reasons why modern societies adopted the one-man, one-vote rule in the first place. It is entirely possible that some significant proportion of the original support for universal suffrage came from people who wanted it because they expected it to lead to a redistribution of income. A casual glance at the bourgeois groups who often accounted for the adoption of universal suffrage, and their classical liberal or laissez-faire bias, does not altogether support this supposition, but it probably contains some degree of truth. To the extent that it does, there is a case for putting public redistributions from the rich to the rest in the grants economy. It is, however, also important to realize that there are many things besides a desire for redistribution that could lead to the adoption of a one-man, one-vote rule. Most notably, such an institution could readily be the outcome of a bargaining process because it is a "prominent" or "focal" solution, and Schelling has shown that there is often a tendency for bargaining to lead to such solutions.

As Boulding himself has so eloquently emphasized, the governmental redistributions of income that are counted in the grants economy are all too often not *from* the rich, but *to* the rich, or at any event to those who have average or above-average incomes. Though this point has by now been made many times by different writers, much of the empirical research needed to determine its dimensions has not been done, and the point itself is often forgotten. Thus there is some purpose in reminding ourselves of some notable examples. In the American setting—and examples are quite as numerous in a variety of other societies—the public subsidies to "general" (i.e. mainly private) aviation obviously provide disproportionate benefits to those who can afford an airplane of their own.[3] The subsidy in the form of the income-tax exemption on the imputed rental value of owner-occupied homes is also clearly regressive, since homeowners are on the average richer than renters.[4] Similarly, the public subsidies inherent in most American state universities and colleges (and private subsidies in the form of contributions to private institutions of higher learning) surely also have regressive effects on the income distribution. This case deserves emphasis because of the fact that the potential student or his family must be able to raise the money needed for living expenses and tuition, and also forego the earnings that could be earned through full-time employment, before access to the subsidy inherent in tuition at a fraction of total cost. The system has something in common with those situations in pre-Revolutionary France, in which occasionally men of great wealth could obtain patents of nobility which then exempted them from taxation. Though Boulding has

---

[3] Jeremy Warford, *Public Policy Toward Aviation* (Brookings Institution, Washington, D. C., 1971).

[4] Henry Aaron, *Shelters and Subsidies* (Brookings Institution, Washington, D.C., 1973).

done as much as anyone to call attention to such examples as these of redistribution from poor to rich, it nonetheless remains true that it is very difficult indeed to explain this adequately with his conception of the benevolent motives in integrative systems.

In addition to its apparent tendency to neglect the role of self-interest in explaining governmental redistribution, the grants-economy literature also has what might be called a "private-goods" bias. According to Boulding, "the economic system may be divided roughly into the 'exchange economy', which studies bilateral transfers of exchangeables (A gives something to B, B gives something to A) and the grants, or transfer economy, which studies one-way transfers of exchangeables (A gives something to B, B gives nothing in the shape of an exchangeable to A)".[5] This division of reality neglects goods that are not, in any strict or helpful sense, exchangeables. If a good has the characteristic that it is either available to some group (or perhaps an entire country) or else available to no one, it is not helpful to think of it as something subject to bilateral exchange. The consumption of the good is inherently "multilateral" and the good in most cases cannot be provided through a voluntary exchange or market process. In the most typical case, the resources needed to provide the good can only be obtained by taxation, which is of course compulsory. In other words, collective goods and externalities cannot in general usefully be put in the category of "exchangeables" or regarded as bilateral. It is true that Lindahl and others of his vintage once spoke of the "Voluntary Theory of Public Exchange", but their conception of the problem of collective goods was intended to show the formal similarity of the necessary conditions for an optimal allocation of resources in the private and public economy.

There is, to be sure, nothing wrong with the practice of confining a given system of thought solely to individual or private goods, provided that the limited applicability of the system has been made clear. But in the grants-economy literature this point has not been made clear, or at any rate clear enough. The notion of an integrative system has indeed often been applied to governments and other organizations that primarily produce collective goods. Boulding, for example, has in some of his writings left the impression that most public expenditures, except perhaps defense expenditures, fall into the grants economy. Government spending on research and education in this country, and the whole investment sector of the economy in socialist countries without a capital market, have explicitly been put into the grants economy.

The emphasis on exchangeables and the neglect of collective goods or

[5]"An Invitation to Join a New Association', *op. cit.*, p. 2.

externalities in the grants-economy literature leads to an overestimate of the quantitative importance of the grants economy. A large part of the government budget, especially after government businesses are excluded, is surely explained by the fact that the objects of the government expenditure are, or are thought to be, collective goods or goods with externalities. If the citizens of a country express a demand for a collective good, or for the regulation of activities with externalities, they presumably do so because they feel that it is in their interest. It is hard to see why benevolent or self-sacrificing motives would in general lead to the provision of such goods through public expenditure. Take the case of government spending on research (which Boulding puts in the grant economy) as an example. Pure or basic research is a collective good, but there is no reason why motives of self-sacrifice should lead a people to insure that their government finances such research through taxation. Indeed, self-sacrifice could equally well lead a people to forego an advantageous collective good as to provide it. And if the assumptions of self-interest and rationality are *both* discarded, there is no longer any way to explain why governments need compulsory taxation; in the absence of self-interest and rationality they would presumably finance appropriate philanthropic expenditures out of receipts from contributions. If we assume that behavior is philanthropic, but at the same time rational, we can, it is true, see that the philanthropic motive might lead a people to provide some collective goods out of tax revenues because of the benefits that these goods provided to others. This might be quite important in the case of programs providing benefits to the poorer groups in a society. These programs might, say, reduce the crime rate for the whole society, and in that respect benefit everyone. Yet it is possible that most of the supporters of these programs are thinking, not of the external economies to themselves, but rather of the moral worth of programs for the poor. In this case, the expenditures on them do indeed belong in the grants economy. Since many government programs have, however, no special benefits for the poor, and since even those that do can also be explained in terms of the rational self-interest of those who perceive that they will prove advantageous to society as a whole, it seems unlikely that the foregoing case accounts for any very large share of total public expenditure.

A further disadvantage of the tendency to put collective goods in the grants-economy framework is that it apparently leads to analytically arbitrary distinctions. If expenditure intended to protect people from the threat of floods is put in the grants economy, and expenditure intended to protect them against a foreign enemy is not, then analytically identical problems are given very different treatment. These analytically arbitrary distinctions do in fact occur in the grants economy literature, which tends to include most public goods but to exclude defense, presumably because it is thought to belong in the threat system. This criticism does not deny that there often is an enormous moral difference between defense expenditure and expenditure on other collective goods. But this is another matter. Defense expenditures and expenditures on other collective goods, however different morally, may still be explained in the same way, irrespective of whether the hypothesis of self-interest is used, or whether some variety of selfless, e.g., country-above-self, behavior is assumed.

If we assume that integrative institutions, such as the government and the family, involve not only gifts or trades of exchangeables, but also collective goods, some of the characteristics that Boulding sees in them become easier to explain. As indicated earlier, Boulding has observed that integrative or love systems sometimes show a paradoxical tendency to degenerate into threat systems. This is hardly surprising in light of the nature of collective goods. The nonexcludability of nonpurchasers of these goods, which is one of their defining characteristics, means that they can't be withheld, either from those who don't pay or from those who don't want any. A collective good goes to everyone in some group, perhaps even everyone in a nation, whether he wants the good or not. Often everyone gets more or less uniform quantities, however much or little he might have wanted. Thus if a nation is composed of half militarists and half pacifists, at least half of its population is sure to be dissatisfied with its defense budget and its foreign policy. Similarly, if some want a high level of spending on a particular type of public education, and others want a low level of spending or a different approach to education, there will again be dissatisfaction and conflict. Whenever a group or society is concerned about a collective good, or whenever it provides otherwise private goods through a bureaucratic or nonmarket process that makes them available only in prescribed amounts (i.e., supplies them as collective goods), any dispersion of tastes (or of income, unless the good has a unitary income elasticity of demand) will lead to conflict. Where an entire country or other large group is at issue, the collective good can be supplied only through coercive collection of taxes, so that those who don't want a given collective good may find that they not only have to put up with it, but are *forced* to help pay for it as well. In very small groups, such as the family, collective goods can exist without any need for coercion to obtain the needed resources, but the problem of divergence of tastes remains. The house that they will live in, and the number of children that they will

raise, are a collective good to the husband and wife. If their tastes
diverge greatly, each has an incentive to threaten the other with divorce
or other sanctions in order to obtain the desired family decision.

This point can be stated more precisely in geometrical form. If, as
in fig. 1 below, quantities of a collective good are measured along the
horizontal axis, and quantities of a private good (or money, if we assume
constant price ratios among the private goods and no complementarity
between any of them and the collective good) on the vertical axis, then

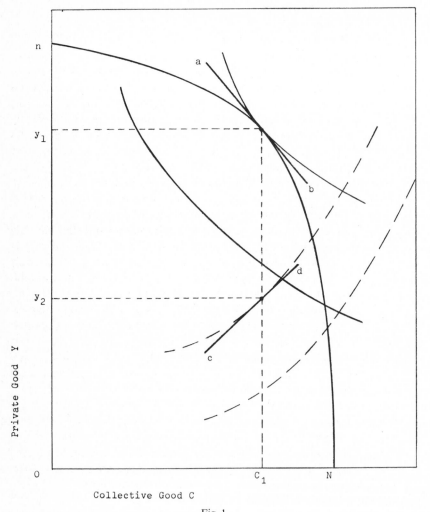

Fig. 1.

the different preference orderings or values as well as different incomes can be depicted. The preference orderings of a homogeneous group of individuals with a fondness for the collective good at issue are shown in solid lines, and preference orderings of the members of a corresponding group who regard the collective "good" as a "bad" are depicted with broken lines. These latter indifference curves show higher levels of utility with moves in a northwesterly direction, and are concave when seen from that direction to reflect an increasing willingness to give up private goods to obtain a reduction in the collective bad as the amount of the bad, and supply of private goods increases, and *vice versa*. The production-possibility frontier is shown by the curve *MN*, and the amount of collective good provided by OC_1. The incomes of individual members of each of the two groups are shown by points OY_1 and OY_2.

Though it is not necessary to the general argument that is being made, fig. 1 is for illustrative reasons drawn on the assumption that the group which values the collective good is a majority, or for other reasons controls the political system, and that it completely ignores those who detest the collective "good". Thus the dominant group has chosen the allocation of resources which is optimal if it were to consider only its own preferences, and had to forego all the private goods needed to produce the collective good. The slope of the tangent ab gives the price that each member of the dominant group is willing to pay for the marginal unit of the collective good when amount OC_1 is provided.

A glance at the indifference curves given in broken lines reveals that each member of the politically weaker group would, by contrast, be willing to pay a roughly comparable amount to have one unit *less* of the public good. By choosing an allocation in which the tangent cd would have the same steepness of slope as ab, but an opposite sign, we could readily get a point where each member of the weaker group would be willing to pay exactly the same price to have a unit *less* of the collective good-bad as the members of the stronger group would pay for an additional unit. (If there were a "symbolic" collective good-bad which could be "produced" without resource costs, and the two groups under discussion here were equal in number, this condition would define the Pareto-optimal level of provision!)

The figure makes it obvious that the provision of collective goods in societies in which values are so divergent that what is a "good" to some is a "bad" to others is likely to promote bitterness and sometimes even violence. If there were depicted the common institutional arrangement by which the weaker group is not only required to stomach the collective "good" but to pay taxes to help finance its provision as well, the weaker group would have even more incentive to want to change or destroy the

system. If a depiction of this commonplace arrangement were added to
fig. 1, and if the fact that in a democracy logrolling or other bargaining
would usually give the weaker group *some* influence on the allocation
(resulting in a somewhat lower level of provision of the collective
good-bad), we should have a rather realistic portrayal of the position of
the pacifist minority in most societies today, or of the *laissez-faire*
minority in a democratic welfare state, or of a black minority in an
American city who wants a totally black police force, or of the citizen
anywhere who doesn't like his country's foreign policy. Such an elaboration of the figure would also nicely depict the situation of anti-war groups
in the United States during the period when American troops were
participating in the Vietnam War, with the exception of the fact that
there was then a special tax (conscription) which placed a larger burden
on a subset of the young male population.

One can imagine institutional arrangements that might reduce the
degree of dissonance or the "need" for repression, though these institutional arrangements are all too rare in practice. It is logically possible that
a government or other institution could bribe those who detest a
collective good that the majority desires at a level that would make them
as well off as they would have been had none of the collective good been
provided. (The compensations paid to those whose homes must be
destroyed to make room for a road could be interpreted in this way.) This
could solve the problem of the disaffected minority and end any "need"
for forcible repression of it,[6] but it could hardly be expected to be
popular with the majority. The majority then not only has to pay the full
resource costs of the collective good, but also has to meet the often far
larger costs of the bribe needed to compensate those with "deviant"
preferences—and such preferences are more often considered reprehen-
sible rather than an entitlement to subsidies. Because of the fact that, as
Paul Samuelson has most clearly shown, individuals will often have an
incentive to conceal their true preferences with respect to public goods,
there would also be no way of determining how much compensation the
minority should receive. If there were a policy of compensating
minorities fully for the provision of the collective goods that they abhor,
there would often be no way of knowing how great this abhorrence was
without asking the individuals affected by the collective good what their
evaluation of it was. Those who actually put a positive value on the
collective good would then have an incentive to state falsely that they
abhorred it and deserved compensation, and each person who claimed

---

[6] I am thankful to Bruno Frey for calling this point to my attention.

compensation would have an incentive to exaggerate the degree of his abhorrence to obtain greater compensation.

In summary, the logical possibility of bribes to minorities with deviant preferences usually does not and often can not keep integrative systems in which there are opposing values about collective goods from disintegrating or degenerating into threat systems. Boulding's observation that integrative or love systems can paradoxically become threat systems is an extraordinarily insightful observation, but there is no need to introduce a change in motivation to explain it. The paradox to which Boulding has called our attention is exactly what the "new political economy" and particularly the theory of collective goods, when developed along the lines suggested here, lead us to fear. The political-economy or public-choice approach, as we have seen, also offers an explanation of many of the public expenditures and income transfers that do not fit at all simply into grants-economy framework.

When the foregoing argument was first put forward at a session of the Allied Social Science meetings on the Grants Economy,[7] Boulding offered an extraordinarily fascinating and suggestive rejoinder. It is not within my powers to do justice to the extemporaneous and coruscating wit with which he argued his case, so I shall instead refer the reader to a paper which Boulding delivered two months after his oral rejoinder which developed in a most systematic way the same arguments that he had made orally.

This paper is entitled 'The Network of Interdependence'[8]; it will amply repay the attention of any thoughtful reader and should be compulsory reading for anyone who has read or heard the argument that I have just presented. Though Boulding's paper is far too rich to summarize, the importance of its counter argument can perhaps be discerned with the aid of a few quotations. Boulding concludes that

the importance of this analysis for the theory of public choice arises because in the absence of benevolence or malevolence there is no concept of the "public" at all .... The theory of public goods cannot simply *assume* that there is a public. Why the publics are what they are is part of the problem, not part of the assumptions. A public requires some sort of organization, an organization implies a community, a community implies some kind of clustering in the benevolence function. This is true whether the organization or the community consists of the national state, a corporation, a profession, a university, a trade union, a church or a family .... The very concept of public goods, therefore, implies the concept of a public, that is, a cluster in the benevolent matrix .... The assumption which economists are all too apt to make is the size and the composition of the public is simply

[7]On December, 1969.
[8]Delivered at the meetings of the Public Choice Society, Chicago, February, 1970; mimeographed.

given is one that can only be justified at a level of analysis so primitive that it hardly seems worth doing.

One of the most interesting and difficult problems in the theory of the integrative system is the relation between the benevolence matrix ... and the grants matrix. I have argued elsewhere that there is indeed a close relationship, that if we are looking for an objective measure of the integrative structure the grants matrix is at least a good place to start ....

It is clear that in a theory of public choice, the definition of the public is a much more important and difficult problem than the definition of choice.[9]

Just as my argument seemed to strike at part of the foundation of Boulding's concept of the grant's economy, so Boulding's argument in his rejoinder seemed to strike at part of the foundation of my argument. The parallelism of the situation presumably gives my own criticism more importance in relation to Boulding's thought than it deserves—he is such a perceptive and detached critic, even of his own work, that we must suppose he would have developed my criticism on his own and thereby gone on by himself to the ideas in his most creative rejoinder. It is nonetheless instructive, I think, to continue to deal explicitly with the relationship of the two arguments: they confront each other very nicely. An appreciation of both arguments and of the fundamental difference between them helps one think about the great task of developing a more general theory that would subsume all that is true in each. For all the destruction that each argument directs against foundation stones of the other, there is still the possibility that with enough remodeling each of the intellectual structures could be accommodated within a still more capacious framework. This framework would have to take account of independent changes in patterns of benevolence and malevolence, and at the same time the logic of collective goods and decisions that must constrain the outcomes of any given pattern of preferences. Science is cumulative, and the ultimate, even if possibly utopian, aspiration must be to integrate whatever is true in the opposing arguments into a more general argument that encompasses both the causes of changes in preferences and the implications of given preferences.

What help can the tools of public choice and public goods be when the question is enlarged to the point where the genesis of the "public" at issue must also be explained? It might seem at first that the question completely eludes current theory, but this is not in fact the case. There are *some* features of the current patterns of institutions, boundaries, and publics that are rather readily explained with the language of collective goods and public choice.

These features are those—surely a minority—that can be traced to

[9]Kenneth Boulding, 'The Network of Interdependence'.

public goods which have a "domain" or "catchment area" that is defined by nature or the existing technology. The prevention of water pollution can be considered a public good in a given watershed, the control of boat traffic a public good in a given port, the abatement of air pollution a public good in a given airshed, a levee against floods a public good for a determinate flood plain, and so on. In cases such as these, there is clearly no problem for the economist in defining the "public" to which a "public good" applies: a relevant public is given by the boundaries of the public good itself.

Because of what I like to call the principle of "fiscal equivalence" there is also a modest tendency for jurisdictional borders to match boundaries of the collective good. Suppose first that the government or jurisdiction that provides a public good does not encompass all of the beneficiaries of that public good, as when a city center government attempts to abate air pollution that reaches the whole of a metropolitan area, or builds an airport that everyone in the metropolitan area can use. In such a case there is obviously an external economy of the jurisdiction's action that will make it provide a less than Pareto-optimal quantity of the collective good. This reality largely explains the creation of Councils of Governments for each of the major metropolitan areas of the United States, and it sometimes brings about full metropolitan governments in many other countries. It might seem that there is no corresponding problem if the jurisdiction covers more than the catchment area of the public good, yet in fact there is. Suppose that only a minority of the citizens in a jurisdiction benefit from a collective good, as happens particularly often in a country like France, where there is very little in the way of local government, yet there are inevitably many unique local or regional problems calling for government action. Even if a local public good would bring gains far in excess of its costs, and thus would have to be provided to meet the necessary conditions for a Pareto-optimal allocation of resources, there will still be more losers than gainers if the benefits are localized and the taxes are national. Logrolling on packages of local projects or other forms of bargaining will mean that local public goods will sometimes be provided even by completely centralized national governments, but bargaining is a costly and highly uncertain process that often will not be able to provide optimal quantities of collective goods. Since the logic of fiscal equivalence has been set out elsewhere,[10] I will not go into it further here, except to say that there are often gains to be made from making jurisdictional boundaries match

[10]'The Principle of Fiscal Equivalence', *American Economic Review*, Proceedings Issue (May 1969) 479–487.

catchment areas of public goods, and that there is an incentive for the relevant groups to continue bargaining about public-goods provision and jurisdictional arrangements until "fiscal equivalence" has been obtained. The bargaining may fail more than often than not, but it unquestionably does succeed at times. Think not only of the Tennessee Valley Authority and of Soil Conservation Districts that clearly have boundaries given in nature, but also of the frequency of complex federal systems of government (which by the theory are required for optimality), of the lately increased interest in local government in countries like France, and of many of the regional and world-wide organizations of governments that have been set up to deal with problems that transcend national borders. Thus I conclude that in an important minority of cases there is not only a public good that can be defined without reference to the benevolence and malevolence matrices, but even some tendencies for governmental boundaries to approximate the domain of the public good.

Public goods like law and order can of course be provided over almost any size or shape of domain, and thus are provided to whatever "public" exists within given boundaries. Defense—or what might better be called military capability, since it can be used for offensive purposes as well—has a somewhat similar malleability. In this latter case, however, "natural boundaries" in the form of "defensible frontiers" can also be relevant. The size of the relevant "public" for defense is also strikingly affected by the enormous economies of scale: a country of 200 million people can finance a military capability of a given cost for 1/40th as much per capita as a country of five million people.[11] This fact helps to explain the rarity and questionable independence of Monte-Carlo-sized countries, in spite of the probable prevalence of a strong benevolence matrix in most small communities. It also helps to explain the more active foreign and military policies of larger countries and the frequency with which large nations have gobbled up smaller ones. The greater military potential of large and prosperous countries has, of course, always been recognized, but what is being asserted here is that there is also (because of the economy of scale at issue) a distinct *incentive* for larger countries to take on more "costly" foreign and military policies. This incentive has to the best of my knowledge usually been overlooked in the literature, but it could be quite as important as the difference in military potential of countries of different size.

    The considerations brought out in the prior paragraph would suggest that large countries would historically have tended to expand at the

[11]If a large country were more of a temptation to an attacker than a small one, the advantage of size is reduced.

expense of smaller countries, at least up to the point where they come up against oceans or other "defensible frontiers." Though this tendency has undoubtedly been manifested with frightful frequency, there has been a countervailing factor that was often decisive in pre-industrial times, and in less-developed countries even today. This is the extraordinary and sadly-neglected difficulty of administering large territories without modern systems of transportation, communication, education, and public administration. There are records showing that in Medieval Europe, for example, the cost of a measure of wheat doubled if it had to be transported as much as thirty miles by land. Distant tax receipts or feudal dues were then of limited value. In times and places in which runners or horses were the only means of communicating over substantial distances, monarchs had little idea what was going on even a hundred miles away, so subordinates could often become essentially independent rulers. In the absence of "mass media" and widespread literacy, traditional leaders did not have the capacity (used so effectively by the totalitarian regimes that are now possible) to indoctrinate large and dispersed populations with a common ideology or respect for a distant authority. In pre-industrial societies, moreover, the characteristic diseconomies of large-scale enterprise have nurtured a loyalty to extended families, tribes, manors, communal groups, city-states, or other small and relatively unspecialized institutions, rather than to the "organization man" needed to make large-scale bureaucracies operate without nepotism or other forms of corruption. These considerations among others suggest that parochial or "feudal" government is a natural and appropriate arrangement for really poor countries without modern means of transportation and communication. Since I have been working intermittently for nearly two decades on this difficulty of governing large-scale institutions in primitive conditions, and hope eventually to write a book about it, I shall say no more about this difficulty here,[12] except that it underlines the importance of some insightful comments that Boulding made about "power diminishing over distance" in his most useful book on *Conflict and Defense*,[13] and that it has massive implications for the size and shape of the boundaries of the "publics" that provide public goods.

If the problem of transportation and communication and the other difficulties to which I have alluded are of decisive significance, they would not only countervail the tendency on "economies-of-scale"

[12]See my 'Social and Political Implications of Economic Development', *World Politics*, XVII, No. 3 (April 1965) 525–554; and 'Economic Growth and Structural Change' (unpublished manuscript).

[13]Kenneth Boulding, *Conflict and Defense* (Harper and Row, New York: 1962).

grounds for the bigger baronies to absorb smaller ones, but would also suggest the hypothesis that the "publics" for "variable-boundary" public goods would in at least pre-industrial times tend to have the size and shape given by advantageous routes of transportation and communication, especially water routes. There is a good deal of evidence for this hypothesis, running from the first really sizeable Kingdom along the Nile, to the Mediterranean-centered borders of the Roman Empire, to the great role of navigable canals and rivers in making China the first nation-state, to the national power of island domains like Great Britain and Japan. To the extent that the hypothesis is correct, it would greatly help to explain why the world is divided up into the "publics" that Boulding rightly demands be explained. Like the arguments about those collective goods with given catchment areas, it predicts what determines the public without any prior reliance on benevolent or malevolent matrices or any other special assumptions about preferences.

Any historical study of the effect of transportation or communication costs and economies of scale on government borders would also make it clear that many of the events that have determined or influenced many of the boundaries of various publics presumably cannot be explained by any parsimonious theory or general hypotheses—that is, any intellectual device which endeavors to explain a vast variety of phenomena in terms of a limited number of initial facts or assumptions. From any such perspective these events are random. The accidents of the battlefield; the element of chance in the arrangement of marriages among royalty who "owned" various lands; the caprice of explorers who may determine the boundaries of empires—and later of countries—by turning one way or another; the genius or incompetence of individual leaders whose talents or failings bring accumulation or loss of territory; none of these phenomena can be explained either in terms of public choice or of the grants economy.

A more systematic or general determinant of the size and boundaries of jurisdiction is the structure of preferences with respect to both private and public goods. It will be argued here that *diverse* preferences with respect to *private* goods, and *common* preferences with *public* goods, are favorable to the creation, development, and survival of a government, and that the reverse works against the creation, prosperity, and viability of a jurisdiction. It will be helpful to consider preferences with respect to private goods now, and to turn (or return) to preferences for public goods immediately thereafter.

There will probably not be any significant disagreement between Boulding and me about the fact that differences in preferences with respect to private goods can lead to harmonious cooperation. Nor will there probably be much disagreement among economists in general, for the point is very old and is derived from one of the first great insights in the history of economic science. Some famous sociological paradigms— most strikingly those developed by Talcott Parsons—and some features of popular wisdom or folklore do, however, appear to conflict with the implications of economic theory, so the reasons behind that should be set out explicitly.

The fundamental reason why diverse preferences with respect to private goods should facilitate harmonious cooperation is that trade, in the absence of force, fraud, or mistake, is mutually advantageous. If one of the parties to an exchange had thought the transaction would have led to undesirable or disadvantageous results, he would not if rational have participated in it. It would be easy to prove that the mutually beneficial character of free exchanges between informed and rational actors holds fully as well when there is monopoly or monopsony on one or both sides of the transaction, and when one party is rich and the other poor, as it would in a perfectly competitive society with a relatively egalitarian distribution of income. Differences in income levels between otherwise identical individuals can even bring about mutually advantageous trades that would not have occurred had they had the same income. The social costs of either monopoly or inequality can even reach extreme levels without making trade in private goods a disadvantage to any of the participants.

Clearly people with identical wants and endowments will not normally[14] gain anything from trade with each other, and therefore are without an important incentive for social harmony. If, by contrast, they either want to consume different things, or desire to produce different things, they will tend to gain from exchange. Because the Germans like sausage, and the French demand the better cuts, there is an advantageous meat trade between the two countries. If everyone wants a vacation in August at the beach, there is expensive congestion there at vacation time, and a lack of basic services elsewhere (this is a problem that has received official attention in France). But if some want a vacation in winter instead, or prefer to go to the mountains, everyone can be better off. If some want to work outdoors and others indoors, there will be more job satisfaction than there would be otherwise, provided only that free exchange of the output of men in different occupations is allowed. A

---

[14]When there are decreasing costs, trade among individuals of identical tastes and endowments could be mutually advantageous, but the trading partners would differ in what they specialized in producing.

common market involving the diverse nations of western Europe can possibly prove advantageous and unifying, whereas a common market among the Arab nations (though often supported) makes much less sense (they can't usefully export oil to each other, but can advantageously trade with industrialized economies).

This point about the virtues of diversity is by no means related only to trade in material goods. One does not maximize Motherhood by bringing women together. If one marriage partner likes fat, and the other lean, they can together lick the platter clean. A marriage is more likely to be successful if one of the partners wants to lead, and the other wants to follow, than if both have the same desire. A similar point can be made about any organization. If different leaders or groups want different divisible or private good objectives, they will often be able to trade for their mutual advantage, but if their wants and situations with respect to private goods are identical, the only way that one party can improve its situation through interaction with another is by winning a struggle over how that which is commonly desired should be distributed or divided among them.

All that has just been said obviously supports Boulding's assumption that exchange systems, in contrast to integrative systems, have no tendency to degenerate into threat systems. It is also entirely consistent with his assertion (which he supported, however, with different arguments) that "benevolence is more likely to be fostered through exchange than through gifts."[15]

The situation is very different for collective or indivisible goods. As we know from the analysis of tendencies for integrative systems to degenerate into threat systems, opposite values about whether a given collective "good" is a good or bad can make it impossible for an institution to continue, at least without subjugating one of its constituent groups. In an earlier paper I made an argument about how "fiscal equivalence" should apply to groups that are distinguished by different cultures or values. If this argument is correct, the formation or viability of a jurisdiction or other institution presents some difficulties in providing a collective good whenever the individuals in the institution want different amounts or varieties of a collective good. This observation is valid even if they would not disagree about whether a given collective good had a positive or negative value. Since I have discussed this before, and since others[16] have developed more detailed models with similar implications, there is

---

[15]The Network of Interdependence, p. 4.
[16]See Martin C. McGuire, 'Group Segregation and Optimal Jurisdictions', *Journal of Political Economy* (January 1974).

no need to go into the matter at any length here. The elementary and essential aspect of the question is that the individuals in a jurisdiction or other institution must take more or less of any collective good together. Furthermore, they must agree on some one of several "policies" that determine how a collective good should be produced, and what attributes will distinguish it from similar collective goods that may be provided elsewhere, or could have been provided by the institution at issue. If the individuals who enjoy the same collective good have different evaluations of marginal units of the same collective good, they can agree on how much should be provided only if they face different tax rates. Indeed, there will be complete argeement about how much of the collective good that everyone values should be supplied only if the recipients of the collective good share its marginal costs in the same proportion as they value its benefits (i.e. are in a "Lindahl equilibrium"). Since there are presumably some divergences of taste in every institution, and since Lindahl equilibria (because of the nonrevelation of preferences) must be very rare, this may not seem to be a point of any practical importance. But the degree of divergence in tax rates required to obtain even an approximation to consensus will be greater the less the homogeneity of tastes, and divergences of tax rates that cannot be ascribed to *objective* differences (such as in property holdings, money income, family status, or age) are very difficult to work out. Most democratic constitutions or legal systems for good reasons rule out legislation or policies that single out particular individuals, and they also tend to rule out discrimination against groups unless this can in some sense be justified as the result of the impartial application of some rule that applies to all groups and involves different objective attributes, such as different levels of wealth. Thus it would be very difficult to tax a group that was distinguished only by its greater desire for some public good, more heavily than other persons of the same income, family status, and the like.[17] Even if taxation according to tastes were legally admissible, the nonrevelation of preference for public goods would still make it impossible to know how much each individual ought to be taxed. The only practical alternative for a jurisdiction comprised of individuals with very different preferences orderings is to relate tax rates to the objective states of the individuals in the system, and then hope that the disputes about the level at which the public good should be provided will not be serious enough to keep a jurisdiction at issue from functioning.

Individuals with identical preference orderings but different incomes or situations normally place different marginal evaluations on a collective

[17]I am thankful to Larry Sjaastad for greatly helping my thinking on this point.

good. These different evaluations, however, need not be so much of a problem, since political bargaining over time can work out a progression or system of tax rates which prevents substantial and intense differences about how much of the public good to provide. This distinction is overlooked in some of the literature, which fails to distinguish those differences in demand for public goods that arise from variations in income or other measurable characteristics from differences in preference orderings.

When different groups in a jurisdiction differ about the policies that determine how a collective good is provided, or what detailed attributes it should have (should there be a civilian review board for the police department? or a restaurant in the public park?), similar difficulties arise. If the good is unambiguously a collective good for the whole jurisdiction, everyone in the jurisdiction must put up with the same production policy and attribute[18] choice for the collective good. Those who get just the policy and attributes they prefer for the public good will want more spent on the good than if their tastes were not so well served, whereas those who lost will want a smaller expenditure than if they had won. If all preferences were completely known, it would be possible to work out a Pareto-optimal solution that corresponded to the existing distribution of income and to obtain a tax structure varied enough to bring about a Lindahl equilibrium that would bring agreement about how much of the collective good to supply. Since preferences for public goods are never fully revealed in practice, however, the conclusion must be that even differences about the way that a public good should be produced or the attributes that it should have, are in some degree a problem for an institution, and therefore presumably work against the creation, expansion, or survival of those "publics" in which they are relatively great.

If diverse preferences for private goods and similar preferences for public goods do in fact facilitate the creation, growth, and viability of the "publics" or institutions which Boulding rightly demanded that we explain, then we must next ask: "What in turn accounts for the respective diversities and similarities of preferences?".

It is tempting to say that the diversities and similarities of preferences are produced by the same forces that produce the malevolent and benevolent matrices: by the religious doctrines which Boulding believes are so important to economic[19] as well as political development, to

---

[18]See Kelvin Lancaster, *A Revision of Demand Theory* (Columbia University Press, New York).

[19]Kenneth Boulding, 'Religious Foundations of Economic Progress', *Harvard Business Review XXX* (May–June 1952), 33–40; reprinted in Kenneth Boulding, *Beyond Economics* (University of Michigan Press, Ann Arbor, 1968).

ideological doctrines or secular systems of thought, to different patterns of socialization, and to any other factors which account for cultural differences and similarities. Differences and similarities of preferences, like malevolent and benevolent attitudes, would seem to call for "religio-cultural" determinants, and thus be explained by forces which have little or nothing to do with the explanations offered in economics or even the new political economy.

There is no doubt a good deal of truth in this type of view. Though Boulding is not by any means the only social scientist to emphasize the point that economic theory and collective decision theory could not be intellectually complete, much less sufficient for policy guidance, unless they were integrated with a theory of culture and preference formation, he is unquestionably one of the very most eloquent and forceful advocates of this position. This is in my judgment a major contribution. Though I shall go on to suggest that some commonplace forms of what I like to call "religio-cultural determinism" lead many people to underrate other explanations of changes in preferences, not to mention other causes of social change, that does not deny the fact that, as Boulding has said, the genesis of the "public" that receives a public good has to be explained, and that in many cases this cannot be done adequately without examining religious, ideological, intellectual, and cultural developments which economists have characteristically ignored.

The fact that it is *diverse* preferences with respect to *private* goods, and *common* preferences with respect to *public* goods, that is favorable to the creation and durability of a public should warn us of the diversity and complexity of the forces that determine preferences. A common religion or ideology, such as Catholicism or Marxism, could perhaps, explain common values for public goods in some area, but it could not easily *also* explain a diversity of preferences for private goods. The same problem holds for any other aspect of a group's culture; the pattern of socialization in a group or country may explain similar beliefs about public goods, but is not very likely also to explain diverse preferences about private pursuits. Possibly Hinduism, with some beliefs ostensibly common to all castes and outcasts, inculcates certain common attitudes that could possibly explain any common preferences for public goods in Hindu areas, and yet, because of the diverse occupational roles assigned by the religion to each caste, at the same time could explain differences in preferences that would give rise to mutually advantageous exchange. The hierarchical relationship of the castes, however, makes the observer wonder about the social organization at the time that the religion emerged. The fact that Hindu areas have not had exceptional success in large-scale political organization, at least until after the British united

India, is also suggestive. So it is not at all clear that even Hinduism is very successful in explaining both similarities and differences in belief. The different roles assigned to the sexes in many religions show it is *possible* for almost any culture to inculcate both similarities and differences of preferences at the same time. Different roles for the two sexes, however, are hardly a sufficient basis for the division of labor needed for any large-scale social organization. Given the dominance of "religio-cultural determinism" in some branches of American social science today, and the fact that it is not usually exposed or ridiculed in the way that Marx's type of "economic determinism" is, there will perhaps be efforts to reinterpret the diversity implicit in Calvinistic concept of the "calling," or to emphasize the simultaneous differences and similarities in the manifold sects of Protestantism, or to bring up old sociological notions about how a common culture may socialize different people into diverse "roles." These efforts should be encouraged, for they may reveal heretofore unrecognized ways in which particular religions or cultures facilitated or failed to facilitate the growth of "publics" or other aspects of development. Withal, the fact that it is diversity as well as commonality of preferences that favors the development of a "public" strongly suggests that religio-cultural explanations are very far from sufficient by themselves to explain preference patterns, much less the delineation of the publics that receive particular public goods.

Another, perhaps more powerful influence on preferences can perhaps be seen most graphically in the recent history of the American South. It was a commonplace of American political and scholarly debate about racial segragation and discrimination in the nineteen fifties and early nineteen sixties to say that "values cannot be changed by legislation" or "by force". Plausible as these arguments seemed at the time, they were utterly wrong—it would probably be nearer the truth to say that, if values are going to change at more than a glacial pace, it is government and force that will change them. In little more than a decade the differences in attitudes toward race between the North and the South of the United States have diminished strikingly, and public policy has probably been the major cause.

There are many other examples of how governments, with their capacities to use taxes to finance education and propaganda, and their power to compel some direct changes in behavior, can change preferences. The totalitarian states provide particularly instructive if frightening examples of this. Neither the Communists nor the Nazis apparently had majority support when they took power respectively in Russia and Germany, yet the testimony of observers suggests that both parties obtained a substantial degree of loyalty from most of the populations they controlled. To say that this wouldn't have happened if these regimes had allowed freedom of expression has nothing to do with the point at issue now: historically many governments have limited freedom of expression, and that is one reason why they have often changed preferences. The map of religious preferences in Europe today still shows the traces of the religious choices of monarchs and princes, and the outcomes of battles, in the sixteenth and seventeenth centuries. Governments might not have had such a large or enduring effect on religious affiliation had they regularly welcomed religious diversity and dissent.

If governments change preferences by inculcating ideologies, religions, and civic attitudes, as they manifestly sometimes do, then we have the exact converse of the problem that Boulding posed for economics and public choice: the matrices of benevolence and malevolence derive from the institutions that provide collective goods, and most aspects of behavior that they can explain can be explained more fundamentally and parsimoniously with a genetic analysis of public-choice processes. When the existence and boundaries of a government are explained by the catchment area of a collective good, or by transport and communication costs, or by economies of scale, or even by military or political accidents, and the government itself then forms attitudes, the theories of economics and collective decision-making are on a far stronger position than any explanation that starts from the benevolent and malevolent matrices. This does not deny that these matrices may still be important, or that we should endeavor to incorporate them into our theory, but it does argue that they should have a more modest role than Boulding gives them in his analysis of the grants economy.

The fact that heterogeneous preferences for public goods are most favorable to the genesis or security of a public does not by contrast pose any special problems for the new political economy. In primitive conditions, with poor transport and communication, there is characteristically some variation in culture or tastes as one goes from one tribe, extended family, parish, or city-state to another. If a technological change lowers transportation and communication costs for a government, or a relatively larger political unit exploits the economies of scale in military capability and conquers a smaller neighbor, or a military or political accident leads to a government that includes two or more groups with divergent tastes, the leaders of that government will have a reason to indoctrinate the diverse groups within it to develop a common attitude about government and public goods. In due course, if the expanding government is successful, more nearly homogeneous preferences for public goods will result, which in turn will make it easier for the augmented jurisdiction to survive. This type of scenario would lead one to expect more dissent, turbulence, and instability in newly-conquered areas than in those that have been held long enough for official indoctrination to have taken effect, and this is of course frequently observed. Another factor that helps to determine the boundaries of "variable-boundary" public-goods is of course language. Often governments impose common languages upon those whom they govern, and to the extent that this happens, language is not an independent influence on the shape or size of a public. Many nationalisms are on the other hand delineated by a common language. The simplest application of the theory of economics and public choice would call attention to the great savings of cost that accrue where everyone in a jurisdiction or other institution shares a common language. If interaction in an institution is very frequent, a diversity of language can be prohibitively costly: a nuclear family, for example, without a common language is difficult even to imagine.

Boulding would no doubt point also to the colossal influence that religion has on language, and he would surely be right to do so. The influence of Luther's Bible on the character and use of the German language, and the influence of the Koran (both through its influence on military zeal and its direct effect) on the use of Arabic are obvious examples. Stein Rokkan, the distinguished Norwegian political scientist, has perceptively pointed out that protestantism, with its emphasis on lay reading of the Bible and on popular sermons and songs, created an intellectual elite in protestant countries that used the vernacular rather than Latin. He believes that this partly accounts for the earlier development of stable democracies in Northern than in Southern Europe.

The diversity of the forces that determine the delineation of language groups, and the interaction of these delineations with the formation of publics, are nicely illustrated by the position of the English language today. The pre-eminence of the English language today is due partly to religious dissent in England following the reformation, partly to British naval and maritime skills in this period, partly to the fact that the Industrial Revolution took place in Great Britain, partly to the complex of causes that led to the expansion of the "second" British Empire in the 19th Century, partly to the economic, scientific, and military might of the United States in the 20th Century, and so on.

Clearly the notions in the grants-economy literature are not sufficient to explain the delineation of linguistic areas, much less the domains or the boundaries of the governments and other institutions that provide collective goods. The "publics" to whom public goods are provided are defined in some cases by the technological or geological realities that create a catchment area for a public good, in others by the economies of scale in military capability, in others by defensible borders, in others by transportation and communication costs, in others by random events of military or political interaction, in others by the presence or absence of heterogeneous tastes for private goods and homogeneous tastes for public goods, and in still other cases by a pre-existing common language which itself has a complex explanation. The patterns of preferences are partly explained by the religious or cultural factors which Boulding likes to emphasize, but it is difficult to see how any single religious or cultural force could often account for *both* homogeneities and heterogeneities of preferences. Cases in which a public is formed by some process that can be explained in terms of economics and public choice, or these plus a random term, and in which the jurisdiction then molds preferences to meet its needs, are by contrast quite common. No valid theory of the genesis of governments or other institutions could possible leave out the theory of public goods or the other tools of economics and decision theory.

Neither could it leave out the exogenous changes in preferences to which Ken Boulding has so eloquently called our attention. In doing this, he has made a crucial contribution to economics and to social science generally. He has in addition shown, better than any other writer that I know about, how the systems of market exchange must be understood in the context of a comprehensive conception of the social system that subsumes governments and families, threats and gifts, hate and love. Every economist should concede that we cannot have much confidence in any sweeping or fundamental policy judgment, even about the role of markets, without the aid of a conception, or at least a taxonomy, which reminds us of the intimate interrelationship between markets and other essential social processes. The economist must concede, too, that just as human nature should be expected to be similar in different contexts, so it may be changed to some degree by different social settings—Boulding's contention that threat systems breed malevolence is evidence enough of this. Thus, even if all of the criticisms of the grants-economy idea offered in this paper were totally accepted, that would not deny that Boulding has beautifully posed some inescapable problems that economists have shamefully neglected, and even provided some of the concepts needed to solve these problems.

If this paper is correct, a good many of the other concepts we need can be fashioned now with the aid of the tools of thought already available in economics and collective-decision theory. Unfortunately, the relative significance of these concepts in relation to those that Boulding has developed in his discussions of the grants economy is not yet clear. There is a compelling need for good historical studies which attempt to sort out the relative importance of the considerations that Boulding and I have been arguing about. A massive inquiry into both comparative history and into the developing areas of the present day is finally required, but even studies of individual societies could move our understanding a long way ahead. Is it too much to hope that comparative historians, economic historians, political historians, students of political and economic development, and empirically-minded economists and social scientists of all kinds will endeavor to ascertain the relative role of the forces that are under dispute in various concrete situations?

There is ultimately the heroic task of creating a more general theory that can *simultaneously* consider both the implications of existing preferences and the ways that social processes change preferences. A normative theory must proceed with some given preferences or some criterion of progress, but a positive theory need not; and it is a more general positive theory that we most need now. Schumpeter is supposed to have said that it is sad to be an economist after Walras invented general equilibrium, because the greatest idea that economic science could *possibly* develop had already been invented. Schumpeter was wrong: creating a model of the general equilibrium of a society that changes preferences in the process of satisfying them is an even nobler goal, and it is a goal toward which the grand man to whom this volume is dedicated is leading the way.

B.2. The brotherhood of man and the leadership of Kenneth Boulding

JAMES N. MORGAN

Looked at from one point of view, Kenneth Boulding can be accused of starting a whole series of rabbits running. He was talking about ecology in the fifties when most of us didn't really know what the word meant. He started a faculty seminar at Michigan on income maintenance when the transfer-payments components of the national accounts were only a minor source of confusion to most economists as to whether they belonged in the Gross National Product or if not, how to treat them. He started a society for the study of conflict resolution, and another for the study of the grants economy.

But all this was not just coining new terms, or building empires, or trying to get others to get "with it". Seen as a whole, it expressed a concern that we study and improve the way we relate to one another in the economy and the polity, how we implement our sense of brother-hood, to use an ancient term. The fact is that some aspects of this concern have caught fire (ecology and our responsibility for future generations of man), while others have misfired (dependence and poverty where the elimination of the former proved elusive and of the latter impolitic), and still others have yet to capture the energies of many people in spite of their critical importance (the creative resolution of conflict, and even the development of systematic research on the problem).

I can report from my own biased memory being dragooned into attending a faculty seminar on income maintenance at the University of Michigan in the late 1950's where the mixture of Kenneth's enthusiasm and Wilbur Cohen's trees-and-forest combination of knowledge of the intricate detail and sense for the big problems convinced us that the persistence of poverty after decades of apparent affluence in the United

States deserved some attention. One direct result was a proposal, a national study, and a book jocularly known as the morgan-david volume.[1]

There is a chapter on philanthropy (money only, not time) documenting for the first time its substantial size, religious base, its high income elasticity, and its concentration among older people, the latter leading to speculation about less-generous newer generations of people, versus the alternative hypotheses that the ability to give (or one's concern with the hereafter) grows with age.

There is a great deal on intergenerational transmission of poverty, largely since ignored or even misquoted because like most empirical findings the results fit no stereotype. There is a great deal of intergenerational change, *and* some serial correlation.

Perhaps the most important contribution of that book has been and still is for the most part ignored, namely the focus on the importance of the unit—the family. It might seem that since fewer than a fifth of the families in this country have adults other than the head and wife in them, the family is a perfectly acceptable unit for analysis. But in fact it is the doubled-up families who are hiding much of the dependence, and whose stability in the face of alternative income-maintenance programs becomes a crucial policy issue when one is proposing reforms like a negative income tax. Without unacceptable interference and spying, such a system would have to be self-administering like the income tax itself, hence neutral with respect to who lives with whom. But if any individual adult could qualify in his or her own right for an income supplement, designing a schedule that would encourage at least as much living together as we have now is a genuine challenge. Given the reluctance with which people double up, analysts of income distributions and of poverty need at least to look separately at adult individuals and couples (and their children), if not at individuals.

One way to deal with the problem is to divide families into adult units, as was done in *Income and Welfare in the United States.* Another way to deal with intra-family transfers, which is what is involved, is to make some direct estimates of what living together really means economically. Since one knows in a survey who earns income, and can estimate the fraction of income consumed by the different family members, the difference for each person is his net contribution to, or receipt from, the family. One might think it was overdoing this to include the children, but in a society moving rapidly toward government subsidy of child care, and toward group care facilities, calculations of what total individual irres-

[1]James Morgan, Martin David, Wilbur Cohen and Harvey Brazer, *Income and Welfare in the United States* (McGraw Hill, New York, 1962).

ponsibility (for one's fellow man) would imply are at least interesting. One set of such calculations estimated that the amounts of (implicit, intra-family) transfers involved was well over $300 billion in 1970.[2]

Another way to study the importance and impact of decisions about family structure is to examine its dynamics. It has long been traditional for sociologists to study the expected pattern of life-cycle changes, and more recently to study actual decisions about how many children to have, and with what spacing. But attention to decisions about family patterns as though they were genuine choices has been much rarer. As Jim Duesenberry once remarked:

Economics is all about how people make choices. Sociology is all about why they don't have any choices to make.[3]

It is not just that change in family composition is an interesting subject for study. In our analysis of family-income dynamics, following a panel of 5,000 families and their newly-generated splitoff units, we discovered that indeed, changes in economic status of American families are dominated by the effects of changes in family composition, and related changes in labor-force participation.[4]

And there is clearly some discretion at least as to the timing of such events as the children's leaving home to form separate units, as well as the doubling and undoubling of adults other than the family head and wife. The incentive of children to "split" is clearly affected by their earning opportunities, and by the quality of the education which is available to them as an alternative.

So much for intra-family transfers, except to note that a great deal more research about motivation and behavior, and a great deal more attention to long-range public policy toward the family as an institution, are both in order. What about transfers *between* families? How much do people help their relatives when they are not doing it in the intimacy of living together? The simple answer is: very little. A brief summary of the evidence may help.

Extensive help to relatives means that one provides more than half their support and they become dependents for tax purposes. For years, in order to estimate people's income taxes we have asked about support given to

[2]Nancy Baerwaldt and James Morgan, 'Trends in Intra-Family Transfers', in: Lewis Mandell (ed.), *Surveys of Consumers, 1971–72* (Survey Research Center, Institute for Social Research, The University of Michigan, Ann Arbor, Mich., 1973).

[3]James S. Duesenberry, '*Comment in Demographic and Economic Change in Developed Countries*' (Princeton University Press, Princeton, N.J., 1960) 233.

[4]James N. Morgan, 'Change in Global Measures' in: *Five Thousand American Families — Patterns of Economic Progress*, Vol. I (Institute for Social Research, The University of Michigan, Ann Arbor, Mich., 1974).

dependents outside the household, and whether it was more than half their total support. The proportions reporting such help, and there is no particular reason to suspect under-reporting of such acts of generosity, have never been more than a few percentage points. In the 1973 wave of our panel study, some 10 percent reported *some* such support's being given, $3\frac{1}{2}$ percent to more than one person, but only 4 percent reported anyone dependent on them for more than half their support.

Our estimate of amounts in the 1960 study (for 1959) were some $7 billion, however, compared with $4.5 billion given to the extra adults living with relatives.[5]

All this ignores non-money components, which may well be more important. When people live together it is difficult or impossible to measure the time they spend helping each other, though work is under way on the time-cost of children.[6]

Some data on time spent doing things without pay for church, charity *or* relatives, were presented for the year 1964, without separating that done for other individuals (mostly relatives).[7] The same study asked about help *received* with housework and child care, and whether it was free or paid for, the free help being largely from relatives. There was very little free help from outside.

One bit of evidence on the sense that people have of obligation to relatives comes from a question asked of our current income-dynamics panel, "Would you feel you had to help your parents or other relatives (more) if you had more money?". Some two-fifths said yes, mostly without any qualifications, and, interestingly, the proportion seemed to go up during the period from 1968 to 1972.

In the first wave of the current panel study, we asked respondents whether they spent more than 40 hours in the previous year (1967) helping friends and relatives. Nearly half said they had, and about a tenth claimed to have spent more than 120 hours on such activities.[8]

A final bit of evidence on inter-family help is the number of people who neither own nor rent their dwelling, some of whom are living rent-free in dwellings provided by relatives. (Some 2–3 percent of all families)

[5]Morgan *et al.*, *Income and Welfare in the United States, op. cit.*, p. 279.

[6]C. Russell Hill and Frank P. Stafford, 'Allocation of Time to Preschool Children and Educational Opportunity', *Journal of Human Resources*; and Russell Hill and Frank Stafford, 'Time Inputs to Children', in: *Five Thousand American Families — Patterns of Economic Progress*, Vol. II (Institute for Social Research, The University of Michigan, Ann Arbor, Mich., 1974).

[7]James Morgan, Simail Sirageldin and Nancy Baerwaldt, *Productive Americans* (Institute for Social Research, The University of Michigan, Ann Arbor, Mich., 1966).

[8]*Ibid.*

So much for help to and from relatives, in time and money and things, with and without any reciprocity. One can argue that much of it is a substitute for previous patterns of family life, and ask what its future is. But let us turn to a brief examination of what is more generally called "philanthropy"—gifts of time and money and property to others where there is clearly no reciprocal obligation, nor even a set of implicit family obligations to guide. Strangely enough, in spite of much casual history of philanthropy in America and a unique set of laws and institutions that have stimulated it, the quantitative evidence is not that extensive. We know about philanthropic deductions on the Federal income tax, except that those who give through private foundations or trusts disappear from those data. And those who find the standard deduction is more than what they can itemize, disappear also from these statistics (as well as those who file no return). What the tax data show is clear though: extremely large income elasticity, particularly for non-religious contributions, and yet a substantial number even at the highest incomes claiming no charitable deductions. (In addition to those giving in other ways, some may have so many other ways of reducing taxable income that the tax incentive is no longer relevant.)

We have small-sample survey data, with less precision but a richer capacity to explain interpersonal differences, on money given in 1959, and on time given in 1964, but nowhere both together, or combined with time and money given to non philanthropic (or non-deductible) causes such as political candidates and organizations trying to change or preserve laws. Hopefully that lack will be remedied by studies currently under way funded by a new Commission on Private Philanthropy and Public Needs. Such studies are particularly crucial at this time because of massive changes in our laws and society in the last ten years, and proposed future changes. It may be well to summarize what some of the crucial changes have been, and some of the proposals to study them.[9]

[9]F. Emerson Andrews, *Philanthropic Giving* (Russell Sage Foundation, New York, 1950); Robert H. Brenner, *American Philanthropy* (University of Chicago Press, Chicago, 1960); Richard Carter, *The Gentle Legions* (Doubleday, New York, 1961); Merle Curti, American Philanthropy and National Character', *American Quarterly 10* (Winter, 1958) 420–437; Murray Hausknect, *The Joiners* (Bedminster Press, New York, 1962); Herbert, Hyman and Charles Wright, 'Trends in Voluntary Membership of American Adults', *American Sociological Review 36* (April 1971) 191–206; Helen H. Lamale and Joseph A. Clorety, 'City Families as Givers', *Monthly Labor Review* (December, 1959) 1303–1311; Arnaud C. Marts, *The Generosity of Americans* (Prentice Hall, Englewood Cliffs, N.J., 1966); Marcel Maus, *The Gift*, translated by Ian Cunnison (W. W. Norton, New York, 1967; original 1925); National Opinion Research Center, *Motivations for Charitable Giving*, UAJ Study in an Eastern Area (Chicago, 1961); Carl Rosenfeld and others, *A Survey of Volunteer Work*, U.S.B.L.S., Manpower Administration (In Nov. 1965 Census labor force survey); David Horton Smith

It all began in 1964 with that famous tax-cut, the first time that economists had managed to convince Congress that it was all right to cut taxes when the government was running a deficit. It was much heralded among economists as a successful breakthrough. Only later did it become clear that it was a decision not to abolish poverty—the same fiscal results could have been achieved by giving money to the poor to bring everyone above a poverty line. (The reason, of course, was that people wanted to abolish dependency, not just poverty.) But for the purposes of the present discussion, the tax cut had another effect—it raised the "price of charity" at the very top from 9¢ on the dollar (or less) to 30 on the dollar.

The reason, of course, is that the tax advantage from deducting charitable contributions depends on one's marginal tax rate. If one can reduce taxable income by $100 by giving that much to charity, one's taxes are cut by a fraction of that, the fraction by which an added dollar of income is taxed. Indeed, until recently at least, the tax was neutral with respect to whether one gave time or money to charity.[10] If one gave the time instead of working and earning an extra $100, one saved the taxes on the extra $100 or earnings. If one earned the extra money and gave it to charity and could deduct it, one also saved the taxes on the extra $100. Of course, for those who cannot benefit from itemizing deductions, there is no tax advantage, and giving $100 to charity reduces one's income by $100 and it is better to give time, but more of that later.

At any rate, prior to 1964 the combination of the high marginal tax rates, and the provisions allowing full deductibility of the current value of appreciated assets without paying the capital-gains tax, allowed the wealthy to determine the allocation of large amounts of resources at little net cost to themselves. There are of course arguments for such a system. It preserves diversity, allows initiative and innovation, and perhaps even meets society's needs in a better way than that provided by the political process. One can even argue that the social obligations of the rich are such, and their inability to spend it all on themselves anyway so severe, that it is

---

(ed.), *Voluntary Action Research, 1972* (D. C. Heath, Lexington, Mass., 1972); David Horton Smith, (ed.), *Voluntary Action Research, 1973* (D. C. Heath, Lexington Mass., 1973); Victor Thiessen, *Who Gives a Damn? A Study of Charitable Contributions*, Ph.D. Thesis, University of Wisconsin, Madison, Wisc. (1968); Commission on Foundations and Private Philanthropy, *Foundations, Private Giving and Public Policy* (University of Chicago, Press, Chicago, 1970).

[10]Since the marginal tax rate on *earned* income has a 50 percent maximum, whereas added-on unearned income on top can be taxed at rates up to 70 percent. Therefore a man could earn $100 more, increasing his taxes by $50, but give the $100 to charity, cutting them by $70. But if he gave time directly, he would lose the $50 that he would have earned after taxes rather than the $30.

not really their income that they give to charity, and therefore not taxable as such.

In the decade since 1964 a series of other changes have taken place, some affecting largely the most affluent, some affecting largely the least affluent. The maximum proportion of income that could be deducted for charitable contributions in any one year was raised substantially, though differentially depending on the donee—lower limits on gifts to private foundations. The freedom from capital-gains tax on appreciated assets given to charity was limited, again depending on the donee. The marginal tax rates increased, at the lower incomes, if only because of inflation. And in 1969 a complex series of laws about private foundations and charitable trusts, aimed at eliminating abuses, made the rules far more complex and apparently incomprehensible even to legal experts.

Finally, in 1971 and 1972 the standard deduction was raised in two steps to a maximum of 15 percent of income or $2,000, whichever is less, making it no longer advantageous for millions of taxpayers to itemize. If one is not itemizing, then the tax advantages of deducting charitable gifts no longer apply, and the "price of charity" rises from say 70% on the dollar (if the marginal tax rate is 30 percent) to $1.00 on the dollar.[11] We have some specific data on what people say who have *stopped* itemizing in this recent period. The sample is very small, but the results are interesting. Only a small fraction (less than a tenth) admit that the loss of tax advantage has had any effect on their giving. But a much larger fraction expect it to have an effect on people like themselves, and a still larger fraction expect it to have an effect on people in general. Given the fact that only with the 1972 return filed in the spring of 1973 did the full effect of the law change appear, there might actually be quite a lag before an effect appears. It seems to be a change well worth trying to monitor. The policy implications are serious, since the lower-middle-income groups affected, particularly those older people with the mortgage paid off (and no interest to deduct) are likely to be a major source of support for churches.

Proposed changes include (a) a floor, with contributions deductible only to the amount by which they exceed some fraction of income, (b) a decrease from 100 percent to some lower percentage, in the fraction of an estate that can be left tax-free to charity, and (c) an increase in the marital exemption from estate taxes (so that one could postpone the charitable bequest, leaving it to the surviving spouse to decide). Some would even eliminate the charitable deduction altogether. Perhaps the most important

[11]Of course if one can give *time* instead of earning money and giving that, there is no tax, so these nonitemizers would be advised to give time, if they could. In 1975 the standard deduction was raised again, reducing the numbers who could benefit from itemization.

proposal, however, would be to substitute a tax-credit or matching-grant system for the present deductibility. This would provide the same relative subsidy to anyone's giving, regardless of his income, rather than the present system which gives subsidies varying from zero to 70 percent. The present concentration of giving at the highest incomes may, indeed, have resulted in part from tax advantages. If revisions made those advantages equal, would more philanthropy come from the middle-income groups (where most of the aggregate income is), and thus change the nature and character of the things supported?

Of course, there has been a growing role of government and private-insurance system transfers, and a growing awareness of the complex and often inequitable net of overlapping jurisdictions. Using survey data to cut through to what happens to the people at the end of the line, Katherine Dickinson reports that even though transfers do keep some 10 percent of the population out of poverty, their speed and efficiency in offsetting changes in income does not appear so effective. And those with a little earned income seem to end up worse off than those with none at all.[12] The regional disparities in levels of welfare, even corrected for differences in cost of living, are apparent in these data too. A fertile field for study, hampered by the variety of jurisdictions and the flexibility of interpretation of the rules by social workers, is the equity as well as the adequacy of the whole income-maintenance system.

Added to all the changes relating directly to private philanthropy have been a series of large social changes, particularly the expanded role of the government in helping dependent people, and in providing some amenities. Social-security benefits have been expanded in scope and adequacy. More of those eligible for welfare have found out about it and/or decided to accept it. There has been an explosion both of prices and of real incomes, and some catching up by Blacks and women, and there is Federal support for the humanities and the performing arts. All this can be expected to affect private philanthropy—partly competing with it, partly changing the appropriate menu of activities most requiring private support.[13]

The growing awareness of the failure of most attempts to eliminate dependency may yet force us back to a consideration of the abolition of

---

[12]Katherine Dickinson, "Transfer Income" in *Five Thousand Families, Patterns of Economic Progress*, Institute for Social Research, The University of Michigan, 1974.

[13]For some insightful treatments of this see R. J. Lampman, 'How Much Does the American System of Transfers Benefit the Poor?' in L. H. Goodman (ed.), *Economic Progress and Social Welfare* (Columbia University Press, New York, 1966), and R. J. Lampman, 'Public and Private Transfers as Social Process' in: K. E. Boulding and Martin Pfaff (eds.), *Redistribution to the Rich and the Poor* (Wadsworth, Belmont, Calif., 1972).

poverty, and the changes in the public transfer systems most effective in doing that. Recent increases in prices and the cost of living seem to have exacerbated people's concerns with their own incomes, and their sense of unfairness, and may make it increasingly difficult to tax the middle incomes (where the money is) to raise the floor. Our sense of brotherhood, it seems likely, will be sorely tried in the years to come. If we are found wanting, it will not be because Kenneth Boulding did not try.

B.3.   Pathways toward greater equity

MARTIN PFAFF and ANITA B. PFAFF

1. Introduction

1.1. "LIBERTÉ, EGALITÉ, FRATERNITÉ"?

Only few observers of the human scene could possibly believe that of the three rallying themes of the French Revolution—"liberté, egalité, fraternité"—any one has been achieved anywhere in the world to a completely satisfactory extent.

In the aftermath of the social changes wrought among other things by the French Revolution, the liberalist principle held sway in parts of the Western world. It emphasized the norm of liberty, the freedom of individuals or groups to pursue their fortune according to their own judgement. The role of the state was to "laissez faire, laissez passez!" Adam Smith's Invisible Hand implied nothing else but the notion that out of the manifold plans of individuals striving to seek their own self-fulfillment an economic and social harmony would automatically result.

If one observes the history of the past and the present century, one must seriously question whether this benevolent ideal based on the pure competition of individuals, has really brought the fruits its proponents had envisaged. The market mechanism shows an alarming propensity to adjust to changes in a cyclical mode. The result is unemployment of human and material resources, fluctuations in prices and interest rates. All of these put great stress on the ability of human organizations to accommodate to the unfettered operation of market forces. Indeed, the rise of the labor movement and the socialist movement of the past century can only be explained against the background of the failure of the system to provide for more general human needs—for example, stability, security, and human integration. More recently we have come to conclude that markets do not even function as efficiently as had been envisaged: Due to monopoly elements, externalities, indivisibilities, increasing returns to scale, and lack of information, market mechanisms do not provide efficient signals in the allocation of scarce resources. This is of particular concern in a new era when social costs of production and consumption have to be considered—whether this be the result of pollution or of the energy crisis. The spectre of a stationary economy lends even greater credence to this concern. The notion that society has to provide for institutional rules to safeguard individuals against the misfortunes of the market place has become more generally accepted. Perhaps the goal of liberty can only be achieved if a minimum of security is provided and if individuals acquire the norms of conduct which otherwise would have to be imposed upon them by an outside force. In this sense Rousseau's postulate that freedom results from carrying out the "will of all" acquires an even stronger meaning particularly in a democratic society.

The second ideal, "egalité", appears to be even more elusive. Does it imply a complete equality of all individuals—young and old, men and women, black and white, educated and uneducated, industrious and lazy? How is equality to be defined in operational terms and in concrete situations? In an age when scarcity still prevails and where individualism yields emotional force, the postulate that could receive the greatest approval could be one of "equal opportunity for all." This notion could imply that everyone should start the race of life at the same base line; no one should be carried over the finishing line in a golden chair while the others are just getting ready to start the race. The goal of public policy would thus be to help create roughly equal starting positions to run the competitive race. Indeed this postulate appears to command the consent of many because it seems to them fair and equitable: We have come to think of the right of an individual to earn the fruits of his labor. In the age of scarcity, perhaps such differences in human status and social, political, and economic attainment appear justified. Progress generally appears possible only by the enhanced productivity and the initiative brought to bear over and beyond the call of duty by many motivated individuals. Nonetheless, differences already become obvious between the concepts of equality and equity. An equitable state of affairs could also be one which is not equal: "Those who labor more should receive a larger share of the product". As long as men consider such unequal sharing of the output legitimate, no problems of equity or justice appear to arise. Injustice is generally felt when the perceived state of affairs deviates from the expected or generally legitimated state. This then already brings us to the question of the relevant norm and the shape of the expectations with which perceptions of reality must be compared in order to yield a foundation for the concept of equity.

Even a cursory examination of the starting positions of individuals born into a different social and economic milieu belies the postulate of "equal opportunities for all". Children of wealthier and more educated parents tend to attain higher life incomes than their less fortunate brethren.

The lofty ideal of "fraternité" appears to have been achieved to various degrees in different forms of human organization. Fraternité is perhaps attained by the members of a family under pressure, by a group sworn to attain a common goal, and by soldiers in the hour of battle: In all these cases the degree of integration of the individual in the collectivity attains a rather high level. Nonetheless, if one views the broad scene of human endeavors, fraternité appears more as a goal to be striven toward than as a definite achievement of a particular form of social organization.

1.2. CONFLICTS AMONG SOCIAL GOALS

The principle of equality essentially implies that one should "treat equal things equally and unequal things unequally". This concept of equality is one of the moving principles of modern democratic thinking. Thus we find it also in the declaration associated with the French Revolution. Nonetheless there appears an obvious contradiction between reality and the theoretical ideal of equality: Distinctions are generally based on a set of socio-economic criteria. The antithesis between the ideal of equality and the real world presumably has a very significant impact on the forces tending towards social change. The ideal of equality can be applied not only to the distribution of income and wealth: It applies also to power—the rule of man over men. The ideal of equality would call for a different foundation governing the relations of man: In the place of dominance and subordination it would provide for free contracts, free exchange, and voluntary consensus.

The concept of equality itself explains to a large extent many political movements of our era of history. It emphasizes not only the concept of equality of opportunities, i.e. the possibility for each individual to attain an economic and social state corresponding to his skills and talents. This notion merely represents the application of individualism to social relations. The concept of equality before the law represents a second extension of the notion of the worth of individuals before the structure of power. A similar role is played by the concept of political equality, which is expressed in notions such as "one man, one vote". Similarly the concepts of social and racial equality have influenced modern political endeavors. Finally we find the concept of economic equality. The problem of economic equality, however, is not as simple as it may appear. Very few would advocate a completely equal distribution of income and wealth.

Not even Marxism or other types of socialism would assert that all men should be alike economically, and that all should obtain an equal share of the common wealth. Nonetheless, the continuing presence of poverty at a time when the economic surplus has increased by the means of industrial production and distribution—as well as the increased inequality of wealth and power—indicates that the problems have not been solved. Indeed some would maintain that the forces operating in modern organizations would tend toward even greater inequalities. This appears to be true even though on the surface a larger degree of social equality has been attained than at any other time in history. Alexis deTocqueville already pointed out that there is a conflict between the idea of liberty on the one hand and the idea of equality on the other: The free exercise of personal abilities leads to inequality in the social domain: Therefore greater social equality can be attained only by restricting the will of the individual and thus individual freedom. In deTocqueville's view modern mass democracies would place greater emphasis on equality than on freedom.

The "Declaration of the Rights of Man and the Citizens" of the French Revolution (1789) explicitly recognizes the right to private property as one of the natural rights of man. Private property, however, gives rise to social inequality. Private property, combined with the right of inheritance, leads to a programming of social positions. Thus the problems caused by property and inheritance appear to stand in contrast with the ideal of equality. If one wishes to change the prevailing pattern of inequality one must neutralize the effect of inheritance in influencing the opportunities accorded to individuals. It comes as no surprise that the social movements of the past century and the present one attempt to achieve a state whereby man has both equality *and* freedom. Such a reconciliation of seeming opposites can only be attained by changing on the one hand the concept of property and that of the economic order on the other. There exists a conflict even among these social movements: Marxist socialism attempts to achieve such an ideal through the overthrow of the capitalist social order. Reform socialism or democratic socialism attempts to attain both equality and freedom through a peaceful reformation of the economic, political and social order. Democratic socialism influenced the concept of the modern social state: In the name of equality it attempts to improve the economic position of disadvantaged social groups, by using a variety of instruments such as wage policy, tax-transfer policy, and social policies.

The idea of justice is closely related to the idea of equality: It postulates that everyone should get what he deserves; that equal objects should be treated equally; that each individual should be given equal treatment in line with his state; and that the abuse of power should be avoided.

The concept of justice goes back to Aristotle, who attempted to apply it to the social domain. He recognized that, apart from justice, equality has to be considered. He describes two basic forms of justice: First is the justice in the distribution of goods; it implies that equal individuals should obtain equal parts. This "justicia distributiva" lays down the rights and obligations of the individual toward the community. The second kind of justice—"justicia commutativa"—lays down the rights and obligations of individuals toward each other.

In Aristotle's view justice consists in the harmony of the state. It is accomplished when each individual assumes the task required to maintain the social whole. Thus the individual represents an element in the organic totality of the state. Nonetheless Aristotle extends and modifies this notion by introducing the concept of equality: He views it either as an arithmetical or geometrical concept: The former is based on identity, the latter on proportionality or equivalence. Arithmetical notions of equality lead to a concept of commutative justice whereas geometrical equality presumes distributive justice.

Commutative justice is administered by the judge while distributive justice is the proper subject of a political authority. Political goods and services as well as rights and obligations should be administered in line with distributive justice; punishments and damages should be applied according to the tenets of commutative justice. Nonetheless, even to Aristotle there appears an inherent tension between these forms of justice: He advocates that a moving equilibrium should attempt to reconcile the demands of distributive justice with those of commutative justice.

Thomas Aquinas applied and extended these notions of commutative justice to that of contracts and exchange, i.e. to individualistic relations. Distributive justice in his view is more of a hierarchical concept. According to him one should not rely on a complex equilibrium but rather on the power of the state which is established over and beyond the relations of the community. This notion was advanced further by Locke, Rousseau and Kant: They point to justice in an attempt to integrate the conflicting values of liberty and equality.

Proudhon and the Solidarists attempted to reconcile a similar conflict between justice and fraternity: They strove to rectify the administration of commutative justice in order to reconcile the apparent conflict between the solidarity of man and their inequality in economic and social position. They advocated "a realignment in the positions of the various members of society" brought about by the power of the state and through social legislation, in order to protect marginal and underprivileged groups such as women and children. This was to be accomplished by the use of progressive income taxes and other measures of redistribution.

In the concept of justice, therefore, an attempt is made to arrive at a synthesis of the antithetical values of liberty and equality. Behind these in turn we recognize the ideals of society which have been responsible for the continuing tension inherent in western cultural thought, i.e. those of individualism and universalism. The former sees in society the sum of individuals, the latter an organic entity which is more than the sum of its parts.

When the goals of the French Revolution were proclaimed, their realization in actual affairs was rather remote. It was not necessary to give them operational or practical content or to deal with the conflict arising between these goals.

Furthermore, from the point of view of an atomistic individual there appeared perhaps less potential for conflict inherent in these goals. The liberty of one to express himself by necessity reduces that of the other. A social contract appears to be called for among individuals whose aim is to assure a degree of liberty of the individual precisely by constricting his behavior towards others.

The concept of equity completely ignores the existence of large and by necessity, hierarchically structured organizations. Inherent in these is the existence of inequality due to income, status, and power. The concept of equality therefore has to give way to that of equity.

The concept of equity traditionally is generally identified with the notion of fairness and natural justice in the courts of law. It implied the ability of the court to provide a discretionary treatment to an individual case in accordance with notions of natural justice. Thus it, in fact, supplemented common law. More generally the concept of equity denotes the postulate of providing a more humane interpretation of law in general. Essentially it implies that these tenets obtain a superior status simply because they are based on the ethical equality inherent in the principles to be applied to a particular case. In the social realm the Norman rulers of Britain were already prescribed to carry out their royal duties and to administer justice to rich and poor alike. Thus equity represented "executive justice" rather than justice according to the strict interpretation of the law.

In practical terms one could thus define equity as a norm providing for the "unequal treatment of unequal individuals; but the resultant degree of inequality has to be legitimated by all". Similarly, the concept of fraternité to a degree recognizes the existence of social ties resulting from the pattern of integration. It neglects again the hierarchical nature of relations in large social groups.

2. Concepts of distributive justice

2.1. SOCIAL GOALS AND THE ECONOMIC SYSTEM

The goal of egalité—and to a lesser degree that of liberté—has entered the sphere of economic concerns particularly in the guise of questions regarding income or wealth distribution.

The relationship between the goal of equality and distribution seems more readily apparent. Although no one has been able to provide a universally acceptable and ideal norm for the distribution of income, most economists would agree that a more equal distribution of income and wealth is, *ceteris paribus*, preferable to a less egalitarian distribution. On the other hand many, if not most, economists agree that a completely equal distribution of income would not be desirable.[1] Depending on the income concept analyzed, a completely equal distribution may appear to be less than fair.

If annual income should be equalized for all, it would involve a severe disadvantage for the person who attains a higher level of education and who enters gainful employment at a later age. On the other hand, should life income be equalized, problems of differential life expectancy in different occupations and rates of discount to establish present values of life income enter the scene. Finally some argue that equal income may not only be unfair, but also inefficient. Differential incentives may act as regulators bringing about a more efficient factor allocation in the labor market.

The goal of liberté cannot be seen as unrelated to the distribution of income and wealth. Property, or more accurately control of economic resources, provides a degree of freedom of decision and action. In particular the power to withhold resources from others on the one hand provides liberties or freedoms to an economic actor, at the same time it withholds the good from others. In fact, exceedingly complex trade-off relations between different manifestations of liberty exist in human organizations. One example may be cited: Organized labor conferred certain liberties upon union members and non-unionized labor, as well. The possibility of strikes, i.e. withholding their economic resource 'labor' from others, conferred a liberty or right upon an individual worker which was absent in the pre-union era. Yet this liberty

---

[1]For a persuasive argument in favor of equal incomes in a situation of uncertainty, see Abba P. Lerner, *The Economics of Control*: Macmillan, New York, 1946.

or right, like any right in a social group, had to be acquired at the "price" of yielding other rights to the labor union. Some of these rights were empty or useless in most normal circumstances. Yet, for example, the freedom to negotiate independently, if less favorably, might have been important to some individual laborer who lost his job because of an aggressive and rigid wage policy on the part of his union during a recession.

In any event the individual who enjoys a more favorable position in the income and wealth hierarchy is, in practice, if not in principle, more free or less restricted than his less fortunate and less well-to-do brethren. This freedom ranges from long-run allocation of time to allocation of income, to control over other individuals. Thus even the optimal distribution of liberty, if such a phenomenon could be defined unequivocally and operationally, cannot be seen in isolation from the distribution of income and wealth. A corrective interference with the latter may be a prerequisite for ensuring the former.

The third goal that we addressed ourselves to—fraternité—does not find its economic reflection as readily as do the other two. However, the *homo socialis*, as opposed to the *homo oeconomicus*, is "his brother's keeper", up to a point. He is not only morally responsible to concede the other's rights and liberty, but also to help the unable, the disabled, the destitute, or the weak. In the sphere of economic concern this brings us to the domain of redistribution, or the grants economy.

The three goals associated with the French Revolution to a degree ignore, at least in their simple declaration, the systemic interdependence of social organization. Yet it is equally evident that they have meaning only in a social system with the interdependence of members, its hierarchies, and its conflicts. For a Robinson Crusoe on his island these goals are no problem. Nor are they of interest for atoms or molecules in a gas or fluid, who find an equilibrium state quite different from that of a purposive human social system.

We have touched upon the historic discourse on the potential and actual conflict of liberty and equality. In a social-science context that means that liberty has to be replaced by a system of organized restrictions of liberty—a legal and political system borne and legitimated by society: The material rules have to be legislated according to generally accepted processes (the constitution). The formal or procedural rules have to be laid down to provide the mechanisms for conflict resolution between individuals and groups, and to punish violations of material rules of conduct. The problem of liberty is much rather transformed into a problem of participation in political processes.

The mythical process underlying the establishment of a viable legal and political system—be it a social contract or some other phenomenon—need not concern us at this point.

The goal of equality should be modified to one of equity. Equal rights, which by necessity would entail obligations, would hardly be considered fair or desirable. A child or a disabled or sick person is not equal in every relevant sense to an able-bodied adult and should not be treated as such.

The concept of fraternity should similarly be modified. It should recognize the inherent differences in human beings: From these result safeguards against undue hardship, misery and catastrophe. This concept is implicit in those actions and institutions of the economic system which are guided by "need" and not by merit or narrow allocative efficiency.

Each one of the three principles is thus tied in with distribution and redistribution. However, the theory of income distribution hardly provides a normative framework to judge a distribution as desirable, let alone optimal. The only rigorous normative rule for the functional and personal distribution of income was provided by the marginal-productivity theory. Some theories of personal income distribution are based on the assumption that abilities are normally distributed while income distributions are skewed to the right. These theories suffer, however, from the weakness that abilities can only be measured uniquely up to a monotonic transformation (i.e. they are non-metric in nature). In terms of measurement, the statement that abilities are normally distributed is thus without exact informational value.

2.2. PRINCIPLES OF JUSTICE IN DISTRIBUTION

Different principles or canons have been invoked in discussions of distributional equity. In his book on *Distributive Justice*[2] Rescher summarized these canons. He attempts further to subsume all of them under one single principle.

The pure utilitarian principle which parallels closely the principle of the predominance of growth ("The maximum good for the maximum number of individuals") is inconsistent in many instances with our concept of justice. Rescher distinguishes justice in the narrow sense—in essence implying equality—and justice in the wider sense, incorporating other aspects, such as more for all, over and beyond equal shares for all.

In three phases of development or societal affluence different implications for a just distribution need to be stressed. In an economy of scarcity care should be taken in the interest of justice (in the wider sense) that more be available; this appears more important than fairness. The number of individuals with a utility share falling below the minimum is to

---

[2]Nicholas Rescher, *Distributive Justice.*

be minimized. A more objective standard would postulate that the number of individuals with incomes below a poverty threshold should be minimized.

In an economy of sufficiency the principle of fairness commands greater force. In an economy of abundance, Rescher claims in turn that inequalities of distribution may again be compatible with justice.

Rescher then formulates eight canons of distributive justice; seven of these are monistic.

(1) Equality—"Justice consists in the treatment of people as equals".

(2) Need—"Justice consists in the treatment of people according to their needs."

(3) Ability and/or Achievement—"Justice consists in the treatment of people according to their abilities."

(4) Effort—"Justice consists in the treatment of people according to their efforts and sacrifices on their own or their group's behalf."

(5) Productivity—"Justice consists in the treatment of people according to their actual productive contribution to their group."

(6) Social Utility—"Justice consists in the treatment of people according to the best prospects for advancing the common good or public interest, or welfare of mankind, or the greater good of a greater number."

(7) Supply and Demand—"Justice consists in the treatment of people according to a valuation of their socially useful contributions, these being evaluated on the basis of relative scarcity of product" (not on the basis of canon (6)).

(8) Claims (Rescher's Position)—"Distributive justice consists in the treatment of people according to their legitimate claims."

Each of the above canons represents a particular sort of ground (need, effort, etc.) on whose basis certain legitimate claims can be advanced.

In the actual distribution and redistribution processes of societies aspects of all these canons can be encountered.

Equality is in the back of those arguments that call for a more equal distribution rather than a less equal one.

Need enters as a modifying factor in various social-policy instruments, particularly in certain public transfer programs such as public aid and public assistance, or their equivalents.

Ability or achievement plays a part in setting differential wage and salary levels.

Effort tends to modify income within occupational groups.

Productivity acts as an official guideline in management-labor negotiations.

Social utility as a distributional principle, is perhaps less applicable than the other canons outlined. It would imply a remuneration or subsidy of external economies, which classically has been advocated already by Kahn and others; in practice, however, subsidies are guided by other considerations.

Forces of demand and supply have been considered dominant in determining remuneration in an economic setting. In particular the accrual of rents and quasi-rents can be attributed to these forces.

Finally, canon (8), the claims or rights or titles to receive assets or income, entails nothing more than the recognition that no single cause determines distribution. Rescher, like many others, leaves the question open, how various claims are aggregated; or, focussing on an other aspect of the same problem, how they are weighted.

We can follow Rescher in focussing on three aspects that appear important:

(1) The total amount of goods.
(2) The pattern of distribution.
(3) The distributing procedure.

Little disagreement will occur on some aspects of point (1); ceteris paribus, more goods are always better than less, as most will agree. For quite a while economic growth seemed to save us the conflict of distribution. When we extend point (1) to encompass quality or the expansion of production, consensus between all groups may not and will not be automatic or easy. Very clear preferences for one or the other allocation may prevail.

The pattern of distribution, as most will agree, should be equitable. As to what this should imply, consensus seems unlikely. A generally accepted "good" distribution should, however, take into account certain factors:

(a) The concept of income should be extended to include the real income of persons or families; social goods should be included, and so should be social bads.

(b) Not only economic goods should enter the argument in as far as some substitution relationships to economic goods exist.

(c) Temporal and inter-generation relations should be considered very carefully.

(d) External effects should be considered, particularly in education.

Rescher's canons of distributive justice summarize the ingredients of a norm of distribution quite aptly. The dose of each, however, we too would rather leave undetermined in the abstract.

The distributing procedure presents more acute and touchy problems than one might think at first.

The mode of income receipt, whether through exchange or grants processes, may not be a matter of utter indifference to the recipient. The negative experience associated with the receipt of some public transfer payments is too well-known to bear belaboring. The very intricate matter of achieving an integrative or disintegrative effect through grants requires further investigation.[3]

Generally it should be the goal of a system to provide for an income distribution such that redistribution other than that wrought through the distribution of benefits of public goods should become to a large extent superfluous. The principle of fraternité cannot always be relied upon to provide a necessary basis for granting or accepting grants. After all, Able was killed not because he was selfish and vicious, but, maybe, because he was too kind and selfless.

The principle of equality, on the other hand, would, in its extreme consequence, negate the necessity to give or to be given, unless on a reciprocal basis.

The cultural rules prevalent in a society make some grants acceptable, while others are tied in with status-lowering or status-conferring images.

We require a principle of reciprocity that goes beyond purely economic accounting: It should guide our judgement in determining as to what is equitable in an exchange or a grants relationship.

3. Equity in social exchange

The concepts of equity or justice have not only permeated Western or Eastern philosophical thinking throughout the ages. They have also been investigated by economists in regard to the problems of income and wealth distribution and also by psychologists and sociologists. Anthropologists have described the rules governing social interchanges among tribes and among so-called primitive peoples.[4]

Equity theory analyses the rules whereby an allocator commits resources among competing individuals, on the basis of experimental psychology. In contrast to broader descriptive treatments, it appears to come closest to the paradigms which economists are most familiar with. Furthermore it is likely to provide "operational hypotheses" on the behavior of allocators and recipients which may have more immediate policy implications in our cultural context.

[3]The empirical investigation of social integration sheds little light on the question whether integrative relations foster granting relations or not. Robert C. Angell, for example, constructs an Index of Integration by using the amount of charitable contributions made in a community to operationalize social integration. (R. C. Angell, "The Social Integration of Selected American Cities", *The American Journal of Sociology*, 47 pp. 575–592.)

[4]Marcel Mauss, *The Gift: Forms and Functions of Exchange in Primitive Societies.* (Norton & Company, New York, 1967).

Leventhal, Popp and Sawyer describe the conclusions of equity theory as follows:

Recent theorizing suggests, that an individual (an allocator) who distributes rewards to other persons may follow either of two norms of fairness. The equity model (of J. Stacy Adams) suggests he will reward recipients in accordance with their task inputs, a suggestion which has been supported by numerous investigations. However, others have suggested an allocator may often ignore differences in the recipients' task inputs and divide rewards equally ... Both views are probably justified since it is likely that, depending on circumstances, an allocator may follow an equity norm or an equality norm when distributing reward. Consequently, it is necessary to determine the conditions under which an allocator prefers equality over equity (and vice versa) when distributing reward.[5]

In Leventhal's view equity can be viewed as a norm competing with equality; indeed, it is the opposite. It implies a distribution rule based on relative inputs or contributions of effort or materials. Thus it appears to offer an experimental isomorphism with the marginal-value-product theorem of distribution familiar from neo-classical economics. In any case, such a definition appears to fall short of an essential ingredient of equity or inequity, namely, the presence or absence of legitimacy.

What is of greater interest is the actual behavioral rule applied by an allocator. Leventhal, in fact, points to different rationales that an allocator may follow:

Such a theory has to take into account the fact that an allocator may not only try to divide rewards equitably, but also, under varying circumstances may prefer to divide them equally; or divide them in accordance with the recipients' needs; or divide them so as to minimize dissatisfaction and conflict; or divide them so as to encourage the recipient to quit the relationship; or divide them in accordance with some complex combination of these factors—which is usually what happens.[6]

This unfortunately, only points out alternatives and does not offer conclusions on the nature of equity itself.

The work of the psychological equity theorists was inspired by J. Stacy Adams who uses the notion of "felt inequity" to explain types of apparently baffling behavior. He arrives at the following conclusions:

First, it seems that manifest dissatisfaction and other behavior are responses to acutely felt injustice, rather than directly to relative deprivation. Relative deprivation is a condition occurring naturalistically or an experimental manipulation which elicits feelings of injustice. In turn, feelings of injustice trigger expressions of dissatisfaction ... Injustice, then, may be said to mediate the effects of relative deprivation. A second conclusion is that what is justice is based upon relatively strong expectations ... Thirdly, it is clear that a

---

[5] Gerald Leventhal, Artur L. Popp and Llewlee Sawyer, 'Equity or Equality in Children's Allocation of Reward to Other Persons', *Child Development 44* (1973) 753–763.

[6] Gerald S. Leventhal, 'Equity and the Economics of Reward Distribution', Paper presented at the Meeting of the American Psychological Association, Honolulu, September 1972.

comparative process is inherent in the development of expectations and the perception of injustice, as implied by the term relative deprivation.[7]

This psychological concept of inequity would emphasize that inequity is felt, whenever a person perceives that the ratio of his outcomes to inputs and the ratio of other's outcomes to other's inputs are unequal.[8]

This conclusion brings us back to the kind of input-output reasoning only too familiar from utility theory.

Concepts of equity or inequity pertain, however, not only to the relationship between productive inputs and rewards. A broader view could focus on various levels of human interactions. Humans interact in order to attain also noneconomic resources. These would be, for example, political power, social status, a cultural and personal identity, devotion, affect, love, attraction and so on. Generally, information represents an important resource to the individual.

It becomes apparent that all human interrelationships, even in the noneconomic plane, cannot be viewed simply as a two-way exchange. This is recognized, for example, by Foa:

The fact, for instance, that resources like information and love can be given to others without reducing the amount possessed by the giver, has been considered contradictory to the very notion of exchange since this effect does not occur in transactions of money and goods.[9]

If one pursues this line of reasoning, one would arrive at a "generalized grants concept": In economic terms, a grant represents a one-way transfer of exchangeables; non-economic goods, may indeed flow in the opposite direction. (In contrast, an economic exchange transaction involves a two-way flow of exchangeables). However, as pointed out above, one-way flows of non-economic goods are just as conceivable as one-way flows of economic goods. This possibility shows the limitations of applying the economic concept of exchange to more complex human relationships.

Foa classifies interpersonal resources into goods, services, money, information, status and love. To these we would add power and identity. He notes that the rules for economic exchange are only one set of rules which do not apply for the exchange of other resources. He emphasizes the importance of "particularistic resources" such as love in solving problems of modern society. These resources, no doubt, can, if at all, only be measured through a system of social indicators.

[7] J. Stacy Adams, 'Inequity in Social Exchange', *Advances in Experimental Social Psychology II* (1965) 271 ff.
[8] *Ibid.*, p. 280.
[9] Uriel G. Foa, 'Interpersonal and Economic Resources', *Science* (29 January 1971) 345.

Perhaps a more direct measure of the sense of equity or inequity—say, in the form of avowed satisfaction or dissatisfaction—can offer a more concrete handle to the difficult problem of increasing equity.

4. Strategies for furthering equity

What concrete steps could be taken if a society were truly interested in attaining a higher level of equality, or more generally greater equity in the distribution of income, wealth, and power? Three pathways can be envisaged, depending upon the time horizon within which such a strategy is to be applied.

First, in the short run a greater degree of equality, and possibly of equity, in the distribution of income can be attained by changing the structure of the secondary income distribution resulting from the system of one-way transfers, or simply, from the total grants economy. This involves the systems of transfers made in cash as well as in kind. As an immediate step one could envisage some kind of "distributive impact statement": It should accompany all measures resulting in the disbursement of public funds, whether they be in cash or invested in goods or services which are made available free of charge or at a reduced price to the public at large. Furthermore, information and control systems should be instituted to keep a close check on expenditures of public funds.

Second, in the intermediate run the structure of primary income distribution should be affected in such a way that individuals coming from an underprivileged group will have a better chance of earning income through the market place. The major strategic variable appears to be a reform of the system of education which qualifies individuals to receive different levels of income.

Third, a long-run strategy aimed at greater equality and equity could bring about changes in the distribution of wealth and possibly of power. The major strategic point of departure seems to consist of changes in inheritance laws and in the laws that define rights of property. Finally, the whole question of the distribution of power across individuals and groups would have to be raised if major changes of a very long-run nature are contemplated.

4.1. SHORT-RUN CHANGES IN THE STRUCTURE OF THE GRANTS ECONOMY

In the volume *Redistribution to the Rich and the Poor*[10] it was demonstrated that the grants economy has indeed brought about some measure

[10]K. E. Boulding and Martin Pfaff (eds.), *Redistribution to the Rich and the Poor: The Grants Economics of Income Distribution* (Wadsworth, Belmont, Calif., 1972).

of redistribution toward the poor. This is particularly true for some components of the explicit grants structure, i.e. grants made in cash under various social welfare programs. But we concluded:

Despite this increase the actual distribution of income seems to have changed little even though the number of poor has diminished, as we have all gotten rich together. On the other hand the 'perverse effect' of implicit public grants, conveyed either through special provision of the tax laws, public policy, or administrative practices, tends toward greater inequality: They help the rich propertied more than the poor. Furthermore, many public expenditures aimed at improving economic and social well being in a particular area—for example, education or agriculture—tend to reinforce income disparities or even to augment them.

Apart from the examples cited, we find a variety of programs whose de facto effect is to increase inequality rather than to decrease it. One of the reasons for this perplexing result is found in some specific aspects of the granting formula. For example, the amount of Medicaid funds disbursed by the Federal Government of the United States to the state governments is dependent upon the ability of these state governments to match these funds. Since wealthier states are more able to provide funds for this purpose, they also tend to get a larger share of Medicaid funds. Hence, the net effect of these Medicaid measures is to further increase inequality.[11] It is obvious that in such situations a change in the granting formula is called for. Similar changes are in order for those effects of the grants economy which have a pernicious impact on the structure of the family (such as "the man in the house rule" which would make a woman with children ineligible to receive public aid). There appears therefore a vast scope for immediate changes in the structure of the formulas and rules which are used to disburse public funds.

At the next level we find possibilities for changing the structure of the implicit grants through large-scale tax reforms. The present tax system, for example, in the United States, leaves much to be desired. The structure of exemptions and deductions can be viewed as a system of implicit grants in the sense that they deviate from some equity norm; it favors the middle- and the upper-income groups most dramatically.[12]

What may surprise many is that less than half of the social welfare payments of the United States actually go to the poor; and that the problem of poverty is not and cannot be eliminated by these measures alone. What appears to be called for is some kind of income-guarantee scheme: It would assure for all families a minimum level of subsistence,

---

[11]See Bruce C. Stewart, 'The Impact of Medicaid on Interstate Income Differentials', in: K. E. Boulding and M. Pfaff (eds.), *op. cit*, p. 149ff.

[12]See Martin and Anita Pfaff, 'How Equitable are Implicit Public Grants? The Case of the Individual Income Tax', in: K. E. Boulding and Martin Pfaff (eds.), *op. cit.*, p. 181 ff.

depending on their particular structure, such as the number of children, their ages, geographic location, the ability of the head of the household to work, and so on.

Such a program is consistent with the self-image of an industrialized and wealthy society. Several formulas and schemes for income maintenance have been proposed. The adoption of one of these suggests itself as a major first step in the right direction.[13]

What can be done to assure that a larger share of the public transfers-in-kind provided, say, in the form of public parks, schools, or hospitals, would benefit the lower-income groups? Perhaps what is necessary is for every public project to be evaluated ex-ante on the basis not only of allocative efficiency or productivity but also distributive equity. In other words, who is going to benefit to what extent from this proposed project? If such distributive impact statements become mandatory parts of project funding requests, a means for exerting influence on the distribution of public goods and services can be attained.

Furthermore better sources of information, or in short, better information and controls systems are required. They should be designed so as to enable the legislature, on the one hand, and the general public, on the other, to be better informed and to participate to a greater extent in the planning and in decision making about the allocation of the public grants economy. This is perhaps the only way to make sure that grants once sanctioned will not continue *ad infinitum*. Furthermore, the awarding of grants should be tied closely to specific operational criteria which the recipient has to meet in order to qualify for continuing allocations.[14]

4.2. INTERMEDIATE-RUN CHANGES IN THE STRUCTURE OF THE EDUCATIONAL SYSTEM

Spokesmen for an evolutionary solution to social and economic problems generally point to education as the major key to bring about social change: Individuals with sufficient talents and motivation should avail themselves of the educational system in order to change their social and economic status. Therefore one could view changes in the structure of education as primary means for affecting the primary distribution of income resulting in the market place (For lower-income groups, minimum-wage laws have a similar impact). Thus the educational system would contribute to the reduction of inequality and inequity. It would

[13]See section 4, 'Implications for Redistribution Policy', in: K. Boulding and M. Pfaff (eds.), *op. cit.*

[14]Martin and Anita Pfaff, 'The Grants Economy as a Regulator of the Exchange Economy', in: US Congress, Joint Economic Committee, *The Economics of Federal Subsidy Programs, Part 1, General Study Papers*, (May 8, 1972) 120–155.

increase social mobility and thus contribute to social harmonization. It would also provide for the self-fulfillment of individuals. It was held that by providing education free of charge, equality of opportunity would be furthered if not attained.

These views have been seriously challenged by a series of studies pointing to the predominance of the social environment of the home, or else to the genetic characteristics which determine IQ and the level of life incomes. Others, again, see in education simply a means whereby the working class is being prepared for the hierarchical structure of the capitalist state. Others again see in the educational system a means for the alienation of the individual.

A study of the role and function of the educational system within the Federal Republic of Germany reached the following conclusion:

Participation in the educational process, particularly in schools of higher learning and in universities, is dependent upon the social group in to which an individual is born. The educational level of the parents determines to a large degree the educational level that the children are likely to attain.

Individuals do not necessarily attain higher levels of education simply because of their abilities. Able children among the lower social and economic strata are less likely to attain a higher level of education than those born into higher social classes. Accordingly, an individual's cognitive skills and his performance in school are not the major factors in determining the individual's likelihood of participation. . . .

For the groups investigated, the quantity and quality of education determined to a large extent an individual's life income: The higher the level of education, the higher a person's life income tends to be. . . .

On balance those who do not participate and graduate tend to finance the educational system without receiving from the system an equivalent amount of direct benefits in the form of quantity of education consumed. The group of graduates of university-level institutions . . . are subsidized by the educational system.

Thus it can be argued that the lower-income groups on balance tend to subsidize the higher-income groups via the educational system of the Federal Republic of Germany.[15]

The solution proposed is a reform of the financing of education so as to provide a better mix of exchange and grants instruments. No doubt, such a mixing is consistent with allocative-efficiency considerations, since education can be viewed as a mixed good which has both private and public goods' characteristics. This reform of the financing of education would be based on two pillars: First, market-type instruments, e.g. student loans, should be relied upon to a greater extent to help finance the education of the children from middle- and upper-income groups.

[15] Martin Pfaff and Gerhard Fuchs, with the assistance of Peter Köppl, 'Education, Inequality, and Life Income: A Report on the Federal Republic of Germany', prepared for the conference on Education, Inequality and Life Chances, Directorate for Social Affairs, Manpower and Education, Organization for Economic Cooperation and Development, Paris, 6–10 January 1975, pp. 1–3.

Thus the subsidy component of education provided to these middle and upper groups would be reduced or even eliminated, depending on the financial capability of the parents. On the other hand non-market instruments, e.g. outright grants or stipends should be paid to those children from the lower social strata who have the ability to pursue higher levels of education but who may lack the motivation or the means to do so.

The main aim would be to keep these children out of the labor market at an early age. This would only be possible if one could in fact compete through subsidies with the pull that the pricing mechanism of the labor market exerts on these individuals. This is perhaps the only way to keep them from dropping out of school in order to obtain the benefits of a higher standard of living immediately.

If the present system of education is continued, we cannot expect any great and dramatic reduction of inequality or even of inequity. Only a restructuring of the system of education could assure that the gifted would attend school irrespective of the social background of their parents. It would make it more likely that income inequalities could be narrowed and that obvious inequities could be eliminated. No doubt the whole problem of education is far too complex to be solved by financial means. Other means of communication at the mass-level are required. Individual counselling is needed for students, particularly at those junctures in their educational path which determine their career choices. Nonetheless, a change in the structure of the financial basis of education offers itself as a means for reducing inequity.

4.3. LONG-RUN STRATEGY: CHANGES IN THE DISTRIBUTION OF WEALTH, PROPERTY, AND POWER

It has been well established that in most Western countries the overriding share of productive wealth is held by a relatively small fraction of the population. Changes in the structure of wealth-holding, however, are not very dramatic: Lampman, for example, concludes: "Our finding that the share of wealth held by the top 2 percent of families fell from about 33 to 29 percent from 1922 to 1953, or about one eighth, would seem compatible with . . . the general belief that there has been some lessening of economic inequality in the United States in recent decades."[16]

This group of top wealth-holders wields a disproportionate amount of economic power: "This group of 1.6 percent owned 33 percent of all privately owned wealth, consisting of 82.2 percent of all stock, 100

[16]Robert J. Landmann, *The Share of Top Wealth-holders in National Wealth 1922–1956*, a Study by the National Bureau of Economic Research, (Princeton University Press, Princeton, J.J., 1962) 217.

percent of state and local (tax-exempt) bonds, 38.2 percent of Federal bonds, 88.5 percent of other bonds, 29.1 percent of the cash, 36.2 percent of mortgages and notes, 13.3 percent of life-insurance reserves, 5.9 percent of pension and retirement funds, 18.2 percent of miscellaneous property, 16.1 percent of real estate and 22.1 percent of all debts and mortgages".[17]

On the other hand, half of the people own less than 10 percent of the wealth and have an average estate of $1,800, "enough to cover furniture, clothes, a television set and perhaps a run-down car. Most of these had less; many had nothing at all".[18]

There appears little doubt that a major avenue for long-run changes in the pattern of equality or inequality will consist in abolishing the rights of inheritance. Undoubtedly if such restrictions in inheritance were only applied to productive capital, major changes would already result. This would not prevent inheriting consumer durables including also individual homes. Preventing the inheritance also of consumer durables would perhaps be the most dramatic and far reaching way of insuring a more equal opportunity for everyone at the base line. No doubt this step would lead to some type of meritocracy with all its positive and negative attributes. But everyone would, in principle, be able to attain the position in society as reflected in income, wealth, power, and status—which would be commensurate with his particular talents.

It would be the most far reaching path leading towards reduction in inequity. It would also have a considerable impact on increasing the pattern of equality. No doubt the system based on performance alone would not eliminate the pattern of inequalities; and individuals would differ in terms of their attainments. However, felt or subjective inequity may be greatly reduced.

These three strategies offer alternative pathways applicable to different time horizons. What appears to be called for is not the selection of one over the other: In the short run, no doubt, only changes in the structure of the grants economy appear feasible. In the intermediate run, educational reforms may be possible. Whether the long-run changes envisaged by abolishing differentials in wealth and power are attainable in a free society, is a question worthy of a separate investigation. For after all, ownership of property and wealth commands power. And the question of the inequality in the distribution of power itself is worthy of a further investigation. Perhaps the movement felt currently in the western world, aiming at greater participation of citizens in the affairs of their

[17] *Ibid.*, pp. 23, 192–193.
[18] Ferdinand Lundberg, *The Rich and the Super-Rich* (Bantam Books, New York, 1968) 9.

towns or of public affairs in general, will lead to a greater redistribution of power. It remains to be seen, however whether the more articulate and educated groups are not also in a position as they have been thus far of wielding the instruments of participation for their particular advantage.

The great and overriding question remains: How can we combine greater equity with freedom in the kind of open society which Western man has come to cherish? The conflict in these two goals, no doubt will create the kind of tension which will shape the political dialogue of the next few decades. Undoubtedly, problems of equity will become more dominant at a time when economic growth becomes more questionable or even unattainable in a quasi-stationary economy. Measures designed to redistribute income, wealth, or power will go a long way toward improving the quality of life in such a society. Ultimately, however, it is changes in human nature which are required in order to transcend the limits imposed today by inequality.

C. *The international grants economy*
and
the economics of imperialism

C.1. The scope of the international grants economy: The case of the Eximbank

JANOS HORVATH

1. The issue in a nutshell

Writers, businessmen, academicians, politicians, whose judgment carries weight in shaping the international commerce of the United States hold diverse views about the government's main promotion agency: the Export-Import Bank (Eximbank). Diametrically different opinions claim uncompromising validity. Critics of the system argue that through easy credit terms economic aid is given to foreigners, even to adversaries. Others reject the belief that Eximbank credits involve U.S. Government subsidies. The resultant uncertainty confuses policy making and hurts business activities. Given such predicament, the question which calls for answer is whether or not the problem must remain beyond the realm of economic analysis, left to influence peddlers and guesstimates.

On the ensuing pages I shall outline a method adapted to the illumination of the issue at hand. A review of the current subsidy debate over East-West commerce sets the stage for designing techniques which can identify implicit subsidies in credits. Then follows the quantification of grant with the use of cases, actual and illustrative. The findings reveal that Eximbank credits do embody a modest amount of implicit grant: around 13 percent on the average, varying in accordance with the actual contract terms. The net benefit of such grant flows does not normally accrue to the foreign importer but rather to the domestic export sector. This recognition warrants further empirical studies which quite likely will provide new impetus to Eximbank-type operations.

*The need for problem solving models which can penetrate the political rhetoric of international policy issues, particularly between different systems, was impressed on this author while a senior fellow at Columbia University's Research Institute on International Change. The present study is one offshoot of that impetus. During the quantitative analysis assistance has been received from Butler University's Holcomb Research Institute where Messrs. Michael Gibbons and Tony Cherry designed the computer program.

2. The subsidy debate over East–West commerce

During the summer of 1974 an unprecedented controversy erupted when
the charter of the Eximbank came up for renewal in the United States
Congress. A sample of the related statements may best illuminate the
situation.

The opposition came from various sources. *The Wall Street Journal*
editorialized: "There being no economic justification for the bank,
Congress should feel no qualms about letting its authority lapse"[28].
Senator Lloyd Bentsen, a Texas Democrat, alledged the use of U.S.
taxpayers money to directly subsidize foreign oil operators in the
purchase of drilling and refining equipment[11]. The chief objection
centered on the Eximbank's dealing with Communist countries. For
example, Republican Congressman John Conlan of Arizona said that
Eximbank has become an "international pork barrel whose dealings with
Russian and other Communist countries are at best bad business, at most
suicidal"[11]. Even *The Washington Post*, a longtime supporter of
Eximbank, has editorialized that the bank's recent loans are "a tremendous subsidy" to foreign interest which are in direct competition with
American industry[11].

The defenders of the status quo reiterated: (i) The Eximbank use no
tax monies—on the contrary, on its initially appropriated $1 billion stock
it pays dividend to the Treasury; (ii) If we do not have the facilities to
match the marketing terms of foreign manufacturers, then the United
States will lose the sale—which means loss of jobs, profits, and taxes.

The fact that professional economics owes some definitive analysis to
the problem at hand has remained evident. Based on institutional
surveys, there seems to prevail an array of opinions which in turn fuel
the ongoing debate among various business and public policy advocates.

The sceptics could quote Gunter Dufey who states: "Subsidized
credits and financing terms which are not commensurate with the free
market cost of funds ... represents ... a net transfer of resources to the
trading partner, i.e. a gift"[8, p. 38]. Stanley D. Metzger writes that "the
difference between the more favorable government terms and the
available less favorable terms of private financing institutions constitutes
a subsidy"[19, p. 122]. Murray L. Weidenbaum underscores the statement in the President's Commission on Budget Concepts, that if there
were no subsidy elements in governmental loan programs, "a serious
question could be raised about the appropriateness of such activities
being conducted by public rather than by private financial
institutions"[29, p. 106].

A criticism of the Eximbank critiques has been offered by Paul Marer and Egon Neuberger. It reads:

Many economists, Congressmen, and the general public believe that Eximbank credits to Eastern Europe involve U.S. Government subsidies. This appears not to be true. In essence, this is because (a) Eximbank interest rates to all borrowers are the same; (b) the Bank borrows the money it relends on the open capital and money markets; (c) over any reasonable period . . . it makes a profit . . . part of which it turns over to the Treasury [18, p. 584].

Perhaps there is no need to belabor further the above "yes or no debate".[1] Within the next section of this paper I shall help in resolving much of the controversy. At the two opposite poles, the Gunter Dufey versus the Marer-Neuberger propositions will have to undergo some modification. Likewise, the identification of implicit grant values will lay the groundwork for reliance on more fact and less intuition in policy debates.

3. Identifying subsidy elements: The analytical model

The grants economy concept, as it has developed in the course of the last five years lends itself to analyzing choices which have public as well as private implications. That a network of governmental subventions— frequently in the form of implicit income and wealth transfers—regulate the national and international economy may well be the most important single message of grants economics. The *modus operandi* of such an instrument has universal bearing, to wit, "whenever government policy intervenes in the market system in such a way that the terms of trade of contracting parties—or the market prices of factors of production and of goods and services—are affected, an explicit or implicit grant structure results" [21, p. 122]. These operational definitions have their root in Kenneth Boulding's dictum that the grants economy represents the heart of political economy, because it is precisely at the level of one-way transfers that the political system intervenes in the economic system.

---

[1] It was apparently a mistaken premiss that prompted Professors Marer and Neuberger to deny the existence of subsidies. (i) The fact that Eximbank allows lower interest rate to *all* borrowers does not negate the presence of an implicit grant. Indeed, all of its customers receive some amount of subsidy, depending on the size and the maturity years of the loan. The privileged position of Eximbank beneficiaries becomes even more visible when compared to those exporters who do not avail themselves of this particular credit facility. (ii) Even though Eximbank raises some of its operating funds on the open market, it does so from a privileged position. Also, much of its funds originate, directly or indirectly, from the U.S. Treasury. (iii) Just the fact itself that someone makes profit does not exclude the possibility of generosity.

Naturally, the size and performance of such an instrument will very much interest both the analyst of efficiency and the maker of policy. By now, the investigator can consult a growing list of sources to familiarize himself with grants economics—the sub-discipline of economics concerned with interdependence both on the production and consumption sides, and with the techniques which reinforce or alter the price mechanism[3; 4; 12; 21]. Apart from its normative propositions, a primary task of grants economics is to identify its object, which means the sorting out of grant elements, sometimes explicit but mostly implicit, in a varying admixture of transactions. The measurement of grant elements, not unlike a medical diagnosis, paves the way toward therapy. In turn, corrective policies will inject into or withhold from the economic organism grant flows in doses conducive to the desired goals.

Vehicles for transmitting grants are numerous. Elsewhere, I have surveyed over twenty regulations that generate some magnitude of foreign trade related implicit grant. For example: concessionary credits, tax preferences, variable tariff levies, "buy domestic" rules, "most-favored-nation" provisions, exchange restrictions, and so on. The grant equivalents embodied in these policy measures may vary significantly, depending on the terms of concessions and stipulations.

The model building usually begins with basic concepts, as described in several studies[13, p. 267–281; 12; 15]. The crude approximation of the grant equivalent (G) of a loan (L) is obtained through discounting the stream of repayments due by a chosen comparative discount rate (opportunity cost) and deducting the sum of the discounted payments from the face value of the loan. The grant ratio (g) is the proportion of grant equivalent in the loan ($g = G/L$). The more tractable expression of this grant ratio is found in the formula:

$$g = \left[1 - \frac{i}{q}\right]\left[1 - \frac{e^{-qM} - e^{-qT}}{q(T - M)}\right] + g_1 + \cdots + g_n, \tag{1}$$

where
g is the grant ratio
i is the rate of interest
q is the opportunity rate of discount
T is the time of maturity in years
M is the moratorium years on repayment (grace period).

An advantage of expression as grant ratio is that the sensitivity of the ratio with respect of various policy measures can be calculated. The procedure identifies in ratio units (i.e. percentage points) the effect of any alternative of the policy measures utilized or their individual contract terms. By thus measuring the respective weight of each concession and stipulation, it also becomes possible to calculate trade-offs between them.

In general, the sensitivity of a mathematical function with respect to one of its variables is defined as the change in the value of the function when a change occurs in the variable. The process is partial differentiation. Two distinct measures of sensitivity can be defined. Firstly, the absolute sensitivity of a contract term (or policy measure) gives the "percentage point" change in the grant ratio when the term is changed by a certain degree. Secondly, the relative sensitivity of a contract term indicates the relative weighting (i.e. contribution), of that term toward the grant ratio.

The absolute sensitivity formula may be introduced with the use of one of the independent variables. For example,

$$S_g^T = \frac{\partial g}{\partial T} \tag{2}$$

is the sensitivity of grant ratio with respect to the time length of repayment. In a similar fashion one can prescribe the partial differentiation for each contract term:

$$S_g^M = \frac{\partial g}{\partial M} \tag{3}$$

$$S_g^i = \frac{\partial g}{\partial i} \tag{4}$$

to read as: the sensitivity of grant ratio with respect to the moratorium years (3), and the interest rate (4).

Sensitivites may have positive or negative signs depending on the case. A positive sensitivity indicates that the change in the function is in the same direction as the variable. In other words, an increase in the variable will increase the function, or vice versa. A negative sensitivity indicates that the changes in the variable and the function are in the opposite direction. For example, an increase in the maturity period of a loan will increase the grant ratio of the aid, hence the sensitivity of grant ratio with respect to maturity period will have a positive sign. However, an increase in the interest rate will decrease the grant ratio, hence the sensitivity of grant ratio with respect to interest will have a negative sign because the changes are in the opposite direction.

The relative importance of each independent variable is shown in terms of a proportion. Relative sensitivity of the length of repayment, for instance, expressed in percentage points, is

$$RS_T = \frac{S_g^T}{\sum S_g^j},$$

where j is the general notation for the variable, i.e. T, M, i, etc. Of course, any group of variables can be chosen as a base. However, the relative sensitivities of the terms taken, in this particular example three, must add up to 100 percent as prescribed below:

$$RS_T + RS_M + RS_i = 100\%.$$

4. The Eximbank loans during fiscal year 1973

In order to demonstrate the tractability of the model, I shall introduce the analytical techniques stepwise. Table 1 includes selected Eximbank credit authorizations, arranged according to transactions with four important countries. A sketch of the transactions and the credit figures are adopted from the Eximbank official report. [9, p. 31–53]. The analysis begins with the calculation of the grant ratio, which when multiplied by the face value of the loan will give the grant equivalent.

For example, the second item in table 1 is the sale of "model 1370-W dragline" by a United States exporter to Costain Australia Ltd. The contract terms specified that part of the financing, $2,340,000 will come from the Export-Import Bank of the United States with 6 percent interest rate, 5 years of repayment after six months of moratorium on the initial installment. Based on these data, the grant ratio is 0.1005, which amounts to about 10 cents in each dollar. So the Eximbank in offering a $2,340,000 promotion loan, also sacrifices a grant equivalent of $235,125. When this export transaction from the USA to Australia is combined with others also subsidized by Eximbank, they amount to $20,695,500 authorized credit. The grant equivalent embodied in this sum, $2,339,634 is the result of a weighted average grant ratio of 0.1131.

To provide further illustrations, also listed are Eximbank supported export transactions to three other countries: Switzerland, Poland, and the Soviet Union. Within this sample, the lowest grant ratio, 0.0781, applied to shipments of a computer system to Australia and tractor components to Poland. The highest grant ratios, 0.1667 and 0.2114, have occured in the case of exports to Switzerland. Three export shipments to the Soviet Union have embodied grant ratios of 0.1005, 0.1310, and 0.1495.

For the sake of a global perspective on the matter, table 2 lists by countries of importers the export credits authorized by Eximbank from July 1972 through June 1973. Altogether 67 countries are involved. The computations show that out of $2,314 million export credit the grant equivalent amounted to $307 million, with a weighted average grant ratio of 0.1327.

Before proceeding further with the analysis, a few comments on the data seems appropriate at this point. Time of the loan is the only contract term which varies significantly, from about 2.5 to 10 years. The other concessionary contract terms are constant. Namely: 6 months moratorium on repayment; 6 percent interest rate (to which three minor exceptions were the 6.5 percent rate in financing the sale of steel plant facilities to Brazilian importers); the opportunity cost (i.e. comparative rate of discount, q) was assumed 11.75 percent on the average, the rate charged by commercial banks on their share of export credits. Another matter concerns those smaller transactions involving 4–5 percent of the whole volume, which the Eximbank Report[9] did not specify. Yet these minor discrepancies will not affect the main findings of present study.

Turning now to the analytical findings in table 2, the observer may obtain some illumination by ranking the figures.

(1) The gross value of Eximbank credits varied widely: at the lower end $216,750 in support of exports to Dahomey and at the upper end $236,354,963 to Iran. The other large items in declining order are: Algeria $186 million, Spain $171 million, Mexico $166 million, Taiwan $150 million, Brazil $113 million, USSR $101 million, Japan $96 million, Canada $82 million, Sweden $77 million, and so on. Altogether there are 7 countries over $100 million, 30 countries between $10 and $100 million, and 30 countries below $10 million.

(ii) In terms of grant equivalent the declining rank order is: Algeria $27 million, Mexico $27 million, Spain $27 million, Iran $25 million, Taiwan $22 million, USSR $15 million, Brazil $14 million, Sweden $14 million, Canada $11 million, and so on. There are 11 countries figuring with grant equivalent over $10 million, 27 countries between $1–$10 million, and 29 countries below $1 million, the lowest Dahomey with only $19,404.

(iii) In terms of grant ratio the German Federal Republic leads with 0.2114, followed by Sweden 0.1793, Switzerland 0.1780, Liberia 0.1667, Mexico 0.1628, Spain 0.1572, and so on. There are 6 countries over the mark of 0.1500, 49 countries between 0.1500–0.1000, and 12 countries below 0.1000. The lowest grant ratios are associated with exports to Japan and Costa Rica, 0.640 and 0.0781 respectively.

Further utilization of the grant analysis is offered in table 3 through the

TABLE 1

Selected Eximbank credit authorizations, arranged according to transactions with four importing countries

Obligor	Purpose and contract terms	Amount	Grant ratio	Grant equivalent
Australia				
Commonwealth of Australia	Aircraft jumbo jet (1) 747 6% interest, 5 years	$11,284,000	0.1310	$1,477,978
Costain Australia Ltd. (Richard Costain Ltd.)	Model 1370-W dragline 6% interest, 3.5 years	2,340,000	0.1005	235,125
Utah Development Company (Utah International Inc.)	Coal mine development 6% interest, 3 years	6,500,000	0.0895	581,878
Conzinc Riotinto of Australia	Computer system 6% interest, 2.5 years	571,500	0.0781	44,653
Total CFF & relending loans	Details in supplementary report	(25,940)[a]	[a]	[a]
		$20,695,500	0.1131[b]	$2,339,634
Poland				
BK Handlowy w Warszawie Sa (Gov. of Polish People's Rep.)	2 meat processing plants 6% interest, 5 years	$8,910,000	0.1310	$1,167,031
BK Handlowy w Warszawie Sa (Gov. of Polish People's Rep.)	Sendzimir rolling mill 6% interest, 4.5 years	1,989,000	0.1212	241,055
BK Handlowy w Warszawie Sa (Gov. of Polish People's Rep.)	CYBER 72-14 computer system 6% interest, 2.5 years	1,094,850	0.0781	85,543
BK Handlowy w Warszawie Sa (Gov. of Polish People's Rep.)	Components for Crawler tractor 6% interest, 2.5 years	696,600	0.0781	54,427
BK Handlowy w Warszawie Sa (Gov. of Polish People's Rep.)	9 high temperature furnaces 6% interest, 4.5 years	2,610,000	0.1212	316,316
BK Handlowy w Warszawie Sa (Gov. of Polish People's Rep.)	2 meat processing plants 6% interest, 5 years	22,320,000	0.1310	2,923,472
		$37,620,450	0.1273[b]	$4,787,845

Switzerland				
Swiss Air Transport Co. Ltd.	Aircraft, DC10's (2) 6% interest, 7 years	$11,736,000	0.1667	$1,956,164
Swiss Air Transport Co. Ltd.	Spare engines and parts 6% interest, 10 years	4,000,000	0.2114	845,454
		$15,736,000	0.1780[b]	$2,801,617
USSR				
Bank for Foreign Trade (Gov. of the USSR)	500 submersible elec. pumps 6% interest, 3.5 years	$11,671,650	0.1005	$1,172,774
Bank for Foreign Trade (Gov. of the USSR)	2 tableware plants 6% interest, 5 years	3,101,912	0.1310	406,289
Bank for Foreign Trade (Gov. of the USSR)	Truck and engine plant 6% interest, 6 years	86,450,000	0.1495	12,923,406
		$101,223,562	0.1433[b]	$14,502,469

[a]Smaller transactions, not included in report.
[b]Weighted average grant ratio.

Source: Export-Import Bank of the United States, *Statement of Condition Fiscal Year '73*. (Government Printing Office, Washington, D.C.).

TABLE 2

The grant analysis of export credits authorized by Eximbank, July 1972 through June 1973, arranged by countries of importers

Country of importer	Years to repay[a]	Grant ratio	Eximbank credit	Grant equivalent	Absolute sensitivity of grant ratio with respect to			Relative sensitivity of great ratio with respect to		
	weighted average		in million dollars		Interest	Time	Grace	Interest	Time	Grace
Algeria	5.86	0.1468	185.6	27.3	−0.0255	0.0180	0.0222	0.3879	0.2743	0.3378
Argentina	4.46	0.1199	30.9	3.7	−0.0208	0.0200	0.0234	0.3238	0.3123	0.3639
Australia	4 13	0.1131	20.7	2.3	−0.0197	0.0206	0.0237	0.3069	0.3224	0.3706
Barbados	4.00	0.1110	0.5	b	−0.0193	0.0207	0.0237	0.3028	0.3248	0.3724
Belgium	5.00	0.1310	2.0	0.3	−0.0228	0.0192	0.0229	0.3510	0.2960	0.3529
Brazil	4.89	0.1272	112.9	14.4	−0.0222	0.0194	0.0229	0.3429	0.3012	0.3559
Brunei	4.00	0.1110	4.5	0.5	−0.0193	0.0207	0.0237	0.3028	0.3248	0.3724
Cameroon	5.00	0.1310	2.0	0.3	−0.0228	0.0192	0.0229	0.3510	0.2960	0.3524
Canada	5.48	0.1379	82.5	11.4	−0.0240	0.0187	0.0226	0.3657	0.2876	0.3466
China-Taiwan	5.82	0.1441	150.3	21.7	−0.0251	0.0183	0.0223	0.3800	0.2792	0.3408
Costa Rica	2.50	0.0781	0.2	b	−0.0136	0.0232	0.0251	0.2195	0.3750	0.4055
Dahomey	3.00	0.0895	0.2	b	−0.0156	0.0223	0.0246	0.2489	0.3572	0.3930
Denmark	4.52	0.1213	18.5	2.2	−0.0211	0.0199	0.0233	0.3274	0.3101	0.3624
Dominican Rep.	3.72	0.1040	10.4	1.1	−0.0181	0.0213	0.0240	0.2841	0.3362	0.3797
Finland	3.50	0.1005	1.5	0.1	−0.0175	0.0215	0.0242	0.2766	0.3408	0.3829
France	5.06	0.1317	41.6	5.5	−0.0229	0.0192	0.0229	0.3524	0.2952	0.3523
Gabon	3.50	0.1005	1.9	0.2	−0.0175	0.0215	0.0242	0.2766	0.3405	0.3829
Germany, F.R.	10.00	0.2114	19.7	4.2	−0.0368	0.0134	0.0193	0.5295	0.1924	0.2781
Greece	5.00	0.1310	4.1	0.5	−0.0228	0.0192	0.0229	0.3510	0.2960	0.3529
Guatemala	5.00	0.1310	13.5	1.8	−0.0228	0.0192	0.0229	0.3510	0.2960	0.3529
Guyana	3.50	0.1005	2.4	0.2	−0.0175	0.0215	0.0242	0.2766	0.3405	0.3829
Honduras	4.28	0.1159	4.9	0.6	−0.0201	0.0204	0.0235	0.3136	0.3185	0.3679
Hong Kong	2.50	0.0781	1.8	0.1	−0.0136	0.0232	0.0251	0.2195	0.3750	0.4055
India	5.00	0.1310	2.7	0.4	−0.0278	0.0192	0.0229	0.3510	0.2960	0.3529
Indonesia	5.72	0.1444	71.7	10.3	−0.0251	0.0182	0.0223	0.3823	0.2776	0.3402
Iran	3.72	0.1049	236.4	24.8	−0.0182	0.0212	0.0240	0.2874	0.3340	0.3786

Israel	4.96	0.1302	19.5	2.5	−0.0226	0.0193	0.0229	0.3491	0.2971	0.3537
Italy	5.75	0.1447	46.7	6.8	−0.0252	0.0182	0.0223	0.3830	0.2772	0.3399
Ivory Coast	3.50	0.1005	2.0	0.2	−0.0175	0.0215	0.0242	0.2766	0.3408	0.3829
Jamaica	6.00	0.1495	7.3	1.1	−0.0260	0.0178	0.0221	0.3943	0.2704	0.3352
Japan	2.13	0.0640	95.6	6.1	−0.0111	0.0242	0.0256	0.1764	0.4019	0.4217
Jordan	4.47	0.1200	5.9	0.7	−0.0209	0.0200	0.0234	0.3239	0.3122	0.3638
Kenya	5.00	0.1310	0.8	0.1	−0.0228	0.0192	0.0229	0.3510	0.2960	0.3529
Korea	4.57	0.1222	58.3	7.1	−0.0213	0.0199	0.0233	0.3296	0.3088	0.3615
Liberia	7.00	0.1667	− 9.4	1.6	−0.0290	0.0166	0.0213	0.4333	0.2476	0.3191
Luxemburg	5.00	0.1310	0.4	0.1	−0.0228	0.0192	0.0229	0.3510	0.2960	0.3529
Malaysia	2.93	0.0878	2.8	0.2	−0.0153	0.0225	0.0247	0.2442	0.3600	0.3957
Mali	2.50	0.0781	0.7	b	−0.0136	0.0232	0.0251	0.2195	0.3750	0.4055
Mexico	7.00	0.1628	166.6	27.1	−0.0283	0.0169	0.0215	0.4212	0.2554	0.3235
Morocco	3.50	0.1005	3.5	0.4	−0.0175	0.0215	0.0242	0.2766	0.3408	0.3829
Mozambique	4.00	0.1110	6.1	0.7	−0.0193	0.0207	0.0237	0.3028	0.3248	0.3724
Netherlands	2.50	0.0781	8.8	0.7	−0.0136	0.0232	0.0251	0.2195	0.3750	0.4055
Nigeria	3.34	0.0965	4.3	0.4	−0.0168	0.0218	0.0243	0.2660	0.3469	0.3870
Norway	2.87	0.0862	39.3	3.4	−0.0150	0.0226	0.0248	0.2400	0.3626	0.3974
Pakistan	6.00	0.1495	28.2	4.2	−0.0260	0.0178	0.0221	0.3943	0.2704	0.3352
Panama	3.10	0.0914	52.2	4.8	−0.0159	0.0222	0.0246	0.2531	0.3547	0.3922
Philippines	3.88	0.1082	22.8	2.5	−0.0188	0.0209	0.0239	0.2957	0.3290	0.3753
Poland	4.82	0.1273	37.6	4.8	−0.0221	0.0195	0.0231	0.3419	0.3014	0.3566
Portugal	4.84	0.1276	12.9	1.6	−0.0222	0.0195	0.0230	0.3427	0.3019	0.3562
Romania	4.81	0.1271	36.0	4.6	−0.0221	0.0195	0.0231	0.3414	0.3018	0.3568
Singapore	5.00	0.1310	29.5	3.9	−0.0228	0.0192	0.0229	0.3510	0.2960	0.3529
Spain	6.44	0.1572	171.2	26.9	−0.0273	0.0173	0.0217	0.4099	0.2616	0.3284
Sudan	5.00	0.1310	10.3	1.4	−0.0228	0.0192	0.0229	0.3510	0.2960	0.3529
Sweden	8.05	0.1793	77.5	13.9	−0.0312	0.0157	0.0207	0.4579	0.2340	0.3080
Switzerland	7.76	0.1780	15.7	2.8	−0.0310	0.0158	0.0208	0.4577	0.2336	0.3087
Thailand	3.84	0.1077	4.6	0.5	−0.0187	0.0210	0.0239	0.2945	0.3297	0.3757
New Guinea	2.50	0.0781	5.0	0.4	−0.0136	0.0232	0.0251	0.2195	0.3750	0.4055
Tunisia	3.50	0.1005	3.2	0.3	−0.0175	0.0215	0.0242	0.2766	0.3405	0.3829
Turkey	5.65	0.1415	70.8	10.0	−0.0246	0.0184	0.0224	0.3740	0.2827	0.3433
USSR	5.68	0.1433	101.2	14.5	−0.0249	0.0183	0.0224	0.3794	0.2793	0.3413
United Kingdom	4.24	0.1148	22.7	2.6	−0.0200	0.0204	0.0236	0.3110	0.3200	0.3690

Country of importer	Years to repay	Grant ratio	Eximbank credit	Grant equivalent	Absolute sensitivity of grant ratio with respect to			Relative sensitivity of great ratio with respect to		
	weighted average		in million dollars		Interest	Time	Grace	Interest	Time	Grace
Venezuela	4.36	0.1180	14.0	1.7	−0.0205	0.0202	0.0234	0.3191	0.3151	0.3658
W. Indies-N.	5.00	0.1310	3.1	0.4	−0.0278	0.0192	0.0229	0.3510	0.2960	0.3529
W. Indies-Br.	3.50	0.1005	3.1	0.3	−0.0175	0.0215	0.042	0.2766	0.3405	0.3829
Yugoslavia	5.23	0.1349	40.0	5.3	−0.0235	0.0189	0.0227	0.3599	0.2908	0.3493
Zaire	5.35	0.1365	42.7	5.8	−0.0237	0.0188	0.0227	0.3629	0.2892	0.3479
Zambia	3.15	0.0919	9.1	0.8	−0.0160	0.0221	0.0245	0.2538	0.3544	0.3918
Total	5.23	0.1327	2,314.1	307.0	−2.3078[c]	0.0191	0.0228	0.9797[c]	0.0094	0.0109

[a]Time of the loan is the only contract term which varies significantly from case to case. The other concessionary contract terms are constant. Namely: 6 months moratorium on repayment; 6% interest rate (three minor exceptions were the 6.5% rate in financing the sale of steel plant facilities to Brazilian importers); the opportunity cost (i.e. comparative rate of discount) was assumed 11.75% on the average, the rate charged by commercial banks on their share of export credits.

[b]Grant equivalent less than half-a-million dollars.

[c]Weighted averages for absolute and relative sensitivities with respect to the comparative rate of discount (i.e. the opportunity cost, q).

Source: Export-Import Bank of the United States, *Statement of Condition Fiscal Year '73*, (Government Printing Office, Washington, D.C.).

TABLE 3

Grant elements in export credits authorized by Eximbank, July 1972 through June 1973, arranged by importer country groups

Classifications	Years to repay	Grant ratio	Eximbank credit	Grant equivalent
	weighted average		in million dollars	
I. Grouping by economic status				
Industrially developed countries	5.42	0.1345	803.1	107.9
Industrially underdeveloped countries	5.11	0.1310	1,296.6	169.9
Communist Bloc countries	5.30	0.1362	214.4	29.2
All transactions considered	5.23	0.1327	2,314.1	307.0
II. Grouping by regions				
Canada	5.48	0.1379	82.5	11.4
Latin American countries	5.42	0.1354	422.0	57.1
European countries	5.91	0.1448	595.9	86.3
African countries	5.52	0.1399	281.4	39.4
Asian countries (including Near East)	4.63	0.1216	902.2	109.6
Near East countries	(3.83)	(0.1071)	(261.8)	(28.0)
Oceania countries	4.57	0.1063	30.1	3.2
	5.23	0.1327	2,314.1	307.0

Source: Table 2.

grouping of importing countries. Naturally, the result of grouping 67 countries into 6 regions does narrow the variation of the grant ratio: the spread is between 0.1448 for European countries and 0.1063 for Oceania. If the weighted average grant ratio were regarded as an expression of "relative sacrifice" then exports to European countries are subsidized most, followed by Canada, Africa, Latin America, and Oceania. Alternatively, when the country grouping is arranged according to economic status, the pattern is still similar to the former one, namely transactions with the industrial advanced countries are subsidized more than those with the less-developed countries. A notable point is that both of these groups are slightly surpassed by the weighted average grant ratio of the Communist Bloc countries.

The grouping of countries in table 3 also illuminates how the $307 million grant equivalent subsidizes exports to the areas in focus. Viewing grant equivalent as an expression of "absolute sacrifice", the leading region is Asia with $109 million. The corresponding figures for Europe is $86 million, Latin America $57 million, Africa $39 million, Canada $11 million, and Oceania $3 million. From the viewpoint of economic status, the underdeveloped countries figure with $170 million, the developed countries with $108 million, and the Communist Bloc countries with $29 million dollars.

Beyond ferreting out the grant elements and subjecting them to cross-sectional scrutiny, the techniques outlined in the preceding section make available another working tool, namely the sensitivity analysis. As already reviewed, the expression of grant ratio and grant equivalent enables the analyst to state findings with a high degree of confidence. Evidently, each of the concessionary factors (i.e. interest rate, time of maturity, and grace period) make their weight felt. Now measuring the respective weight of each contract term, it also becomes possible to calculate trade-offs between them. Table 2 includes the coefficients of absolute as well as relative sensitivity.

Taking again United States exports to Australia for illustration, one finds that the coefficient of absolute sensitivity with respect to interest rate is -0.0197. This figure means that one percent reduction in the rate of interest will increase the grant ratio by 0.0197 (i.e. $0.1131 + 0.0197 = 0.1328$). In a similar fashion, lengthening the maturity by one year would increase the grant ratio by 0.0206 (i.e. $0.1141 + 0.0206 = 0.1347$), and lengthening the grace period by one year would add to the grant ratio 0.0237 (i.e. $0.1131 + 0.0237 = 0.1368$). Of course, changing the contract terms in the opposite direction would reverse the adjustment on the grant ratio.

The concept of relative sensitivity refers to the comparative signifi-cance of each contract term. In the present case, the relative significance of the contract terms are: 31 percent for one percentage point change in the rate of interest, 32 percent for one year change in the maturity time, and 37 percent for one year change in the grace period.

The model outlined and demonstrated here makes it clear that there exists a fundamental technique, ready for application. It promises that whatever policy devices are adopted, grant elements can be quantified and, through the use of grant ratios and sensitivity calculations, incorpo-rated into a single analytic body.

5. Who receives the subsidy?

Having analyzed Eximbank loans, a logical next question concerns the incidence of the grant. Certainly the burden falls on the American taxpayer who is the grantor. But the identification of the beneficiary still remains open. For example, to whom does the grant accrue in the formerly demonstrated case of exporting "model 1370-W dragline" by a United States exporter to Costain Australia Ltd.? Does the grant really go to the Australian importer, as conventional wisdom implies? Or does it accrue to the people of Australia, or to the government of that country, or perhaps to the American exporter who may share it with others?

To pave the way toward the resolution of these knotty questions, I have designed several illustrative cases as seen in table 4. The analysis therein points toward a generalized method which can trace the subsidy elements in Eximbank credits extended for the purpose of trade promo-tion. In setting the stage let us assume a homogeneous product, the intrinsic value of which is the same regardless of origin even though costs of production tend to vary from country to country. We also assume that it costs more to produce this particular equipment in the United States than in some of the other major producer countries, and, further, that supply is highly elastic in the relevant range. Under such conditions foreign sellers undoubtedly would capture all orders from third country buyers. However, motivated by the goal of making American manufacturers competitive with lower-price-quoting foreign producers, the Eximbank enters the scene and offers financing arrange-ments with the provision that the shipment is ordered in the United States. Suppose that the contract terms embody, for each $100 financed, a $10.00 grant equivalent.

No doubt that the Eximbank sacrifices $10.00 in pursuit of its target, i.e. export promotion. So $10.00 has been given away. The question is to

TABLE 4

Tracing subsidy elements in Eximbank credit: hypothetical cases

Price of comparable product			Grant equivalent of Eximbank financing (4)	Grant equivalent		
in USA (1)	on competitive world market (2)	difference (3)		to foreign importer (5)	to domestic exporter (6)	to extricate handicap (7)
I Prima facie grant case, when grant equivalent equals price handicap						
$100.00	$90.00	$10.00	$10.00	$0.00	$0.00	$10.00
II. Indulgent grant case, when grant equivalent exceeds price handicap						
$100.00	$95.00	$5.00	$10.00[a]	$0.00–5.00 (cir. $2.50)	$0.00–5.00 (cir. $2.50)	$5.00
III. Subterfuge grant case, when grant equivalent occurs in absence of price handicap						
$100.00	$100.00	$0.00	$10.00[b]	$0.00–10.00 (cir. $5.00)	$0.00–10.00 (cir. $5.00)	$0.00

[a]This should never exceed $5.00.
[b]This should properly stay at zero level.

whom? The answer is that the beneficiary of the grant can be identified only after further scrutiny. Superficially it may be argued that the grant is embodied in the loan, therefore, the foreign borrower receives it. But understandably he resents being labeled a grantee, or the beneficiary of any favor. He just happened to come to the market for a specific product which was quoted at a $90.00 price. While shopping around, he was buttonholed by an American sales representative quoting a $100.00 price but at the same time offering a package deal amounting to $90.00. The contrivance, worth $10.00, was readily available. So much so that it is the seller who files through his banker the credit application forms with the Eximbank. Consequently, the American package deal becomes competitive with third country suppliers. Nevertheless, from the buyer's viewpoint the $10.00 worth of Eximbank contract concessions were only an instrument of *price compensation* (a sales gimmick), but not a conduit of grant.

Continuing our search for the grantee, a logical next candidate could be the domestic producer. His higher price remains competitive only because of the availability of the sweetener in Eximbank financing. Now the analyst may surmise that since the seller himself does not pay for the special trade promotion, who-ever foots the bill de facto gives him a grant. This logic points at the high-priced American exporter as the grantee, who succeeded in putting the burden of below-market terms onto the public sector. He may, however, object to the notion, arguing that he sells at a break-even price and beyond that he receives no additional revenue.

Who then is the grantee? Is this case a sort of Greek tragedy where crime can be committed with no villain? Perhaps the metaphor is not so far-fetched. In fact, the producer operates in a millieu by and large beyond his control. It is the socio-politico-economic climate of the American society which sets the rules of the game—such as wages, raw material prices, interest rates, tax levies. These are the "givens". Under such constraints, so to say handicaps, it is the production function that warrants the price of $100.00. Yet the manufacturer is willing to cooperate in the pursuit of national economic policy goals—expanding employment and improving the balance of international payments—if the society extricates him from the handicap. But he resents the implication of being a leach. He may hasten to underscore that there are other beneficiaries of this export promotion, such as material suppliers, labor, perhaps customers (if the firm operates in the down-swing of the average cost curve), and even certain tax collecting agencies.

Notwithstanding the complexities of identification, table 4 through its three hypothetical cases follows the routes which lead to the grantees.

I. *Prima facie grant case: grant equals price handicap*

Price in USA	$100.00
Price in England	90.00
Grant equivalent of Eximbank financing	10.00

In the absence of Eximbank credit the importer makes the purchase in England. But concessionary financing may bring up the American offer to a competitive level. This is a price compensation. The attractive financing which makes the seller's higher price still acceptable to the buyer is a special trade promotion device. Clearly, the importer receives no subsidy, rather it accrues to the American *export sector* which includes the producer, shipper, material supplier, labor, perhaps customers, and the tax collecting agencies.

II. *Indulgent grant case: grant exceeds price handicap*

Price in USA	$100.00
Price in England	95.00
Grant equivalent of Eximbank financing	10.00

Out of the $10.00 grant at least $5.00 must be used to sweeten the seller's unattractive price. The other $5.00 may be shared by the exporter and importer. Depending on elasticities and on market power, it may accrue fully either to the exporter or to the importer. In the absence of empirical evidence, we may assume an equal split should this case exist, which amounts to $2.50 grant equivalent to each.

III. *Subterfuge grant case: grant with no price handicap*

Price in USA	$100.00
Price in England	100.00
Grant equivalent of Eximbank financing	10.00

Since the foreign competitor offers no lower price than the American exporter, it is likely that even a small sweetener may swing the importer. If so, the exporter could raise his price approaching $110 and thereby reap most of the $10.00 grant equivalent. Market power is the decisive factor. Here we assume an equal split, should this case exist, amounting to $5.00 grant equivalent to the exporter as well as the importer.

With its hypothetical cases table 1 helps in illuminating Eximbank operations from another angle. Clearly, the foreign buyer could not approach Eximbank without the active intervention of an American seller. It is in the seller's interest that financing becomes available to the buyer otherwise the export transaction would not materialize. At this point an intriguing question arises. If the seller's prices were already

competitive on the world market, would he still be motivated to secure
Eximbank credit for the buyer? Normally no, although it is not beyond
the realm of possibility. In fact, lower financing cost may permit the
quoting of higher price and eventually splitting the extra profit with the
foreigner in a separate transaction. Such pampering would amount to an
implicit (and apparently improper) grant to the colluding American and
foreigner from the United States Treasury, the burden falling on the
public at large.

The above reasoning leads to a proposition that the grant equivalent of
Eximbank credits accrues to the exporter, or in a broad sense to the
export sector of the national economy. This follows from the fact that
the Eximbank should enter the scene only when the American exporter
operates under price handicaps vis-à-vis its foreign competitors. If
Eximbank extends concessionary financing when price handicap does
not exist, then the action would be against the intention of the law.
Clearly, Eximbank loan without price handicap, or in excess of price
handicap, would be improper. So, the above exemplified $2.50 "indulgent
grant" and the $5.00 "subterfuge grant" both lack legitimate basis;
neither the domestic exporter nor the foreign importer should have
access to these grant flows. As long as Eximbank operates in the spirit of
its charter, there appears hardly a way for the foreign importing country
to capture the subsidy elements embodied in concessionary credits.
Rather, the grant flows remain within the United States.

6. Policy implications: Where to go from here?

By now we are in a position to draw some conclusions regarding the
issues stated at the beginning of this article. It turns out that much of the
reservations against Eximbank stemmed from suspicions that will be
dispelled under the weight of evidence. After re-appraising the relevant
facts in light of an appropriately designed analytical method, the policy
options are proven to be significantly less controversial than before.
Here are a few salient points; some are concluding remarks while others
offer an agenda for research.

(i) Given the customary Eximbank financing pattern, whereby 10
percent of the value of the goods and services is paid in cash with 45
percent loaned by commercial banks at market rate of interest and the
other 45 percent loaned by Eximbank—the grant value is quite
modest. On the average, the subsidy amounts to six cents in each dollar's
worth of transaction, i.e. 45 percent of grant ratio 0.1327.

(ii) For the grant equivalent to accrue to foreign importers, the chances are rather small. The prima facie case for Eximbank credit is to provide terms competitive with those offered by exporters in other countries. This is simply compensating domestic exporters for their handicap on the competitive world market. To subsidize beyond the price handicap or in absence of any price handicap is not supposed to be part of the Eximbank operations. Such indulgent grant or subterfuge grant would be against the letter of the law and could not even arise without the initiative and illegal dealings of the American business.

(iii) Contrary to conventional wisdom, Eximbank gives foreign aid neither to ally nor to adversary. No economic assistance is extended through Eximbank to the USSR and other communist countries. They certainly benefit from trading with the USA, yet that is the kind of gain from trade which accrues to all trading partners.

(iv) Little wonder that several legislators have made unsupportable and unfounded statements when congressional documents still counsel under the heading of Eximbank that—"Direct recipient: foreign purchasers of U.S. goods and services"[26, p. 146]. As the fog of confusion begins to clear, misleading statements will cease to re-appear in public documents.

(v) Clearly, there is need for a thoroughgoing evaluation of governmental support to trade promotion so that the record can be set straight. In support of its existence Eximbank management could then display more convincing evidence, than such quixotic counter-charges as: "On subsidies, where you stand and what you see depends on where you sit"[7]. The truth is that Eximbank is only one of the family of over twenty governmentally owned or supported agencies which pursue public policy goals, such as home construction, agricultural price support, Amtrak, small business, and so on[17, p. 9–15]. In fact, when compared with other implicit grant flows, the leverage of Eximbank is highly favorable.[2]

(vi) After recognizing that Eximbank does not benefit foreigners at the expense of Americans but, rather, its subsidies end up within this

---

[2]It is spelled out in the various operational manuals that a primary goal of governmentally supported export credit facilities is that of "enabling the supplier to be paid on a cash basis"[24, p. 88]. In fact, there remains little difference between the two techniques that are labelled as suppliers' credit and buyers' credit. A sketch of these methods may suffice here. (i) Since few suppliers selling on deferred payment terms have sufficient resources to bridge the credit period, most of them finance the credit they grant with a commercial bank which in turn refinance them with a special governmentally operated institution[24, p. 1]. (ii) Buyers' credits are given on the basis of an application submitted by an exporter on behalf of the importer[24, p. 17], i.e. "on the initiative and with the active help of the supplier"[24, p. 62]. In all cases, it is a governmentally created organization of the exporting country that guarantees repayment under its insurance or other schemes.

country, we can expect that most of the opposition will peter out. Businessmen interested in the expansion of foreign trade need not feel accomplice to charges against the national interest. Trade associations and other lobbies will have their case strengthened. I predict that the Eximbank will receive much more favorable legislative action in the future.

References

[1] BEN B. BLACKBURN, 'Let's Look Twice at Soviet Trade', *Wall Street Journal* (16 August 1973).
[2] DOUGLAS R. BOHI, 'Export Credit Subsidies and U.S. Exports: An Analysis of the U.S. Eximbank', in: *The Economics of Federal Subsidy Programs*, Part 2, 157–175.
[3] KENNETH E. BOULDING, MARTIN PFAFF, JANOS HORVATH, 'Grants Economics: A Simple Introduction', *The American Economist 16* (Spring 1972).
[4] KENNETH E. BOULDING, The Economy of Love and Fear: A Preface to grants Economics (Wadsworth, Belmont, Calif. 1973).
[5] *Business Week*, 'Bridging the East-West Credit Gap' (28 October 1972) 19–25.
[6] ROBERT W. CAMPBELL and PAUL MARER (ed.), East-West Trade and Technology Transfer (Bloomington, Indiana University IDRC, 1974).
[7] WILLIAM J. CASEY, 'A Long Look at the Ex-Im Bank: Reply', *Wall Street Journal* (2 July 1974).
[8] GUNTER DUFEY, 'Financing East-West Business', *Columbia Journal of World Business IX*, No. 1 (Spring 1973) 37–41.
[9] Export-Import Bank of the United States, Annual Report of 1973.
[10] MARSHALL I. GOLDMAN, 'Who Profits More from U.S.-Soviet Trade?', *Harvard Business Review* (Nov.–Dec. 1973).
[11] LOU HINER, 'Eximbank Running Into Opposition', *The Indianapolis News* (8 July 1974).
[12] JANOS HORVATH, 'Recording Actual Grant Flows in the Balance of International Payments: An Analytical Clarification', *The Quarterly Review of Economics and Business*, 14, No. 1, (Spring 1974) 89–102.
[13] JANOS HORVATH, 'On the Evaluation of International Grants Policy', *Public Finance XXVI*, No. 2 (1971) 267–281.
[14] JANOS HORVATH, 'Rural America and the Grants Economy', *American Journal of Agricultural Economics 53*, No. 5 (December 1972) 740–749.
[15] JANOS HORVATH, 'The Grants Economics of Foreign Aid', a paper presented at the University of Augsburg Summer Institute on Comparative Urban and Grants Economics, 1972, Mimeographed.
[16] JANOS HORVATH, 'On the Leverage of Subsidies as Policy Tools in East-West Trade Promotion' (1973) mimeographed.
[17] ANNE MARIE LAPORTE, 'The New Federal Financing Bank', *Business Conditions* (Federal Reserve Bank of Chicago, May 1974) 9–15.
[18] PAUL MARER and EGON NEUBERGER, 'Commercial Relations Between the United States and Eastern Europe: Options and Prospects', *Reorientation and Commercial Relations of the Economies of Eastern Europe*, 556–598.
[19] STANLEY D. METZGER, *Lowering Nontariff Barriers* (Brookings Institution, Washington, 1974).

[20] OECD, *Flow of Resources to Developing Countries* (Paris, 1973) 257–265.

[21] MARTIN PFAFF and ANITA B. PFAFF, 'The Grants Economy as Regulator of the Exchange Economy, in: *The Economics of Federal Subsidy Programs*, Part 1, 120–155.

[22] HOWARD SAMUEL PIQUET, *The Export-Import Bank of the United States: An Analysis of Some Current Problems* (National Planning Association, Washington, 1970).

[23] WALTER C. SAUER, 'Eximbank Credits Back East-West Trade', *The Columbia Journal of World Business VIII*, No. 4 (Winter 1973) 57–60.

[24] United Nations, Ec. and Soc. Aff. Dept., *Export Credits and Development Financing: National Export Credit Systems* (1969) E. 69, II. D. 7.

[25] U.S. Congress Joint Economic Committee, *Reorientation and Commercial Relations of the Economies of Eastern Europe* (Washington, 1974).

[26] U.S. Congress Joint Economic Committee, *The Economics of Federal Subsidy Programs* (Washington, 1972).

[27] U.S. Congress Joint Economic Committee, *Soviet Economic Prospects for the Seventies*, A Compendium of Papers (Washington, 1973).

[28] *Wall Street Journal*, 'A Long Look at the Ex-Im Bank' (28 June 1974).

[29] MURRAY L. WEIDENBAUM, 'Subsidies in Federal Credit Programs', in: *The Economics of Federal Subsidy Programs*, Part 1, 106–119.

C.2. A critique of theories of imperialism *

TAPAN MUNROE

> There is hardly any question which divides the world
> community of social scientists as sharply as that of the
> nature and significance of imperialism. Unfortunately the
> division runs rather sharply on ideological lines, which
> makes communication difficult as it tends to be assumed that
> those who do not agree with us are hampered by some
> ideological commitment which interferes with social
> perceptions.†

Given the vastness of the literature of imperialism and its various
streams and tributaries in this paper I will try to limit myself to what I
think are some of the landmark contributions to the theories of imperialism. I will begin with some clarifying definitions, then briefly review the
the theories of Hobson and Lenin, Schumpeter, Ronald Robinson, Harry
Magdoff, and finally that of Johan Galtung. This by no means is an
exhaustive review of the vast literature, but is a small selective sample of
the totality.

The theories that I have tried to discuss in my presentation may be
classified as follows. The first set comprising Hobson and Lenin's theory,
although not exactly the same, deals with the political economy of
private capitalism and affirms the primacy of economic imperialism. The
second is that of Schumpeter. It is basically a noneconomic interpretation of imperialism. One could almost classify it under a social theory of
imperialism. Both these sets of theories are definitely eurocentric. The
third set is represented by Robinson's work. This appears to be an
important sample of non-eurocentric theory of imperialism. The political
economy of the colonies become as important as that of the imperialist

*An earlier version of this paper was presented at an International Studies Seminar at
Stanford University, Stanford, California, January 1974.
†Kenneth E. Boulding and Tapan Mukerjee, 'Unprofitable Empire: Britain In India,
1800–1967: A Critique of the Hobson Lenin Thesis on Imperialism', *Peace Research Society
Papers XVI*, The Rome Conference, 1970.

country. The fourth set is represented by Magdoff's work. This is particularly important since it attempts to explain the post WW II phenomenon of imperialism without colonies. His work, however, is entirely devoted to economic interpretation of imperialism. The fifth and final set is Galtung's work and in a sense is a synthesis of the earlier theories of imperialism. But it is also more than that, it is theory which attempts to weave together the social, political economic, military, cultural, and communication aspects of contemporary imperialism.

Confusion and ambiguities abound in the literature of imperialism. For one thing, there does not appear to be a general agreement about the meaning of the word. The word in itself is a linguistic casualty which has been drained of its intellectual content by its emotive use in propaganda battles. A word like imperialism can be used to describe almost anything for which the author has developed a strong dislike.

For some the theory of imperialism is for all empires at all times; for some it relates to the formal colonial empires of the 19th and 20th centuries; for some it is the late 19th century new imperialism of Hobson's, and for some it is the neo-imperialism of Magdoff. The word is used ambiguously by Marxists also. Sometimes they refer to it in the technical sense, i.e. the final stage of capitalist development, and at other times they use it in the colloquial sense, i.e. the relations between developed countries and countries of the third world.

Another source of confusion has been the context in which the theories of imperialism have been developed. The authors of early theories of imperialism, liberals like Hobson, or Marxists like Lenin and Luxemburg, were not just interested in theorizing, but they were also interested in devising ways of ending imperialism—their aims were political. The debates were certainly more than academic exercises. The different theories of imperialism can be classified as a set of dichotomies—Marxist and Anti-Marxist, economics and history, theory and practice, 19th century and 20th century.[1]

There is little doubt that the core meaning of the word imperialism implies domination by persons of one nation over another. To clarify some of the confusion surrounding the concept, we can ask ourselves the question—"Is the relationship between two nations imperialistic or not"? In order to answer it we have to identify a number of different elements in the relationship. These are (1) The relationship is between groups rather than individuals; (2) the relationship implies inequality of status—the imperialist, of course having the dominant status, the subject

[1] E. R. Owen and R. Sutcliffe (eds)., *Studies In The Theory of Imperialism* (Longmans, 1972).

a lower status; this inequality of status usually arises out of the exercise of threat; (3) threat in the relationship has to be legitimated and hence has to be made part of the political system. Imperialism in this respect is then related to the degree of legitimation of the dominance relationship. The dominance of a capital city and a political elite over the provinces of a given country is not usually regarded as imperialistic because the people regard themselves as part of a single integrative system. We do not regard the Mafia or the bandit as imperialist even though they exercise threat and extract tribute. In contrast to this Portugal and its overseas colonies were defined by most people outside the Portuguese elite as imperialistic in spite of Portugal's assertion that it was a single country.[2]

The theory of imperialism had its birth in the underworld of economics. John Hobson gave a place to the concept with the publication of his work on imperialism.[3] His major theme can be traced back to the underconsumptionists—Malthus, Rodbertus, Sismondi. Hobson's major purpose was to provide exposure to his theory of underconsumption and not necessarily to propagate his theory of imperialism. According to him slumps and underemployment in developed capitalist economies were due to the fact that consumption failed to keep up with production. What was the cause of this malady in capitalist economies? According to him, maldistribution of wealth in a capitalist society occurred because labor had less bargaining power than the owners of capital. His solution was to achieve a more equitable distribution of income through state action by the regulation of monopolies and taxation of surpluses that were accumulated over and above that necessary for the maintenance of economic growth.

There appears to be slim evidence that colonies were essential as export markets or as outlets for surplus capital. Historical data shows that most colonies were economically underdeveloped and thus were too poor to be attractive export markets for manufactured goods. Although some of them were suppliers of important raw materials, their contribution amounted to a relatively small portion of the world's raw materials market. The significant part of the trade of the imperial countries seem to have been with each other. Trade did not appear to have followed the flag, but it may have followed effective aggregate demand.[4]

---

[2]Kenneth E. Boulding, in: K. E. Boulding and Tapan Mukerjee (eds.), *Economic Imperialism* (University of Michigan Press, Ann Arbor, Mich. 1972) IX–XVIII.
[3]John A. Hobson, *Imperialism: A Study* (University of Michigan Press, Ann Arbor, Mich. 1967).
[4]Hans Dalder, Capitalism, Colonialism, and the Underdeveloped Areas: The Political Economy of Anti-Imperialism', in: E. de Vries (ed.), *Essays in Unbalanced Growth* (Mouton & Co., The Hague, 1962) 141.

As far as capital flow is concerned, the evidence appears to be similar to that of trade. Most of the British capital appears to have gone to the United States, Latin America, and the self governing dominions such as Canada, and Australia. In 1913, less than 25 percent of the outstanding foreign investment seems to have gone to the remainder of the British Empire. The story is the same for France and Germany; together they did not invest more than 10 percent of their over-seas capital in their colonies. It is interesting to note that some of the more aggressive imperial powers at the turn of the century—Russia, and Portugal—were not capital exporters but importers.[5]

Lenin's work *Imperialism —the Highest State of Capitalism* although substantially based upon Hobson's work, gave imperialism its dogmatic nature. To the political leaders of 19th century, to their liberal critics, like Hobson, and to politicians and intellectuals in the colonies, the definition of imperialism related to two things. First, the policy pursued by the major powers in conquering and administering colonies and second, the political and economic relations between the advanced and backward nations of the capitalist world. To Lenin, imperialism was more than this. It was a stage which the capitalist system on a world scale entered around the end of the 19th century. There were three essential features of this stage—(a) the decisive role of monopoly, (b) the merging of industrial and finance capital, and (c) the predominance of export of capital over export of goods.

The Leninist theory that describes imperialism as a stage of capitalist development runs into difficulties if one considers the fact that early precapitalist states such as the Roman, Greek, and the Egyptian were highly imperialistic, or if we take into consideration the fact that contemporary non-capitalist Soviet and Chinese states have been highly expansionary. In the recent history of man the most aggressive and imperialistic states have been National Socialist Germany, Fascist Italy, and pre World War Japan.

Schumpeter's contribution is important since it is one of a few that tends to reject the view that economic factors explain the phenomenon of imperialism.[6] It may be worth exploring since it has obtained little exposure. Imperialism to Schumpeter implied aggressiveness—an aggressiveness which was renewed by each success of the aggressor. It was aggressiveness for the sake of aggression. Imperialism to him was the objectless disposition on the part of a state to unlimited forcible

[5]Benjamin Cohen, *The Question of Imperialism* (Basic Books, New York, 1973) 64.
[6]Joseph A. Schumpeter, *Imperialism and Social Classes* (A. M. Kelley, New York, 1951).

expansion. Although at one point he seems to accept the economic motivations behind the forces of imperialism, he insists that the major explanations lie in the needs that have molded people into warriors. According to Schumpeter psychological dispositions and social structures acquired in the past tend to maintain themselves long after they have lost their meaning. Imperialism was thus atavistic in character. It was derived from the living conditions of the past, and from past production relationships.

Schumpeter was attempting to provide a strong defense of capitalism. He said that in a capitalist system energy for war becomes energy for labor of every kind. A purely capitalist system cannot offer a true environment to imperialist impulses (K. E. Boulding echoed Schumpeter when he said "with the development of science based productive processes it became possible to squeeze ten dollars out of nature by production and exchange, for every dollar that could be squeezed out of subject, class, people, or colony by the use of imperial power and the exaction to tribute").[7] Capitalism, according to Schumpeter was anti-imperialistic.

Some of the evidence that Schumpeter mustered in support of his thesis, although impressionistic, is interesting to examine: (a) Pacifism is a phenomenon of the capitalist world; (b) Wherever capitalism penetrated, peace parties of considerable strength arose (c) Capitalism creates anti-imperialistic workers; (d) Among all capitalist economics the U.S. is least burdened with pre-capitalist elements, shows weakest imperialistic trends; however, we should not expect it to be free from imperialism since most of the immigrants came from Europe and brought with them pugnacity. Considerable data can be amassed that contradict the last two points. In a sense Schumpeter was reacting against Lenin's work. He wanted to show that it was a fallacy to describe imperialism as a necessary phase of capitalism.

The majority of works on the theory of imperialism, developed in the west, have been eurocentric. They have been about the economies, the societies, the political systems of the European states. Ronald Robinson's contribution is important in the respect that he gives significant weight to the social system of the colonies in explaining imperialism.[8]

In his view a meaningful theory of imperialism must find room for

[7]Kenneth E. Boulding, *op. cit.*, pp. IX–XVIII.
[8]Ronald Robinson, 'Non-European Foundation of European Imperialism: Sketch for a Theory of Collaboration', in: *Studies in Theory of Imperialism, op. cit.*

inclusion of local collaborating groups as mediators between the European powers and the political and economic system of the colony.

The idea of a collaborative mechanism appears to have several advantages—(1) it explains why Europe was able to rule large areas of the world so cheaply and with so few troops, (2) it explains the process of decolonization in terms of the growing ability of the independence movements in the colonies to disrupt the arrangements for collaboration. According to Robinson, imperialism was as much a function of its victims' collaboration or non-collaboration as it was of European expansion.

Imperialism in the industrial age has been a process by which agents of a dominant society have gained influence or control over weaker societies by dollar diplomacy, by gun-boat diplomacy, by ideological suasion, by conquest, or by planting colonies of its own abroad. Imperialism has implied the use of power and the transfer of economic resources. According to Robinson, without the voluntary or coerced cooperation of the colonial elites, economic resources could not be transferred. Indian Sepoys and Indian Revenue conquered and kept for the Raj the so-called brightest jewel in the imperial crown (although there is evidence to suggest that in aggregate terms the Indian jewel may have been a paste jewel for Britain after all. See Tapan Mukerjee, *The Economic Impact of Decolonization: The Britain-India Case*, Doctoral Dissertation, University of Colombo, Boulder, Colo. (1970)). China and Japan did not provide such collaboration as India and therefore, perhaps, could not be brought under submission.

With the invasion of less developed agrarian societies by large scale industrial societies the glamour of what the big society had to offer in trade, capital, technology, military aid and simple threat elicited colonial collaborators. In India and Africa up to 1947 there was an abundance of indigenous collaborators. They were of many kinds, most were traditional elites, some collaborated at central, some at provincial levels, some in education, some in administration. A large number were in the non-commercial ruling oligarchies and landlord class. Another significant group were the civil servants. From a European standpoint the secret of a successful system lay in the variety of choice and combination of indigenous collaborators. The latter were concerned with exploiting the wealth, the prestige and the influence to be derived from association with the colonial government. This, in many instances, may have increased their traditional followings.

The collaborative mechanism made imperialism a relatively low-cost process; as a matter of fact it perhaps made empires viable for a long time. One could theorize that apart from loss of legitimacy of empire, one of the major reasons for decolonization was the breakdown of the collaborative mechanism.[9]

Imperialism appears to have survived decolonization. According to some customary identification of imperialism with colonialism is an obstacle to the proper study of the subject. Harry Magdoff attempts to explain the phenomenon of imperialism without formal colonies.[10] The basis of the continuity of imperialism, according to Magdoff, is foreign investment in a large scale. In a search for its causation, Magdoff rejects explanations like that of Hobson's (which deal with surplus capital) or the falling rate of profit argument. He finds the underlying cause to be continuing capital exports and the monopolistic structure of industry in the advanced capitalist countries.

Magdoff states that it is incorrect to assume that modern imperialism would have been possible without colonialism. Colonialism seems to have been essential for reshaping the social and economic institutions of many dependent countries to the needs of the metropolitan centers. Once the reshaping was accomplished, economic forces such as international market and financial systems were sufficient to perpetuate the relationship of dominance and exploitation.

The primary determinants of imperialism according to Magdoff remain—(1) the monopoly structure of big business in metropolitan centers, (2) the need for these economic centers to grow and to control materials and resources and markets, (3) the continuation of an initial division of labor which serves the need of metropolitan centers, and (4) national rivalry among industrial powers for export and investment opportunities in each others markets.

It is Magdoff's contention that the essential structure of economic dependency has persisted in the period of imperialism without colonies. Dependency relations that were embedded since the days of mercantil-

---

[9]Another perspective is obtained on this issue from the work of Harold and Margaret Sprout: "The British Empire was maintained as long as lowly folk in the United Kingdom and in the colonies could be controlled and kept working at a relatively low cost in money and violence. The British Empire became progressively insupportable as rising demands within Britain and resistance to imperial rule in the colonies coincided with escalating costs of maintaining Britain's historic role on international politics. The British experience also suggests to us the possible utility of thinking about imperialism in terms of viable and unviable types—the former evolving into the latter when erosion of the imperial powers moral claims ("civilizing mission", "white man's burden", etc.) necessitates progressively heavier reliance on violence to sustain the imperial authority."—Harold and Margaret Sprout, 'Dilemma of Rising Demands and Insufficient Resources', World Politics (1968) 660–693.

[10]Harry Magdoff, The Age of Imperialism (Monthly Review Press, New York, 1969).

ism have not been easy to eradicate. International prices structure, income distribution, and resource allocation patterns, combined with the superior military power of the west have maintained the pattern of dependency. The real-world price-market mechanism is after all not an impartial regulator of the economy. Allocation of resources is distorted by forces such as wars, colonialism, manipulation by industrialists, monopolistic industries, and international financial arrangements.

The economic and political structures of former colonies appear to have been suited to the perpetuation of economic dependence along with political independence. There appears to have been one weakness in the neo-imperialistic set-up, i.e. the political instability and the transitory nature of the power structure of the former colonies. The retention of influence and control by the metropolitan centers in the post colonial period has required some special measures. The techniques according to Magdoff fall in the following categories:

(a) Wherever possible economic and political arrangements have been created in order to maintain former economic ties such as preferential trade agreements and maintenance of currency blocks;

(b) Local elite groups have been manipulated and supported with a view to keeping the special influence of the metropolitan centers and prevent internal social revolution; institutional arrangements such as C.I.A. operations, military assistance programs, and officer training programs have helped towards attaining these goals;

(c) The direction of economic development have been influenced through bilateral economic aid and the policies and practices of the world bank and other international organizations. These activities in addition to influencing the direction of economic development have tended to intensify the financial dependence of aid recipients on the metropolitan money markets.

In Magdoff's theory one of the major features of the period of imperialism without colonies has been the pivotal role of the U.S. in the international system. The greatest gains to the U.S. in the early post WW II era was perhaps the triumph of the U.S. dollar and the establishment of New York as a maor international banking center. This development allowed the U.S. to enlarge the economic base of U.S. business abroad through expansion of exports and enlarged the economic base of U.S. business abroad through expansion of exports and enlarged capital investments. In addition to this the U.S. stepped up its efforts to enter the preserves of the former colonial powers by (a) becoming the major provider of military and economic aid, and (b) by constructing a global network of military bases and staging areas.

One of Magdoff's major contention is that a close relationship exists between the large Multinational Corporation and their Governments in modern capitalist societies. His conclusion is very similar to that of Baran and Sweezy.[11] Their theory raises some crucial questions—can the Multinational Corporations call for the support of their government whenever they need it? Is the government in capitalist societies subservient to the needs of the giant corporation? Reality seems to suggest that there is as much conflict as coincidence of interest between the two. Politics, power, national prestige, and national security are also important considerations of governments. Economic factors are involved, but they are not the sole determinants of policy.

United States policy in the middle east certainly does not appear to be in the interest of the multinational oil companies. As a matter of fact the U.S. support of Israel runs in opposition to the interests of the giant oil companies. Some have suggested that the U.S. policy in Viet Nam was motivated as a result of creating new opportunities for American enterprise.

One of the explanations put forward is that the policy was designed to preserve Southeast Asian markets for Japan, without which Japan would become economically dependent upon China. This would very adversely affect the U.S. economic status in the Pacific. Another explanation for U.S. military involvement in Indo-China is that it was designed to preserve the offshore petroleum rights for the U.S. oil companies. There appears to be very little persuasive evidence to support either of these explanations involving the support of U.S. business interests in Viet Nam. What may be an acceptable explanation is that what was at stake in Viet Nam was not the interests of specific groups but a system and a set of rules, a system in which the United States had a preeminent position. It was not physical threat to America that precipitated U.S. involvement, but the threat to the social and economic system dependent upon America's hegemonial position in the world.[12]

Magdoff, following along the lines of Baran and Sweezy[13], theorize that capitalist societies are imperialistic because it is necessary for them to be

---

[11]Paul Baran and Paul M. Sweezy, *Monopoly Capital* (Monthly Review Press, New York, 1966).

[12]Benjamin J. Cohen, *The Question of Imperialism* (Basic Books, New York, 1973) 126, 250, 251.

[13]Baran and Sweezy also talk about the need for capitalist societies to absorb an ever rising surplus, which can only be attained by imperialistic behaviour on their part. The problem with this theory is that there is little evidence that capitalist societies would have difficulty in absorbing the surplus, if there is one, since the demand for payments and expenditures on social goods appears to be ever increasing, and can always be expanded.

so. Both say that there is need for the state to protect the monopoly position of the giant corporations. The problem with this theory is that there is perhaps as much conflict of interest between the state and the Corporation as there is coincidence.

Cohen in his recent work aptly concludes that:

> The trouble with modern economic theory of imperialism—old or new lines—is that it tries to prove too much. Marxists and radicals do not simply accept that trade and investment in LDCs are important to advanced capitalist societies.
>
> .... There is no question that without such connections the profits in at least some industries of the metropolitan center would be lower, their costs higher, and their goods scarcer. Marxists and radicals unfortunately insist on trying to demonstrate much more— that trade and investment connections are *necessary* (in the sense that without them center countries would unavoidably sink into stagnation and unemployment), that economic imperialism is *inevitable* (in the sense that the capitalist system as a matter of course must generate behavior classified in this way). In terms of these more ambitious targets they fail.[14]

The theory that I propose to discuss last has significant linkage to Robinson's work and to some extent to that of Magdoff's. I would like to dwell upon Johan Galtung's work to a much greater depth than the previous ones since it attempts to construct an integrated theory of imperialism. The basic notion in Galtung's theory is that the center of an imperialist nation establishes a bridgehead in the center of the dominated nation by virtue of mutual interests.[14] The peripheries of the two countries are kept apart by having less inequality in the dominating than in the dominated nation. Imperialism in Galtung's model is a combination of intra-national and international relations. Galtung's theory is not reductionist in the sense of Marxist–Leninist theory which conceives imperialism as an economic relationship under private captialism alone. According to the latter view imperialism will cease when capitalist conditions for dominance no longer exist.

Specifically imperialism in Galtung's model is a relationship between a center (C) and a periphery (P) nation such that—(i) there is harmony of interest between the center of the center nation (cC) and the center of the periphery nation (cP), (ii) there is more disharmony of interest within periphery (P) nation than the center (C) nation; (iii) there is disharmony of interest between the periphery of the center nation (pC) and the periphery of the peripheral nation (pP).

Galtung's theory is based upon two mechanisms of imperialism along with five different types, and three phases of imperialism. The two

---

[14]Benjamin Cohen, *op. cit.*, pp. 133–134.
[14]Johan Galtung, 'A Structural Theory of Imperialism', *Journal of Peace Research*, pp. 82–117.

mechanisms of imperialism in his theory are (a) vertical interaction relationships, and (b) feudal interaction relationships. Vertical interaction relationships are those where the dominating nations enriches itself more as a result of the interaction than the dominated nation (the dominatee). This type of relationship in its modern form is concerned with situations where the imperialist exchanges manufactured goods for raw materials from the dominatee. The concept of processing gap becomes important in this context; this idea relates to the difference between an extractive economy and a manufacturing economy. The spin-off effects of a manufacturing society can be numerous and far reaching compared to the processing nation. The effects that one needs to consider are in the realm of economics, political status, military standing, communication, knowledge and research, skill and education, social structure and psychological effects.

Vertical interaction relationships involve unequal or asymetric exchange or exploitation. Galtung talks about three distinct types of exploitation. These are (i) looting and slavery, the case of pure one way transfers; (ii) the case of unequal exchange, a situation where the imperialist offers something in return, but the price paid may be ridiculous or unfair; (iii) the case where there may be balance in the flow between nations but among nations there is great structural difference as a result of processing gap; an obvious case of such an exploitative relationship would be where country A produces tractors and country B produces wheat. Imperialism in its contemporary form is due to a gap in processing level between countries. The center country provides processing and means of production, the peripheral country provides raw materials and markets.

Feudal interaction relationship is the mechanism by virtue of which the dominated nations in the periphery are kept apart with little communication and trade among themselves. International inequality is maintained and protected by this mechanism. Moreover it provides the stabilizing factor in contemporary imperialism. This type of a relationship is characterized by four different rules: (1) interaction between C and P is vertical; (2) interaction between P and P is missing; (3) multilateral interaction involving all three is missing; and (4) all interactions with-the-outside world is monopolized by the center nation (c). The economic consequence of this type of relationship for the dominatee are: (a) concentration of trade partners—i.e. periphery nation has most of its trade with its center nation; (b) commodity concentration, i.e. the peripheral nation specializes in the export of one or very few primary products. The combined effect of these two economic consequences is increased dependency of the P nation on the C nation. Galtung in this connection says that only imperfect and amateurish imperialism needs weapons to sustain the dominance relationship, professional imperialism on the other hand is based upon structural rather than direct violence.

Next we consider the five types of imperialism in Galtung's model. The classification scheme is based upon the type of exchange that occurs between the center and the peripheral nation. These are economic, political, military, communication, and cultural imperialism.

Political imperialism occurs when the mother country (C) provides decision models and technical assistance; the peripheral country (P) provides obedience and immitation. In military imperialism, the center (C) provides protection by means of destruction, and military advisers, whereas the periphery (P) provides discipline and traditional hardware. In communication imperialism, by virtue of advanced communication and transportation technology the C nation obtains substantial advantages over the P nation in terms of news management. Center news takes up a large proportion of periphery news publications, and the P nations do not read much about other P nations, but read more about C nations. This accentuates the dependence of the P nation on the C nation. In cultural imperialism we are not very much concerned with the division of labor between the teacher and the learner, but more concerned with the location and origin of the teacher and the learner. If the C always provides teachers and selects teaching material (from Christian gospel to technology) and the periphery always provides the learners, then we have cultural imperialism. The center likes to be the model, it likes to be emulated, the periphery provides a humble culture seeking strategy. The center ultimately creates culture and then manages its demand.

In his discussion of the different types of imperialism, Galtung mentions that one type is convertible to another. For example, political imperialism can be transformed into economic imperialism by manipulating the terms of trade. Military imperialism can be converted into communication imperialism by centralizing communication and transportation networks by invoking needs of terretorial security. Communication imperialism in turn may be changed to cultural imperialism by controlling and manipulating information flow. Cultural imperialism may be transformed into economic imperialism through technical assistance programs. The expert from C country not only provides technical advice, but ultimately creates a demand in the P country for the goods of the C country. It is his contention that complete inter-convertibility of the various types of imperialism would allow us to refute the assumption of primacy of one particular form of imperialism over others. It is on this basis that he rejects the reductionist causal chain of Marxist–Leninist theory that imperialism can be eliminated if its main element—private captialism—can be abolished.

We will now consider the three phases of imperialism as described in Galtung's theory. Phase one consists of the colonial era. In this the two centers belong to the same nation, the cP physically consists of cC people who engage in occupation of P. This is now a thing of the past. One of the few remaining examples are Portugese territories of Africa.

Phase two is the neo-colonialist phase. In this the centers are tied together by means of international organizations. This is the contemporary form of imperialism. Phase three is the neo-neo-colonialist phase, in which ties are established by means of rapid communication techniques. The cC interacts cP via space-age international communication. In all three phases, the center nation has a hold over the center of the periphery nation. The precise nature of the hold has differed and has been instituted through the means of transportation and communication. The essential fact is that historically the quicker the means of transportation, the less has been the need for permanent settlement in the dominated nation.

Phase one of imperialism became firmly entrenched with the advent of new means of production and transportation. This gave Europe a decisive edge over peoples in other regions. Decolonization came, partly due to the weakening of cC and partly due to the strengthening of cP. In Phase two control over the dominatee became indirect and was exercised through international organizations. These organizations which act as vehicles of transmission of dominance are well known for the five types of imperialism discussed above. According to Galtung's scenario, in the third phase of imperialism the international organizations will eventually go into disrepute and dissolve, these will be substituted by instant international communication networks. Guided by large data banks, they will permit the participants in the international system to find their opposite numbers without having them installed in a permanent institutional framework.

Galtung sees the role of the international organization as the most important instrument of imperialistic dominance at the present time. To understand its role clearly Galtung distinguishes between five different stages in the development of an international The organization in its first stage operates only on a national scale. In the second stage the national organization goes abroad, and a subsidiary or a branch office is established by its agents. This is a crucial stage where the major problem for the emerging organization is to gain a foothold abroad. In the third stage the organization goes multinational. Several national companies are started with the mother country organization in a dominating role. At this stage elites who are collaborators emerge in the P nation. Clearly this is the beginning of the imperialistic phase. In the fourth stage the multinational organizations became relatively more independent. In the fifth and the final stage we have the emergence of global or transnational organizations where national identities dissolve. This will be the age of super-imperialism with its accompanying rule by a world elite.

Several things stand out in Galtung's theory. First, in order to understand the nature of contemporary imperialism, one cannot ascribe primacy to one form of imperialism alone. One has to look at all the five types of imperialism. Second, imperialism is not just a product of private capitalism, it is a form of international and intra-national dominance system that exists in all the different political arrangements. Third, for imperialism to sustain itself the center of the imperialist nation has to create harmonious relationships with the center of the peripheral nation. Fourth, and final, imperialism cannot be eliminated by eliminating unfavorable terms of trade for a nation. Unequal exchange or exploitative relationships emerge because of processing gaps between nations.

One of the major problems of Galtung's theory stems from the definition of the "vertical interaction" mechanism of imperialism. Based upon this concept whenever there is trade between two countries, where manufactured goods are exchanged for raw materials, a processing gap develops, and we have an exploitative situation. The nation dealing in manufactured goods is the imperialist and it exploits the nation dealing with raw materials. The validity of this particular mechanism is very difficult to defend in the light of the recent situation existing between the oil exporting Arab countries and the oil importing industrial countries of the west. It is indeed difficult to make a case for the existence of exploitation of the oil rich LDC in the present case. If the existing terms of trade are maintained, and the world political situation does not alter drastically against the middle eastern countries, the processing gap existing between the Arab countries and the West most likely will narrow significantly as a result of the tremendous inflow of wealth and its subsequent investment into the industrial sector. The present situation by many has been described as one where the West is being exploited by the Arab countries rather than the conventional perception of the developed society exploiting the LDC.

On further scrutiny the implications of Galtung's theory become problematic. According to Galtung, even if two countries happen to be trading on the basis of comparative advantage, there could be imperialism and exploitation, as long as one of them deals with raw materials and the other in manufactured goods. Based upon this theory, a country would then have to eliminate exportation of raw materials in order to prevent itself from being exploited. Galtung's theory in itself becomes imperialistic in that it tries to label a large variety of legitimate, mutually agreeable transactions between nations as imperialism. I think that this is a major fault of his work.

Galtung's theory itself again becomes imperialistic when it goes into the discussion of the various types of imperialism—economic, political, cultural, military, and communication. The problem with the classification is that any interaction between two countries, one strong the other weak, be it cultural, economic, political, can be considered as an imperialistic relationship. For example, if a less developed society willingly embraces certain cultural attributes of the more developed society, then according to Galtung the situation will be imperialistic and will eventually spill over into economic imperialism, since the citizens of the LDC will become avid consumers of the products of the developed country, and so on. It is indeed difficult to accept such a wide and all embracing definition of the concept of imperialism.

D.   Ecology (the spaceship earth)
and
the stationary economy

D.1.   Must growth stop?

EMILE BENOIT

This paper may look somewhat inconsistent. I first argue that the limits to growth are real, and are sufficiently close so that a policy of restraining growth is urgently necessary. However, I then go on to argue *against* a "stationary state" of stable population and production. I shall try to show that there is no real incompatibility between these two positions.

The belief that the fixed dimensions and finite resources of the earth will not permit an indefinite continuation of exponential economic growth, and will require a timely transition to a "steady-state" economy (of stable population and production levels) has deep roots in classical economics, especially Ricardo's theory of declining returns to land, Malthus' theory of the trend toward overpopulation, and J. S. Mill's theory of the stationary state. These classical elements have been imaginatively integrated with the contemporary insights of ecology and eloquently expressed in the imagery of the space age by Kenneth Boulding in his seminal essay on "The Economics of Coming Spaceship Earth"[1] — which provided the main intellectual stimulus for the present paper.

The new view of the world and of the problem of economics implied by this line of thought, I recently summarized as follows:

Our earth, we now begin to realize, does not and can not supply us with an unlimited amount of usable energy, raw materials, foodstuffs, safe dumping grounds for our waste products—or even standing room. It is not an inexhaustible cornucopia. It is much more like an inter-planetary vehicle, where resources must be carefully conserved, waste products must be minimized and recycled, and where the number of passengers must be carefully limited to those that can be taken aboard without overcrowding.... We have, in effect, a revolution of rising expectation, superimposed on a population explosion, in a world of fixed dimensions and limited productive capacity. Therein lies the problem.[2]

---

[1]Kenneth E. Boulding, 'The Economics of the Coming Spaceship Earth', in: Henry Jarrett (ed.), *Environmental Quality in a Growing Economy*, (Resources for the Future, Inc., Johns Hopkins Press, 1966).
[2]Emile Benoit, 'A Survivalist Manifesto', *Society* (March–April 1974) 14.

That the finitude of the earth and its resources set some sort of limit to unrestricted growth would seem difficult to deny, though some growth enthusiasts hesitate to admit it explicitly. Most of them argue only that the ultimate limits—if they exist—are so far away from where we are now, and are so modifiable by further technological innovation, that no deliberate action to control growth is necessary in the foreseeable future. The more optimistic among them such as Herman Kahn argue that a continuation of present growth trends will in time produce such a high level of material welfare that the incentives to continue growth will weaken, leading to a voluntary slowdown of growth through satiety. Others whose optimism is more qualified foresee that growth will be slowed down automatically by rising costs of foods, and raw materials, and antipollution equipment. But they agree that continued rapid growth poses no imminent danger, and that any required slowdown can be expected to occur of itself without a deliberate change in public policy.

The contrary viewpoint, which will be argued here, is that a continuation of unrestricted growth threatens human survival through raw materials, energy and food shortages, as well as pollution problems.

1. Raw-materials shortages

The Limits to Growth[3] has been most seriously criticised for its calculation that if past growth trends continue the world will exhaust its reserves of most nonrenewable raw materials within the next century or two. Coal, for example, of which world reserves are generally thought to be enormous are estimated by *Limits* to be exhausted in 111 years if demand keeps rising at past rates.[4]

Critics, however, allege that known reserves constitute only a small part of "ultimately recoverable resources". Professor W. D. Nordhaus proposes to substitute a U.S. Geological Survey estimate of "Ultimately Recoverable Resource" based on a fraction of the resources which, based on prior experience, seem likely to exist in the top kilometer of the earth's crust. For coal this amount of "Ultimate Recoverable Resource" turns out to be equal to 5,119 years of consumption at recent rates. On the basis of this and similarly large estimates for other minerals he concludes: "The clear evidence is that the future will not be limited by sheer availability of important materials; rather any drag on economic growth will arise from increases in costs."[5]

[3]Dennis Meadows *et al.*, *The Limits to Growth* (Universe Books, New York, 1972).
[4]*Ibid.*, table 4, pp. 56–59.
[5]William D. Nordhaus, 'Resources as a Constraint on Growth', *American Economic Review* (May 1974) 23.

This could turn out to be one of the more celebrated *non-sequiturs* in economic literature. Any attempt to measure the impact of future growth by means of a static reserve index—comparing the estimated stock of the material with the *present* rate of consumption—can be thoroughly misleading. For this purpose only an exponential index will do: one which compares the estimated stock with a rate of consumption projected to continue growing in line with past trends. The difference in these two ways of measuring the adequacy of the stocks is enormous. In the case of coal, for example, using Nordhaus's own figures, but extrapolating a continued growth in coal consumption at 4.1 percent a year (it could easily go higher as other fossil fuels run short) my rough estimate shows exhaustion of the "Ultimately Recoverable Resource" of coal in only *135* years, not 5,119 years!

As another example, Nordhaus estimates ultimately recoverable resources of aluminum as amounting to *68,066 years* of consumption at the present rate. An exponential index, however, using Nordhaus's figure for the size of the stock, but extrapolating a continued growth of consumption at the past trend of 6.4 percent a year, comes up with a very different sort of figure—around *140 years*. These examples illustrate that static indexes are utterly misleading in assessing the effects of *growth*, and, that how long the stocks will last is much less sensitive to the size of the stocks than it is to the rate of growth in consumption. Because the long-term effects of sustained growth are intuitively so very unobvious (and indeed are so hard at first to believe), it is dangerous to base policy in this field on general impressions—or even on estimates if the assumptions on which they are based have not been systematically checked for appropriateness and consistency.

But *is* it realistic to assume a long-term continuation of recent trends? Any statistician will tell you that a long-term projection of recent trends is almost *bound* to be wrong. Here we must be careful not to misunderstand. To discover what would happen if growth did continue is not to predict that growth *will* continue. The purpose, indeed, may be to find out whether growth should not be slowed. And it ill befits those who argue that continuing growth is possible and desirable to object when the "unrealistic" multiplicative implications of continuing growth are pointed out.

Many economists have been critical of estimates of materials shortages which give no significant role to substitution between commodities and to the effect of prices in stimulating such substitutions, and in encouraging conservation, recycling, or more exploration and intensive exploitation of commodities that are in short supply. However, if we are primarily concerned with the very long run, and with all non-renewable resources taken as a group, then substitutions and price movements may have only a limited role. Many of the substitutes would themselves be running short, and rising prices would no longer serve to stimulate substituted or additional output, but only to register the fact that irremediable shortages exist, and to force corresponding cuts in consumption. As for recycling, *Limits to Growth* projects catastrophic shortages *despite* very extensive recycling which could reduce by 75 percent the amount of virgin raw materials per unit of output.

There is a widespread impression that the mining of the manganese nodules of the seabed may solve our raw-materials problems—at least with respect to certain important non-ferrous metals. According to some experts (though this is questioned by others) these nodules may in ten to twenty years be providing copper equal to a quarter of current output, nickel equal to three times current output, and manganese equal to six times current output—with the potential of ultimately quadrupling these quantities.[6] This sounds impressive, until one realizes that if past growth trends continue, annual demand one hundred years from now would be at *90* times the present level for copper, *28* times the present level for nickel, and *17* times the present level for manganese. Thus the additional quantities supplied by the nodules could significantly delay the appearance of shortages with respect to a few important minerals, but could not change the essential character of the long-term depletion problem arising from continued growth of demand.

A number of economists have questioned the thesis of growing raw-material scarcity because of the lack of any evidence of it in the movement of relative prices. In essence, they ask: "if raw materials have been getting increasingly scarce, why is it that their price has not been rising relative to other things?" Nordhaus, for instance, points out that the relative price of most minerals relative to wages per hour in industry steadily declined between 1900 and 1970 (Nordhaus, table 2, p. 24). This is undoubtedly true—though the movement *since* 1970 was in the opposite direction. But what does the increasing relative cheapness of raw materials from 1900 to 1970 really prove? Between 1900 and 1970 the labor costs of developed countries (the measure here used is based on the U.S.) were being driven up by trade-union monopoly control over key areas of the labor market. On the other hand the cost of materials was being held down by vast new finds of highly concentrated and easily exploitable minerals and energy—especially oil and gas—particularly in

---

[6] *Report on the Limits to Growth*—A study by a Special Task Force of The World Bank—(Sept. 1972) 43. There are other experts who believe the potential of the nodules is much smaller.

developing countries under colonial or neo-colonial governments which were unable to limit the rate of exploitation to the degree necessary to obtain prices that would include appropriate depletion charges reflecting the long-term value of the materials to future generations. The presence of absurdly cheap energy supplies made it possible to mine more deeply and smelt lower grades of ores without raising the cost of the refined metals by nearly as much as the price of labor was being raised by trade-union activity in developed countries. The world markets for energy and basic metals were far more competitive than the U.S. market for labor. Therefore it was possible to raise the price of U.S. labor a lot faster than the world prices for energy and metals. But this does not mean that the available stocks of energy and metals were not being run down—as we are now beginning to realize.

The last line of defense for the cornucopian view is the existence of awesomely vast amounts of minerals thinly diffused in the earth's crust, or in the seas. From this viewpoint it is argued that "The literal notion of running out of mineral supplies is ridiculous. The entire planet is composed of minerals, and man can hardly mine himself out . . . . A single cubic kilometer of average crustal rock contains 2×10^8 (metric) tons of copper . . . . We are not suggesting that such dilute materials will ever be mined, but only indicating that exhaustion in a physical sense is meaningless."[7]

This is unfortunate hyperbole. The notions of literally "running out of mineral supplies" and "mining ourselves out" are by no means meaningless. Annual consumption of ten leading minerals is now about 2.7 billion tons. At even a 3-percent growth rate, *annual* consumption would in about 1,000 years exceed the *weight of the earth* $(6 \times 10^{21}$ tons). Thus even if the earth were made 100 percent of usable ores and energy sources, and even if recycling were extraordinarily advanced, we *know* that growth in mineral consumption would have had to stop long before that. And between a 1,000-year maximum and, say, a 200-year minimum (based on estimated amounts of minerals actually likely to exist in usable concentrations) the 200-year figure is obviously a great deal closer to the ultimate limits of the achievable than the 1,000-year figure. And even 1,000 years is not eternity—it is only a quarter of recorded history.

What we can agree on is that "utilizable resources," as usually interpreted, excludes enormous amounts of minerals in extremely diffuse concentrations that would never be economically utilizable unless industrial power for its extraction and refinement (and for rectifying the

[7]David B. Brooks and P. W. Anderson, 'Mineral Resources, Economic Growth and World Population', *Science* 185, No. 4145 (July 1974) 13.

ensuing environmental damages) were *extremely* cheap. If such cheap power is not going to be available then the existence of these very-low-grade minerals is largely irrelevant—in which case we can continue to talk quite meaningfully about the possibility of "running out of mineral supplies" (even in the relatively short term)—in the elliptical sense of running out of those supplies whose exploitation would yield more refined materials than the raw-material inputs required to extract and refine them. We must now consider why the prospects of such cheap power must be dismissed as chimerical.

2. The energy problem

The crucial reason is that in the production of industrial or commercial power, the cost of the fuel or the energy source itself accounts for only a small part of the total cost. The bulk of the cost is for equipment for gathering and concentrating the energy source, converting it into alternative forms, conserving it, transporting it, and delivering it in usable forms and amounts to the ultimate user. These various costs reflect the required large inputs of minerals, power and labor. Thus even if the fuel itself could be made extremely cheap, delivered usable power would not necessarily be so. After all, in the case of hydroelectric power there is no fuel cost at all, but delivered power from this source is far from free. In the case of nuclear power plants, industrial users have received a large indirect subsidy from the defense funds which provided the original R & D and isotope-separation plants, which made the nuclear power program possible. And yet it has taken a quarter of a century before the program has been able to generate as much as five percent of public-utility power.

"Traditional" nuclear plants having failed to usher in the age of limitless cheap energy, the hopes of the cornucopists are now shifting over to the nuclear breeder plants, which could further lower fuel costs since they would manufacture more fuel than they would consume. W. K. Hubbert has calculated that with this technology in hand, energy would be available for 1.1 million years, at the current rate of consumption[8]—providing what Nordhaus calls "virtually unlimited energy".[9]

Such energy, however, would not necessarily be cheap and would be far from "unlimited". The cost saving over conventional nuclear plants is solely with respect to the fuel. The equipment and operation would be

[8]W. K. Hubbert, 'Energy Resources', *National Academy of Science U.S.A.*, *Resources and Man* (San Francisco, 1969) 157–172 (cited by Nordhaus—*ibid.*).
[9]Nordhaus, *op. cit.*, p. 25.

more expensive since the process is a far more difficult and dangerous one requiring extremely close tolerances and elaborate safety precautions, plus heavy insurance coverage. Moreover, if one projects world energy consumption not as stable, but as rising at its historical rate of only 3.4 percent a year, this energy source would be exhausted not in 1.1 million years, *but in 320 years*! And, well before that point, it would be annually generating waste heat equal to 4,260 times as much as produced from present annual energy consumption, which would be equivalent to several times the incident solar energy—and well beyond the maximum that we could probably sustain without grave environmental damage: e.g. violently changing the world's weather, melting the glaciers and the polar cap and submerging the great port cities of the world. This thermal barrier would strongly reinforce the other barriers to growth that we have been discussing, based on shortages of irreplaceable resources. (Power from nuclear fusion, if it ever becomes commercially practicable, would be equally subject to this thermal barrier.)

There is, however, one *renewable* energy resource the use of which does not add to waste heat overall (though it may redistribute it somewhat) and that is solar energy—either in the direct form of sunlight, or in various indirect forms such as wind energy, hydroelectric energy, the energy of the tides and currents and of thermal gradients in the oceans, or the stored energy of plant and animal life based ultimately on photosynthesis. The use of such energy to do "work" creates no additional waste heat and therefore does not assault the thermal barrier.

Although direct solar energy involves no fuel costs, it does, however, involve high capital costs for concentrating the energy, conserving it for when the sun is not shining, transporting it, and making it utilizable for industrial activity. Sunlight itself is too diffuse an energy source to do much economic work directly (except via photosynthesis), and rendering it industrially usable requires too much in scarce inputs of metals, plastics, labor, etc. to make it appear an economical use of resources, except for quite limited purposes. Up to now, we would get more *net* energy[10] by using these scarce resources to produce other energy sources (e.g. mining and processing coal or uranium, etc.). Moreover, so far as we can see, even if we make tremendous progress with our solar-utilization technology in the future, large inputs of scarce resources will always be required to obtain utilizable power of this type—and the real costs of

[10]It is clearly the *net* energy derived over and above the energy absorbed in the energy-producing process that is economically relevant. It is the ignoring of this simple point that underlies the unrealistic optimism of the cornucopists, as is noted by Howard T. Odum, the University of Florida ecologist. (See 'Energy, Ecology and Economy', in: *Ambio* (Swedish Royal Academy of Science) Vol. 2, No. 6 (1973) 220–227.)

these inputs will continue to rise as the most concentrated energy sources and metallic ores are progressively depleted. Thus despite the ubiquity of solar energy, economically utilizable solar *power* never promises to become unlimited or cheap.

A more fundamental explanation of this is given by Nicholas Georgescu-Roegen in terms of the physical laws of entropy.[11] In this view the economic process is largely the finding and dissipation of concentrated low-entropy energy sources or materials. Such products, like petroleum, coal, and high-quality ores, are in a form in which much of the energy, or material is concentrated, unbound, or low-entropy. Industrial use involves dissipating the free energy, and converting it into bound or unconcentrated, and unstructured forms. Because of the second law of thermodynamics, concentrations of low-entropy or unbound energy or material tend to be dissipated into relatively high-entropy or bound forms. Since sunlight is already a high-entropy type of energy it has a limited potential for industrial purposes, in its original form.

3. Food shortages

The current situation with respect to food is essentially as follows. Some ten to twenty million deaths a year officially attributed to various diseases are possibly the primary result of inadequate nutrition, which reduced the body's ability to resist the effects of various diseases— particularly in childhood. In addition we are now faced with the prospect of large-scale famines in poor countries, and embarrassing shortages and rapidly-rising food prices even in the rich ones. Wheat stocks in the main exporting countries, which fell from 49 million tons in 1971/72 to 29 million tons in 1972/73, are by now running dangerously low. Reserves of rice are nearly exhausted. Total food stocks are now equal to only 27 days consumption—a level too low to insure against calamity in the event of serious crop failures.[12] During the fifties and sixties the developing countries were expanding their food demand by 3.5 percent a year (mainly as a result of their rapid population growth) compared with 2.5 percent a year for the developed countries. But this 3.5-percent rate was made possible largely by U.S. food aid from excess stocks. About a third of their food imports were financed in this way. With the disappearance of these excess stocks, most of these imports will now

---

[11]N. Georgescu-Roegen, *The Entropy Law and the Economic Process* (Harvard University Press, Cambridge, Mass., 1971).

[12]According to a statement of Lester R. Brown of the Overseas Development Council at the UN World Population Conference at Bucharest on August 10, 1974.

have to be financed commercially. The non-oil-producing developing countries will find this increasingly difficult to do, at a time when shortages and price-hikes for oil and fertilizer (and higher food prices) gravely reduce the purchasing power of their foreign-exchange earnings. Thus the governments of these countries may be forced to divert all available foreign exchange from their development programs to food imports, or else to accept large scale starvation.

The long-term outlook is even less encouraging. About half the land potentially suitable for agriculture is already in cultivation—and this comprises the most fertile and accessible land. Although substantial new acreage is put into cultivation each year, this is offset by the land taken out of cultivation for roads, houses, airports and other uses, or lost from erosion, waterlogging, the spread of desert areas, etc. The costs of putting new land into cultivation is very high; averaging $150 per hectare in unsettled areas, according to the FAO. This investment reflects the inputs of energy, minerals, labor, etc. required to clear the land, irrigate it and stock it with the necessary fertilizers, insecticides, barns, machines, etc. Moreover, even increasing the agricultural output from *existing* land requires heavy investment of this sort. Thus increasing the food output is not simply a matter of using agricultural labor more effectively, or applying miraculous technological discoveries, like the improved varieties of seed connected with the "green revolution". Improved seeds require more water, fertilizer, insecticides, machinery, petroleum to run the machinery, etc., to be effective, and the additional crops require storage space, processing capacity, transportation facilities etc., if they are to be useful.

Thus increasing the agricultural output involves the using up of mankind's heritage of nonrenewable metals and fuels in much the same way as increasing the industrial output. It is not even clear that the advantages thereby achieved are permanent. Excessive use of synthetic fertilizers may damage the natural fertility of the soil, synthetic insecticides may damage the natural enemies of predators, as well as breeding of resistant strains of predators, and damming and irrigation may lower the water table, increase salinity, and ultimately reduce the amount of dependable water for agriculture as well as stimulate certain waterborne diseases.

What of the much-advertised possibility of supplementing food production by utilizing synthetic production under controlled conditions: of producing a large part of the world's food in "food factories"? Undoubtedly there are important possibilities here for production of proteins. But when it comes to the production of sugars, starches, and fats, it is difficult to imagine a more economical mode of production than the use of sunlight and the automatic drawing of nutrients from the soil by plants selected by mankind over thousands of years for their efficiency in this regard. While industrial techniques can certainly increase the output of food per acre of space utilized for food production, the real question is whether it can increase the output of food per unit of all scarce inputs utilized.

As for fish, which supplies the bulk of the protein available for a number of poor countries, we are coming close to (if we have not already surpassed) the maximum sustainable catch—at least unless we use a more scientific and controlled technique for fish *farming* rather than fish *hunting*. Indeed, present levels are severely threatened by overfishing and by pollution.

4. Pollution as a limit to growth

Economists have generally thought of pollution primarily as a disamenity, rather than as a source of disease and death. They have usually argued against trying to ban pollution completely, and in favor of taxing emissions or effluents so that pollution would be reduced only to the point where the costs of additional controls would equal the welfare benefits of further reducing disamenities.[13]

However, pollution functions as a limit to growth primarily by raising the rate of disease and death, and by lowering productivity. Moreover, as society seeks to guard against pollution by imposing controls, it burdens production with the additional costs of the anti-pollution equipment and processes, or through the discontinuance of types of production which cannot avoid excessive pollution.

There is little question that several persistent pollutants in the environment are growing in some linear relationship with industrial and agricultural production and that some of them tend to become heavily concentrated in human tissue. While it is possible in some cases to identify with fair assurance the critical levels of concentration that will cause disease or death, it is much harder to assess the clinical significance of subcritical concentrations, especially their long term significance.

For this reason, long-term projections about the amount of pollution that we may encounter in the future, and the amount of damage that this

---

[13]"Air quality alone should not dictate entire patterns of economic and social growth," said John R. Quarles, Jr., Deputy Administrator of the Environmental Protection Agency, as reported in the *N.Y Times* of August 17, 1974—arguing that areas with above-average air quality should be allowed to pollute them up to the level of already badly polluted areas, if they would prefer more economic growth rather than maintaining existing high standards of air purity.

may do to our health, are extremely speculative. In this case, however, ignorance is not a sound basis for complacency. In the one country where industrial pollution has gone furthest, namely Japan, there are already hundreds of thousands of persons with diseases believed to be pollution related. And in New York, taxi drivers, or others who are much in traffic, already have a level of carbon monoxide in their blood which would make it dangerous to use their blood for blood transfusions to persons with heart ailments.

Pollution can of course be "controlled"—but only in a relative sense. There are wastes inherently involved in all production—indeed in all living. So long as the volume of these wastes is sufficiently small, these wastes may be readily disposed of and will be recycled by natural processes, without creating much of a problem. However, this ceases to be true when the volume of waste products goes beyond a certain level. From then on, more and more of the previously innocuous wastes become noxious and require controls. This means that more and more energy and equipment must be invested in reprocessing, transporting and recycling the wastes to prevent their becoming a source of disamenity, contagion and biological danger.

Anti-pollution investment must be envisioned not merely as a financial outlay but as involving the diversion of vast amounts of raw material and energy into the production, transportation, installation and operation of the requisite anti-pollution machinery, filters, catalysts, and other equipment—thereby indirectly adding further to pollution as well as depletion. To keep these real costs in some reasonable relation to benefits, pollution control must always be limited to only a small number of pollutants, and to a limited percentage even of these.

If an industrial growth rate of five percent (the historic rate was closer to seven percent) could be maintained until the year 2100, then industrial output would be more than four hundred times the present level. Even with great progress in pollution controls, the control of pollution at that level of output would pose formidable (and possibly insoluble) problems. Even at the best, the burden of pollution control would become one of the main industrial costs, comparable to that of energy, or labor, or materials, Annual investment in anti-pollution equipment by industry in the U.S. is already estimated by the U.S. Department of Commerce to be close to $5 billion and is expected to rise by nearly a third in one year. Thus the sheer cost of pollution controls will become an important constraint on growth, and despite such controls the volume of pollutants may well reach very dangerous levels.

World pollution levels will be affected by the fact that a considerable share of the world's future growth of industry will be in developing

countries, which may be unwilling to sacrifice maximum growth for the
sake of amenities or even of public health. Some, indeed, may deliberately assume the character of "pollution havens" to increase the inflow
of foreign investment.

5. Can technology guarantee growth?

Growth enthusiasts usually depend on technological breakthroughs to
circumvent the limits to growth: supplying substitutes for depleted
resources, controlling pollution, and increasing agricultural output in new
ways. In the words of Carl Kaysen:

> Once an exponentially improving technology is admitted into the model, along with
> exponentially growing population and production, the nature of its outcomes changes
> sharply. The inevitability of crisis when a limit is reached disappears, since the "limits"
> themselves are no longer fixed, but grow exponentially, too.[14]

This treats technology as a separate and exponentially growing production factor, which moreover is infinitely substitutable for any other
production factor so that it can be used to offset growth failures
anywhere else in the system.

We question whether this is a realistic interpretation of technology's
role. What technology has chiefly done is to economize on human labor
or time at the expense of nonrenewable natural resources, or substitute
one such resource for another. But there is no indication that it can
modify natural built-in limits. For example there is now virtually no
research on increasing the speed of non-military aeroplanes. The world is
so small that there would be little advantage in further increases in flying
speed except for military purposes. Similarly, there is little further
research on increasing the speed of message transmission, in view of the
fact that our communications are already close to the fixed speed of light
and of electro-magnetic impulses. Technology does not make these limits
"grow exponentially"—as Carl Kaysen suggests. Rather technology
accepts these limits as fixed barriers to further progress along these
particular lines, and shifts to other areas.

Technology is thus not an omnipotent force that can be counted upon
to solve whatever problems we create. Nor would its exponential growth
guarantee that it could solve the problems created by the exponential
growth of everything else. In the first place, we must remember that most
technology is dedicated to improving our ability to kill each other, and
various other matters which contribute little to our long-term survival

---

[14]Carl Kaysen, 'The Computer that Printed out W*O*L*F', *Foreign Affairs* (July 1972),

capability. Indeed technological progress may create almost as many problems as it solves—some would say more problems than it solves! Thus part of technology's growth is devoted to dealing with problems created by the growth of technology itself. By no means all of it is available to deal with the problems created by growth of the economy. And a speedup in technological progress will not assure that more technology will automatically be available for protecting the environment. Furthermore the exponential growth of R & D may not, in fact, continue. United States R & D expenditure declined from 3 percent of GNP in 1967 to 2.6 percent in 1971, and there were declines also in France and the UK. There may well be social resistance from the older establishment of politicians and business leaders to the continued increase in the salaries, fees, prestige and influence of the learned professions.

6. The "doomsday" complex

The point of view here expressed is sometimes criticised as "doomsday thinking"—ignoring the fundamental difference between flatly predicting a diaster, and saying that a disaster is likely unless there is a change in policy.

But why should the existence of built-in limits to growth create a danger of catastrophe? Why should not a growing variable approach the limits gradually and asymptotically, stabilizing before the limit is actually reached, rather than crash into or through the limits in the catastrophic manner that *The Limits to Growth* calls the "overshoot and collapse" mode of adjustment? Of course, the gradual and noncatastrophic adjustment mode is a theoretical possibility, providing that future growth is placed under appropriate social controls designed to provide such an adjustment. In the absence of such controls however, the overshoot-and-collapse mode is far more probable.

For one thing the price system is not very helpful in steering the economy away from potential dangers. Prices reflect expectation of long-term shortages only to a very limited degree, reflecting the short-planning span of companies and individuals exploiting or stocking these commodities, and the high discount placed on income in the distant future.[15] Although prices may be helpful in inducing a switch from a high to a low-priced commodity, they are much less helpful where the prices of most of the commodities that one needs rise simultaneously—as we see in the current inflation. Similarly a general rise in prices signaling the

[15]See Colin Clark, 'The Economics of Overexploitation', *Science* (Aug. 17, 1973).

approach to exhaustion of a variety of essential commodities could not produce any "solution" other than to stop growth—but such an abrupt cessation of growth as this would require would, in fact, be the catastrophe that one was hoping to avoid, since sharp cutbacks would be unavoidable.

Negative-feedback delays of this sort comprise one of the main reasons why an overshoot-and-collapse type of adjustment may be inescapable. As another example, it may take years before a given emission or effluent is identified as dangerous, and a considerable further period before it is effectively controlled—by which time the environment may already be heavily polluted. Similarly, a decline in the death rate does tend to bring about a decline in the birth rate, but only after a considerable lag during which the population grows rapidly and may crash into the limit set by the capability to produce food.

A second source of danger arises from the syndrome which has been called "The Tragedy of The Commons".[16] This is a conflict between collective and individual interest, with respect to resources held in common. It is often to the interest of an individual to overutilize resources held in common even though if others act similarly the final effect will be damaging for everybody. The reason why it may still be rational for the individual to act in that way is that even if he abstained he could not count on others abstaining. Hence he would lose a short-term advantage without necessarily averting the final catastrophe anyhow.

The standard examples of this syndrome are overgrazing on common pastureland, and overfishing in the sea. The same principles apply, however, to overutilization of the two common "sinks", the atmosphere and the sea, as a dump for pollutants, including thermal pollution and the approach to the thermal barrier. In all these cases individuals or governments may continue on an ultimately disastrous course of activity because they cannot find a way to subject themselves to restrictions that, if generally enforced, would be in their common interest.

A third danger of transcending the limits of safety arises from simple ignorance (not knowing) and "advanced ignorance" (knowing what isn't so!). One of the most sinister aspects of pollution is precisely that in advance of experience it may be impossible to estimate at what concentration a given pollution becomes lethal. With respect to thermal pollution it would be difficult to know how close one is getting to the thermal barrier. It now appears that the climatic equilibrium is relatively unstable, and that a set of self-reinforcing changes could be set off by a relatively small external change such as an apparently innocent scheme

[16]Garrett Harden, 'The Tragedy of the Commons', *Science* (Dec. 13, 1968).

for diverting the flow of a major river. In another field we have just been given a dramatic illustration of the perils of ignorance of limits in the disclosure by Dr. Fred Ikle, Director of the U.S. Arms Control and Disarmament Agency, that a major nuclear exchange could very likely destroy the ozone layer in the stratosphere that protects all living things from the destructive effects of the ultra-violet rays of the sun. We then learned that the rapid increase in the use of aerosols may do the same thing.

Why not continue growing now, but cease growing later, "if necessary"? This solution essentially asks our grandchildren to make the sacrifices for their descendants that we are unwilling to make for ours. (Indeed, because of our growth the sacrifices that we would impose on them are far more grave than those we would impose on ourselves!) If unrestricted growth is dangerous, we cannot delegate to others the responsibility of stopping it. Our contribution to our children will be as much in the example we set as in the physical patrimony we transfer to them. If we dodge the issue, we make it harder for them to face it.

7. Steady-state vs. dynamic-equilibrium economy

The main alternative hitherto considered to the "Unrestricted Growth Economy" is the Steady-State Economy, in which there is no further growth in population or production. As I see it, the Steady-State Economy has two serious shortcomings. The first is that despite its laudable objectives it does not actually offer a very long future for mankind. The "Ultimate Recoverable Resource" of coal (as estimated by the U.S. Geological Survey) would provide only 5,119 years of consumption at existing rates. The comparable figure for iron is 2,657 years, for lead 162 years, *et cetera.* The total amounts that could be found might be somewhat greater than this of course, and additional amounts of some metals might be made available by recycling and substitution—partly at the cost of the additional fuel and metals required for such activities. However, even if we multiply the above figures by some small multiple to take account of such potential supplements, we are still left with a period of future survival for our civilization which is negligible in relation to man's past career on this planet, not to mention his potential future career. When planning for the future of human civilization we should be thinking in terms of millions, not thousands, of years.

The other objection which I see to a Steady-State Economy is that it would freeze per capita GNP more or less at present levels—subject to improvement only very gradually as productivity improvements permitted increased production without increases in the volume of material or energy inputs. In 1973, world GNP per capita was around thirteen hundred dollars, about at the level of GNP per capita in Yugoslavia and only a fifth or so of the level achieved in Germany or the United States. I doubt that this is a satisfactory standard for mankind during the rest of its career. It may seem more or less tolerable to some of us in the developed nations, but only because our incomes are a large multiple of the incomes in the poorest countries. According to the World Bank, 800 million people are living in "absolute poverty" on the equivalent of 30¢ a day. It is their terrible deprivation which makes it possible for the relatively affluent middle classes of North America and Europe and Japan to enjoy a reasonable degree of material prosperity without total environmental improverishment. If the world as a whole enjoyed a similar level of consumption, the situation would quickly become unmanageable. Even with the maximum feasible income redistribution achievable without violence and the destruction of wealth, present income levels imply inhumanly low incomes for a large fraction of the world's population, and less than adequate nutrition, medical and educational services, privacy, quiet and dignity for a large part of humanity. It would be a great disappointment to have to settle for such an imperfect solution as this.

It is our task, then, to find a genuine alternative, offering *both* rising living standards and minimal adverse environmental impacts. This will seem self-contradictory to many, but I believe a real solution exists. I call it the "Dynamic Equilibrium Economy".

This is not (like conventional economic equilibrium) a self-maintaining stable relationship among various components *within* the economy, functioning automatically through the working of the price system. On the contrary, it is a *non*-automatic more or less stable relationship *between the economy as a whole* and the physical environment, maintained by conscious policy. The relationship is such that the environmental deterioration from the operation of the economy is minimal, and the economy is capable of continuing indefinitely in that environment—or at least until the earth becomes uninhabitable because of astronomic-geologic changes, like the explosion, overheating, or cooling of the sun. In short we have in mind an economy which is in very long term balance with the environment, and can expect to be indefinitely sustained by it.

The value judgment underlying this concept is that the preservation of the human race and the human culture is the most fundamental moral obligation that we have, and that future generations have as much right to a share in the world's resources as we have. We may not therefore foreclose their options by appropriating more than our fair share, or live by the maxim of "Après moi le deluge". We propose instead, an ethic of "Intertemporal Egalitarianism" which calls for a fair deal for *future* generations. This contrasts with *interspatial* egalitarianism (the dominant social philosophy of our era) which regards the achievement of a greater degree of equality among members of the *present* generation as the moral issue of overriding if not exclusive importance.

The extent to which such an ecological equilibrium is achieved depends on three primary conditions: (1) the size and rate of change of population; (2) the size and rate of change in the production of goods (not services), and (3) the amount and rate of change of environmentally oriented technology, which by controlling depletion and pollution reduces or controls the adverse impact of the economy on the environment.

Is the notion of an economy in ecological equilibrium anything more than a theoretical possibility? Could such a thing really exist? I am convinced it could, and that we can easily specify some hypothetical examples, though we don't yet know enough to be sure just where the parameters would have to be set. One example, would be a world population of ten million people living by hunting in the style of our remote ancestors. Another might be a population even of a billion, with a $100-billion GNP equally divided. Finally, it might be safe to have a rich economy, with let us say a $25,000-a-year per-capita GNP if the population was stabilized at 100 million and a third of the GNP was spent on environmental-protection measures. These are, of course, extreme and oversimplified cases, and we cannot be sure even about them. More realistic parameters could be established only by extensive research, research, incidentally, that could have great long-term value for human survival.

Can an economy in ecological equilibrium with indefinite survival capabilities also be a dynamic economy providing high and rising standards of living? This sounds like a contradiction, yet it is a major thesis of this paper that such a combination *is* possible. It is precisely this that we call a "Dynamic Equilibrium Economy."

How could it be done? It would require, as we see it, three basic policies: (1) Economic Simplification, (2) Technological Renewal, and (3) Negative Population Growth—plus a primary commitment of government to the solution of substantive problems of growth and human survival, rather than to traditional political partisan and nationalistic objectives.

8. Economic simplification

It is clear that our economy produces and consumes a great deal that renders very little net satisfaction to the population as a whole. Some of these items involve sheer waste. A number of American companies found during the recent fuel crisis that they could readily make substantial savings just by tightening up their inspection procedures and eliminating sheer waste of fuel in their regular operations—by such simple means as shutting off idle engines, reutilizing waste heat, repairing broken steam lines, etc. There are also considerable wastes from crime, graft, absenteeism, featherbedding, etc. that could be greatly reduced if a new survival ethic took over. Perhaps it could even be extended to the vast wastes of the arms race. Furthermore there is a large element of convention, fashion, and symbolism in consumption, including conspicuous consumption to exhibit social status. Less expensive inputs of scarce materials would often be required to provide the same intrinsic satisfactions: people could use mass transit, car pools, motorcycles, or bicycles instead of private cars, etc. The symbolic satisfactions could be served in other more direct ways—as e.g. by awarding titles, honors, priorities etc., by providing access to *services*, or by allowing people to earn more money but restricting their right to spend it on luxury goods by a spending tax with exemptions for services, and low rates for goods up to low levels of consumption.

The traditional economic goal of productivity seeks to achieve a given output of goods and services with the least input of labor and/or capital in the interest of shifting redundant units of labor and/or capital to alternative uses, thereby maximizing total output and consumption. Economic simplification, on the other hand, seeks where possible to have economic progress take the form of services and leisure, rather than goods, and to eliminate production of those goods whose consumption does not provide sufficient intrinsic satisfactions to justify the environmental costs thereby imposed on future generations. Economic simplification does not mean that the preferences of existing consumers would be ignored, but it does mean that "consumer sovereignty" (in the sense of the *present* generation of consumers) can no longer be accepted as absolute. Moreover, the right of private companies to reinforce or modify consumer preferences by advertising—particularly manipulatory advertising—can no longer be accepted where this creates or strengthens preferences opposed to the goals of economic simplification.

9. Technological renewal

Many environmentalists have been hostile to technology, which they have blamed for the deterioration of the environment. Actually technology is neutral and will serve any objective to which it is applied. The damage to the environment derives from the Unrestricted Growth policy, which technology has been made to serve. But with a Dynamic Equilibrium policy, technology would provide those measures of conservation, pollution control, population control etc. vital for the preservation of the environment.

This, however, would require the development of an affirmative, unified and dynamic technological policy, for its own sake—such as we have never had. Up to now our technology is largely an incidental side effect of the interaction of a variety of *other* policies and programs such as: higher education, national defense, and space exploration, with the patent laws (and their complex incentives for private companies to develop, or to suppress, various innovations).

Technological Renewal would require the acceptance of the idea that developing a high technological capability is one of the most important functions of government, justifying one of the largest budgets in the government, to subsidize the needed R & D and the advanced training of the people to do the R & D, as well as to support the fundamental planning activities on the basis of which technological priorities would be radically revised.

Top priority might well be given to developing the large-scale production of a renewable fuel like methanol to supplement fossil fuels, and to other indirect forms of solar power such as winds, tides, oceanic thermal gradients, etc. At the same time urgent efforts would be required to identify and control the more dangerous pollutants. As opportunity afforded, there would no doubt be an increasing effort to conserve and recycle all scrap containing non-renewable resources—perhaps designing the objects initially in such fashion as facilitate the recovery of these materials, and to expand the use of renewable materials like wood, glass and stone. For the long run, the most crucial technological project of all would be to find ways of using direct solar energy—not only for space heating—where it already is quasi-practicable—but for a whole range of other energy uses. Also urgent is R & D on contraception, genetic improvements in food plants, and biological methods to control insect pests.

10. Negative Population Growth (NPG)

Starting from where we are now, the only possible way to raise average material consumption *and* reduce pollution and depletion is to cut back population. NPG is therefore an essential component of Dynamic Equilibrium. The environmental benefits are almost self-evident. Other things being equal, fewer people tend to utilize smaller amounts of scarce resources, require less land less intensively cultivated to feed, and generate less pollution.

Population reduction would not only benefit the environment but also raise per capita incomes. Studies of developing countries have strongly indicated that reductions in population growth might be many times as effective (perhaps 100 times as effective) as traditional development programs in raising per capita incomes.[17] These studies are based on a variety of analyses and assumptions in particular countries. A preliminary and unpublished cross-section study that I have been doing myself of 140 underdeveloped countries (with under $1,000 per capita income) showed a decisive negative correlation, of −0.2783, between population growth and growth of per-capita income. (With this size sample, such a correlation is significant at better than a one-percent confidence level!) Multiple regression with a smaller sample and for an earlier period also showed a significant negative correlation. For a group of developed countries there was also a negative correlation but it was not strong enough to be significant.

Such studies do not rigorously demonstrate a causal connection, or the direction of causation if a causal bond does exist, but they do support the expectation that a reduction in the rate of population growth would help to increase per capita income. The essential mechanism that would bring this about is not hard to visualize. The reduction in new births is likely to promote an increase in savings and an increase in investment relative to consumption. More important, it is likely to promote a shift in the type of investment, with less emphasis on housing, sewerage, clearing new lands, etc. as required to keep up with a rising population, and more emphasis on investment in machinery and equipment, advanced education and technical training etc. as required to raise productivity and output. In general, productivity would benefit from the improved man-land and man-capital ratios—and the offsetting loss from the smaller growth in the labor force would be relatively small where there was already substantial unemployment and underemployment. Note that even if NPG made total output increase more slowly, there might still be a more rapid increase in *per capita* incomes because of the smaller number of people.

Several who accept that slower population growth would raise per-capita incomes, are reluctant to accept the further conclusion that *reductions* in population might raise per-capita incomes even more. They buttress their reluctance with a variety of arguments—which I find quite

[17]Stephen Enke, 'Economic Effects of Slowing Population Growth', *Economic Journal LXXVI* (March 1966) 41–56, and *Description of the Economic Demographic Model* (TEMPO, Santa Barbara, Calif., 1971).

unconvincing.[18] To be sure, population reduction is not one of those good things of which one can say, "the more of it the better": a high *per capita* income with no *capita* would be a *reductio ad absurdum*. But up to a certain point NPG does promise large benefits. Research is urgently needed to help us determine where that point is beyond which the adverse effects of slower growth in the labor force outbalance the benefits of having fewer consumers.

11. The survivalist movement

The programs we have been discussing are obviously unlikely to be adopted by governments and electorates as they are today. Over the years, however, an increasing number of people will become aware of the vast risks entailed in continuing present policies, and those who care will, I expect, band together in a social movement for human survival— building upon and bringing together various precurser movements such as those for conservation, pollution control, population control, energy planning, disarmament and arms control, etc. This unified "Survivalist Movement" will be strengthened not only by the increasingly clear and increasingly ominous view of the future, but by actual portents of that future in the shape of famines, epidemics of disease from pollution, war dangers arising out of political struggles to get or keep control over remaining sources of high-quality, low-cost energy and raw-materials sources, and inflations, depressions, and war dangers resulting from energy and raw-materials shortages.

The Survivalist Movement will, I expect, attract to itself a large share of the world's scientific and technical leaders, as well as most of those whose primary loyalty is to the human race as a whole, rather than to particular national, class or ideological interests.

The Survivalist Movement will not be merely a mechanism intended to achieve the adoption of a particular set of policies. For most of its members, it will also involve entry into a confraternity dedicated to a new set of values and a more elemental and integral way of life, largely

[18]For example it is argued that NPG would reduce the share of the labor force in the population. Even on a straight demographic basis this is questionable. (See Timothy King, 'The Measurement of the Economic Benefits from Family-Planning Projects and Programs', Economic's Dept. Working Paper No. 71, IBRD (March 23, 1970), 6, footnote 1.) Besides, if more growth of the labor force is desired, it would be easy to remove existing impediments to enlargment of the labor force—as e.g. low compulsory age requirements for retirement, unreasonably high minimum-age requirements for leaving school, and inadequate child-care facilities which impede the entry of more women into the labor force.

free of the superfluities, trivia and clutter that now dissipate our energies and distort and demean our lives.

Today mankind meets its evolutionary challenges not through genetic changes, but by modifying its social institutions. Survivalism will represent the most self-conscious and ambitious attempt in human history to achieve such modification—in keeping with the unprecedented seriousness of the challenge. It is here, in the attempt to fashion and adopt institutions appropriate for spaceship earth, that human viability will meet its ultimate test.

D.2. The sustainable economy

ROBERT U. AYRES and ALLEN V. KNEESE

Another very important aspect of ecological economics which is receiving more and more attention is the problem of pollution and exhaustion. Economists frequently tend to dismiss this problem with cheerful platitudes.

Kenneth E. Boulding, *Economics as a Science* (McGraw-Hill, New York, 1970) 41.

I have been gradually coming under the conviction, disturbing for a professional theorist, that there is no such thing as economics—there is only social science applied to economic problems. Indeed there may not even be such a thing as social science—there may only be general science applied to the problems of society.

Boulding, from the preface of *A Reconstruction of Economics* (Wiley, New York, 1950).

We cannot escape the proposition that as science moves from pure knowledge toward control, that is, toward creating what it knows, what it creates becomes a problem of ethical choice and will depend upon the common values of the society within which the subculture is embedded, as well as the common values of the scientific subculture.

Boulding, *Economics as a Science*, p. 122.

The origin of this book in my own mind can be traced back to a passionate conviction of my youth that war was the major moral and intellectual problem of our age. If the years have made this conviction less passionate, they have made it no less intense.

Boulding from the preface of *Conflict and Defense—A General Theory* (Harper, New York, 1962).

1. Introduction

While his contributions to it have been many and important, Ken Boulding, as the first two quotations show, has always been somewhat dubious of his chosen profession. His reservations about current doctrine have sometimes been hard to understand at first, because they were subtle and reached out of the near-term context, and when they were understood, sometimes they were hard to take. But they have played no small role in helping to produce healthy and constructive changes in the theory and practice of economics.

One of his main areas of uneasiness has been about economic growth based on ever-increasing "throughputs" in the economy. This reservation far predates the present crop of zero-growth advocates. It is a main theme, for example, in *A Reconstruction of Economics*, his 1950 book in which he tried to persuade economists, without much effect it must be admitted, that they should give attention to assets in their thinking and not focus so single-mindedly on income as conventionally measured. In later years, his concern came to include the environmental pollution and resource depletion which he saw was an integral result of the nature of our contemporary growth processes. He contributed such evocative terms as "cowboy economy" and "spaceship earth" to the lexicon of environmental and natural-resource discourse. His ideas helped stimulate others to work along related lines — including the present authors.[1]

The third quotation illustrates Boulding's concern for the ethical content of science as an influence in human decision making. Such concern often sits uneasily with "scientific" economists who continue to strive manfully for a "wertfrei" discipline. But as one tries to use economics on today's pressing questions of conflicts in human values, unresolvable by the market, and even further on the large issues surrounding humanity's future, it becomes clear that his enduring concern for the moral aspect of this discipline, and of the sciences more generally, was not misplaced.

The fourth quotation displays Boulding's deep concern about the insane level of violence in our contemporary society. In the few years since it was written, the world has seen several more major wars.

In this essay we consider a set of Bouldingian questions, epitomized by the opening quotations, about whether humanity can converge to an indefinitely sustainable economy in a way that is reasonably orderly, peaceful, and safe, or whether it is on a one-way track to disaster. As we contemplated these cosmic issues, we grew increasingly aware of how

[1]See Robert U. Ayres and Allen V. Kneese, 'Production, Consumption, and Externalities', *American Economic Review 59*, No. 3 (June 1969).

complex these matters really are and how foolhardy it is for ordinary mortals to write about them—and yet, the questions won't go away. Recently constructed global models, despite some of the claims made for them, don't answer them. Simple solutions for avoiding the risk of disaster like "stop growth" are not persuasive. Wishing growth away won't make it so and, if it did, clear and present disasters would certainly take the place of more remote and problematical ones.

2. A look at the present context of the growth issue

Contemporary interest in no-growth economics seems to stem from two general causes.

The first is the exponentially soaring rise in world population in the last few hundred years and especially in the post-World War II period.

The second is strongly increasing resource-extraction rates and associated environmental pollution, again at an accelerated pace in the post-World War II period.

Both these phenomena are contributing to large-scale and, many fear, strongly adverse imbalances in ecological systems and irreversible depletion of resources.[2]

Since 1920, the world's population has about doubled, and the gross load of materials and energy residuals returned to the environment has probably more than quadrupled. Because of mass conservation, the mirror image of the extraction of material and energy resources from the earth is the residuals load on the environment. The disposition of the types of residuals now emitted to the environment can probably not grow very much beyond present levels without highly adverse effects on ecological systems and human health, and, clearly, the only imaginable, really long-term sustainable equilibrium involves stationary populations and very low levels of net use of non-renewable resources from earth sources.

These harsh facts have caused some to jump to the conclusion that the world must immediately achieve stable population *and* no-growth economies. But achieving these goals quickly involves complexities and side effects which are coming to be more widely understood—the apparent simplicity of such "solutions" is dissolving in the cold light of reality. For example, population growth is the result of complex interac-

[2]The laws of thermodynamics are often invoked to explain why irreversible depletion of resources in inevitable. Someone has paraphrased them as follows:
  (1) You can't win the game.
  (2) You can't even break even.
  (3) You can't get out of the game.

tions in a system which is excruciatingly slow to adjust into full equilibrium with current changes in birth rates, and stopping economic growth has widespread ramifications—especially in the face of continuing population growth.

2.1. THE GENERAL SITUATION IN DEVELOPING COUNTRIES

Given the huge inertia in population growth, even if active population policies were to come into being soon, a stationary economy for most of the world seems clearly out of the question as a policy objective for some decades to come. This inertia stems from presently high fertility rates and the youthful age structure of the population. Even if fertility rates were to drop drastically, say, to where each family had only two surviving children, the youthful age structure would propel population growth forward for a number of decades. The developing countries, where most of the world's population growth is, have no real choice for the time being but to increase production or face the grim old Malthusian checks on population increase. Furthermore, production must rise fast (5 percent a year or more) if the impoverished state of the masses is to be improved even slightly over the next few decades.

This does not mean that developing countries dare neglect objectives other than growth, such as environmental-quality management. Because of extreme congestion, poor combustion processes, bad local sanitation, and frequently adverse meteorological or hydrological conditions, major cities in developing countries experience some of the most intense pollution in the world. Sao Paulo, Seoul, Taipei, Accra, and Mexico City are only a few examples. Moreover, these problems, unless brought under effective management, will get rapidly worse as industrial production grows and the size of cities continues to grow spectacularly.[3] Whether developing countries will be *able* to grow at rates needed to prevent increasingly grinding poverty and in addition avoid disastrously deteriorating environmental conditions is an open question. But they have no alternative but to try.

We might add that it is the opinion of many ecologists and others, shared by the authors, that *if* the world does finally manage to arrive at some sort of low-birth-rate and low-death-rate equilibrium through non-catastrophic means, it will be at a level of population several times higher—perhaps 15 to 20 billion persons—than would be optimum for the human condition. But there really seems to be nothing that can be done about that—at least not for a very long time to come.

[3]We assume that in the longer time horizon the present "energy crisis" will have been resolved—but presumably at considerably higher prices for energy than have prevailed in recent decades.

To understand why this tremendous inertia in population growth in developing countries exists, it is necessary to look at the reasons for the recent rapid population growth there. It appears to be primarily due to the sudden transfer of a very specialized technology, that of disease control, to the developing countries after World War II.[4] Because of this lopsided technology transfer, death rates dropped much faster than ever happened in the developed countries. Unfortunately, birth rates have remained generally at a high level and even increased—although there are a few cases of decreases as well. Today the world's seven largest nations have about three-fifths of the world's population. These are China, India, USSR, United States, Pakistan, and Indonesia. Only two of these have reached advanced stages of economic development, and the population of poor countries is growing much faster.

One heritage of rapid rates of mortality reduction, centered on infants and children, is an extremely youthful population in the developing countries. On the average, about 41 percent of the population in these countries is below 15 years of age. There are about 76 dependents for every 100 persons of working age (15 to 64 years). That this presents immense difficulties for raising the standard of living needs no elaboration. Moreover, it foreshadows a long period of continued population pressure as these massive numbers move through the childbearing ages, even if birth rates among those in these age brackets should fall. By contrast, in the economically developed world, because both mortality and fertility have been declining for a long time, only around 30 percent of the population is under 15. But even where the situation, as in the United States, is much less extreme, youthful populations will nevertheless drive population growth for a long time. For example, in the United States the net reproduction rate has recently approached unity. Should this situation persist, the nation's population will still increase by about one-third before equilibrium is reached sometime in the next century. This is because the young people move into childbearing age brackets and will be represented there in disproportionate numbers for a period of many years.

Thus, the stage is set not only for continuing difficulties in achieving a high quality of life for vast existing populations but for further unusually rapid population growth in those large areas of the world that are already grindingly poor. The projections displayed in Table 1 show population growth in the developing countries to be five times as great as the growth in the more developed countries during the second half of this century.

[4]This point is, however, controversial. For a conflicting interpretation, see Roy E. Brown and Joe D. Wray, 'The Starving Roots of Population Growth', *Natural History* (Jan. 1974) 46.

TABLE 1

Population estimates according to the UN "medium" variant, 1960–2000, for major areas and regions of the world (population in thousands)

Major areas and regions	1960	1970	1985	2000
World total	2,998,180	3,591,773	4,746,409	6,129,734
More developed regions[a]	976,414	1,082,150	1,256,179	1,441,402
Less developed regions[b]	2,021,766	2,509,623	3,490,230	4,688,332
(A) East Asia	794,144	910,524	1,104,903	1,287,270
(B) South Asia	865,247	1,106,905	1,596,329	2,170,648
(C) Europe	424,657	453,918	491,891	526,968
(D) USSR	214,400	245,700	296,804	353,085
(E) Africa	272,924	345,949	513,026	767,779
(F) Northern America	198,664	226,803	283,105	354,007
(G) Latin America	212,431	283,263	435,558	638,111
(H) Oceania	15,713	18,711	24,793	31,866

[a] Including Europe, the USSR, Northern America, Japan, Temperate South America, Australia and New Zealand.
[b] Including East Asia less Japan, South Asia, Africa, Latin America less Temperate South America, and Oceania less Australia and New Zealand.
Source: World Population Prospects as assessed in 1963 United Nations Population Studies No. 41.

Probably more than three-fourths of the world's population will live in the poor countries by the end of this century as contrasted with about two-thirds at the present time. Furthermore, as population continues to increase after the turn of the century, the balance will weigh even more heavily in the direction of the low-income countries.

In the face of this situation, the income gap between the developed world and the poor countries seems bound to grow inexorably unless some rather spectacular things happen. We indicate some that possibly might in the scenarios we present later.

2.2. THE GENERAL SITUATION IN DEVELOPED COUNTRIES

It is only in the developed countries—which after all use the lion's share of non-renewable resources and produce the bulk of residuals—where one can seriously discuss zero growth as a policy objective in the near-term future. But there are major difficulties and complexities and problems associated with this objective, even in developed nations, especially if they strive to achieve it quickly. Another aspect of the situation is also now becoming more widely recognized. Environmental problems do not have to grow in a one-to-one relationship with either population growth or economic growth. We would, in fact, argue that environmental improvement is compatible with growth in the developed countries, and, because of more rapid replacement of obsolete technology and increased economic capacity to meet various objectives, it may, within limits, even be made easier by it. The urgent question is whether advanced countries will adopt the policies necessary to protect the environment.

A recent careful study of the U.S. situation until around the year 2000 shows that environmental pollution can be reduced by large amounts by the end of the century without large negative effects on economic growth if active abatement policies are followed. Considerable changes in relative prices and life styles may be *on* the cards, however.[5] While the same result would, it seems, be applicable in other developed countries, both economic growth and environmental management are in several cases heavily dependent on their ability to meet energy demands from external sources—a major uncertainty at the moment.

But since they are so much discussed, we proceed to discuss the objectives of zero population growth and zero economic growth in a little detail in the U.S. context. This situation may be considered very roughly typical of the general situation prevailing in many of the more developed countries.

The main source of economic growth in the developed countries has not been rising population and labor force but increases in the productivity of capital and labor. In the United States, for more than a century, the average output per worker-hour has risen at a mean rate of between 2 and 3 percent a year. The figure is lower for the service sector and somewhat larger for the manufacturing, mining, and agricultural sectors (which are exclusively concerned with processing material resources). As we already noted, population growth even in the United States will respond with a very long lag to the reductions in birth rates now occurring. The age structure in a number of other developed countries will lead to a similar result. The labor force for the next couple of decades is already born, and most of these people must work to earn a living unless the world changes its ways quite drastically.

If measured productivity keeps climbing at recent rates, around 3 percent a year, and we continue to have growth in the labor force of around 1 percent a year, and this is likely under any reasonably acceptable population policy, measured national product will grow at about 4 percent a year for at least a few decades. This implies that the

[5]See Ronald G. Ridker (ed.), *Population, Resources, and the Environment*, Vol. III of Research Reports of the Commission on Population Growth and the American Future (U.S. Government Printing Office, Washington, D.C., 1972).

level of measured GNP in 1980 will most likely be something of the order of 50 percent higher (in constant dollars) than it is now. The only way to bring this tendency to a halt quickly would be to reduce labor input either through unemployment or increased leisure. It seems unlikely that there would be large increases in voluntary leisure under circumstances where a major portion of the labor force still lives at comparatively low levels of affluence—median income of American households is still under $10,000. And one does not have to be an environmental Luddite to point out that the enforced leisure (unemployment) alternative also seems very unattractive.

Similarly, and closely related, the ending of population growth presents problems even in developed nations if they have youthful populations, such as the United States and the USSR do, in both cases largely as a result of World War II.[6] Because of this, if the United States, for example, were to attain zero growth rate immediately, it would be necessary to cut the birth rate about in half, beginning instantly. In other words, over the next 15 or 20 years, women would have to bear children at a rate that would produce only a little over one child per completed family. Leaving aside the ways and means of achieving such a situation, at the end of that time we would have a very odd population distribution skewed sharply toward old age.

The more desirable and feasible goal would seem to be to reduce fertility as soon as possible to a level where just enough children are produced to assure that each generation exactly replaces itself and, as we have mentioned, the United States is now at about this point which will nevertheless yield a residual population increase of about one-third. One should be clear that stabilization, even by this process, may have some undesirable features. Assuming that present mortality levels persist, a stationary population achieved in this way would be much older than any that the United States has ever experienced. It would have more people over 60 than under 15, and half of the population would be over 37 rather than over 27, as is the case today.

In this society, the number of people aged, say, 20 would be only slightly larger than the number of people aged 50. This distribution would no longer conform to our traditional social structure—to the distribution of privileges and responsibilities in the society. In the growing population, the diminishing numbers at higher ages and the smaller number of high positions relative to low positions in the economy and the society tend to reduce (though not eliminate) friction between the generations. In

---

[6]The USSR has been in a state of very low birth rates for some years. They now seem to be rising.

the stationary-population case, there would be a much reduced expectation of advancement as a person moves through life.

Furthermore, the present ratio of units in the net reproduction rate may well be fortuitous since there is no logical reason to believe that in the long run people would voluntarily choose a level of fertility that the society would deem desirable. So it seems important to consider what other policies might be applicable. Certainly a good place to start would be to reexamine the enormous direct and indirect subsidies which public taxation and expenditure policy grants to those who choose to have large families.

3. Some summary thoughts about growth in the next few decades

It seems to us incontrovertible that the world's population will continue to rise inexorably for several more decades, at least. This will be so, even if the effectiveness of birth-control measures is greatly increased and even if the underlying dynamics of population growth is such that it will tend toward an equilibrium combining low birth rates and low death rates. This means that many countries (containing most of the world's population) will have little choice but to strive hard for economic growth, in some cases for a very long time, perhaps a century or more. Also, it will probably not prove desirable for the major developed countries (especially those with youthful populations) to develop policies which will end population or economic growth suddenly. Over this period, however, it will be essential to stringently limit the discharge of harmful by-products of production and consumption activities to the environment. If this is done by policy instruments, such as appropriately high emissions taxes which bring social and private costs into conjunction, it will result in more recycling, increased durability of articles, and a price shift which will tend to favor services over goods. Perhaps most important, technical advances in the handling and reuse of residuals will be induced. It should be possible to reduce the rate of discharge of residuals—except CO_2, heat, and possibly organics—while continuing to achieve economic growth in the developed countries. The effects of CO_2 and heat rejection to the atmosphere are still somewhat problematical, and their occurrence, if any, is some decades off.

If prevailing incentive systems are appropriately revised in developed countries to reflect environmental values, it seems reasonable to expect that industrial skills and technology will evolve toward a situation in which the rate of use of non-renewable material reserves per unit output might be greatly moderated.

But even if materials-saving technologies are introduced, there will continue to be a heavy net draft on non-renewable resources as growth continues over the next few decades (and indeed there would if it stopped, unless the nature and scale of economies changed drastically, and probably catastrophically) with quantities used shifting increasingly toward developing countries if they can sustain a high rate of growth.

In point of fact, the deflated price of most natural-resource commodities has been going down more or less steadily, or been about constant, for several decades. However, for a variety of reasons, some of which we explore on, we believe that this tendency will begin to reverse itself in the next few decades—if not immediately. Nevertheless, in terms of the sheer availability of adequate supplies of resource commodities—food, fuels, metals, water, and the like—the outlook to the end of this century for the more developed countries seems rather favorable—if channels of international trade remain open. But as the energy crisis of 1973–74 showed, the position of several of them is rather precarious, and existing growth policies may be reconsidered. It is also not out of the question that some countries will be motivated to pursue military solutions or push the development of hazardous technologies in their quest of greater self-sufficiency—possibilities to which we return later.

For the densely-populated, high-population-growth, poor countries, the outlook is even much more dubious and uncertain. However, a combination of production increase internally and "rescue operations" on the part of developed countries makes it likely that the levels of population foreseen for the end of this century will actually be achieved. The combined result of population and economic growth, at least for the next few decades, will be greatly increased discharges of harmful residual materials in the developing countries. The developed countries should be able to check pollution of the worst kinds and, indeed, even reverse it, while continuing to grow, if they develop effective and efficient policies for doing so. Accordingly, it is reasonable to suppose that the proportion of environmental pollution contributed by developing countries will shift considerably in their direction by the end of the century.

It seems inevitable too that, at the end of the next few decades, there will be vastly more malnourished and grindingly poor people in the world than there are now. The situation will be one in which many incentives to hostility and violence inhere. Higher-income countries may be increasingly heavily dependent on poor countries for resources inputs. Poor countries with crushingly dense populations will be cheek-by-jowl with relatively thinly populated rich countries. Thermo-nuclear and biological weapons will be readily available to numerous countries. Major issues will arise as to whether it is permissible to use certain high-risk technologies in the interest of continued growth or, in the case of some countries, even survival. Nuclear fission and persistent pesticides are current examples. The poor countries will probably be predisposed, if not forced, to take risks unacceptable to the richer ones—some of which risks may have global implications.

Eventually, banning catastrophe in the interim, the world will have to face the question of whether a sustainable world economic system, one that emits vastly lesser amounts of harmful residuals per unit output than the current one and simultaneously makes a much smaller draft on non-renewable resources—is possible while sustaining a world population of 15–20 billion persons. This is the level at which populations may stabilize late in the next century in the absence of large increases in death rates. And, furthermore, there arises the question as to whether the planet can achieve this stabilization in the face of vast differences in wealth, motivations and imperatives, technological competence, and longevity and effectiveness of public institutions among the world's nations. In the next section we develop some scenarios which, we hope, will illuminate some of the possibilities and problems bearing upon the feasibility of evolving toward a substainable world economy. Whether this goal is attainable at all depends heavily on the paths of development which evolve in the interim period. In the next section we look at these paths in a bit more orderly way than we have so far done.

4. Some paths to the future economy

As we turn more directly to the prospects and prerequisites for a "sustainable" world economic system, a number of caveats are necessary. Among the more important of them seem to be the following.

First, the "future" is not predetermined, but some key driving forces can be projected with a fairly high degree of certainty,[7] whereas others are essentially indeterminate or their relevance is not understood at present. We will try to distinguish between the two (or three) kinds.

Second, some imaginable future scenarios are actually impossible for technical reasons, but there are many futures that are both imaginable and possible. However, no particular future scenario can be regarded as "probable" or even "not unlikely." A so-called "surprise-free" future would, in fact, be extremely surprising! However, the degree of "unlikelihood" of possible future events is tremendously variable. All scenarios are inherently unlikely, but some scenarios are very much

---

[7]Long-continued population growth is, as we have seen, one of these.

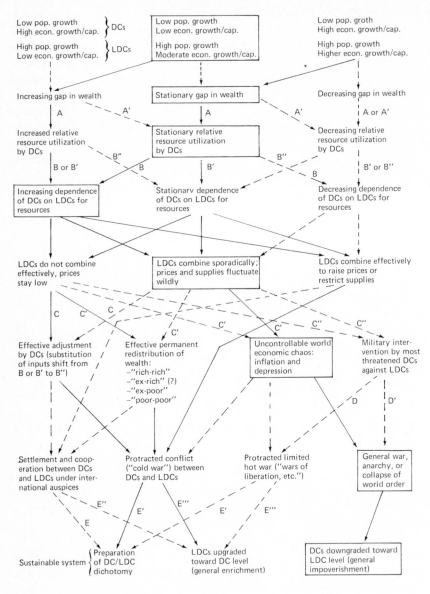

* Solid arrows = "more likely"

Fig. 1. *A*: Developed countries increase consumption of material goods *faster* than material/energy content is reduced by technology and design innovations. *A'*: Converse of above. *B*: Developed countries export resource extraction technology and capital to LDCs

more unlikely than others.[8] Again, we will try to distinguish some of the less and more likely cases and their interrelationships.

Third, not all future world economies are "sustainable". The possibilities of a major war or world-wide economic collapse cannot be ignored. Moreover, it seems inadequate to us to simply mention the possibility and pass on to other topics. In fact, one purpose of this paper is to explore—at least superficially—how some of these unpleasant outcomes might occur, in order to begin to understand what, if anything, can be done to avoid them.

A scenario can be played out by simply connecting any sequence of logical possibilities from the various levels shown in fig. 1. For illustration we have specified a scenario containing the following ingredients:

(1) Low per-capita economic growth by advanced countries and moderate growth by less-developed countries, combined with a higher population growth rate, results in a stationary gap in per-capita wealth.

(2) Resource *utilization* per capita in developed countries remains roughly constant, the increases in population and income per capita being compensated by moderately greater efficiency in the use of raw materials and energy.

(3) Resource *availability* in developed countries decreases relative to less-developed countries (i.e. historical trends continue) and, as a consequence, DCs become increasingly dependent on LDCs for resources. DCs do nothing effective to check this trend.

(4) Because of cultural, economic, political, and geographical differ-

---

[8]One that strikes us as essentially too unlikely to consider is the scenario in which the rich and poor countries of the world voluntarily agree to settle their differences and set aside their sovereignity under the framework of a world government!

---

in order to exploit cheapest available sources of raw materials (free trade policy). B': Developed countries seek to protect domestic resource development activities through tariffs, import quotas or subsidies for domestic producers. B'': As above, but where domestic sources are unavailable, or absolute exhaustion of the resource occurs, substitutes are developed deliberately regardless of cost. C: Developed countries respond to the challenge through rapid technological substitution. C': The challenge is too great, because insufficient time for adjustment is available or institutional rigidity prevents adequate adjustment. C'': Frustration leads to a military response by most threatened DC. D: "Rich rich" (less threatened) remain passive or help to end the conflict. D': "Rich rich" countries enter the conflict on opposite sides. E: Despite assistance (or because of it), "poor poor" countries cannot close the gap. E': Without assistance, "poor poor" countries cannot (or do not) close the gap. E'': Because of assistance, "poor poor" countries are able to develop. E''': *Because of* external pressures (cold or hot), "poor poor" countries achieve necessary internal cohesion and sense of direction to overcome obstacles.

ences, LDCs do not respond to the opportunity (as they might) by creating a worldwide cartel to raise prices and restrict supplies. However, there are sporadic attempts to do so, with varying degrees and duration of impact. The net result is increasing instability in raw-material markets, wildly fluctuating supplies and prices, increasing amounts of speculation and hoarding both by private producers and by nations (including some countries with large cash surpluses).

(5) This syndrome leads to rapid inflation of major currencies, and a breakdown of confidence in the economic system, finally resulting in a "crash" of worldwide dimensions.

(6) The postulated economic crash produces intolerable strains on some of the more fragile parliamentary democracies of the world, both among DCs and LDCs. Totalitarian regimes of the extreme left and extreme right come into being, and there is a reprise of the 1920s and '30s with a high level of violence, disorder, and conflict.

(7) Even if there is no major nuclear war, the likely outcome of this scenario would be general impoverishment.

Of course the reader is free to disagree with our subjective assessment of what might follow from what. Fig. 1 is, essentially, a "do-it-yourself" scenario kit.

Letters (A, A', B, B', . . .) represent apparent alternatives, many of which seem to us to be either indeterminate or unknowable at present. These alternatives are defined in the attached set of notes. For instance, it is by no means clear to us whether a large international program of foreign development assistance would be effective in closing the "gap" between developed and less-developed countries. On the contrary, it seems possible that a moderate degree of xenophobia and self-reliance induced by real (or apparent) external pressure would be more effective in many cases. The recent examples of China and India may be relevant: China appears to have accomplished far more by turning its back on the outside world than India has by actively seeking assistance from the developed countries.

1. DEVELOPING COUNTRIES

One striking feature of figure 1 which deserves comment is that there is no path leading to an automatic favorable outcome for LDCs simply by raising prices for raw materials exported to developed countries. The outcome of recent price increases for petroleum will materially improve the relative economic position of the Arab countries (except Egypt and Syria), Iran, Venezuela, and Nigeria. These may be described as "ex-poor". On the other hand, India, Pakistan, and the rest of Africa and

South America will become poorer even than they were before. It is less likely, but not altogether inconceivable, that Europe and Japan will be hurt badly enough to fit the term "ex-rich".

A major predictable impact of the sharp increase in resource prices, if it is sustained, and it seems likely to us that it will (not ruling out some cyclical behavior),[9] will be large-scale substitution. In North America the development of oil shale, tar sands, and geothermal energy will proceed rapidly—along with other, less immediate, technological possibilities. In India, Japan, and elsewhere, it can be presumed that efforts to develop nuclear power will be redoubled. The case of India is particularly pertinent, in this regard, since the uranium-bearing sands of Kerala constitute one of the major energy resources of that country. Large-scale hydroelectric developments in the Himalayas are another obvious possibility. It would be understandable if these technological alternatives were pursued with rather less concern for safety or care for the environment than might be the case in the United States. It would also not be surprising if border conflicts between India, Pakistan, Bangladesh, Burma, or China should be exacerbated as a result of this situation. In short, many parts of the world may become more turbulent and dangerous as more and more LDCs become dependent on others for basic resources and correspondingly vulnerable.

[9]To see the significance of this statement, one must understand that the long-term trend of real prices for resources commodities has been down. The reasons we think this tendency will not persist indefinitely—while recognizing that considerable fluctuations will probably occur—are as follows:

(1) Lower-quality ores in some important materials do not necessarily exist in exploitable quantities. This appears to be the case for lead and zinc. The same is probably true for practical purposes with regard to hydrocarbons as such (i.e. for non-fuel purposes) since hydrocarbons are not simply dispersed by consumption but are actually used up—that is, chemically transformed into CO_2 and H_2O.

(2) The increased output of the extractive industries in the last century can be attributed in part to the opening up of previously un-explored areas (e.g. Canada, Siberia, Africa, Brazil, Australia). Except for the ocean bottom—which is not easily accessible or easy to exploit—"new" sources will become rarer and rarer in the future.

(3) The prices of mineral commodities historically did not—but in the future must—reflect social costs arising from pollution and waste disposal. But these costs evidently increase non-linearly as the amount of processing increases (requiring more energy and more technological inputs), and as human settlement becomes more dense.

(4) The increased productivity of the extractive industries in the last century is also partly due to economies of scale and the application of mechanical technology. Both are probably subject to the law of diminishing returns.

(5) The developed countries (except for the Soviet Union) are rapidly using up their domestic high-grade sources of minerals and fossil fuels and becoming dependent on the less-developed nations. It seems likely that raw-material exporters will increasingly band together to multiply their bargaining power and increase their revenues from this source.

Indeed, it is very difficult to see how the "poor poor" countries—LDCs with large and growing populations in relation to arable land and other basic resources—can ever catch up to the developed world, or even become much better off than they are, except by undertaking very harsh universal programs to control population growth, reduce consumption, and increase labor productivity and investment. Whether this is possible at all for a country like India is doubtful, but it certainly cannot be imposed successfully from outside. External pressure in favor of birth control, for instance, is very likely to generate internal opposition to it. Yet, external aid *without* such measures can only postpone the day of reckoning, and then probably not much, and consequently increase its severity.

A rich-poor dichotomy between nations may be economically sustainable if the poor countries are, at least, self-supporting. Whether it is *politically* (or ethically) sustainable is another matter, of course. We cannot throw light on this question here.

4.2. DEVELOPED COUNTRIES

We return now to a consideration of some of the implications of "zero growth" within an advanced country such as the United States. We assume, for purposes of discussion, that this state occurs as a result of evolutionary (rather than revolutionary) changes. In other words, for the present discussion we assume that the transitional problems (which will reach at least into early the next century) considered in an earlier section are successfully resolved.

Some of the more interesting and salient issues emerge when one asks the question: is it possible to combine sustained *economic* growth without a stationary (or declining) population, and do so in the presence of a much more limited supply of non-renewable resources? A number of salient interactions are illustrated schematically in fig. 2.

To illuminate these issues, it is necessary to survey briefly the relative roles in the past of raw materials, labor, and technological change in increasing productivity.

One of the classic boosters of productivity in the past—especially in the United States—has been the opening up, at intervals, of access to large, cheap new sources of raw materials. The settlement of the rich agricultural land of the Midwest had a dramatic impact on grain and beef prices, for instance. Similarly, the immense timber resources of the West—especially redwood and Douglas fir—brought lumber prices down to very low levels. These, along with the great discoveries of coal (Pennsylvania, Kentucky, etc.), oil (Pennsylvania, Texas, Oklahoma, etc.), iron ore (Minnesota), gold (California, S. Dakota), silver (Nevada),

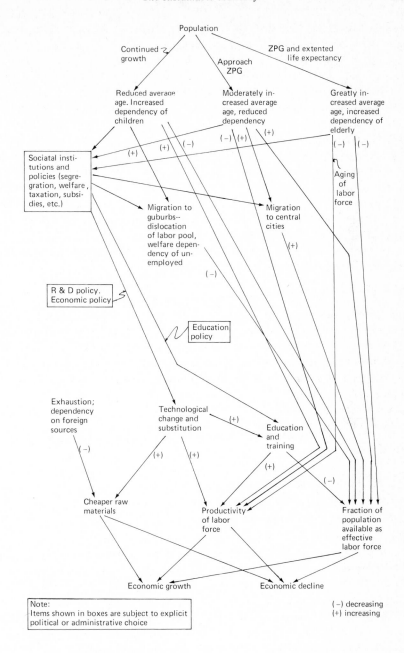

Fig. 2.

copper (Montana, Utah, Arizona), lead (Missouri), and natural gas (Louisiana) had a tremendous cumulative impact on the rate of U.S. industrial development in the 19th and 20th centuries vis-à-vis European countries lacking in comparable sources of wealth.

Evidently, this "cream-skimming" phase of U.S. development is clearly over, and unexploited resources (such as oil shale)—though still vast in quantity—will, especially including environmental costs, not be nearly so cheap to extract. The same is true of coal resources in other developed countries. For the moment, cheap resources reside mainly in the less-developed countries. Judging by recent experience with oil, we would be unreasonable to expect these countries not to "skim the cream" for themselves and sell raw materials to the more advanced countries at prices more nearly reflecting the cost of finding suitable substitutes. Clearly, the level of technological capability is critical in determining the marginal cost of substitution. In any case, however, cheap raw materials do not appear likely to contribute to economic growth of the developed countries from now on. In the much longer term—which is our main concern here—there will be no cheap non-renewable resources any-where. A scenario of more or less continuing increases in the real prices of virgin raw materials into the indefinite future seems quite probable.

Clearly, the *size* of the labor force has also in the past been an important contributor to growing production, and extended schooling has contributed to this effect. Moreover, other demographic and sociological factors have contributed to increased real productivity in the past few decades:

• Urbanization and the end of the self-sufficient (non-cash) family farm.

• Smaller families releasing some women to the work force, both before and after having children.

• Better health and longer life, extending the ratio of productive to non-working periods.

These trends have been counteracted to some extent, however, by trends toward longer schooling, earlier retirement, and shorter work-weeks.

In a stable state of ZPG, as noted previously, the number of younger vis-à-vis older persons will shift markedly toward the latter. If length of schooling, length of work week, and age of retirement remain constant, the number of dependents will decrease—relative to the work force, with a favorable impact on per capita income. This would be reflected by apparent economic growth between now and the time when a stable population is achieved, but most of the impact would occur in the first two decades. Eventually the increased availability of women to the work force resulting from demographic shifts will also work itself out, and there is not much further room for shifting workers out of agriculture into urban pursuits—even if technology continues to permit it.

In the very long term (ZPG—no vast new discoveries of resources to be exploited—this is what we will henceforth mean when we speak of a stationary economy), technological improvement can be the only source of economic growth in developed countries. Indeed, if one considers the dispersion of materials and the necessary resort to lower-grade sources, which even a stationary economy implies, it can be the only possible source of a sustainable economy whether growing or not.

In this connection, it seems important to emphasize the complex relationship between societal institutions in general, the education/training institutions more particularly, and the "process" of technological innovation. A high rate of technological change and innovation certainly requires a willingness to take risks on the part of industry and financial institutions, a flexible educational system, and an adaptable and retrainable labor force. It also requires a flexible legal and institutional framework to cope with change. All of these are much more compatible with a youthful population than with the older and stationary one which must characterize the zero-growth situation. (The correlation between voter age and conservation is well documented, for instance.) We shall return to this point later.

Apart from sociological factors, there is—at first sight—no inherent reason why technology should not continue to improve, nor does there seem to be any basic reason why wealth should not increase, even in the extreme case where total inventory of physical materials (except energy) remains unchanged. Material goods may increase in value (i.e. by offering more services to the user) without increasing their basic resource inputs. A good example of this evolution is the history of radio and TV; thirty years ago even a crude AM radio was both expensive and bulky. Today, the same or better services (i.e. quality of sound reproduction and accessibility to programs) are available in a miniature transistorized radio at a far lower price requiring only a tiny fraction of the physical resources.

Clearly, if wealth is to grow without increasing the requirements for resources, it will be necessary to find ways of greatly reducing the physical resources "frozen" in material objects. That is to say, the material component of physical wealth must decline sharply. What is embodied must be carefully maintained and extensively reused, both to reduce the use of resource inputs and to control the discharge of residuals.

The use of energy in the postulated stationary economy would also have to be far more conservative than is now the case in so-called "developed" countries. This is true not only because of rising prices but also, among other things, because the residual energy "rejected" to the atmosphere might become a severe problem. Present emission of energy is about 1/15,000 of the absorbed solar flux. But if the present rate of growth continued for 250 years, emissions would reach 100 percent of the absorbed solar flux. The resulting increase in the earth's temperatures would be about 50°C—a condition totally unsuitable for human habitation.[10]

It is almost axiomatic in the conventional wisdom that energy consumption per capita is an index of wealth. It is perfectly true, of course, that rising GNP and rising energy consumption have been historically correlated. It is true, also, that the current pattern of increased output of fabricated goods derived from extractive industries tends to result in a non-linear increase in demand for energy, since the declining quality of raw materials necessitates greater expenditures of energy for processing. In a very real sense, however, energy has been utilized in the development of our industrial society as though it were (nearly) a free resource. One recent estimate puts the average efficiency with which energy is utilized in producing "final" (household) services at 4.5 percent for the United States. The figure is higher—but not much higher—for Europe, where energy has been historically more expensive. To double or even quadruple, this efficiency figure should not be beyond the realm of possibility during the next half century or so.

Thus, processing of virgin materials (e.g. metals) is a major use of energy. In an economy based on nearly total recycle of non-replaceable materials, the energy expanded on raw-materials processing could and would be cut drastically—depending upon the specific manufacturing and fabricating technology in use. The details of the technology, in turn, would presumably evolve (given the appropriate incentive structure) in such a way as to reduce both the energy and dollar cost of reprocessing. To give one example of the likely direction of technological evolution, most tasks currently carried out by complete machines built for the purpose, could equally well be accomplished by programmed modular assemblies of flexible multi-purpose components. These modules would be, increasingly, electronic or fluidic rather than mechanical in mode of operation. These modules would be replaceable and repairable individually. Since the most efficient form of recycling (from a materials and energy point of view) is that which involves the least change in form or

---

[10]William R. Frisken, *The Atmospheric Environment* (The Johns Hopkins University Press for Resources for the Future, Inc., Baltimore, 1974).

composition, it is apparent that repair or rebuilding of modules would be highly favored over replacement by new or different types, since the latter would involve the use of virgin materials. Thus, conservation of energy and materials, also would seem to be incompatible with a rapid rate of technological change.

For several reasons, then, there are grounds for believing that technological change is likely to slow down, rather than speed up, in a society where the level of population is constant, and where most physical resources are non-renewable and must therefore be conserved and recycled.

It appears, then, that one cannot expect a continued increase in wealth, and that decline is quite possible, in a stationary society (stationary in the sense defined earlier) unless special incentives are created to "institutionalize" technological innovation. The usual notion is that technological change is a consequence of research and invention. If this were so, it would be simple enough to institutionalize technological change by diverting a significant amount of economic resources into research and development. Historically, one observes a strong correlation between periods of rapid technological change and periods of great fertility of invention as measured, for instance, by numbers of patents filed. However, examination of the historical evidence does indeed suggest that invention may be stimulated by rapid change, rather than the reverse.[11] In any case, there is no guarantee that inventions and discoveries will be implemented, simply because they exist. Innovation is often a fairly painful process which corporations and institutions embrace reluctantly, if at all.

Under the present "rules of the game", technological progress is one of several mechanisms for gaining a competitive advantage, or an increased return on investment. Technological progress often stagnates, however, when the market is not competitive (i.e. in a monopoly or oligopoly), or when other competitive strategies, such as heavy advertising, are more effective. On the other hand, even a natural monopoly may be quite innovative if it is constrained for some reason against raising prices for the same product, and can only increase its earnings by cutting operating costs or providing new services which can be sold at a higher price. The telephone company seems to be an example of this. "Japan Incorporated" is, perhaps, a better illustration, since Japan has maintained a high rate of economic growth for more than two decades, with a rather rigid social structure, a nearly stationary population, a centrally-

---

[11] J. Schmookler, *Invention and Economic Growth* (Harvard University Press, Cambridge, Mass., 1966).

guided oligopolistic economy, and an elderly leadership echelon. This pattern may be generalizable. A more reliable guarantee of institutionalizing technological change, at least in a regulated industry, would be to depreciate the rate base, as the "embodied" technology ages. Various revisions of the incentive system might be devised to induce innovation even in a relatively static system, and no doubt human ingenuity will turn in this direction as the stationary society approaches.

5. The minimum imperatives — energy and food

Even assuming that the world economy is capable of operating on much reduced quantities of non-renewable natural-resource commodities, and that the rich-poor gap turns out to be maintainable without catastrophe, if it is to have any hope of achieving a sustainable economy at a population level of 15–20 billion persons—must be able to produce energy and food in huge amounts—even if much more conservative ways of using the former are found.

We do not believe that energy as such will prove to be an ultimate constraining factor. Although available reserves of petroleum and natural gas must inevitably begin to run out—probably by the end of the century—there are very large reserves of low-quality coal, lignite, and oil shale, which could supply large amounts of energy for a number of decades, probably at something like present (1974) prices, provided that society is willing to tolerate what is sure to be a substantive amount of unavoidable environmental degradation accompanying their use.

The developed countries have put their very-long-run hopes primarily in nuclear power, and this may become a major source for developing countries, too. High-quality uranium sources are limited, also, but plutonium breeder reactors could make it possible to vastly extend the availability of nuclear fuel. Thorium, also, is a potential source of nuclear power, and vast quantities exist in recoverable quantities in granite. Fusion power may be limited by the availability of lithium-6 (to produce tritium), rather than deuterium, but lithium is not a rare element on the earth's surface. Both solar and geothermal power can also be tapped in large quantities—though their cost is uncertain. Technologically speaking, it is probably feasible to capture solar power outside the earth's atmosphere and ship it back to earth either in the form of a high-intensity coherent electromagnetic beam or as synthetic chemical fuels. (It must be remembered that we are speaking of a very long-run scenario in which space technology is highly developed and by no means exotic.)

Also, we do not believe that food availability as such will necessarily be limiting in the very long run if population stabilizes—leaving aside the question of whether the needed technology can be developed rapidly enough. Food is, basically, biologically available energy—in the form of carbohydrate, protein, or fat—plus some needed chemical building blocks which the human organism cannot synthesize from basic elements. These essential components of food include some twenty amino acids. Food must also include a number of minerals such as sodium, potassium, calcium, phosphorus, and iron, of course.

Much remains to be learned about the chemical synthesis of amino acids and vitamins, but most of the basic steps have already been duplicated in the laboratory. In the long-run future, there is absolutely no reason to doubt that food could be manufactured in a chemical plant, given the availability of sufficient energy, capital equipment, and knowledge. This is not to imply that synthetic food would necessarily replace food derived from biological origins. Certainly as far ahead as one can foresee, the latter is likely to be both more palatable and more economical to produce. Ultimately, however, chemical synthesis of food may have to be introduced, too.

Food production, whether based on photosynthesis or chemical synthesis, is evidently energy-limited. We are confronted with an apparent paradox here. World food production, based on photosynthesis, is apparently quite limited. Some experts have predicted world-wide famine within a decade or two. Others, citing the "green revolution", are much more optimistic. But it is painfully clear that conventional agriculture is beginning to approach its limits, and that even though the present world population could probably be fed adequately (though two out of three people on the globe are now receiving inadequate diets), and conceivably even the year 2000 population and beyond could be supported if new strains of grain and the use of fertilizers spread rapidly enough through Asia and Latin America, it is almost impossible to see how conventional agriculture could support 15–20 billion people at the present U.S. or European dietary standard, with 40 percent (or more) of dietary calories derived from animal sources. But unconventional agriculture perhaps could.

By unconventional agriculture, we mean a system based mainly on harvested or recycled cellulose—rather than carbohydrates—which is converted by bacterial action into feed for cattle, hogs, poultry, or fish. All solid organic wastes, whether cornstalks and cobs, brush, grass clippings and leaves, food-processing wastes, waste paper, animal manure, and even sewage, can be converted into animal feed and thus recycled without benefit of additional photosynthesis. The overall efficiency of conversion of solar energy to food can thus be increased manyfold—probably by an order of magnitude—without increasing the intensity of cultivation or altering the primary ecology. Whatever agricultural processes might be found compatible with the indefinite high-level maintenance of a population of 15–20 billion, one thing is clear—they must be arranged so that much less pesticide and plant nutrient is lost to the environment relative to output than is true of present "developed" agriculture. The results of not achieving this would be profoundly destructive effects on ecological systems.

6. Two more big questions

Without commenting further about how mankind got itself into an idiotic race between population growth and technological development, if technical progress can be sustained or accelerated—despite the incentives to slow it down which seem inherent in stationary societies, it is not ridiculous on the face of it to suppose that an ultimate world population of 15–20 billion people could be maintained at a reasonable standard of living. This would necessarily be in an economy using very large amounts of energy, but not so large as to greatly damage the livability of the planet, yet having drastically lower material throughput per unit product than the developed countries of today.

But we cannot conclude on this even vaguely optimistic note without calling attention to two more truly major reservations that we have about the ability of mankind to achieve this relatively favorable outcome.[12] The first is a question of whether the potential for technological progress is truly limitless for practical purposes. The second is whether coping with the increased human interdependence and the risks of some of the more promising new technologies is not beyond the capacity of human institutions.

6.1. IS TECHNOLOGICAL PROGRESS LIMITLESS?

One may suspect that scientific R & D is ultimately subject to diminishing returns. The classical economists of the 18th and 19th centuries felt that economic growth would be brought to an end as an increasing amount of labor was applied to a fixed resource stock so that, eventually, further increments of labor would not yield any additional output. Actually, technology turned out to be the main factor which permitted this dismal result to be avoided—or at least put off for a long time. Labor productivity has been rising almost steadily and fast since the beginning

---

[12]This means relative to perfectly disastrous ones. It puts us in mind of a remark once attributed to Maurice Chevalier. When asked how he felt about getting old, he said, "it's not so great, but much better than the alternative".

of the industrial revolution. In fact, as we have seen, increased productivity has been the main element in economic growth. To get this result, the developed economies have been increasing technology as a production factor faster than the other inputs for a long period of time. Most projections of economic activity and resource use implicitly assume that we will continue to achieve at least constant returns from scientific and technological input. In other words, labor productivity will continue to rise as it has in the past few decades. In the United States this means at about 3 percent per year. This may be quite justifiable if one is looking a relatively few decades into the future. But on the longer-time scale, doubts may well arise, even if institutional arrangements can successfully sustain a higher level of scientific enterprise and innovative behavior.

The noted classical economists, Malthus and Ricardo, were products of the enlightenment which restored Western man's confidence in his ability to understand the workings of the world through reason. And their works are strong testimonials to the power of this confidence. But the Enlightenment's systematic, analytic engine, the scientific method, was just starting to evolve. A method of discovery was being discovered. It is not hard to understand why the classical economists could not grasp fully the implications of this other product of the Enlightenment. The industrial revolution at first produced enormous productivity gains through the application of reason and ingenuity to mechanical devices without the benefits of systematic science. For example, Cartwright, who made the first power loom and other important textile equipment, was not a scientist, but a clergyman who wrote verses, and Benjamin Huntsman, who first made cast steel, was a clockmaker. It was only gradually that industrial innovation moved beyond the basically mechanical and began to incorporate more esoteric accomplishments of formal science, such as chemistry.[13] But science, once it took hold, continued to propel productivity forward despite the fact that some of the more obvious improvements permitted by the spirit of the Enlightenment had been made. As Sir John Hicks, the eminent British economist, has stated in his recent commentary on economic history, "There might have been no Crompton and Arkwright, and still there could have been an industrial revolution; in its later stages it would have been much the same. The impact of science, stimulating the technicians, developing new sources of power, using power to create more than human accuracy, reducing the cost of

[13]A fascinating account of this process is found in 'Machines and Men', Ch. XI, in: G. D. H. Cole, *Introduction to Economic History*, 1750–1950 (MacMillan, London, 1952).

machines until they were available for a multitude of purposes; this surely is the essential novelty, . . .".[14]

The application of science to industry has continued to increase the productivity of labor and more or less steadily to push back resources scarcity, despite huge increases in labor and capital inputs. Perhaps it will continue to do so for a long time to come. But it would seem strange if the application of effort to science and technology were entirely immune from diminishing returns. One may speculate that the return from the applications of resources to scientific discovery and technological development in certain important instances has already begun to diminish. For example, most of the basic mathematical concepts which are used in today's applied science were well known by the beginning of this century. In this connection, it is worth noting that a former president of the American Association for the Advancement of Science (Bentley Glass) has forecast, in a speech before the 1970 AAAS meetings, that we cannot expect continued basic scientific discoveries on the scale of the last 100 years.

While new discoveries always do remain to be made, although not necessarily at an undiminished pace, there are some basic reasons why quantitative technological improvements may require greater efforts to bring about, and why the percentage rate of improvement in many fields. as measured in terms of functional indices, will inevitably begin to decline. The efficiency of energy conversion is a good illustration of the point. Power plants have increased in efficiency from 1 or 2 percent to over 40 percent in the most advanced power plants today. Thus we have already experienced a 40-fold improvement in two centuries. The next 30 years may conceivably see a further increase to 60-percent overall efficiency, but this only represents a 50-percent improvement over the present level. Obviously the rate of advance thereafter must slow down markedly if only because 100-percent efficiency is the absolute upper limit, and it can never be actually reached. In many other areas, also, this same phenomenology holds true.[15]

Should we encounter strongly diminishing returns to scientific technological development, it may well prove to be impossible to converge to a stable, sustainable economy of 15–20 billion persons in which labor productivity is relatively high. Indeed it may not be possible to indefinitely sustain that level of population at any level of living. Thus, as far as we can see, science and technology is not the villain but rather the

[14]Sir John Hicks, *A Theory of Economic History* (Oxford University Press, London, 1969) 147.
[15]For a more detailed discussion, see Robert U. Ayres, *Technological Forecasting and Long Range Planning* (McGraw-Hill, New York, 1969).

potential hero of the piece, if it can be properly developed and directed and if it continues to be highly productive of improved ways of doing things. But we cannot have high confidence that it will do so indefinitely.

6.2. CAN HUMAN INSTITUTIONS COPE WITH NEW TECHNOLOGY?

A second nagging doubt has its basis in the imperfections of social organization and social institutions. We have already hinted at this before but it seems useful to spell it out a little. It is a commonplace that the industrialization has increased interdependence. So although it can produce high levels of material welfare, it can do so only if a high degree of social order is maintained. The system becomes not only vulnerable to breakdowns in the technological chain, but also to human error and malevolence. Some of the technologies which can be foreseen for simultaneously increasing productivity over the long-run future and reducing dependence on non-renewable resources, seem to carry with them huge extensions of interdependency in both space and time. Even without an all-out catastrophic war, which we cannot, unfortunately, rule out as entirely unlikely, such interdependencies may come to be viewed as intolerable and may severely limit the application of certain technologies.

Another possibility is that presumed necessity may dictate their applications anyway—with possibly disastrous results. This may be particularly a possibility in the less-developed countries. The large-scale and continued use of persistent pesticides could be an example here. Other examples of technologies which might be vastly productive of useful work serving great numbers of people but vulnerable to catastrophic failures are tapping energy from extraterrestrial sources, transmitting vast amounts of energy in a limited number of superconductors, and nuclear fission.

That these problems are not remote and hypothetical is amply demonstrated by the debate going on even now over whether the world should become dependent upon a large-scale nuclear-fission energy economy. This debate illustrates very nicely the interrelation of the moral and economic questions and the limits of conventional economic analysis, both of which have so occupied Kenneth Boulding. Therefore we discuss the matter in a little detail.

The Atomic Energy Commission has suggested that the problem of whether to develop such a large-scale fission economy can be solved by benefit-cost analysis.[16] It is our belief that this, frequently very valuable,

---

[16]*Environmental Survey of Nuclear Fuel Cycle: Power Reactor Licensing and Rule Making*, U.S. Atomic Energy Commission (Nov. 1972).

mode of analysis cannot answer the most important policy questions surrounding this issue. To expect it to do so is to ask it to bear a burden it cannot sustain. This is so because these questions are of a deep ethical character. Benefit-cost analyses certainly cannot solve such questions and may well obscure them.

These questions have to do with whether society should strike the Faustian Bargain, as Alvin Weinberg describes it in evocative terms, with the atomic scientists and engineers.[17] If so unforgiving a technology as large-scale nuclear-fission energy production is adopted, it will impose a burden of continuous monitoring and sophisticated management of a dangerous material, essentially forever. The penalty of not bearing this burden may be unparalleled disaster. This irreversible burden would be imposed even if nuclear fission were to be used only for a few decades, a mere instant in the pertinent time scales.

Clearly, there are some major advantages from using nuclear fission technology, else it would not have so many well-intentioned and intelligent advocates. Residual heat is produced to a greater extent by current nuclear-generating plants than by fossil-fuel-fired ones. But otherwise the environmental impact of routine operation of the nuclear fuel cycle, including burning the fuel in the reactor, can very likely be brought to a lower level than will be possible with fossil-fuel-fired plants. In general, the costs of nuclear and fossil-fuel energy, with the latter having a fuel cycle in which residuals generation is controlled to a high degree, do not seem to be so greatly different.

Unfortunately, the advantages of fission are much more readily quantified in the format of a benefit-cost analysis than are the associated hazards. Therefore there exists the danger that the benefits may seem more real. Furthermore, the conceptual basis of benefit-cost analysis requires that the redistributional effects of the action be, for one or another reason, inconsequential. Here we are speaking of hazards which may afflict humanity many generations hence and distributional questions which can neither be neglected as inconsequential nor evaluated on any known theoretical or empirical basis. This means that technical people, be they physicists or economists, cannot legitimately make the decision to generate such hazards based on technical analysis. The society confronts a moral problem of a great profundity. In a democratic society the only legitimate means for making such a choice is through the mechanisms of representative government.

In his excellent article referred to above, Weinberg emphasized that part of the Faustian Bargain is that to use fission technology safely,

---

[17]Alvin M. Weinberg, 'Social Institutions and Nuclear Energy', *Science* (July 7, 1972).

society must exercise great vigilance and the highest levels of quality control, continuously and indefinitely. In part this is because of the great hazards involved in imperfect operation of reactors and the nuclear fuel cycle. Especially the breeder reactor involves large quantities of plutonium which is one of the most toxic substances known to man and which could be used to fabricate nuclear weapons. As the fission energy economy grows, many plants will be built and operated in countries with comparatively low levels of technological competence and a greater propensity to take risks. A much larger amount of transportation of hazardous materials will probably occur, and safety will become the province of the sea captain as well as the scientist. Moreover, even in countries with higher levels of technological competence, continued success can lead to reduced vigilance. We should recall that we managed to incinerate astronauts owing to a very straightforward accident in an extremely high-technology operation where the utmost of precautions were allegedly being taken.

But even deeper moral questions surround the storage of high-level radioactive wastes. Estimates of how long these waste materials must be isolated from the biosphere apparently contain major elements of uncertainty, but current ones seem to agree on "at least two hundred thousand years."

In the United States, heavy emphasis has been given to the storage of these wastes in salt formations, and a site for experimental storage was selected at Lyons, Kansas. This particular site proved to be defective. Oil companies had drilled the area full of holes, and there had also been solution mining in the area which left behind an unknown residue of water. But comments of the Kansas Geological Survey raised far deeper and more general questions about the behavior of the pertinent formations under stress and about the operations of geological forces on them. The ability of solid-earth geophysics proves very limited to predict for the time scales required. Furthermore, there is the political factor. An increasingly informed and environmentally aware public is likely to resist the location of a permanent storage facility anywhere.

Because the site selected proved defective, and possibly in anticipation of political problems, emphasis is now being placed upon the design of surface storage facilities intended to last a hundred years or so, while the search for a permanent site continues. These surface storage sites would require continuous monitoring and management of a most sophisticated kind. A complete cooling-system breakdown would soon prove disastrous, and even greater tragedies can be imagined.

Just to get an idea of the scale of disaster that could be imagined, consider the following scenario. Political factors force the federal government to rely on a single above-ground storage site for all high-level radioactive waste accumulated through the year 2000. Some of the more obvious possibilities would be existing storage sites like Hanford or Savannah, which would seem to be likely military targets. A tactical nuclear weapon hits the site and vaporizes a large fraction of the contents of this storage area. The weapon could come from one of the principal nuclear powers or a lesser-developed country with one or more nuclear power plants, or it might be crudely fabricated by a terrorist organization from black-market plutonium. The radiation fallout from such an event would exceed that from all past nuclear testing by a factor of 500 or so, with radiation doses exceeding the annual dose from natural background radiation by an order of magnitude. This would be a drastically unfavorable, and long-lasting, change in the environment of the majority of mankind. That massive numbers of deaths might result seems clear, but the exact magnitude of the disaster is apparently quite uncertain.

Furthermore, by the year 2000, high-level wastes would have just begun to accumulate. Estimates for 2020 put them at about three times the 2000 figure.

Sometimes, analogies are used to suggest that the burden placed upon future generations by the "immortal" wastes is really nothing so very unusual. The Pyramids are cited as an instance where a very long-term commitment was made to the future, and the dikes of Holland as one where continuous monitoring and maintenance is required indefinitely. These examples do not seem at all apt. They do not have the same quality of irreversibility as the problem at hand, and no major portions of humanity are dependent on them for their very existence. With sufficient effort, the Pyramids could have been dismantled and the Pharaohs cremated if a changed doctrine so demanded—also, it is worth recalling that most of the tombs were looted already in ancient times. After World War II the Dutch dikes were in fact opened. Tragic property losses, but no destruction of human life, ensued. Perhaps a more apt example of the scale of the Faustian Bargain would be the irrigation system of ancient Persia. When Tamerlane destroyed it in the 14th century, a civilization ended.

But none of these historical examples tell us much about the time scales pertinent here—one speaks of two hundred thousand years. Only a little more than one-hundredth of that time span has passed since the Parthenon was built. No government has ever existed whose life was more than an instant by comparison with the half-life of plutonium. There also seems to be a noticeable upward trend not only in the capacity for, but in the frequency of, large-scale violence. Much of this has happened in our lifetime and several notable "incidents" have happened quite recently or are still in progress. As we have seen, the occasions for hostility are very likely to increase further in the future.

It seems clear that there are many factors here which a benefit-cost analysis can never capture in quantitative, commensurable terms. It also seems hard to claim that the nuclear fuel cycle will not sometime, somewhere experience major unscheduled events. These could range in magnitude from local events, like the fire at the Rocky Mountain Arsenal, to an extreme disaster affecting most of mankind if a large part of the high-level wastes in storage were released. Whether these hazards are worth incurring in view of the benefits achieved is what Alvin Weinberg has referred to as a trans-scientific question. As professional specialists, we can try to provide pertinent information, but we cannot legitimately make the decision, and it should not be left in our hands.

Whether the benefits exceed the risks is partly a scientific and economic question and partly, even mostly, a value-judgment question which, as we have said, can only be legitimately answered through our system of representative government. But the committee structure of the Congress, dominated as it is by jurisdictional problems and the special interest orientation of committee memberships, is not a suitable arrangement. The Congress has unfortunately had great difficulty in reforming itself even on issues of much less moment. This is another facet of the institutional challenge that we face.

7. Concluding comment

Can mankind converge monotonically toward a state in which human life is both pleasant and more or less indefinitely viable? This is a very open question, it seems to us. It is one on which, despite our congenital optimism, we are rather pessimistic. But the uncertainties are so great that it is difficult to see how we could rationally influence present policies to take account of possibilities on the pertinent time scale. The only clear signal seems to be that if we fail to bring world population under control soon—very soon—humanity's future problems may be totally insoluble. If we do succeed, there is a chance.

The dangers that perhaps impress us most are subtle ones. They revolve around the probability that, as human society makes greater and greater demands on available resources, margin for error decreases. As it decreases, a more and more interdependent, elaborate, and fail-safe organization is required simply to prevent the system from collapsing at the first perturbation. Recent unhappy experiences with massive break-downs or tie-ups of essential public services—electric power, telephones, sanitation, transportation, international distribution of petroleum—suggest very clearly the magnitude of potential instabilities inherent in a system which depends, for example, on maintaining regular communications in space or beneath the ocean, or the timeless "fail-safe" monitoring and management of certain materials. The elemental need to prevent catastrophic breakdowns or hold-ups may conceivably result in the development of a rigidly structured, rather inhuman "1984" type of social system which subordinates individual talents, needs, or desires to the survival of the social organism as a whole. Or else, the world may "solve" its otherwise insoluble problems of war, famine, or anarchy. We hesitate to dwell on this possibility, and it is distasteful to us to end on such a note. We cannot help but hope that others will soon begin to find positive answers where we have uncovered grounds for pessimism. What does seem clear is that humanity faces a future full of stresses and strains, and that life will not be comfortable for any persistent periods for a long, long time to come—if ever. Analyses, of which there have been many, that address the question of the long-term viability of a very numerous humanity solely in terms of potential technological, or even economic, capabilities miss some of the most central questions. The large Boulding-ian questions of man and nature, war and peace, and private and international morality cannot but come more and more into the forefront of civilized man's preoccupations.

D.3 Stagnation, welfare, and the efficiency of consumption*

BURKHARD STRUMPEL†

Faster than expected even by most prophets of doom, the unprecedented boom of the postwar era has ended. Notwithstanding the recent criticism surrounding economic growth, its demise has been received with suspicion, fear, even alarm. Inflation coupled with lack of investors' confidence has cut stock values in half. Consumer sentiment is at an all-time low: The majority of adult Americans foresee a major crisis. Distributional conflict is on the rise; about every other worker feels he receives less income than he is entitled to.

The passionate response to stagnation, while seemingly plausible, raises puzzling questions: Why is it that we are so vulnerable to even a slight decline in our economic fortunes at a time when mass incomes remain at historically very high levels? Was Ezra J. Mishan wrong in stating that in prosperous industrial societies, command over material resources is neither the only nor the main source of human welfare? If growth does not make people happy, why is its disappearance generally deplored?

We might take a temporary decrease in the sense of well-being more lightly were it not for the possibility of repercussions for the larger system. Individual deprivation, unless accepted as legitimate, is being passed forward to the polity or back to the economy. The question is not only how people experience stagnation but whom they blame and what they do about it in their roles as citizens, workers, consumers. There are signs of alienation, protest, even withdrawal. The current widespread cynicism about government and institutions has been partly attributed to

*Contribution to the volume *Frontiers in Social Thought—Essays in Honor of Kenneth E. Boulding.*
†The author is program director, Institute for Social Research, University of Michigan, and for 1974/75 visiting professor of economics, University of Frankfurt, Germany. Analysis on which the paper is based was made possible through the National Science Foundation.

adverse economic experiences (Miller, 1974). At the time of this writing, strike activity is on the rise, and a growing number of investors prefer gold or highly liquid assets with short maturities over productive long-term capital commitments such as equities or bonds.

The first section of the paper tries to explain the present malaise in the face of stagnation by pointing to our collective inefficiency in converting economic production into well-being. The second section deals with the conditions under which "ill-being" is tolerated and legitimized or, respectively, translated into felt inequity. In the third section, some tentative evidence on behavioral consequences of felt inequity will be presented.

1

Welfare economics and psychology bring to bear two entirely different traditions, approaches, and terminologies to the problem of well-being and its measurement. According to welfare economics the command over goods and services determines welfare and its distribution. This relationship is not assumed to be linear: the principle of "decreasing marginal utility" postulates the amount of welfare increments following resource increments to be a negative function of the initial command over a resource. The more you have, the more you must gain in order to experience progress. Nevertheless and in all instances, it assures that person A, by virtue of his more extensive command over valued resources, is better off than B, no matter where A and B are located in time, cultural setting, or social structure.

While the welfare function in economics is entirely dominated by situational determinants, psychological adaptation level theory assumes an almost unlimited capacity of man to adjust to reality his yardsticks for judging his situation. As the environment becomes more pleasurable, subjective standards for gauging pleasurableness will rise (Brickman and Campbell, 1972). If, according to Kurt Lewin, aspirations rise with accomplishment and stagnate or even diminish with failure, the successful will be captives of the "hedonistic treadmill," while the unsuccessful could look forward, if not to a "humble but happy" life, at least to the same degree of contentment to which the successful will be reduced through habituation. Neither of these extreme approaches is of much help in elucidating societal phenomena, such as the recent apparent accentuation of economic dissatisfaction during times of continuing prosperity.

Welfare has been conceptualized as the quotient of how much people have over how much they want or feel entitled to. ($W = m/a$ where m

stands for means and *a* for aspirations). While the economic approach centers on the numerator, the psychological tradition deals with the dynamics of the denominator. In this line of thinking, the manifest recent diminution of welfare in the face of constant mass incomes can only be explained by an increase in aspirations, a notion lacking merit albeit not resonance. Indeed one reads frequently that in industrial societies, expectations (in my terminology, aspirations) are rising quasi-automatically with income and consumption. Instead I posit that the miserable welfare performance of the industrial economy is a feature of our social condition rather than of human greed. The undisputably rapid expansion of aspirations must be seen as the result not of prosperity but of the growing inefficiency with which production is converted into need satisfaction. Aspirations rather than serving as an evaluative criterion must be seen as a problem.

This approach leads to some important modifications of the above paradigm. As to the denominator, we replace aspirations by needs, recognizing that a person aspires goods and services not for themselves but for the need satisfaction they provide. In the vast body of literature on this topic, needs such as health, comfort, security, self-actualization are considered relatively stable attributes of the human condition. The urgency or priority accorded a given need by society depends to a large extent on its stage of development. Within industrial society, there is a considerable conformity of priorities: a "decent" level of living in excess of the physical minimum of subsistence, health care commensurate with the state of medical knowledge, consumption maintenance in case of adversity are almost universally shared public priorities in East and West alike. If the level of welfare (here defined as need satisfaction) stagnates, higher levels of production notwithstanding, or if a richer country fails to provide her citizens with more welfare than a poor country, goods and services are less efficiently employed in the former than in the latter. A larger volume of goods and services is required for achieving a given level of need satisfaction. People aiming at a given level of needs may, under these conditions, be forced to expand their level of aspirations for market output. This leads to the following representation:

$$w = \frac{m \cdot e}{n}$$

where *n* stands for needs (such as comfort, security, self-actualization, belonging) and *e* represents the efficiency with which a given quantity of command over goods and services is translated into need satisfaction or welfare.

In the theory of production, Harvey Leibenstein (1966) has introduced the term X-efficiency in order to describe the contribution to the production of goods and services of a factor outside of the range of inputs customarily considered. Productive units utilizing the same quantity of factors of production achieve different quantities of output of goods and services. In this paper, I try to demonstrate that private households operating in different societies but using the same quantity of inputs (goods and services) achieve different quantities of need satisfaction or welfare. Pursuing further what was said before about generally shared need priorities, I posit: The welfare efficiency of an industrial society operating within given resource constraints depends on its ability

(a) to guarantee a "decent" minimum level of comfort to everybody,

(b) to arrange income and consumption streams for individuals such that their requirements for comfort over the life-cycle are met ("permanent consumption"), and

(c) to develop tastes that gravitate toward "higher order" needs rather than remaining oriented toward comfort.

A recent survey-based comparison of various dimensions of economic welfare in Bulgaria and Greece demonstrates how income continuity in conjunction with an egalitarian distribution can support welfare with given means (Apel and Strumpel, 1975). Average real incomes per capita are roughly equal in both countries. Yet Bulgarians judge their economic situation, in particular their future, much more cheerfully and optimistically than Greeks. First, there is more equality of income and consumption in Bulgaria, both across the population and within its occupational subgroups. Second, there is more protection from material hazards in Bulgaria than in Greece. Few Bulgarians, but many Greeks, live in fear of unemployment and poverty in case of retirement or disability. These differences are manifestly based on a full-employment policy as practiced in most socialist countries, and on the availability of a voluminous package of fringe benefits such as universal health insurance. Third, the Bulgarian system, more than the Greek, manages to impart the experience of improvement to its constituents. There is a more even, more regular pattern of income increases, not eroded by inflation. Also, there is a wider use of seniority as a basis for remuneration, providing workers with continuously rising wage rates as they go from relatively low paid labor force entry to retirement. Fourth, the data document an impressive mobilization and integration of the agricultural population in Bulgaria, but there are symptoms of economic alienation in Greece. Greek farmers are clearly the most disaffected, even threatened, part of the population, least able to cope with the rapid transformation occurring around them. Their experience is in accord with most farm populations in periods of rapid industrialization. Bulgarian farm workers, on the other hand, during the last two decades have achieved an economic status equal to, if not slightly superior to, the rest of the Bulgarian society.

How to apply the preceding thoughts to the diagnosis of the present malaise in the United States? A large part of American poverty results from insufficient intertemporal transfers or underinsurance, i.e. from the failure of individuals and/or the system to provide for old age, "rainy days," sickness, disability, etc. Much more than in Western Europe, there is in the U.S. a heavy overlap between the aged and the poor. The discrepancy between needs and effective demand can be clearly observed here. The majority of Americans are dissatisfied with both how much they save and how many liquid assets they have. Yet needs for future welfare, while recognized "rationally", are often forgotten or overruled in the consumption spree of the moment. Rates of saving out of disposable income—both financial and total saving—during the last two decades have amounted to only about half of what they were in Germany and Japan (as to the reasons see Strumpel, 1975).

Nevertheless, the inefficiency of the American system of welfare has been obscured through the long period of prosperity. Most working Americans had become accustomed to quasi-automatic increases in their real incomes. This was even true for workers without "careers" who did not experience upward social mobility. What Kenneth Boulding (1973) stated for population change is true for economic change as well: In a growing economy, more workers will experience their income peak late in life than in a stationary one. If the future looks bright anyway, why should there be much effort to prepare for it? The deficiencies of institutional provisions for social security come to fore with the manifest demise of growth affecting prospects for future income and consumption levels more than present consumption.

There is another explanation for the described sudden welfare deficit. Through the past century, in particular the period after World War II, the relative prices of physical goods (more exactly: of goods and services that embody a large proportion of physical "throughput" = resource depletion ending up in waste effluent or pollution) have decreased. Prices of energy, cars, refrigerators, furniture, hardware, food products—raw or processed—have been rising less than doctor's bills, education, domestic services. This trend—brought about mainly by the spectacular increase in the productivity in the primary and secondary sectors as observed by Clark and Fourastié reinforced the American taste for instant buying (Katona, Strumpel, and Zahn). Since consumer durables and other goods produced by the secondary sector most typically serve to satisfy the need for comfort, the "thing-mindedness" of Americans contributed to the neglect of security and other "higher order" needs. There are indications, however, that these trends of sectoral productivity have been coming to an end and may actually have reversed themselves for two reasons:

(a) Physical production is increasingly being blamed for external or social costs connected with pollution, agglomeration, or even social disruption. The internalization of these costs by way of legislation is underway.

(b) Productivity increases in the production of physical goods appear to be more difficult to achieve in the future. In the past, such increases were largely a result of artificially low prices for raw materials, especially energy. For example, labor productivity in agriculture increased at the expense of profligate use of energy, leading to drastically reduced "energy productivity." Recently, raw materials and agricultural land have become more resistent to further expansion in production. Correspondingly, the owners of natural resources have become more aware of their wealth, and set the price accordingly in order to prevent early depletion.

It then appears that throughput-intensive production will remain, as in the last several years, in a situation of rising relative prices as well as marginal private and social costs. While the intervention of technical progress may, in the view of some observers, obscure the picture for the long-term, I am willing to defend this diagnosis for the short and medium-term (10 to 15 years).

Tastes are learned and persistent albeit not immutable. No wonder that an unexpected change in relative prices, as has occurred recently, cannot be countered by a fast shift in tastes from tangible, highly symbolic materials-intensive consumer durables to goods or services that make use or embody a high proportion of recently more abundant resources such as highly qualified labor. There are then at present two sources of welfare slippage: First, prevailing tastes, fixated on comfort, are at odds with a more balanced hierarchy of needs, and second, the economy is less capable than before of catering to the existing range of tastes.

For the future, two kinds of consumer reactions are conceivable, one cooperative, one competitive, the first clearly preferable from the point of view of consumer well-being. The first reaction would be flexible and price-elastic. Responding to moderate changes in prices and public priorities, people would turn to a different basket of goods and services that are less demanding in terms of non-renewable resources and other social costs. They may buy an education instead of a car for their child, or cross-country skis instead of a snowmobile. The second reaction would be defensive, inelastic, and painful: a determined attempt to preserve the customary market basket, or to achieve the aspired one. The desperate competition between buyers of scarce goods with rigidly limited supply would force drastic price increases and impose welfare sacrifices that could be avoided through a more adaptive consumer response. In both cases the price would serve as a mechanism for allocating less ample supplies to consumers. Yet in the first case, the price mechanism could be greatly aided by a shift in tastes.

2

Economic "illfare" or deprivation affects the larger system mainly through the intervening variable "felt inequity". Inequity and deprivation—both defined as subjective characteristics—are by no means identical. Rather, for feeling inequitably rewarded someone must experience a condition as both unpleasant and illegitimate. The standards applied for judging the fairness or equitability of a situation, while tainted by self-interest, express in part a social consensus about the rules of remuneration and their application. Neither does felt inequity necessarily follow from an adverse situational ("objective") condition or change. Sometimes, particularly during times of war or national emergency, austerity and even sacrifice is accepted as necessary or inevitable. The sense of equity then can be seen as a symptom of societal integration as manifested in the prevalence, vitality and authority of commonly shared norms about the distribution of products and resources. If very many people disagree with the rules applied or feel that the rules agreed upon fail to be implemented, the orderly give-and-take that links individuals in any social system is in jeopardy.

Table 1 exhibits survey-based attitudinal distributions on two operational versions of the sense of equity. For the first one, the frame of reference is a comparison with others in the same occupation (within-group equity). For the second one, the respondent compares the rewards of his occupational group with those of other groups (between-group equity). The table makes clear that many Americans feel they are inequitably treated and shortchanged by their contemporaries and that this feeling has grown considerably. According to equity theory, inequity exists whenever a person perceives that the ratio of his outcomes to inputs and the ratio of others' outcomes to their inputs are unequal. Neglecting the case of overpayment, inequity can be schematically represented as follows: (Adams, 1963):

$$\frac{O_p}{T_p} < \frac{O_a}{T_a}$$

where O = outcomes; T = inputs, both as perceived by the person (p).

TABLE 1

Feelings of inequity among some population subgroups percent feeling they get less than they deserve

	Within-Group Inequity		Between-Group Inequity	
	Fall 1972	Fall 1973	Fall 1972	Fall 1973
All workers	28	43	39	53
Less than 35-white collar	28	42	41	51
35 and over-white collar	28	38	40	48
Less than 35-blue collar	37	42	37	49
35 and over-blue collar	20	50	36	62
Blacks	26	66	36	69

The questions in the Fall 1973 study were: "How fair is what you earn on your job in comparison to others doing the same type of work you do (what people in your line of work earn *in comparison to how much people in other occupations earn*)? Do you feel that you get much than you deserve, somewhat less than you deserve, about as much as you deserve, or more than you deserve?"

The Fall 1972 questions were similar but referred to getting more or less than your "fair share."

The subscript (a) denotes the reference person or group. From the strictly relativistic viewpoint of equity theory, there is no *a priori* reason to expect that deterioration as such leads to felt inequity. What then could explain the shift?

Although the year 1973 has not brought a deterioration of living standards for the average American, it has slowed his income advance. As a worker moves through the life cycle, he proceeds from a relatively low work income to a higher relative income toward the end of his working life. These increases during the life cycle are usually higher for white-collar than for blue-collar workers. During most of the past 25 years, they have been confounded psychologically with the positive real income trend due to productivity increases in the economy. Individual workers naturally did not distinguish between the two components of their raises. Both were considered deserved by own performance, and not just windfalls. In the highly inflationary environment of the early 70's, the nominal increases have been generally maintained thus institutionalizing the expectation of continued real income increases. The unexpectedly large inroads of inflation into real incomes under these circumstances must be deeply resented. In the language of equity theory, the individual, on the basis of earlier learning experiences, revised upwards the notion about the value of his own input without seeing his outcomes being adjusted correspondingly.

There is still another version of "money illusion" generated. Price increases also affect the sense of equity in that they inflate the individual's notion about the outcomes of others. If everything becomes more expensive, someone must reap the benefit. Thus, others in the distributional game—who may just catch up with inflation—are perceived as gaining, thereby accentuating the sense of deprivation. Yet in 1973 these conclusions were not entirely illusionary. As is well-known, not all of the price increases were of the cost-push type and served solely to catch up with inflation. Selective price increases, i.e. changes in *relative* prices of consumer goods or services, as particularly frequent in 1973, tend to be resented as illegitimate by those who must pay more, particularly if they are steep and occur repeatedly in brief succession. The recent clamor over the "wind fall profits" of the oil industry is a case in point. The market frequently leads to outcomes considered inequitable by the market participants. It forces many people to put up with changes in real incomes and relative status. By doing so, it also strains the fabric that keeps society together.

3

What are the correlates and consequences of inequity? Rising inequity is a special case of social disintegration. It symptomizes the weakening grip of social norms: the norms are not fully shared by the members, and/or they are not perceived as implemented. The sense of inequity may give rise to disintegrative orientations and behavior. We explore one example of each of these links.

Almost every social system is composed of members and leaders carrying special authority. Its cohesion depends on loyalty, horizontal and vertical. Members must be loyal to other members and the leadership. For a democratic society, disloyalty to other members is more threatening to the system than alienation from leaders. This is so since in such a system the leadership is exchangeable within the rules of the game, but the members are not. Indeed, democracy can be seen as a mechanism defusing the disintegrative effects of discontent with leadership through exchanging the latter by popular will.

Who in 1973 was being blamed for what was considered by many increasing inequity? One could easily imagine a polarization scenario: these groups who think they have fallen behind would heap blame on those groups that are suspected or observed to expand their share. Alternatively, the blame could be directed toward the government charged with the task of assuring distributional justice; here a growing sense of inequity would be accompanied by alienation and distrust.

Following the polarization hypothesis, we should, during inflationary periods, expect mounting jealousies between subgroups—blacks against whites, blue-collar workers against white-collar workers, employers against business, young against old—and there should be some congruence between these orientations and felt inequity, i.e. those individuals who feel unfairly treated should be more likely than others to harbor ill feelings against other groups. According to the analysis of the same data set by my colleague, Arthur H. Miller, neither is the case. Increasing one's income share at the expense of others does not appear to occupy a place in any code of public ethics. The evidence strongly favors the alienation hypothesis. Not only has trust in government during 1973 further declined from an already low level—a phenomenon due to both economic and noneconomic factors. Moreover, the data from Fall 1973, unlike those of Fall 1972, show a significant link between inequity and alienation: those who feel they get less than they deserve are most likely to distrust the government, its intentions and competence.

Inequity, like unemployment and inflation, for better or worse, has become an evil the government is being held responsible for, rather than the multitude of individual decision-makers who raise prices or demand higher wages. We conclude, then, that the sense of inequity of working Americans with their pay has not been expressed to a considerable extent in the scapegoating of other groups. On the other hand, it has not been confined either to the incumbents of leadership positions. It appears to translate into skepticism and alienation from institutions of political leadership.

It cannot clearly be determined whether it is the alienation from the institutions and leaders that shapes the sense of equity of whether it is the response to personal experience that shapes the interpretation of the system. Most likely, both orientations reinforce each other and must be analyzed jointly. The lackluster performance of the government and a prevailing aura of distrust and malaise generated doubt about the legitimacy of conditions which otherwise might have been endured without great ado.

Equity theory posits that people employ a variety of strategies in order to reduce their sense of inequity. From the range of reactions listed, we select two: the individual's attempt to increase outcomes with given inputs, and the reduction of inputs while he tries to retain outcomes. Examples for these reactions were operationalized and tested in our survey. Respondents were handled a scale ranging from "always right" to "never right" and were asked the following question:

Some people think they get *less* pay from their job than they feel they justly deserve. What would be right for them to do in this situation?

The modes of behavior offered for evaluation, ranging from a generally accepted "asking for a pay increase" to the rarely condoned "protesting in public places even if it disrupts order" are listed in Table 2. Since the question explicitly refers to actions taken *in case of inequitable* treatment, Table 2 exhibits both the percentage abstractly favoring the action (although the respondents counted there may not themselves feel inequitably treated) and of those feeling simultaneously deprived of what they deserve *and* favoring the action involved. Some of the actions listed are taken individually, others collectively. Some observe, others violate the prevailing laws or norms pertaining to such behavior. With regard to the societal goals of integration, economic production and monetary stability, the following generalizations are suggested:

TABLE 2
Actions justified in the event of inequitable pay

Action-Type	% Justifying actions	% Inequitably treated *and* justifying actions
A. *Individual-legitimate*		
Asking for a pay increase	95	36
Quitting the job	65	24
B. *Collective-legitimate*		
Participating in union-approved strikes	72	27
Non-violent protest like picketing	59	23
C. *Individual-illegitimate*		
Not working as hard on the job	25	11
Taking longer lunch or rest breaks	14	6
Not coming to work regularly	7	3
Doing work poorly or incorrectly on purpose	4	1
D. *Collective-illegitimate*		
Participating in strikes not approved by the union	22	9
Participating with co-workers in work slowdowns	31	14
	$N = 795$	

Question: Some people think they get *less* pay from their job than they feel they justly deserve. What would be right for them to do in this situation? How about...........
Note: Data for this table and table 1 are based on a national sample of American adults 18 years of age and over, living in the coterminous United States (excluding Alaska and Hawaii).

Success in increasing outcomes above productivity gains (with given inputs) or reducing inputs (with given outcomes) tends to increase unit labor cost and will have an adverse effect on monetary stability;

Reducing inputs, in addition to a possible inflationary effect, is likely to have an adverse effect on production;

Any collective action aimed at improving the outcome/input ratio for a group will have a detrimental effect on societal integration, in addition to its possible adverse effect on monetary stability and production. This will be so in particular if: (a) inputs are temporarily withheld (e.g. strikes); and (b) if laws or norms governing protest behavior and collective bargaining are not observed (disruptive demonstrations, non-union approved strikes, etc.).

Table 2 leads to the following conclusions: The most accepted types of reactions to felt inequity are those involving *individual* action conforming to market rules, such as asking for a pay increase and quitting the job. Second best accepted is a *collective* effort to change distributional rules as long as it makes use of the proper procedures. Since societal integration as well as productivity is at stake here, and also personal sacrifices or risks are involved, people are somewhat more hesitant to approve these actions. The next-best accepted type of action involves *collective illegitimate* action: wildcat strikes, work slowdown. Individual illegitimate action, e.g. taking longer lunch or rest breaks or doing work poorly or incorrectly on purpose is condoned by very few workers. However, there is a considerable minority approving the strategy of "not working as hard on the job". Acting outside the rules as long as it is not manifest and does not affect the pride of workmanship, is by no means unanimously rejected. Collective illegitimate action is frequently favored even though it is inherently manifest.

Conclusion

In following up the societal impact of stagnation, we dealt with three subsystems: The productive system, transforming labor and natural resources into goods and services, the welfare system, converting goods and services into the experience of well-being or need satisfaction, and the integrative system, resolving the conflicts arising from the deficits passed on from the welfare system. Viewing the performance of the three systems in perspective, the productive system must receive the highest marks. Over the past decades, its output was sufficiently ample so as to subsidize the otherwise miserable performance of the welfare system: Quantity in terms of goods compensated for quality in terms of need satisfaction, and the rising income trend tended to obscure the need for institutionalized income continuity. Only recently has the performance surplus of the productive system discontinued, thereby revealing the inability of the welfare system to do its job under conditions of stationary affluence. A mere stagnation of production has led to a drastic increase in felt deprivation. Neither did the integrative system perform well. If failed to legitimize deprivation. For instance, the external challenge of the oil embargo led initially to a sense of common threat resulting in voluntary conservation of energy. After the government had lifted the sense of urgency (Nixon: "We don't have a crisis, we only have a problem"), and after the widely publicized profit explosion of the oil companies, conservation decreased and there arose a widespread feeling of inequity.

Felt inequity to-date seems to have resulted less in social conflict, and more in withdrawal from participation in economic and political processes. Since Tocqueville, Americans have been described as a nation heavily partaking in civic affairs. Our own research has shown that American households provide more paid labor (mainly wives' work) than Europeans, acquire higher education and invest their savings in equity capital more frequently. Felt inequity and estrangement not only has reduced voter turnout and the effectiveness of government leadership, it also has increased strike activity and may even affect the pride of workmanship, as we have seen in our data. It certainly has diminished the willingness of capitalists to take risks as is obvious from the present condition on the finance markets. In short: the failure of both the welfare and the integrative systems feeds back to the productive system.

We located the inefficiency of the welfare system in its fixation on tastes geared to comfort but neglecting other needs. The change of tastes then emerges as an important condition for obtaining welfare without growth. Consumer tastes or budget choices must not be seen as individual or psychological attributes but rather as characteristics that have been generated by concrete cultural and institutional conditions. The peculiar expansion of consumer wants for physical, "throughput-intensive" products, mainly consumer durables, was clearly stimulated by declining relative prices for these goods. It was facilitated by a variety of government interventions and non-interventions such as the Federal Highway program and the deductibility of interest payments for mortages in the United States as well as the failure to legislate the internalization of external and social costs such as environmental damage and resource depletion. And the present malaise is due to no small extent to "withdrawal symptoms". In contrast to the recent past, the productive system fails to respond readily to the traditional catalogue of aspirations. Now we live in the worst of all worlds. Our aspirations are inefficient, and besides, we do not achieve our aspirations. And it would be erroneous to assume that a reversal of these economic conditions and a mere elimination of explicit or implicit public subsidies to the exploitation of raw materials and the processing and consumption of physical goods would be sufficient to assure smooth adaptation. Tastes and consumption styles are shaped during childhood and early adult socialization. Their modification requires cultural change that unfolds very slowly—for instance, by way of generational change—or can be brought about by major disruptions (wars, catastrophies) or social innovation coupled with ideological change. It is the latter scenario that appears most promising in our present context.

The successful response to the threat of overpopulation in some industrial countries may serve as an example for effective adaptation facilitated by social innovation. Easy availability of contraception and abortion coupled with a change in ideologies and norms pertaining to the appropriate number of children in a family, followed by the deterioration of economic expectations brought about the most drastic decline in fertility in the recorded demographic history of both the United States and Western Europe. The analogy to consumer behavior is obvious. Behavioral change away from materials intensive expenditures presupposes first the availability of alternative life-styles: smaller cars, public transportation, consumer goods of high durability, effective institutional provisions for health and income continuity must be in reach of the average consumer. Second, there must be financial incentives favoring the change; here is the role of pricing. And third, there must be a change in belief systems and ideologies, in short: a new image of the merit and role of alternative ways of consumption for society and saving. Under which circumstances can we expect such new images to emerge? In times of war and national emergencies, people are often ready for economic sacrifice and a reorientation of their life-styles. Contrariwise, according to the theory of revolution, a group is most likely to engage in demands, protest, and disruption after a period of progress when its expectations have been disappointed *and* other groups are perceived as achieving further gains. Society in both cases deals with deterioration. What conditions distinguish the successful adaptation of the first scenario from the unsuccessful adaptation of the second one?

(a) a climate of solidarity, equity, sense of burden sharing assuring social integration and facilitating a rearrangement of individual behavior in order to accommodate collective goals,

(b) the perception of an entirely new environment weakening the adequacy of old beliefs and behavior patterns.

Publicly emphasizing, even dramatizing the common challenge, providing for alternative consumption goods and patterns, and creating or preserving a climate of equity and solidarity, these three general strategies by government and other institutions then seem to be indicated in order to facilitate adaptation of consumer tastes and demand.

References

J. STACY ADAMS, 'Injustice in Social Exchange,' in L. Berkowitz (ed.), *Advances in Experimental Social Psychology, Vol. 2*, New York: Academic Press, 1965.

HANS APEL and BURKHARD STRUMPEL, 'Economic Well-Being as a Criterion for System Performance: A Survey in Bulgaria and Greece,' in Burkhard Strumpel (ed.), *Economic Means for Human Needs*, Ann Arbor: Institute for Social Research, University of Michigan, 1975 (forthcoming).

KENNETH E. BOULDING, 'The Shadow of the Stationary State,' *Daedalus*, Fall, 1974, *Vol. 102*, No. 4, pp. 89 ff.

PHILLIP BRICKMAN and DONALD T. CAMPBELL, 'Hedonic Relativism and Planning the Good Society,' in M. H. Appley (ed.), *Adaptation Level Theory: A Symposium*, New York: Academic Press, 1972.

GEORGE KATONA, BURKHARD STRUMPEL and ERNEST ZAHN, *Aspirations and Affluence: Comparative Studies in the United States and Western Europe*, New York: McGraw-Hill, 1971.

HARVEY LEIBENSTEIN, 'Allocative Efficiency Vs. X-Efficiency,' *American Economic Review, Vol. LVI*, No. 3, June 1966, pp. 392–415.

ARTHUR H. MILLER, 'Political Issues and Trust in Government: 1964–1970,' *American Political Science Review, Vol. LXVIII*, No. 3, September 1974, pp. 951–972.

BURKHARD STRUMPEL, 'Saving Behavior in Comparative Perspective: The Cases of Western Germany and the United States,' *American Economic Review, Vol. LXV*, May, 1975, pp. 210–216.

D.4.   The multiple futures*

ALBERT G. HART

All decisions, as Kenneth Boulding makes clear in *The Image*, must shape themselves out of the decision-maker's image of the setting in which he is operating. Since decisions take time to execute, any decision that is in any degree rational must involve aspects of the image that relate to future events. These events in the large are of course beyond the control of any decision-maker. Nevertheless, any meaningful decision is a choice between alternative futures: a decision-maker feels able to shape at least those aspects of the future that consist of actions that he can direct, and will strive to choose actions whose consequences are in accord with his value-system.

In speaking of "the future", we commonly use language which hints at a simplistic view that the future (aside from our own acts) is single-valued—that of the conceivable states of the world in which our decisions are to take effect, only one is "really" possible, and that our problem is simply to sift the list of conceivable future states down to the one which corresponds to the "real future". But such single-valuedness is a property of the past, not of the future. When we contemplate the choices open to ourselves, we must remember that others as well have choices to make. The only strictly correct answer to a question about the events that will set the framework for our own activities would be: "The decisions by other people that will determine these events have not yet

*Besides the obvious general influence of Kenneth Boulding upon this paper, I take occasion to acknowledge the influence of Franco Modigliani and of Henri Theil. For specific suggestions that led to the present paper, I am indebted to a number of participants in a 1974 meeting on "adaptive expectations" at MIT—especially to my Columbia University colleague John Taylor and to Georges De Menil. Marshall Kolin and John Taylor have clarified substance and method in numerous conversations. My assistants on the project of which this paper is an outgrowth (Victor Glass, David Green and Helena Hessel) have helped with substantive analysis as well as with programming and data processing. I am grateful to the Columbia University Center for Computing Services and to Dean Bernard Friedman for generous provision of computer time.

been taken, and are uncertain." Having faced this fact, we may proceed to consider the evidence as to what image of the future other decision-makers hold, and as to how they will respond both to these expectations and to the surprises that they are sure to experience as events unroll. But it is plain that from the standpoint of any rational decision-maker there are *multiple futures* to take into account—differing from each other not only in respect of the actions that he himself may take, but in respect of the context that will be created by the decisions of others.

1. *Possibilities of observation*

In the large, we must be skeptical about the possibility of systematically observing the way that the multiple futures enter the images of decision-makers. Observation is indeed possible and almost commonplace. The view—which has altogether too much currency among economists—that views of the future and related value-systems are inherently inscrutable because they are locked up inside some individual's skull should not be taken too seriously. For most of the important decisions are made by groups rather than by individuals, and the necessary communication within the group is observable. Not only do participants sometimes describe the process to social scientists, but decision-making groups on occasion permit observers to sit in on their conversations. Furthermore, there are often written minutes of decisions and collections of background materials that entered the decision process. The difficulty lies in making observation "systematic". The very richness of the materials that an observer can collect tends to defeat system: he is swamped with detail (much of which cannot be so handled as to be comparable with other case material); he loses track of key questions, or is unable to press them when the initial response is off the track. So much time is absorbed by each case studied in depth, and so many opportunities turn up for improving the pattern of inquiry as the case is studied, that it is very difficult simultaneously to observe the process in depth and to build up an archive of observations so designed as to admit of systematic analysis—holding some variables constant while examining differences in respect of other variables.

We must reckon besides with the fact that important parts of the image may not be explicit in the minds of participants (and may or may not be held in common by all members of the group). Many decisions, furthermore, must be based on intuition rather than on calculation about future circumstances and about the consequences of proposed actions. Where intuition dominates, it may be fruitless to seek systematic assembly of observations about the decision-makers' image of the future. The "black box" view of decisions—where we observe the output, can make good guesses as to what are the actually-used inputs, but really do not know what goes on inside—in such situations may be our only recourse.

There is an interesting decision-domain, however—important in its own right, and likely to offer valuable cross-lights upon other domains— where it is part of the folkways to build into the decision process a whole structure of calculations, and to systematize and document these calculations. I refer to the decision-complex that centers around fixed investment (plant-and-equipment expenditure) of large companies, particularly in manufacturing. For the short run, investment decisions are formalized in capital appropriations, contracts and orders for plant and equipment, and the like. For the medium term, decisions are formalized—it cannot be too much stressed, on a provisional basis—in capital budgets, backed by formulation of explicit views as to what will happen in the next few years to a number of variables.

The processes of capital budgeting and capital appropriation have turned out in our generation to lend themselves to study by survey techniques—by mail questionnaires, or by questionnaires administered by interview. These surveys focus on a few questions designed to tap the respondent companies' records relating to (notably) capital appropriations and capital budgets. The present paper is devoted chiefly to study of a segment of this archive, dealing with materials related to companies' capacity targets and sales forecasts, drawn presumably from capital budgets.

2. Alternative futures as pictured by ex post and by ex ante data

The empirical study of fixed investment takes the form of a search for "determinants of investment decisions". The basic conceptual framework which economists use for such studies is one wherein a decision-maker ascertains an accessibility-locus which describes actions open to him and the consequences thereof and then makes his choice by applying a value-system to choose the "best" action.

In principle, the data-book for such a search should be made up of evidence about the alternative futures visualized by decision-makers, with "alternatives" varying along two dimensions:

(i) Alternative sets of external circumstances viewed as time-series of future values of the relevant exogenous variables—no single set being adequate in principle because developments are uncertain.

(ii) Alternative sets of actions that the decision-maker's firm might take, viewed as time-series of future values of such variables as flows of investment expenditures or levels of manufacturing capacity.

A third set of variables is of course implicit—endogenous future
time-series measuring consequences of alternative sets of actions, and
comprising both costs and benefits. A set of consequences can be
specified for every intersection of a set of exogenous variables with a set
of actions.[1] Each set of consequences can be reduced to a present net
discounted value—to be supplemented by memoranda about other
aspects of results that decision-makers include in their preference-scales.
For each set of actions, then, there will be a distinct set of consequences
for each set of exogenous variables considered. Since in the end it is sets
of actions which must be valued to determine the choice, each set of
actions is to be thought of as having a matched collection of alternative
sets of consequence-values attached, for which the decision-maker is
presumed to have a distribution of subjective probabilities. Choice of
actions will then be seen as depending on the expectation value of this
probability distribution—and also presumably on other aspects of the
distribution.[2]

Relative to such a utopian description of the data-book that one should
have for an adequate analysis of investment decision, the poverty of the
accessible collection of data is appalling. In conventional investment
studies, this situation is compounded by an acceptance of voluntary
poverty—a self-denying ordinance renouncing use of *ex ante* data.
Standard patterns for such research rely exclusively on *ex post* data—
that is, on reports as to what actually (or should we say "purportedly"?)
took place prior to the viewpoint date as of which information was

[1]Though in principle each of the dimensions of variation may be a continuum, it is plain that
the field of alternatives can be mapped to any specified degree of precision by working out a
moderate number of discrete sets which intuition suggests are sufficiently representative;
so that we are not bound to adopt the inevitably clumsy semantics that goes with continuity
assumptions in such a discussion.

[2]Since it really contributes to vagueness rather than to definiteness to visualize decision-
makers as having a view of the future that extends indefinitely, we may choose to think of
the "future time series" as defined only up to some specified number of future years which
we may call the "frontier of estimation". If so, we must take as one of the elements of
discounted value as of the viewpoint-date, a discounted value of the net worth which the
estimates attribute to the firm at the frontier date.

In these terms, we may well imagine that decision-makers will operate with a taboo on
lines of action which raise the probability of zero net worth above some modest level. This
remark should not be interpreted as an assertion that decision-makers are necessarily
"risk-averters". For any manager, assuming that he has enough self-confidence to be viable
in top management of a business, must reckon that if the firm survives as a going concern to
and past the estimation frontier, there is sure to be some way that management can wring a
profit out of the situation. "Zero net worth" will therefore represent a situation where
values realizable by competent management after the frontier date are made inaccessible
by letting insolvency put the firm out of action.

assembled. Since the past is single-valued, such data do not explicitly describe any alternatives in either of our two dimensions: anything we can know from the *ex post* data-book about the alternatives visualized by decision-makers is inferential. True, we are informed what actions were taken under what external circumstances, and with what consequences. But to try to transform this information into inferences about alternatives is risky. It is a trap to suppose that the actions and consequences observed over (say) two decades represent simultaneously-existing alternatives. On the contrary, we know that there is no path back from 1975 to 1955—and that there was no path forward from 1955 to 1975 that did not entail a long series of moves which could not possibly have been visualized at a 1955 viewpoint. We are of course closer to comparing simultaneously-available alternatives if we put the study on an incremental footing. It is reasonably safe to suppose that the action taken in 1964 could have been replicated in 1965—though perhaps not that the action taken in 1965 could have been taken in 1964. Whether we work with levels or with increments, we must remember that *ex post* records mingle inextricably the execution of previous plans with improvisations to adapt to external situations that were not contemplated when plans were laid. In a world of surprises, many of the actions taken may never previously have been visualized as possible, and would never have been taken if the decision-maker had visualized in advance the circumstances in which they were adopted.[3]

When we introduce *ex ante* data, we have much better prospects of finding out about the field of alternatives among which decision-makers thought they were choosing.[4] Ideally, we might hope that surveys of *ex*

[3]Improvisation, of course, is also an aspect of decision. If we think of investment-decisions as relating to "projects", we must see decision as a process rather than an event. The early stages of decision on a project will include go-ahead decisions (substantially equivalent to actions) on some of its aspects, and the framing of plans (that is, sets of provisional decisions) for the rest of the sequence of actions that the project entails. Unless the course of events is surprisingly unsurprising, the plan must be adapted to circumstances in the course of execution. (A plan may be defined informally as "a statement of what we will do unless we change our minds"—and we normally do change our minds.) But the setting for the later stages of decision is compounded of new perceptions of external conditions (including technology and the like) and the consequences of actions taken at earlier stages. Go-ahead decisions at earlier stages, in turn, must be scrutinized by a rational decision-maker to make sure that they do not needlessly close off options for later plan-revisions. To try to explain the sequence of actions without allowance for the fact that the plans evolved between initiation and completion of the project is to leave systematic characteristics of decision-making out of account.

[4]I assume implicitly that the *ex-ante* data are "authentic" in the sense of being serious statements from members of a decision-making group about considerations that actually entered their decision process. It is certainly conceivable that this sort of authenticity may

ante data would elicit multi-valued responses which would exhibit several of the alternatives considered at the viewpoint date as of which the survey was taken. Experience with surveys, unfortunately, indicates that contingent questions are asked only on special occasions, in relation to momentarily topical contingencies such as possible renewal of the energy shortage. Hence the systematically-collected bodies of *ex ante* data are limited to single-valued statements about actions or external circumstances at specified horizon-dates.[5] But as against *ex post* data they have the advantage of describing points declared to lie on the feasibility locus as seen at the viewpoint.

Special interest attaches to *ex ante* data from surveys with fairly long horizons. The typical investment survey concentrates on getting investment-expenditure plans and sales-forecasts for the oncoming year—or sometimes for shorter periods measured in calendar quarters. But there are surveys that look farther into the future. In the United

---

be lacking. Americans are notorious for their willingness to formulate survey-responses based on little or no information. If the person who filled out the questionnaire was not a participant in the decision, he may write in irresponsible surmises as to what happened. If decisions were reached in a much less rational way than the questionnaire implies (for example, if investment decisions were taken without any serious consideration of actual sales-prospects), the respondent may write in his *ex post* rationalization of the process.

My own impression (based on the work done for this paper and a great deal of other work with the same data-archive) is that the data are "authentic". But it is hard to see how such impressions could be turned into hard findings of fact without a prolonged and expensive field study of respondents' mode of handling the questionnaires, their capital-budgeting process, and their "actual behavior".

[5]Survey-takers at meetings of CIRET (Centre Internationale de Recherches Economiques Tendencielles), which is an association of those who work with *ex ante* data, have repeatedly shown strong intellectual interest in G. L. S. Shackle's schema for representing expectations by "focus-gain/focus-loss" estimates purporting to describe the most favorable and least favorable situations that would be regarded as "unsurprising". But no survey taker seems to have regarded this schema as sufficiently workable to base a series of surveys upon it.

Since there must be a good deal of two-way communication between survey takers and their respondents, this behavior of survey takers has value as evidence to the effect that respondents typically think in terms of central values (means? modes?) of their subjective probability distributions. For the basic participation incentives of respondents must be some mixture of pleasure in finding that outside experts agree with them that their doings are interesting, and of curiosity about the survey responses of their reference group (competitors, customers and suppliers). What endangers response rates in a survey is a sense of frustration on the part of respondents who feel that the questions asked do not give them a framework for explaining their views in an interesting and revealing way. If decision-makers really found a central-value presentation unrepresentative and felt that Shackle-type focus-gain/focus-loss formulations were more illuminating, survey takers could not afford to go on working solely with central values of expectations.

States, we now have two decades of data accumulation from an *ex ante* survey conducted by the McGraw-Hill Company, in which respondents grouped into fourteen manufacturing industries are asked to look ahead four years. With four horizon years covered by surveys at each of twenty survey viewpoints, we have for each industry no fewer than eighty viewpoint-horizon combinations.[6] Although each of the eighty observations is in itself single-valued, the observations can be regrouped to give us four observations each for seventeen viewpoint dates (1958–1974), three each for another two (1957, 1975), and two each for another two (1956, 1976). In view of revision of plans and forecasts, the estimates for each horizon date spread out over a considerable range in the dimension of action-alternatives. In the dimension of external-condition alternatives, each of the four estimates (coming from different viewpoints) for a given horizon will contain a different sales forecast.[7] The four estimates will have in common essentially constant pictures of a number of relevant pre-determined variables of a sort that is very hard to measure—notably the respondent firm's organization, structure, and position on the market, its product-list, and in broad terms its technology. For the spread of viewpoint dates is small enough that we can properly suppose that respondents are not forced to speculate about radically unfamiliar situations.

It will be observed that the list of variables covered by the survey is very skimpy. The list is reasonably adequate to represent investment decision by the planned investment expenditures and the capacity targets. But a number of other variables relevant to investment and presumably used as inputs in capital budgeting are omitted from the survey—such as the company's view of the future of corporate cash

[6]The sense in which we actually have four horizon-dates covered at each viewpoint date will be closely examined in the next section of this paper. In the survey questionnaire, it is only for planned plant-and-equipment expenditures that the respondent actually supplies four distinct *ex ante* figures. For the other two variables for which McGraw-Hill collects *ex ante* data (forecast sales and targeted manufacturing capacity), explicit data appear only for the change to the viewpoint year from the base year, and for the change from the viewpoint year to a horizon year starting three years later. But for reasons to be explained below, I hold that it is meaningful to supply the missing sales-forecast and capacity-target entries for the next two years after the viewpoint year by log-linear interpolation.

[7]It will be noted that I am treating sales forecasts as exogenous. It is plain that in the broadest view of a firm's decision structure, decisions about product-prices, sales-promotion, and the like that can affect sales, must be taken into account; and in the perspective of five or ten years, changes in product-line and geographical structure of a firm may have considerable impact on sales.

It seems to be normal in capital-budgeting, however, to regard sales as exogenous—a point of view which presumably regards product line and the like as set for the next four years or so, and price as predetermined. I am following this usage in the present paper.

flow, interest rates, prices of capital goods, wage rates, and prices of output and of materials. Though we may hope that *ex ante* surveys of some future date will inquire into these variables, they are missing from the archive of data which we must use for the investment studies of the next few years, except as we can use a shorter series on cash-flow prospects.

The best available remedy for these data gaps is to fill them with expectations-proxies—by which I mean constructs from *ex post* data that are designed to simulate the kind of estimation likely to be used by respondents in the context. Since each of the four viewpoint dates that we draw on for variant estimates has a different antecedent set of *ex post* data, the variant estimates will differ in the alternative-external-conditions dimension for these variables as well as for sales. But by treating the 80 observations for each industry in battery fashion (while taking careful account of the viewpoint-to-horizon spreads involved), we can expect to get meaningful results when on another occasion we come to the analysis of investment expenditure. In the present paper, I am deliberately adopting a narrow focus where the object of explanation is the capacity target; and here on the assumption that prospective sales are the only highly important external-conditions variable we can do so well that these complications can be avoided.

3. Descriptive account of the expectations under analysis

The sector of the image-structure examined in this paper is part (but only a part) of the McGraw-Hill collection of *ex ante* data. The core of the McGraw-Hill survey is a set of questions asked early in each year, starting with 1955, of a stratified sample of manufacturers.

The first of these questions calls upon respondents to report how much they plan to spend on plant and equipment in the viewpoint year and in each of the ensuing three years (in the 1974 survey, for example, in 1974, 1975, 1976 and 1977); for calibration, they are also asked about spending in the base year (in the 1974 survey, 1973).

The second question asks by what percentage the respondent's productive capacity will expand from the opening to the close of the viewpoint year, and from the close of the viewpoint year to a date three years later (in the 1974 survey, the end of 1977), if the investment plans are executed. For capacity there is also an *ex post* question about the percentage expansion during the base year.

The third question then asks by what percentage the respondent's "sales in physical units" are expected to expand from the base year to the viewpoint year, and from the viewpoint year to a horizon year three years later (in the 1974 survey, the year 1977).[8] A retrospective sales question serves only for weighting sales-forecast responses in McGraw-Hill's tabulations of sales forecasts by industries.

In this paper, I concentrate on the sales-expansion and capacity-expansion estimates in their relation to each other, leaving the explanation of sales forecasts and the planning and execution of capital expenditures for analysis in another place. It should be noted that I am treating McGraw-Hill's summary figures for each of the 14 industries analyzed as if they were data for single decision centers—incurring risks of distortion by aggregation which are sufficiently familiar in investment studies. To give visibility to what is here an assumption (though in other parts of my project the object of special analysis) that for these decision-makers sales are exogenous whereas capacity is endogenous, I adopt the semantics of sales "forecasts" as against capacity "targets".

To illustrate the character of the *ex ante* data on sales and capacity, and to set forth the transformations by which I prepare the data for econometric analysis, Table MF-1 presents a set of original and transformed data for the industry "machinery, except electrical" (Standard Industrial Classification number 35). This industry, because of its special role as simultaneously a major demander and a major supplier of capital goods, is perhaps the most interesting of the fourteen industries studies. Its data-processing problems, furthermore, are reasonably representative.

Table MF-1 falls into two sections—each with a line for each of the 20 years of McGraw-Hill surveys that make up the data-book. The left half deals with sales forecasts, the right with capacity targets. In each half, the first column of data presents *ex post* base figures. The next three columns contain McGraw-Hill's *ex ante* figures (expressed for convenience as change ratios rather than percent changes). Then come two columns in which the *ex ante* magnitudes are transformed into absolute levels by applying the change ratios to the base figures. On both sides of the table, absolute figures are stated in "(billions of) value-added dollars of 1967".

---

[8]By an aberration, the 1972 survey put the sales-forecast question in terms of "dollar sales". Rather than introduce what would have to be a highly arbitrary price correction, I have assumed that respondents gave the same answers that they would have given to the usual form of question. Scrutiny of the resulting computer printouts suggests that this assumption does little violence to the facts.

In the 1973 survey, McGraw-Hill reverted to asking about "physical units" and in addition asked about dollar sales. In the 1974 survey, a further question was inserted about expected price changes. I have assumed the comparability of "physical unit" responses of the 1973 and 1974 surveys with those of 1955–1971.

Table MF-1

USA: Manufacturing, industry 35: machinery, except electrical.

Illustration for industry 35 of derivation from McGraw-Hill Survey Data and FRB Production Index of levels for sales forecast and capacity target in 1967 value-added dollars (billions). For definitions of variables see footnotes.

Viewpoint (opening-of-year date)[a]	Variables relating to actual and forecast "sales in physical units"[b]							Variables relating to actual and targeted capacity[c]				
	QVABY	SFR1Y	SFR3Y	SFRIN	SFL1Y	SFL4Y	CAPVP	CTR1Y	CTR3Y	CTRIN	CTL1Y	CTL4Y
1955.0	12.61	1.05	1.19	1.060	13.24	15.77	14.23	1.06	1.13	1.041	15.15	17.12
1956.0	13.83	1.13	1.17	1.054	15.63	18.30	15.39	1.09	1.20	1.063	16.77	20.13
1957.0	15.84	1.11	1.25	1.077	17.58	21.96	17.35	1.08	1.17	1.054	18.74	21.93
1958.0	15.81	0.93	1.27	1.083	14.70	18.68	18.55	1.04	1.10	1.032	19.29	21.22
1959.0	13.28	1.09	1.29	1.089	14.47	18.69	19.10	1.04	1.11	1.035	19.86	22.05
1960.0	15.48	1.09	1.20	1.063	16.87	20.26	20.08	1.05	1.09	1.029	21.08	22.98
1961.0	15.56	1.03	1.24	1.074	16.03	19.85	20.84	1.04	1.10	1.032	21.67	23.84
1962.0	15.14	1.07	1.22	1.069	16.20	19.79	21.28	1.04	1.12	1.039	22.13	24.79
1963.0	16.95	1.05	1.21	1.066	17.80	21.56	22.37	1.05	1.11	1.035	23.49	26.08
1964.0	18.12	1.07	1.15	1.048	19.39	22.32	23.25	1.04	1.12	1.039	24.18	27.08
1965.0	21.04	1.09	1.22	1.069	22.94	28.02	23.90	1.06	1.14	1.045	25.33	28.88
1966.0	23.58	1.11	1.28	1.086	26.17	33.52	25.86	1.08	1.16	1.051	27.93	32.40
1967.0	27.73	1.09	1.31	1.094	30.22	39.56	27.81	1.08	1.19	1.060	30.03	35.74
1968.0	27.84	1.07	1.30	1.091	29.79	38.68	29.69	1.07	1.19	1.060	31.77	37.80
1969.0	28.00	1.09	1.32	1.097	30.52	40.30	31.38	1.06	1.16	1.051	33.26	38.58
1970.0	29.51	1.06	1.25	1.077	31.28	39.07	33.82	1.06	1.23	1.071	35.85	44.09
1971.0	27.98	1.04	1.27	1.083	29.09	36.96	35.51	1.06	1.17	1.054	37.64	44.04
1972.0	26.25	1.06	1.16	1.050	27.82	32.21	36.81	1.05	1.15	1.048	38.65	44.45
1973.0	29.42	1.09	1.21	1.065	32.07	38.74	38.59	1.07	1.19	1.060	41.29	49.14
1974.0	34.80	1.08	1.17	1.054	37.60	44.00	41.56	1.10	1.27	1.083	45.72	58.06
Statistics of variables:												
Mean	21.44	1.070	1.234	1.073	22.97	28.43	25.87	1.061	1.155	1.049	27.49	32.02

Standard deviation	6.74	0.040	0.050	0.016	7.35	9.32	7.91	0.018	0.046	0.015	8.61	11.09
Increment without regard to sign: average	1.82	0.043	0.043	0.013	2.11	2.85	1.44	0.013	0.032	0.010	1.61	2.16
per cent of above mean	8.5	4.0	3.5	1.2	9.2	10.0	5.6	1.2	2.8	1.0	5.9	6.7

[a] "Viewpoint" denotes opening of year in which relevant McGraw-Hill survey was taken. This year is designated as "viewpoint year", the preceding calendar year as "base year".

[b] Variables for "sales" (with FRB production index in 1967 value-added dollars as proxy) are designated as follows:

QVABY: FRB production index for base year relative to viewpoint given in stub.

SFR1Y: McGraw-Hill's average of industry's stated ratios of expected sales in viewpoint year to actual sales in base year. This and other "ratio" variables are set up by adding unity to per-cent-change reports in the source, for convenience in further transformations.

SFR3Y: McGraw-Hill's average of industry's stated ratios of expected sales in horizon-year that opens 3 years after viewpoint to sales expected for viewpoint year.

SFRIN: Compound-interest rate of expansion during period from viewpoint to horizon year: cube root of SFR3Y.

SFL1Y: Sales-forecast level for viewpoint year: QVABY multiplied by SFR1Y.

SFL4Y: Sales-forecast level for horizon-year opening 3 years after viewpoint: SFL1Y multiplied by SFR3Y.

[c] Variables for "capacity" are designated as follows:

CAPVP: Capacity at viewpoint date (opening of viewpoint year), from McGraw-Hill index.

CTR1Y: McGraw-Hill's average of industry's stated ratios of capacity targeted for close of viewpoint year to capacity at viewpoint.

CTR3Y: McGraw-Hill's average of industry's stated ratios of capacity targeted for date 4 years later than viewpoint to capacity targeted for 1 year after viewpoint.

CTRIN: Compound-interest rate of expansion during period from 1 to 4 years after viewpoint: cube root of CTR3Y.

CTL1Y: Level of capacity targeted for end of viewpoint year: CAPVP multiplied by CTR1Y.

CTL4Y: Level of capacity targeted for date 4 years later than viewpoint: CTL1Y multiplied by CTR3Y.

On the left side, the base figures represent "sales" for the base year. Since the McGraw-Hill survey gives no information on the change to the base year from the year preceding, there is no way to build up a time-series for "actual" (*ex post*) sales in physical units from within the McGraw-Hill data-book, and we must draw on other sources. After laborious sifting of other ways to measure *ex post* sales, I conclude that the best series for the purpose is the relevant industry's componeni of the Federal Reserve Board Index of industrial production. This choice may perhaps seem arbitrary, since the FRB index purports to measure output rather than sales as such. But we must bear in mind that the primary role of the sales forecast in capital budgeting is to serve as a proxy for the future output against which capacity is to be provided by investment; this is why McGraw-Hill asks for "physical units". Hence the fact that the FRB index is designed to measure output in physical units is a reason for (rather than against) its use as the base series for "actual sales".[9]

In principle, what manufacturing firms produce is the *service of manufacturing*: the physical-goods 'output' which they sell is the joint product of this service with the materials flow to which this service is applied. The current-dollar counterpart of this service flow is of course the flow of value-added-by-manufacture. Hence it is appropriate to transform the base series and forecast-level series for "sales" into units of value-added at 1967 prices. I do this by multiplying each industry's component of the FRB index (taken with the industry's 1967 output as

[9]Two alternative sources exist which might be used, with price-deflation to transform current dollars to 1967 dollars. The Federal Trade Commission and Securities Exchange Commission publish quarterly data denominated "sales" in the *Quarterly Financial Report for Manufacturing Corporations*. And the Census publishes monthly data denominated "shipments" (a more precise expression for the journalistic term "sales") in monthly releases about manufacturers' orders, shipments and inventory. When McGraw-Hill in recent years has expressed sales-forecasts in base-year dollars, it has used Census shipments for its base-year sales.

Although the BLS index of wholesale prices includes components that correspond rather well to a few of the 14 industries under study, matching is rather poor for others. For a good proportion of the industries, my assistants and I have found that deflated "sales" or shipments show movements that look incongruous when compared with related series on output, employment, materials-throughout, etc. Even though sales or shipments deflated by relevant BLS components may for various reasons be superior to FRB output as measures of "actual sales" in a few industries—and this list of industries could be extended by finding or generating better-adapted price indexes—the attainable margin of improvement does not seem to warrant the labor involved. Besides, it is plainly preferable in a paper of this sort to transform the data in ways that are easy to describe and to reproduce, avoiding elaborate descriptions of the adhockery entailed in handling different industries by different procedures.

unity) by Census figures from the 1971 *Survey of Manufactures* which state the industry's value-added (excess of value of shipments over the value of purchased materials and energy) for the 1967 year. The resulting series (like components of "GNP in 1958 dollars") have the convenient property of permitting aggregation or disaggregation by simple addition or subtraction.[10] Hence the series of base-year "sales" (column QVA67 in the table) gets its time shape from the FRB index, and its level from the Census data for value-added of 1967.

On the capacity side, the base figures represent actual capacity at the opening of the viewpoint year. The figures get their time-shape from the index of actual capacity published by McGraw-Hill in its survey releases—an index obtained by chaining together the *ex post* data for each industry arising from the inquiry about actual capacity growth during the base year. The level of the base-capacity series is determined in a slightly more complicated way. Starting from the FRB index used to measure "sales", I apply the convenient "Pennsylvania method" to estimate the opening-of-1968 level of capacity in 1967 value-added dollars.[11] The resulting series should be constructed to yield some sort of

---

[10]Technically, this property is useful in the present study because one of the "industries in the *ex ante* data-book of McGraw-Hill (and also in that of the Conference Board) is the sum of "fabricated metal products" (SIC number 34) and "instruments" (SIC number 38)—a combination which arose by peeling off various elements from what was originally an aggregate of "metal-processing industries". Besides, two of the two-digit industries— primary metals (SIC 33) and transportation equipment (SIC 37)—are broken in two in the investment statistics; and flexibility in disaggregation simplifies data-processing.

For various purposes, besides, it is worthwhile to build up industry-figures to aggregates for durable-goods industries, non-durable-goods industries, and their total.

[11]Although the Pennsylvania method is not so new as one might suppose from recent literature (I for one have been using the same method in published work since the 1948 edition of *Money, Debt and Economic Activity*), its systematization and its bold application by University of Pennsylvania economists to relatively narrow aggregates make it appropriate as well as convenient to give it the label now current. It rests on locating unsubmerged peaks in a seasonally-unadjusted output series, and treating these points as measures of capacity.

The logic behind this method rests on the unduly neglected principle that what happens is possible. In the present case, this principle tells us that every observation of output (unless for a period so short that its level may be non-sustainable) gives us an under-estimation of the output attainable. Among these underestimates, most are so far down the scale that they give no good indication of capacity; but the unsubmerged peaks may be presumed to underestimate only slightly the attainable level.

If the resulting series of peak values behaved capriciously, we could rest little weight on the results. But in fact the high points in a semi-log chart of seasonally-unadjusted 3-month moving averages of the FRB production index show a very reasonable course in the 1955–1974 period for all the industries studied. By this statement I mean that (a) there are no serious disagreements in a semi-log chart between the set of "unsubmerged peaks" and

effective capacity level, which is less than total capacity by whatever
reserve of unused capacity the industry may hold at times when seasonal
and cyclical peaks coincide.

In relating the "sales" and capacity variables, we have to bear in mind
that the derivation of base figures from disparate sources introduces an
element of incomparability. Investment statistics are compiled with the
company as the basic unit; this is as it should be, since the company must
be viewed (with minor reservations) as the decision center for investment. But production statistics (like statistics for employment, shipments, and a host of other variables) are compiled with the establishment
as basic unit. Thus establishments which in the production index
contribute to one industry may contribute to quite another one in
statistics on investment or capacity, since the company including all its
establishments is placed in the industry of "principal activity". Furthermore, shifts of "principal activity" sometimes cause companies to be
reclassified; and additional interindustry shifts result from mergers. Still
further, it is to be suspected that the production index may for some
industries be biased by its reliance on counts of physical quantities
passing prescribed check-points, which may fail to register quality
increases related to an increase in the degree of fabrication.[12] My main

---

the McGraw-Hill index of actual capacity as to which subperiods show rapid and which
show slow expansion; and (b) the peaks chosen in the first place by visual inspection as
"unsubmerged" pass muster on closer scrutiny. Almost without exception they represent
either a coincidence of seasonal and cyclical peaks or a situation where a strike just
impending or just completed created an intensification of demand. Besides, the unsubmerged peaks generally are confirmed as such either by records of unusually long working
hours, or by spreading out of a seasonal peak over more months than usual, or both.

Several industries, though, show serious disagreements between the McGraw-Hill index
and the course of "unsubmerged peaks", as to the overall growth-rate over the two
decades. I construe these differences as arising from differences in industrial classification,
and deal with them econometrically by using "trend" terms as rectifiers.

To estimate capacity as of date 1968.0, I locate the two unsubmerged peaks for the
industry that are closest to that date (one before, one after). The corresponding 3-month
moving averages (taken with the industry's 1967 level as unity) are multiplied by the
industry's 1967 level of value-added; and the figure for date 1968.0 is obtained by log-linear
inter-polation.

[12]The case of the primary iron-and-steel industry is particularly puzzling. If we take at face
value the official statistics, we must say that over the twenty-year period 1955–1974 this
industry invested heavily, reduced its man-hour labor input very slightly, and ran a
peak-to-peak output trend (whether measured by the FRB index or by such quantity terms
as tons of steel ingots) that was virtually level. Admitting that the US steel industry is no
paragon of efficiency, it is hard to believe that with so much investment, and with
introduction of various improvements in technology, it can scarcely have stagnated in its
output per man hour to this extent. The McGraw-Hill capacity index, though showing some

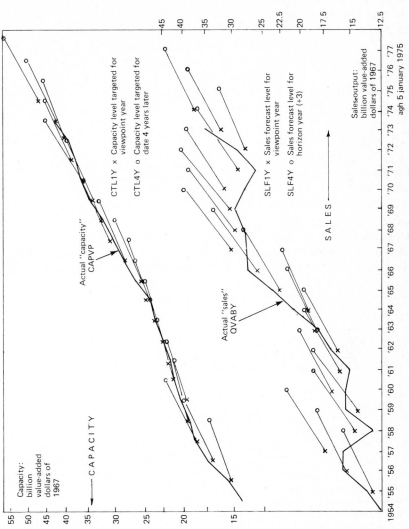

Chart MF-1. *Ex post* and *ex ante* levels of capacity and "sales = output", 1954–1977
(Industry 35: Machinery except electrical).

reliance for curing these defects is the introduction of trend terms, justified by the presumption that the relative drifts of "capacity" and "production" will be fairly smooth through time.[13]The trend variables have in addition the function of safeguarding the analysis against making causal attributions which rest on the mere fact that, for both sales and capacity, later-is-bigger.

4. Some characteristics of the data

By way of a halfway-house between mere description and econometric analysis, I offer in chart MF-1 a graphical view of the data in table MF-1, from which some analytically-useful impressions emerge. As the description in the following few pages shows, the most important of these may be listed as follows:

Sales

(a) We must allow for a marked tendency of sales-forecasts to run high relative to actual sales—which however I see as a matter of "strategic assumptions" rather than of "biased error".

(b) It would seem that the latest year's experience supplants rather than supplements previous experience in the formulation of sales forecasts, to such a degree as to move medium-term forecasts proportionally with short-term forecasts.

(c) Extending the inferences from point (b), it seems that we are in a position to make meaningful estimates of sales forecasts by log-linear interpolation for the two years between the viewpoint-year and the horizon year starting three years later.

(d) Cumulative effects of experience on the gradient of sales forecasts can perhaps be inferred; but this point is peripheral to the present paper.

---

years of zero growth, indicates a two decade annual growth rate of some 2.3% per annum, low but appreciable. If pressed, I would rather believe the McGraw-Hill capacity index than the production index in this case—inferring that the FRB index has somehow overlooked increases in the degree of fabrication. Incidentally, deflated sales or shipments would agree with the FRB-index picture of stagnation—presumably because prices used to construct the deflators also underrate quality changes.

[13]My trend formula is cubic. The reason is that in most industries we can detect an early period of rapid capacity-expansion, relative stagnation in the late 1950's and early 1960's, and then renewed rapid expansion. A trend capable of showing an inflection seems to be called for.

Capacity

(e) Although revision of capacity targets is much milder than that of sales forecasts, parallel treatment appears to be justified.

The exaggeration of sales-forecasts (point (a)) is clear to the naked eye in the chart. In the lower half of Chart MF-1, devoted to sales forecasts, the heavy line shows actual (*ex post*) "sales", measured by the 1967-value-added-dollar series based on the FRB production index. The thin lines trace sales-forecasts. They are drawn to show how the actual curve would have continued had the announced forecasts been precisely correct. The x-point at the left-hand end of each thin line represents the forecast-level for the viewpoint year (which could be linked back to the actual level of the base year). The circle at the right-hand end represents the forecast level for the horizon year starting three years after viewpoint. The gradient of the thin line represents the rate of increase (variable SFRIN in table MF-1) forecast for the period between the viewpoint and horizon years. Not only do the circled points fall above the actuals (except for forecasts framed at viewpoints 1961.0–1965.0), but the gradients are very high relative to experienced rates of expansion. On a peak-to-peak basis (17 years from 1956.5 to 1973.5), actual sales expanded at an annual rate of 4.75%. Not one of the 20 entries in column SFRIN of table MF-1 is lower than this *ex post* expansion-rate; and the mean level of variable SFRIN shows expected expansion at an annual rate of 7.3%.

My interpretation of this discrepancy is not an absurd degree of optimism on the part of the people who forecast for manufacturing firms, but rather the appropriateness of erring on the high rather than the low side. (i) The sales forecasts "adopted" in the framing of capital budgets cannot be concealed from the company's sales managers; and it might be a source of serious loss to put them too low to keep the salesmen on their mettle. And (ii) we must suppose that most companies are wary of getting into a position where for lack of sufficient capacity for a given product line they must offer customers discouragingly slow deliveries. It seems likely that costs in permanent loss of market-share from such episodes are more formidable than the costs of estimating high and thus providing needed capacity expansion a year or two ahead of actual need.

The indications of strong reliance on the most recent experience in revision of sales forecasts (point (b)) are again conspicuous in the chart. If we look at the thin lines, it is striking that from viewpoint to viewpoint these lines move bodily up or down the chart, with few sharp changes of gradient between adjacent viewpoints. If new experience were always treated as an interesting addition to the previous stock of information, without restructuring of the sales image, we would expect to find a degree of stability in levels forecast for horizon years 2 to 3 years into the future. We should then see numerous intersections of the successive thin lines—which we might think of as pivoting on a point (say) three years ahead of the new viewpoint and four years ahead of the old. But only one such intersection appears for the machinery industry, and the picture for the other industries studied is similar. In terms of the descriptive statistics at the bottom of table MF-1, it will be seen that the average change (without regard to sign) for the gradient coefficient is only 1.2% of the mean level of the coefficient, as against an average change in the forecast level amounting to 9.2% for the viewpoint year and to a remarkably-similar 10.0% for the horizon year four years ahead.[14]

The relative stability of the gradients of the thin lines from viewpoint to viewpoint (in contrast with the instability of levels) points the way to filling in by log-linear interpolation the missing sales-level forecasts for the first and second years after the viewpoint year. Remember that what we want the interpolated values for in the analysis is to make comparisons between estimates framed at different viewpoints for the same horizon date. What difference will it make to these comparisons whether the "true" curves which correspond to my semi-log straight lines are concave upward or concave downward? Looking at the chart, it will be plain that if the sign of the concavities is positively correlated as between adjacent viewpoints or the degree of concavity is slight, the ratios between successive estimates for the same horizon (measured by vertical distances between curves on the chart) will be essentially the same whether we use the "true" curves or my linear interpolations. Only if the concavity is both well marked and randomly distributed (or negatively correlated) as between successive viewpoints will the use of the linear interpolations distort this relationship. It strikes me as intuitively implausible that the concavity should be marked and also that what concavity exists should not be positively correlated between adjacent viewpoints. Hence I argue that the linear interpolation is appropriate. This argument can be reinforced by considering communication between survey-takers and respondents. If the respondents are aware of a tendency to make non-linear forecasts of sales and capacity between

[14]On the hypothesis that the latest year's experience ordinarily supplements rather than supplants previous information relevant to sales, we should expect the change from viewpoint to viewpoint to be smaller for the longer horizons.

It might well be more meaningful to compare the forecasts at the new viewpoint with forecasts at the previous viewpoint for identical horizon dates, as I do in the regression analysis below. But this comparison depends on interpolation to obtain forecast levels for the first and second years after the viewpoint year, which is a move ahead of the present stage of the argument.

viewpoint and horizon year, will they not be so interested in this aspect of the forecasting of their reference groups that the survey takers will find it rewarding to ask questions making room for the concavity?

Traces of cumulative influence of experience on sales forecasts (point (d)) do seem to appear in chart MF-1. As a broad generalization, we may see that after a few years of sustained expansion the gradients of the thin sales-forecast lines grow steeper, whereas after a few years of stagnation they grow flatter. This comment is intended to safeguard against exaggeration of the predomince of the latest experience. But closer scrutiny will show enough exceptions to make this generalization useless without actual econometric scrutiny; and since the explanation of sales-forecasts is not being dealt with in this paper, I do not pursue the point.

The behavior of the capacity-target data (pictured in the upper half of chart MF-1 with the same conventions that I have used for sales forecasts) differs from that of the sales forecasts primarily in its much smaller amplitude of movement. The x-points at the left-hand end of the thin lines uniformly lie close to the curve of actual capacity, indicating that the 1-year targets come rather close to realization. This finding of course represents the fact that many of the projects whose completion will expand capacity during the viewpoint year were already started or covered by firm contracts by the viewpoint date, whereas the list of projects on which expenditure in the viewpoint year is uncertain will consist largely of projects which in any case will not be complete enough to expand capacity till after the end of the viewpoint year. But even though the revisions in capacity targets for the first year are small, they are still large enough to abate the degree to which capacity-target revision alters the gradients of the thin lines between adjacent viewpoints. Although intersections of the thin lines are not so rare for capacity targets as for sales forecasts, it is still true that most of the time the capacity-target lines shift bodily up or down the chart, with great stability of gradient over short periods. The case for using log-linear interpolation to fill in the missing targets for horizon dates two and three years after the viewpoint is thus just as good as for sales-forecast interpolation. The apparent cumulative effect of successive years of rapid or slow expansion of actual sales seems to be much the same (with reduced amplitude) as for sales forecasts.

5. Underlying logic of the econometric analysis

The relationship of sales forecasts to capacity targets is to be seen as one equation in a recursive realization/planning/forecasting model of the type that we owe to Franco Modigliani. In such a recursive model, actual capital expenditure is seen as the "realization" of antecedent investment plans, with over-realization or under-realization according as surprises about the variables underlying the plan are agreeable or disagreeable. The investment plan is seen as a design for acquiring capital goods between viewpoint date and horizon date, so as to fulfill capacity targets set for the horizon date in the most advantageous way, all within a complex framework that takes account of financing costs and of the prospective relative prices of capital goods, cooperating inputs (above all labor), and products. Capacity targeting is seen as aimed to gauge the capacity stock that will enable the investing company to fill the orders which (as estimated by its sales forecasts) its salesmen will be able to bring home. The sales forecast, in turn, is seen as generated out of the company's experience and observation.

It will be seen that this schema diverges substantially from the format typical of investment-studies based on *ex post* data. It diverges also from the Modigliani schema from which it is derived in that it splits Modigliani's planning stage into two sub-stages—one devoted to capital expenditure, the other to capacity. Furthermore, it implies that the logic of stock adjustment is to be applied to capacity rather than to a stock variable regarded as a physical quantum of capital. This shift of emphasis is unavoidable if we wish to use the McGraw-Hill data effectively, in view of the pivotal position of capacity as an intervening variable between sales and investment. The emphasis on capacity enables us to bypass major difficulties in the measurement of the putative physical quantum of capital—difficulties that grow out of the incomparability of "vintages" of capital goods stressed by Solow and Phelps.[15] I would emphasize the fact that we lack convincing evidence of the ability of business men to organize their thinking in terms of a quantum of capital. If a survey like McGraw-Hill's tried to get respondents to estimate *ex post* changes in their physical stock of capital, the result might well be a mishmash of historical cost and capacity data. On the other hand, despite

---

[15]Whereas for many periods we can take refuge in the supposition that changes between "vintages" take place gradually, the period under study is one where this supposition seems unacceptable. For a large part of the first-line equipment of the late 1950's and early 1960's must have been items produced during the war years 1942–1945 and 1950–1953. Because of the wartime allocation system, projects of high long-term yield were barred during the wars unless they promised a quick acceleration in the flow of critical materials, whereas projects of low long-term productivity may have been pushed through because they did promise such an acceleration. The normal presumption that marginal investment dollars represented a reasonably uniform "marginal productivity of capital" (which is fundamental to the logic of capital-stock estimation by the standard perpetual-inventory methods) must therefore be rejected for this period.

all the uneasiness that the economic theorist feels about capacity as an economic quantity, field experience shows that the concept is in regular use and is viewed as indispensable in capital budgeting. Besides, as Solow and Phelps point out, capacity is a framework within which new and old capital goods can be expressed in common units; and the question of capital-labor substitution in the "putty" stage of capital formation lends itself to formulation in terms of the capital intensity of increments of capacity.

Taking the capacity-target/sales-forecast relationship at its simplest, we could imagine writing it as:

$$_vC_h = C[_vS_h] \triangleq {}^0c + {}^1c(_vS_h) \tag{i}$$

where C measures target-capacity, S measures forecast-sales, v is a viewpoint-date, and h is a horizon-date. The symbol $\triangleq$ denotes "equals-for-example". To obviate scaling problems, we may think of this as an equation in logarithms, so that coefficient ${}^1c$ becomes an elasticity-coefficient. If we imagine fitting this equation to data-sets each of which is limited to a stated viewpoint-to-horizon interval, we must take into account that each year's increment of capacity must realize upon complementaries between installations of that year and of earlier years. Hence we should expect the response elasticity of capacity on sales forecasts to be smaller when the horizon is so close that the effect of previous installations is likely to predominate.

It must be recognized, besides, that the accessibility-range for future capacity will be much influenced by viewpoint-date capacity. At the lower end of the range, we must bear in mind that the capacity represented by now-existent capital goods will almost all be still available a year hence, and not much will disappear even in four years. Furthermore, any capacity-reducing gaps that may appear among these pre-existing capital goods are likely to be of the sort that can be filled by replacing a few components. Hence we should not be surprised by the fact that in the entire array of 1955–1974 capacity-change ratios for 14 industries, there is not a single capacity decrease among the reported targets. Looking in the other direction, a stated absolute level of capacity must be much easier to reach from a starting point fairly close to the target than from one which is far below. We should expect enlargement of capacity increments within a stated time span to be subject to increasing costs. Hence we are likely to find that viewpoint-date capacity enters as an argument in the equation, and may prefer the form:

$$_vC_h = C[_vS_h, _vC_v] \triangleq {}^0c + {}^1c(_vS_h) + {}^2c(_vC_v). \tag{ii}$$

For very short horizons, it would not be surprising to find the initial-capacity variable dominating the sales-forecast variable; presumably the influence of initial capacity will be attenuated for longer horizons.

Because of data considerations mentioned above, we should not state the relationship in a form that is too rigid to make sense of the data even if there is a coverage-drift between our indexes of "sales" and of "capacity". Hence we will do well to generalize the relationship slightly by introducing a trend term. We might write:

$$_vC_h = C[_vS_h, _vC_v, v] \triangleq {}^0c + {}^1c(_vS_h) + {}^2c(_vC_v) + {}^3c(v). \tag{iii}$$

Without going outside the "accelerator" framework where only sales-variables purport to be explanatory, we can if we wish complicate the relationship by introducing lagged terms. Going outside this framework, we can if we wish introduce into the capacity-target function some variables that measure the difficulty of financing investment, or the price relationships likely to affect incentives to vary the capital intensity of increments of capacity, or to carry more or less reserve capacity.[16] Experimentation with a number of variants, however, has persuaded me that the simple framework sketched in this section of the paper is more satisfactory than more complex formulations.[17]

The equations so far suggested imply that for each length of the viewpoint-to-horizon span we will carry out a separate analysis. But to work in this way would reduce the benefit of a data book that is full of information about "multiple futures" from each viewpoint-date. Hence we will want to pool the observations within each industry over the different viewpoint-to-horizon spans.[18] This is readily done by introducing dummy variables to tell the computer which of the four possible spans is expressed by a given observation. It would be possible to use the

[16]A "pure-accelerator" model of capacity targeting would mean that cost-of-capital and price variables would affect the incremental quantity of capital and the capital intensity of the capacity increment without affecting the size of the capacity increment itself. It is certainly conceivable that if financing costs or capital-goods prices are high, companies may decide to make do with a smaller capacity increment. In this case, any variable capable of affecting investment incentives may enter the capacity-target function. But my provisional impression is that financial and price variables have only a small effect on capacity targets.

[17]As a control operation, I have run all my regressions with an extra variant which includes as an additional "explanatory" variable the sum of capacity targets of all 14 industries. Since finance, capital-goods prices, etc. should influence all the industries in the same direction, this variable should be useful as a proxy for such additional influences on capacity targets. In some early regression-runs, this proxy showed impressive T-values; but as my work converged upon the "standard equations" reported in the next section of this paper, these T-values became non-significant. This outcome is the evidential basis of the impression cited in the previous footnote.

[18]This pooling operation was suggested by John Taylor.

dummies simply as additional separate variables, with the effect of getting different intercepts for the different spans. But it is more logical to use them to modulate the sales-forecast and initial-capacity variables, giving expression to the presumption that the response of capacity targets to sales forecasts will be smaller as there is less time to turn around between the revision viewpoint and the horizon, while the importance of initial capacity will rise.

After considerable experimentation (which consisted chiefly of trying and rejecting more complex equations) I arrived at the "standard-equation" format of the equations reported in table MF2. The presence of no fewer than twelve "magnitudes" in the stub of table MF2 might seem to belie my claim of extreme simplicity. But a closer look will show that in fact only five substantive variables enter the equation: the dependent capacity-level variable with symbol LCL; the sales-forecast level variable with symbol LSL; the initial-capacity term with symbol LCA67; the date of the horizon year with symbol AD; and the length of the viewpoint-to-horizon span which is taken care of by the dummies. The additional "magnitudes" (aside from the intercept) arise from multiplying variables LSL and LCA67 by the dummies that register the viewpoint-to-horizon span, and from using the second and third moments of the date around its midpoint (AD2 and AD3).

In table MF-2, each industry has a column, and the "magnitudes" just discussed are represented by rows—in the first section of the table for parameters, in the second for the T-values of these parameters. Some summary statistics for the standard equation and for a non-explanatory "baseline equation" make up the third section of the table.

6. Analysis of econometric findings

The results reported for the 14 branches of manufacturing in table MF-2 confirm strikingly my hypothesis that there exists a coherent image structure within which the capacity-targets for the various viewpoint/horizon combinations are strongly and positively linked to corresponding sales forecasts. This relationship is clearly there, together with the predicted downward gradient of the capacity-on-sales respon-siveness as we shorten the viewpoint-to-horizon span while holding the horizon date constant. In terms of the logic of the model, the initial-capacity terms and trend terms are present only to clarify the role of the sales forecast, not for their own sake. Nevertheless the regressions for the initial-capacity terms conform to the expectation that the relationship will be positive—and more so for the shorter viewpoint-to-horizon spans than for the longer.

TABLE MF-2
USA: 14 Manufacturing industries

Parameters and statistics of equations to explain capacity-target levels as function of sales-forecast levels, viewpoint-date capacity, available adjustment interval and cubic trend, for all four horizons estimated at viewpoints 1955.0–1974.0. dependent variable: LCL = natural log of capacity target. Underlying quantity unit: billion value-added dollars of 1967. For industry code and variable-designations, see footnotes.

Magnitude[b]	331	333	35	36	371	372	3438	32	28	26	30	29	20	22
							Industry[a]							
i. Parameters of standard equation														
Sales-forecast terms														
LSL	+0.315	+0.496	+0.269	+0.302	+0.341	+0.187	+0.277	+0.367	+0.414	+0.569	+0.193	+0.283	-0.147	+0.240
D3LSL	-0.029	-0.001	-0.027	-0.029	-0.031	-0.007	-0.043	-0.000	-0.018	-0.093	+0.011	-0.059	+0.022	-0.038
D2LSL	-0.101	-0.038	-0.070	-0.063	-0.088	-0.020	-0.093	-0.025	-0.020	-0.280	+0.015	-0.119	+0.048	-0.076
D1LSL	-0.205	-0.078	-0.133	-0.100	-0.161	-0.034	-0.145	-0.091	-0.010	-0.463	+0.016	-0.174	+0.079	-0.117
Initial-capacity terms														
LCA67	+0.257	+2.143	+0.606	+1.394	+0.838	+0.217	+1.202	+0.830	+1.053	+0.630	+1.531	+0.498	+1.579	+0.432
D3LCA	+0.023	-0.008	+0.018	+0.016	+0.025	-0.003	+0.035	-0.011	-0.008	+0.093	-0.028	+0.050	-0.039	+0.026
D2LCA	+0.086	+0.021	+0.051	+0.036	+0.072	-0.001	+0.075	+0.005	-0.001	+0.275	-0.049	+0.099	-0.083	+0.052
D1LCA	+0.179	+0.048	+0.100	+0.057	+0.133	+0.002	+0.115	+0.059	-0.022	+0.445	-0.067	+0.141	-0.130	+0.077
Trend terms (note floating decimal: for AD, -1; for AD2, -3; for AD3, -4):														
AS	+0.141	-0.649	+0.063	-0.313	-0.086	+0.447	-0.225	-0.001	-0.357	-0.077	-0.393	+0.068	-0.172	+0.184
AD2	-0.427	+0.457	+0.621	+0.289	+0.182	+0.232	-0.059	+0.414	+0.262	+0.234	-0.180	+0.881	-0.514	+0.894
AD3	-0.285	-0.596	+0.638	-1.390	+0.663	-0.355	-0.062	-0.420	-0.089	-0.564	-0.120	+0.001	-0.254	-0.010
Intercept	+1.252	-3.061	+0.560	-1.938	-0.358	+1.598	-1.333	-0.308	-1.205	-0.350	-1.148	+0.435	-1.222	+0.786
ii. T-values of above parameters														
Sales-forecast terms														
LSL	+5.37	+8.03	+8.42	+4.53	+5.53	+7.40	+4.97	+5.24	+5.37	+5.47	+1.51	+2.32	-1.70	+3.69
D3LSL	-0.36	+0.01	-0.61	-0.36	-0.44	-0.25	-0.59	-0.01	-0.22	-0.59	+0.19	-0.53	+0.42	-0.47
D2LSL	-1.23	-0.49	-1.57	-0.78	-1.20	-0.65	-1.20	-0.26	-0.25	-1.59	+0.25	-1.07	+0.89	-0.89
D1LSL	-2.48	-1.01	-2.89	-1.23	-2.21	-1.07	-1.78	-0.87	-0.13	-2.44	+0.28	-1.57	+1.42	-1.27
Initial-capacity terms														
LCA67	+1.97	+10.94	+7.43	+12.09	+4.28	+2.26	+5.05	+5.49	+5.34	+2.50	+2.86	+2.14	+4.30	+1.93
D3LCA	+0.28	-0.11	+0.40	+0.20	+0.35	-0.01	+0.46	+0.11	+0.09	+0.55	-0.47	+0.46	-0.71	+0.32
D2LCA	+1.05	+0.28	+1.13	+0.45	+1.02	-0.04	+0.95	+0.04	-0.01	+1.51	-0.83	+0.91	-1.47	+0.60
D1LCA	+2.19	+0.66	+2.20	+0.72	+1.90	+0.06	+1.40	+0.55	-0.28	+2.31	+2.31	-1.31	-2.26	+0.85

Magnitude[b]	Industry[a]													
	331	333	35	36	371	372	3438	32	28	26	30	29	20	22
Trend terms														
AD	+5.32	−8.07	+1.71	−4.35	−1.25	+7.98	−1.90	−0.03	−3.05	−0.66	−2.06	+1.22	−1.05	+2.15
AD2	−4.12	+4.10	+8.83	+1.65	+1.35	+2.60	−0.55	+3.68	+1.76	+2.08	−0.62	+4.56	−1.43	+2.52
AD3	−1.36	−2.42	+3.55	−4.48	+2.14	−1.59	−0.26	−2.38	−0.41	−2.27	+0.37	+0.03	−1.11	−0.04
Intercept	+4.25	−7.55	+2.37	−5.49	−0.61	+7.74	−1.84	−1.09	−2.34	−0.71	−1.40	+1.16	+1.11	+1.96
Mean values of variables														
LCL (dependent)	2.72	2.11	3.34	3.26	2.85	2.55	3.25	2.20	3.15	2.28	1.98	1.76	3.26	2.17
LSL	2.63	1.86	3.19	3.04	2.66	2.40	3.16	2.17	3.00	2.24	1.77	1.66	3.28	2.08
LCA67	2.64	1.98	3.21	3.10	2.77	2.44	3.12	2.08	2.99	2.17	1.85	1.70	3.14	2.07
Statistics of standard equation														
Durbin-Watson[c]	1.89	2.40	1.77	1.05	2.57	2.16	2.11	2.37	1.29	2.95	1.22	1.64	1.75	2.47
R-squared, adjusted	0.9715	0.9835	0.9970	0.9931	0.9764	0.9960	0.9937	0.9915	0.9963	0.9893	0.9864	0.9790	0.9958	0.9934
Statistics of base-line equation[d]														
R-squared, adjusted	0.9539	0.9545	0.9920	0.9905	0.9640	0.9913	0.9910	0.9866	0.9931	0.9824	0.9869	0.9783	0.9957	0.9917
"Multiple partial" R-squared for sales-forecast variables[f]	0.382	0.637	0.625	0.274	0.344	0.540	0.300	0.366	0.464	0.392	[e]	0.032	0.023	0.205

iii. *Statistics of standard and base-line equations*

[a] Industry codes are standard SIC numbers so far as applicable, with adaptations where 2-digit industries must be combined or split:

331: Iron and steel subtotal within industry 33: sum of SIC numbers 331, 332, 3391.

333: Non-ferrous component of primary metals; besides SIC 333 includes minor components.

35: Machinery, except electrical: identical with SIC 35.

36: Electrical equipment: identical with SIC 36.

371: Motor vehicles and parts: identical with SIC 371.

"372": Other transport equipment (chiefly aerospace); SIC 37 less SIC 371.

"3438": Fabricated metal products plus instruments: sum of SIC 34 and SIC 38.

32: Stone, clay and glass products: identical with SIC 32.

28: Chemicals and products: identical with SIC 28.

26: Paper and products: identical with SIC 26.

30: Rubber and plastics: identical with SIC 30.

29: Petroleum products (almost entirely refining); identical with SIC 29.

20: Food and beverages: identical with SIC 20.

22: Textile mill products: identical with SIC22.

The sequence in which these industries are listed, based on FTC/SEC practice early in the period of observation, follows that used in most survey-reports by McGraw-Hill and the Conference Board. Note that McGraw-Hill does not publish data for several industry groups (apparel, publishing and printing, furnitures, lumber products, ordnance ...) and these are not covered in my study. The 14 industries listed above, however, account for 78% of manufacturing value-added as of 1967.

bVariable-codes are as follows:

LCL: natural log of capacity-target valued in billion value-added dollars of 1967.

LSL: natural log of sales-forecast valued in the same units.

LCA67: natural log of capacity-level at viewpoint date.

For each industry, there are 80 observations, representing respectively 4-year, 3-year, 2-year and 1-year horizons (for sales 3.5-year, 2.5-year, 1.5-year and 0.5-year horizons if we date the year's sales-flow at midyear) for LCL and for LSL. Dummies are used of which D1 equals unity when the horizon for capacity is 1 year, D2 equals unity when the horizon for capacity is 2 years, D3 equals unity when the horizon for capacity is 3 years; except as stated each dummy has value zero. The dummy-string '000' denotes that the horizon is 4 years.

D3LSL denotes LSL multiplied by dummy D3.

D2LSL denotes LSL multiplied by dummy D2.

D1LSL denotes LSL multiplied by dummy D1.

Similarly:

D3LCA denotes CAP67 multiplied by dummy D3.

D2LCA denotes CAP67 multiplied by dummy D2.

D1LCA denotes CAP67 multiplied by dummy D1.

AD denotes "adjusted date"—that is, date minus midpoint of 1964.500.

AD2 is square of AD.

AD3 is cube of AD.

cDurbin-Watson statistic is biased in the direction of its ideal value of 2.00 by the presence in each industry's data-series of three large arbitrary jumps (from 1974-viewpoint down to 1955-viewpoint levels) where strings of observations for different horizon lengths are placed end to end.

dBaseline-equation is non-explanatory relation using cubic trend and initial capacity terms, but excluding the sales-forecast terms which appear in the standard equation.

eAdjusted R-squared for baseline equation exceeds that for standard equation.

f"Multiple partial" is the proportion of the variance left "unexplained" by the baseline equation which is cleared up by adding sales-forecast variables to produce the standard equation—representing variance "explained" by the R-squared adjusted for degrees of freedom.

Examining the parameters in section i of the table, we find that with the sole exception of industry 20 (manufactured food and beverages) all industries show a positive response coefficient for capacity target in relation to sales-forecasts. Of these 13 positive parameters, all with the exception of industry 30 (rubber and plastic products) show T-values in excess of 2.00; with the exception of industry 29 (petroleum refining etc.), with its T-value of 2.32, all the remaining T-values exceed 3.69.[19]

The regression coefficients for the three additional sales-forecast terms are in the nature of adjustment coefficients to correct the coefficient in line LSL—which stands for what happens when the viewpoint-to-horizon span is four years—for the effect of dealing in shorter spans. Except in industries 20 and 30 (those which failed to yield significant coefficients for LSL) all of these coefficients have the predicted negative sign, and for all twelve industries they march as predicted from smaller to larger negative numbers as we move down the columns toward shorter viewpoint-to-horizon spans. Although the effect is not strong enough to yield significant T-values for the coefficients representing the 3-year and 2-year viewpoint-to-horizon spans, four of the T-values for the 1-year span exceed -2.0, and an additional 6 T-values exceed -1.0.[20]

The magnitudes of the sales-forecast coefficients cluster quite closely; for variable LSL, the partial regression coefficients for the 12 industries where they are significantly positive range only from 0.187 to 0.496, with an inter-quartile range from 0.240 to 0.414. The adjustment coefficients for the length of viewpoint-to-horizon span remove rather substantial proportions of the LSL coefficient, indicating that when the span is only 1 year the impact of the sales forecast is quite small. It is somewhat

---

[19]Observe that the effect of using the sales-forecast variable to "explain" capacity targets is not fully expressed by these T-values, since the terms D3LSL, D2LSL and D1LSL each carry part of the same information as LSL, modulated by the relevant dummies. To gauge the effect of the set of four sales-forecast variables as a whole, see the "multiple-partial R-squared" entries in the final line of table MF-2. These represent the proportion by which the "unexplained" variance—$1-(R$-squared adjusted)—is reduced in going from the baseline to the standard equation. The fact that the non-explanatory baseline equation yields an adjusted R-squared of 0.9957 for the food industry may explain my negative explanatory results: it may not be worth the while of planners in that industry to bother with medium-term sales forecasts.

[20]The stability of all these T-values might be expected to be impaired by multicollinearity. It will be noted that the terms D3LSL, D2LSL and D1LSL all have in common the fact that somewhat correlated values of LSL enter them by multiplication with the relevant dummy. Besides, the variable pairs D3LSL/D3LCA, D2LSL/D2LCA and D1LSL/D1LCA all have dummies in common. In these circumstances, I would be happy to be able to show that the joint effect of these variables was helpful; that each one individually should fall into the predicted pattern in this way is an aggreeable surprise to me—and doubtless in some part accidental.

disconcerting, I find, that these coefficients are so small. The regression coefficient for LCL on LSL (since this is a log/log equation) has logically the dimensions of an elasticity coefficient and might be expected to lie closer to unity. On the other hand, we must allow for the fact that capacity targets do not flap so much in the psychological breeze as do sales forecasts, being more firmly anchored in gradually-evolving reality at the end nearest the viewpoint. Consulting the summary on "increments without regard to sign" at the foot of table MF-1, we find that for the machinery industry the absolute viewpoint-to-viewpoint changes in capacity-target levels were only about two-thirds as great as those in sales-forecast levels. If we allow for a scaling-down factor of about $\frac{1}{3}$ in moving from the sales variable to the capacity variable, the magnitude of the LCL/LSL regression coefficient is less disturbing.

A substantive interpretation of the gap between the LCL/LSL coefficients and unity can perhaps be found in the relation between the medium-term perspective implied by sales forecasts that look only three and a half years into the future, and the long-term-planning characteristics of large companies. Presumably such companies have long-term strategies for developing new product lines, entering new geographical areas, modernizing facilities and the like—all of which will entail expansion of capacity. Changes in medium-term prospects may well alter the timetable of actions in pursuance of such long-term strategies. But there must be many projects which are urgent either to get the full benefit of complementary installations already made (or contracted for), or else to keep the firm's technology up to date and provide a platform for later investment. The inclusion of such projects in capacity-expansion plans is bound to hold down the sensitivity of capacity targets to medium-term sales forecasts.

Turning to the partial regressions of capacity-targets on viewpoint-date capacity, we note that all the coefficients are positive, and the lowest T-values at 1.93 and 1.97 are just at the boundary of being significant at the 0.05 level. Half of these T-values exceed 5.0.[21] The magnitude of these coefficients has a disconcertingly large range, since ideally one would expect them to be of the order of unity. In addition to the coefficients in excess of 1.5 for the industries (20 and 30) where the expected sales-forecast relationship cannot be demonstrated, we find coefficients in excess of unity for industries 333 (non-ferrous metals), "3438" (fabricated metal products plus instruments), and 28 (chemicals). It will be noted that the high coefficients in line LCA67 appear in industry columns where the trend term in line AD is negative. Presumably the

---

[21]In the base-line equations, T-values for this partial regression run higher still.

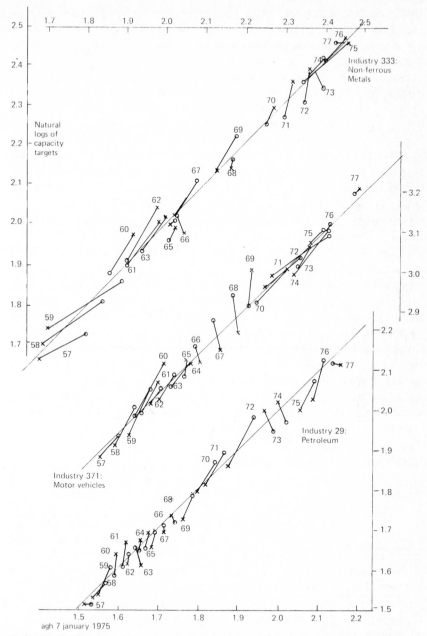

Chart MF-2. Highest and lowest capacity targets reported for each horizon date 1957.0–1977.0, as observed and as estimated from standard equation, selected industries (333, 371, 29). (Natural logs of quantities in billions of value-added dollars of 1967.)

cubic trend and the initial-capacity variable (both of which have some capability to sort out periods of acceleration and deceleration in the growth of capacity) have curious interactions.

As to the trend terms, since their function is in good part to provide flexibility for the oddities that result from drawing capacity and sales data from disparate sources, we start with no particular expectation except that there should be a mixture of positive and negative relative trends. It will be noted that T-values in excess of 2.0 appear for the squared or the cubed trend term (or for both) in 10 of the 12 industries where the LCL/LSL coefficient is significantly positive. Besides, comparison of the standard-equation results with results for an equation which has the same list of variables except for the omission of the higher trend-moments, shows not merely lower adjusted R-squared, but also almost without exception lower T-values for the sales-forecast variables when the linear trend is used.[22]

Readers familiar with investment studies will realize that such collections of regression results commonly represent a good deal of "fishing" for good-looking equations. In candor, I am obliged to warn the reader that my results for the machinery industry should perhaps be viewed with some skepticism, since I always tried out new equation-variants on this industry—a procedure which would make it hard not to reach "successful" equations for machinery. But I should emphasize that I have not resorted to using different variable lists for different industries, and that my numerous trials of variant equations led me toward simpler and simpler rather than toward more and more complex forms. As Jorgenson points out, there is a degree of "safety in numbers" in studies that work with a dozen or so industries: it is not easy to manipulate equations in search of "good" results for one set of industries without obtaining "bad" results for others.

---

[22] As an *a priori* proposition, it would seem plausible that the best way to sort out the partial contributions of the sales-forecast variables would be to match them with a rigid linear trend variable. For may not the failure of actual capacity and of capacity targets to keep up with a linear trend during the Eisenhower/Kennedy stagnation give the sales-forecast variable a change to show its powers by fitting into the stagnation concavity?

Plausible as this argument seems, there is no blinking the fact that on the record the sales-forecast variables do still better at "explaining" residuals from a cubic trend than at "explaining" residuals from a linear trend. I see no reason therefore to reject the cubic trend.

7. Success in mapping alternative futures

For most of the industries analyzed, my regression analysis yields an interesting view of the contingent capacity-target/sales-forecast relationship not merely in a composite view, but likewise horizon date by horizon date. I base this assertion on a set of graphical tests which seem quite clearcut, applied to all 14 industries. Specimens of these graphs appear in chart MF-2.

My test operation begins by locating in the printout the series of "observed" and "estimated" capacity targets (logs of levels) from the standard equation for each of the 14 industries. Of the target estimates observed for each horizon-year, I graph the highest and lowest (using a cross for whichever one was of earlier viewpoint date and a circle for the other, to permit scanning the charts for possible asymmetrics between upward and downward revisions); the two points for each horizon are then linked by straight lines.

The industries seem to fall into three well-defined groups. As may be seen from the "multiple-partial" coefficients in table MF-2, three industries (food, rubber-and-plastics, petroleum) gain no explanatory power by including sales forecasts along with non-explanatory terms. For these industries, we get graphs like the one for petroleum at the foot of chart MF-2. Here the standard equation of course yields the same "estimated" data as would a non-explanatory equation where the variables on the right-hand side are only initial-capacity terms and trend terms. Though the points graphed all lie reasonably close to the 45-degree diagonal which is the locus of "observed = estimation", the lack of a significant sales-forecast term has the effect of randomizing the relation to the diagonal of the points referring to each horizon year. Hence we find negative slopes as often as positive in the lines that link cross points to corresponding circle points.

Two industries (steel and motor vehicles, which incidentally are both near the bottom of the 14 industries in their ex-post growth-rates) show cross-to-circle lines which most of the time are roughly parallel to the diagonal. Such parallelism may be interpreted to say that the regression proceedure has been successful in sorting out for the horizon year in question a pair of extreme capacity-target/sales-forecast values which exhibit the same structure that the standard equation gives us as the average relation over the period of observation. But for these industries there are stretches of horizon years (for motor vehicles, in the middle section of chart MF-2, those from 1966 through 1969) where the relationship does not seem to be working. For these industries we may still see the standard equation as giving a meaningful composite picture of the influence of sales forecast on capacity target. But the standard equation does not seem to go so far beyond the call of duty as to yield corresponding relationships for all the specific horizon years with substantial divergence between high and low capacity targets.[24]

The remaining nine industries show graphs of reasonably steady relationships for specific horizon years, with only scattered exceptions for years of only moderate change. The data for non-ferrous metals at the top of chart MF-2 are typical. Here it would appear that the relationships indicated by the standard equation work at the level of fine detail indicated by the cross-to-circle lines of chart MF-2 as well as in the broad.

What is tested by this operation, as I read it, is the efficicacy of my use of dummy variables and trend terms to sort out capacity-target/sales-forecast combinations that are highly comparable from the standpoint of tracing "accelerator" influences of sales prospects on capacity. Since out of the twelve industries that yield significantly positive relationships, the detailed structure seems to stand very close interpretation in nine, I find myself rather well satisfied as to the appropriateness of my treatment.

8. Conclusions

Within the restricted subject matter of this paper, my finding is that the relation between sales forecasts and capacity targets conforms neatly to what we would predict from the hypothesis that *ex ante* data embody authentic and coherent plans along the lines of the adapted version of the Modigliani realization/planning/forecasting model. The magnitudes of the elasticities, and their gradient, is illuminating about the interplay of medium-term and long-term planning.

Looking at the work reported in this paper as a trial run for the application of the alternative-futures view to the whole expectational structure underlying the formulation and realization of investment plans, we are encouraged. The logic by which we are able to treat each viewpoint/horizon combination rather than merely each survey as a usable observation (with careful use of trend terms, and of dummies registering viewpoint-to-horizon spans, as filters for the relationships under study) seems to stand up under empirical application. Both the explanation of sales forecasts and the explanation of investment-expenditure planning and realization will entail use of variables of types

---

[24]Roughly speaking, a difference of 0.1 between the logs of the higher and lower estimates corresponds to a difference of 10% in capacity-targets, since we are using natural logs.

not involved in the more simple segment of the problem that I have been analyzing here—notably the development of an appropriate collection of expectations-proxies. But the methodological arguments presented in this paper, together with encouraging experience in preliminary rounds of equation-fitting at the other stages of the recursive model, give every reason for confidence that the whole recursive model is workable econometrically.

My main hope in presenting this paper is that I can persuade the profession to repeal the self-denying ordinance that bans use of actual *ex ante* data in investment studies and in large econometric models. Expectations proxies are useful supplements to actual *ex ante* data, but by themselves they do not offer prospects of a meaningful mapping of the field of alternative futures which theories of rational decision suggest should be at the root of investment decisions.

E. Conflict resolution and peace research

E.1.   Threat, trade and love

ANATOL RAPOPORT

Great thinkers have a way of compressing a whole universe of thought into a single sentence: You can't step into the same river twice (Heraclitus); *Cogito ergo sum* (Descartes); War is a continuation of politics by other means (Clausewitz); Those ignorant of history are condemned to repeat it (Santayana); The peasants voted against the war with their feet (Lenin); Some day they will give a war and nobody will come (Sandburg). Boulding's image of the three types of social interaction, the Deterrent System, the Exchange System, and the Integrative System (Threat, Trade, and Love) is another such admirable feat of compression, designed to summarize aspects of social reality that have a profound significance for the human condition.

Are all these aphorisms or evoked images "truths"? Not in the scientific sense. The terms are not "operationally" defined; the implicit predictions (if any) or the generalizations cannot be put to rigorous empirical tests under specified conditions. They are truths in another sense, though, beyond the scope of scientific cognition. They strike a note of recognition of something we have known all along. We cannot "prove" these "truths", because proof is either impossible or superfluous. Thus, Heraclitus's aphroism is a metaphorically disguised truism (everything changes): Clausewitz's, examined closely, is a biased characterization of war and politics (both war and politics are a lot of other things): Sandburg's is a pious hope. The "truth" of the images resides not in their depictions of reality with implicit predictive power expected of scientific generalizations but rather in their potential for fixating attention on what is of prime importance from the point of view of specific world outlooks.

So it is with Boulding's three modes of social interaction. They stand out as archetypes of relations of man to man, group to group, nation to nation. And what is more important than these relations in view of the menace that man's power over nature has become to man's existence?

I find myself writing "Man", "the menace to Man", "Man's power over nature", and so on—a very bad habit, perpetuating the illusion that there is such a thing as Man. I say this not in agreement with the medieval nominalists, who insisted that only individual man has "real existence", that Man is only a name given to men collectively, a word without a referent in the "real world". The nominalist position was naive. Why focus on the individual human being as a "real entity"? Why not insist that only the cells of the human body are "real", that a "human being" is only a name attached to a collection of such cells? And why stop with a cell? Why not reserve the status of "real entities" to atoms? Generally speaking, what is so basic about *objects* as "real entities" compared with their parts or collections of them? Is a page more real than a book, or is a book more real than a library? If, as it appears, the level of being that deserves a name is arbitrary, is not also the level of "reality"? If so, why not speak of Man as endowed with "real existence" apart from the human beings that compose mankind?

Yet the argument of the nominalists has some merit. Whereas an individual human being is a living system, Man is not. Even though Mankind is listed as one of the levels in the hierarchy of living systems, it does not deserve the designation: it lacks a crucial characteristic of a living system, the properties of self-organization and regulatory mechanisms that insure its continued existence as a system. Portions of mankind have these properties and these mechanisms and so deserve to be called systems. Whether mankind will one day acquire them depends on the predominant modes of interaction among its organized portions; whether these are dominated by threats, trade, or love.

One might ask: If portions of mankind interact in one of these three modes, do not these interactions make mankind a system? Do not even threat interactions contribute to the maintenance of the system by acting as inhibitions (deterrents) of destructive conflicts? Definitions are, in principle, arbitrary, but they should be tailored to the context of a discussion. The point of departure of this discussion was whether it makes sense to speak of "Man's power over nature", "Man's lack of control over himself", and the like. Implicitly, these phrases project the image of Man as an *actor*, at times conscious, at times merely reactive, but an actor nevertheless, to whom appetites, hopes, and fears can be ascribed. In that sense, I submit, Man does not exist, whereas individual human beings do. However, I part company with the nominalists when they insist that *only* individual human beings (rather than Man) have "real existence". "Real existence", in the sense that we usually attribute to human beings, that is, as actors, can be attributed also to collectives of human beings, such as institutions or states. The nominalists' criteria of "real existence", for example, the property of occupying a portion of space with clearly defined boundaries, that is the property of objects, was superficial.

To return to our theme. Imagine for the moment a Hobbsian world of individuals waging a Hobbsian war of all against all. According to Hobbes, this was the "natural state" of men. Further, since the natural state would inevitably lead to demise through mutual extermination, it could not last. Thus arose the legend of the origin of the State, according to which individual actors gave up their "autonomy" to a potentate in order to be protected against each other.

Conceivably the problem might have been solved in another way. Each individual could be armed, and the efficiency of armor or weapons, that is, the lengths of swords, thickness of shields, etc. could be carefully calibrated so that each would present exactly the same threat to each. The probability of "victory" in each binary encounter would thereby be exactly one half. Clearly, a series of such encounters under perfect "balance of power" reduces the chances of survival in geometric progression. Consequently, assuming individuals to be "rational" (which Hobbes apparently does), the war of all against all war would be stopped by "deterrence" or a "balance of power".

Ludicrous as this "solution" would appear in the context of a completely atomized Hobbsian world, it is the most prevalent, the most venerable, and the most seriously discussed model of an achievable peaceful world.

To be sure, in drawing the analogy with the Hobbsian model, I am doing the international threat system an injustice. The fact is that Hobbes's world never existed. Man was a social animal, identifying and cooperating with his own kind, long before he became man. On the other hand, the international threat system not only has a long history but continues to exist, and there is no foreseeable end to it. On closer examination it turns out that the international threat system is as much a product of imagination as the Hobbsian "state of nature". The difference is that the Hobbsian war of all against all was imagined only by Hobbes and perhaps by a few other philosophers of similar persuasion, whereas the international threat system pervades the imagination of the ruling circles of all great powers and most of their populations. Threats *are* real if they are perceived as such. The international threat system material- izes in hardware; it determines the allocation of resources. It inspires theories and treatises. It fills the content of courses in international relations. It dictates Ph. D. theses. It promotes bullies like Richelieu, Metternich, and Bismarck to the rank of statesmen, which is to say, sages. It ossifies the Orwellian absurdity "War is peace" as an axiom. But it has never worked in the way intended. Those that say it is working now might ponder the state of mind of the man who fell off the Empire State Building and remarked as he passed the tenth floor, "So far, I am doing fine".

Let us, nevertheless, for the sake of argument, assume that deterrence works (except when it doesn't). How does it work? Why, in the way described, we are told. In the simplest case of two super-powers, the military machine of one protects the society on which it feeds from the military machine of the other. Each machine is thus justified with reference to the other. Consider an analogy: a man, bending under the burden of a yoke with a bucket of stones on each end. Each bucket is necessary to balance the other. Without one of them, the yoke would be useless. Here is a thought: without *both* buckets, there would be no use for the yoke. So the question necessarily arises, *is* the yoke necessary? Yes, if the stones have to be hauled. The yoke is justified by a task that is *extraneous* to it. So the question hinges on whether the military machines (that keep the threat system going) perform a task *aside* from self-maintenance. In other words, what would be left undone if *both* military machines in our simplified model vanished? I can think of one such extraneous function, semi-facetiously suggested in the *Report from Iron Mountain*. An image of an enemy is indispensable for maintaining an organized society. I do not, of course, believe that this proposition is generally valid, although in specific instances there may be some evidence for it. However, in examining instances where the proposition is supported and those where it is not, we would have to go far afield. For example, we would have to inquire into what sort of societies depend on the image of an external enemy for internal cohesion, and we would have to face the question of whether such societies are worth preserving.

On the whole, we are forced to the conclusion that the justification of the threat system, hence its nourishment, is internal. It exists and flourishes, because it exists and flourishes. It provides employment to millions, profits and professional careers to thousands. It presents exciting challenges to ingenuity and imagination, not only through the scientific, logistic, and strategic problems generated by the death technology but also through problems generated by the widely recognized and sincerely accepted duty to keep the system "under control". For the tremendous sophistication of modern weapons systems is partly necessitated by the imperative that they should always remain in a state of readiness for instantaneous activation and also that they should never be activated. For their activation would mean that they failed to accomplish their purpose, that is, to deter.

The solution of problems associated with maintaining the threat system requires not only resources but also talent, and talent is accordingly mobilized. As I write, earnest and technically sophisticated discussions are going on between American and Soviet experts, collaborating in the task of keeping the threat system under control without compromising the reality of the threat that it presents. These are admittedly difficult problems, requiring the dedication of brilliant, creative minds.

Herman Kahn once described the nature of the problem in the following parable.

Assume there are two individuals who are going to fight a duel to death with blow torches. The duel is to be conducted in a warehouse filled with dynamite. One might conjecture that they would agree to leave the lights on. There is undoubtedly powerful motivation for them to do so. While both are agreed that only one is to survive, they would each like some chance of being that one; neither prefers an effective certainty of both being killed. Yet they might still disagree on how many lights? Where? How bright? Should the one with greater visual acuity handicap himself in other ways? And so on.[1]

The variability of the threat system manifests itself in the circumstance that questions of this sort completely eclipse other more important questions. First, is it indeed a "warehouse", in which the duel is to be fought? Or is it rather the basement of a crowded apartment building? And who stacked it full of dynamite and why? And what business have those two imbeciles fighting their idiotic duel in that basement? Why does not some one take them by the scruffs of their necks, bump their heads together and put them away somewhere where they won't be a menace?

Of course such questions are asked all the time, but there is no one to pay heed to them, no one who can do anything about this crazy set-up. So the observation that the threat system is a threat to Man is true enough, but Man is not in a position to get rid of the threat, because Man is not an actor. States *are* actors, and they perpetuate the threat system through historical inertia or through the dynamics of their internal organization or simply because states, conceived as sentient beings, have extremely limited mentalities, devoid of those faculties that one attributes to reasonable or sensitive human beings.

So far we have been examining threat systems composed of "equals". There are also social systems based on threat to insure compliance, for example, societies with slave or serf labor. Although the power in such societies is entirely vested in the elite, the elite itself often feels itself to be constantly under threat. Sparta was a classical example. The complete militarization of Spartan society has been, I think justifiably, attributed to the single-mindedness of its elite, determined to keep the helots in

[1]H. Kahn, *On Escalation: Metaphors and Scenarios* (Frederick A. Praeger, New York, 1965) 16.

subjugation. The constant presence of an internal enemy has a stultifying effect on societies based on threat. Like prisons, they remain static until the system disintegrates cataclysmically and completely.

In a deterrence system composed of "equals", the participants share only a "negative" common interest—that of avoiding actions disastrous to both (or all). In an exchange system, positive common interests come to the foreground. The underlying model is that of Adam Smith or Ricardo rather than that of Hobbes. In a deterrent system, the prospect of receiving "bads" (Boulding's felicitous term) is supposed to keep the system from demise. In an exchange system, coherence is insured by the exchange of "goods". As a result of the exchange, each party is richer than before, for the exchange depends on differential needs and on possession of surplus goods. Each party receives something that he needs or values more than what he gives in return. In a threat system (with equals) each party would prefer that the other were not there; supposedly, that is, for one can argue that the participants in a threat system also fulfill each other's (morbid) needs. In an exchange system, each party needs the other not merely as a hate object or some similar pathological reason, but as a source of satisfaction of "normal" needs. Therefore symbiotic relations are possible within an exchange system.

Classical economics rests solidly on the exchange model of human relations. As in the Hobbsian model, however, society appears atomized. To be sure, the "atoms" need no longer be single human individuals. They can be economic units of arbitrary size. However, the cooperative interdependence of the units is predicated strictly on the benefits that each economic unit receives in the exchanges. In most models of classical economics, each unit is assumed to act in a way as to maximize the benefits accruing to itself (and itself alone). Thus, some acts involve selection of exchange partners (competition). According to the classical economic theory, competition, as well as cooperation, contributes to the "general welfare" by the well-known mechanism of natural selection of efficient units, through stabilization of exchange rates, in short, through the adjustment mechanisms of supply and demand. The critiques and defenses of this model and of its off-shoots and variants are well known and, at any rate, fall outside the scope of this discussion. Of principal interest here, as in the case of the threat system, is the quality of inter-group relations dominated by the exchange system.

The exchange system governs most of the relations among autonomous actors in so-called civilized societies. The chief characteristic of these relations is their impersonal nature. *Who* you are matters little, if at all, in a well-run exchange system. What you want and what you offer in return defines every transaction. Money as a universal medium of exchange removes the necessity of examining each such transaction separately. In fact, even money has been largely supplanted by a vast system of bookkeeping far from the scene of the transactions, so that only records of these transactions need to be made. A rich man does not need to carry more than pocket change. He carries only pieces of paper or cardboard or plastic which identify him as plugged into the bookkeeping apparatus.

With such an identification, one moves through the "civilized" areas of the globe with perfect ease and assurance. One is at home everywhere. The world of airports, hotels, restaurants, and shops is striking in its polylingual uniformity. Armies of attendants stand ready to satisfy every need that can be satisfied in the exchange system. And in fact, the needs that *can* be so satisfied become dominant, *because* they can be satisfied. All these attendants are perfect strangers, whom one has never seen and will probably never see again. They feed you, clothe you, move you over the face of the earth, entertain you, give you first aid if you are hurt and prolonged medical care if you are sick, not because you are a friend or a relative or because they feel a personal obligation to you, but only because you are plugged into the bookkeeping apparatus. Being plugged in is a necessary and sufficient condition for being taken care of.

It is, in a way, a marvelous arrangement. It gives the appearance of an integrated world, where no one needs to be wary of strangers or stand in danger of perishing for lack of friends. But of course, these are only appearances. The benefits of the exchange system accrue only to those who have the wherewithal of exchange. Nevertheless, the exchange system is seen by many as a substantial advance over the threat system as a principle of interaction or organization. I, too, prefer a society based on a market and money economy with its necessarily concomitant "free institutions" and flexibility, to a society based on slave or serf labor, or on quasi-military discipline, that is, one based on institutionalized threats. And of course I would rather see a global exchange system than the present threat system, dominated by delusions of security through military might.

Still, it should be apparent that the exchange system represents no more than a half-way house on the road to integration of mankind. Getting stuck in it would be perhaps not as disastrous as getting stuck with the threat system, but would be most unfortunate nevertheless. For the crucial problems of our time are global, and nothing short of complete integration of mankind (so that Man can be an actor) will set the stage for the solutions of these problems. The exchange system does not provide the means for complete integration, if only because the large majority of the human race can be for a long time only on the receiving end of the flow of goods, resources, and services. They have next to nothing to give in return and so cannot be plugged into the bookkeeping complex. But they *must* be integrated into a living system called Man, or else Man cannot act, and if "he" cannot act, he cannot escape destruction either at his own hands or at the hands of Nature wreaking vengeance for the indignities to which she has been subjected.

It is very difficult to break through the mentality imposed by the exchange system. The system is widely associated with emancipation from the constraints of threat systems, and tightly linked to the notion of freedom. Indeed the term "Free World", coined during the Cold War as a rallying cry to mobilize loyalty to the United States and its allies, hypocritical as it is, is not wholly devoid of meaning. Anyone with wherewithal of exchange is more free in the "Free World" than any human being ever was throughout history, not only in the sense of choice of consumer goods and services and mobility, but also in the sense of being freed from personal obligations to kinfolk, mentor, lord, or vassal. They say alienation was the price paid for de-personalized social relations, but perhaps the escape from the web of fixed personal and status obligations was well worth the price. (We can form an opinion on this matter only on the basis of reading about the vanished world.)

The exchange system also carries a promise to attentuate the dangers of the international deterrence system. Enemies can be turned into customers. Finally, the exchange system provides a conceptual basis for a universal theory of value, linking ethics to economics. Money, with its unlovely connotations of venality, need not remain the universal concretization of value. Instead, the sterilized concept of "utility" can serve in this capacity.

It is instructive to examine the history of the utility concept in economics and decision theory. It first appears in a rather vague formulation as a presumed universal measure of value in Bentham's utilitarian calculus. Later it is introduced into economics in connection with a theory of commodity exchange. Mathematical analysis, however, revealed that the concept of utility is not really necessary for the theory, which can be formulated entirely in terms of so-called indifference curves, plots of utility-equivalent amounts of exchangeable commodities. It turns out that utility so defined can be determined only on an ordinal scale, invariant up to a positive monotone transformation and so of very limited usefulness for a mathematical theory. Finally, Von Neumann and Morgenstern[2] re-defined utility by introducing choices between risky alternatives and so pointed the way of determining utility

[2]J. Von Neumann and O. Morgenstern, *Theory of Games and Economics Behavior*, 2nd Ed. (Princeton University Press, Princeton, N.J., 1947).

on an interval scale, which is stronger than an ordinal scale (being invariant only up to a positive linear transformation). Interval scale utility is of considerable usefulness in a mathematical theory of economics and of rational decision.

Now here is an interesting point about utility measured on an interval scale. The unit and the zero point of each actor's scale must remain arbitrary, because the procedure for determining an actor's utility function on a set of commodities or situations does not permit the determination of either the unit or the zero point. This, in turn, implies that utilities of two or more actors cannot be compared. Neither can they be added. Consequently, the notion of a "welfare function" remains meaningless. For instance, it is not possible to say "By giving up one unit of utility, A makes it possible for B to gain 100 units; therefore it is socially desirable for A to give up a unit". Bentham's utilitarian calculus remains without a logically tenable basis.

Of course the concept of a "welfare function" is by no means dead, even in economics. And, of course, innumerable social arrangements, not to speak of interpersonal relations, explicitly or implicitly invoke inter-personal comparisons of utilities. Social life is impossible without some notion of social justice, and all notions of social justice pose the problem of comparing the losses of some to the concomitant gains of others. But a rigorous, operationally defined concept of utility precludes such comparisons. In order to make such comparisons, a "transferable" and, preferably "conservative" (in the sense of conservation of quantity) commodity must be promoted to the status of a universal concretization of value. Money is by far the most obvious candidate. (In fact, *any* commodity in this capacity would be money by definition.) But to translate all values into monetary terms is to trivialize the formidable problem of value or to side-step it rather than to face it soberly.

Thus, the exchange system and the impressive conceptual repertoire introduced by it into human affairs still does not solve the problem of turning Man into an actor.

There remains the integrative system. Of the three terms, "threat", trade", and "love", "trade" is the easiest to relate to observable referents and so to treat in the context of scientific discourse. Also, events involving trade can be treated without reference to psychological factors. (Whether it is advisable to leave these factors out of consideration is another matter.) Both "threat" and "love" are necessarily linked to psychology, and so discussions involving them must usually be carried beyond the realm of "hard" science. However, in the context of scientific discussion, attempts to operationalize intuitively-appreciated concepts are always in order.

Throughout the Cold War, attempts to bring "hard" analysis to bear on a theory of threat systems became commonplace (cf. the writings of Kahn[3], Schelling[4], Jervis[5]). This is not surprising, because tough-mindedness and "hard" analysis are conceptually compatible. In fact, the work of the above-mentioned authors relies on models based partly on the conceptual repertoire generated by a threat system and partly on one generated by an exchange system. All of this work was quite likely inspired by game-theoretic models of conflict, where calculations in utility terms of possible or probable consequences of decisions are at the center of attention. A "threat" in this scheme is conceived simply as a probabilistically determined loss of utility.

Love, understandably enough, plays no part in these approaches. Not only is this term tinged with connotations that do not lend themselves easily to operational definitions, but also it appears to be completely out of place in an approach that purports to be an embodiment of "realism", especially in politics. It is, nevertheless, possible to purge the term of all sentimental connotations which make it unacceptable to the tough-minded. Whether the proposed interpretation captures the essence of love as it is understood by moralists and poets is an open question. I submit that it does so at least partly.

An integrative system, where love is the regulatory mechanism of social interaction, is one where the definition of "self" of an actor is extended to include other actors. "Feelings" need not enter this interpretation at all, because "extension of self" can be operationalized in terms of re-defining the utilities associated with outcomes of decisions. On the other hand, feelings can also be incorporated in the interpretation without necessarily invoking the notion of love, from which the tough-minded shrink as the Devil from holy water. I do not "love" my arm in the sense that I love my children, but if it is injured, I certainly feel pain. Thus, it is natural to think of my arm as part of my "self" but also unnecessary, since "I" can live without it. It is simply a matter of extending the definition of "self" to include a portion of the world to which I am connected by feelings. As for "feelings", they cannot nor need not be "operationally" defined. For instance, every one knows what "pain" means, and it is fatuous to pretend that one doesn't.

We know, to be sure, that the nervous systems of our bodies are not physically connected with each other. So if my child is tortured and I do not know about it, my feelings cannot be affected. But if my child were

[3]H. Kahn, *On Thermonuclear War* (Princeton University Press, Princeton, N.J., 1960).
[4]T. C. Schelling, *The Strategy of Conflict* (Harvard University Press, Cambridge, Mass., 1960).
[5]R. Jervis, *The Logic of Images in International Relations* (Princeton University Press, Princeton, N.J., 1970).

tortured in my presence, I certainly would feel excruciating anguish, psychologically quite akin to physical pain, in the sense, for instance, of evoking involuntary cries of dismay, impulsive reflex-like movements, etc.

It is an undeniable fact that some individuals are linked in this manner and that this linkage enables the emotional state of one individual (either positive or negative affect) to induce a similar state in another. This linkage on the psychological level is possibly genetically determined, that is, characteristics of our species. That this should be so in mammals and birds is understandable in the light of natural selection: the survival of mammalian and bird species depends on the protection and care of the young. And even adult animals equipped with deadly weapons show evidence of inhibitions against excessive intra-specific aggression. Their fights for territory or mates are seldom fatal. The inhibitions serve as an obvious species-survival mechanism.

It is not unlikely that such inhibitions are also built into the human psyche. Only very few individuals are able to murder in cold blood. The fact that it is usually much more difficult to kill a child suggests that the inhibition is linked to mammalian instincts.

Now these inhibitions have nothing to do with calculations of utilities or foreseeing the consequences of actions. Nor are they necessarily simply products of socialization or indoctrination. That they are at least in part instinctual is evidenced by physiological reactions, for example, vomiting at the sight of torture inflicted on another. It is as if links other than physical connections existed between the nervous systems of human individuals, as if the boundaries of "self" were not quite the boundaries provided by the skin.

This linkage, I believe, is a psychological and physiological basis of love. Now the integrative is one in which the participants are bounded by such linkages to the extent that the definition of self extends to a collective. Certainly such collectives are not unknown among human beings, although the degree of integration varies. The most dramatic manifestations occur in times of great stress or danger, especially when a realization of mutual interdependence for survival has been deeply internalized. It is observed, for example, on the battle field. In fact, somewhat ironically, the strongest personal attachments, acts of self-sacrifice, undertaken as a matter of course, genuine concern for the well being or safety of others, all forms of behavior ordinarily associated with love and empathy (I believe the two terms refer to closely related feelings) occur among soldiers jointly facing death. These attitudes cannot be wholly explained by the usual indoctrination to which soldiers are subjected, because they persist long after the effects of indoctrination aimed to induce loyalty to God, country, leader, etc. have been eroded by disillusionment and cynicism. Loyalty to buddies is the staunchest. It is based on concrete, not abstract, extensions of self to real, immediately present others.

There is no question, then, that love, in the sense of extension of self, exists among human beings. The important and still unanswered question is how far the limits of self can be extended. The question is crucial, because a *partial* extension may aggravate the problem of human survival instead of partially solving it. For a partial extension defines the limits of self short of including some others, hence excluding others. This distinction occurs, of course, also on the individual level. However, assuming for the moment a Hobbsian world, where the conception of self is sharply confined to the individual, who thereby finds himself "at war" with all other individuals, the situation resulting is not nearly so dangerous as one where each self is a much larger unit. For one thing, individuals do not possess the destructive power of groups organized for violence. Also, the prospect of remaining "sole victor" in the war of all against all is very dim. The dream of remaining "sole victor" is the dream of kings, emperors, and dictators, commanding integrated collectives, not of Hobbsian human atoms. The fewer actors there are, the more attainable the dream appears. The most dangerous world is a bi-polar one.

For this reason, I do not share the optimism of those who see the gradual regional integrations as steps to global integration. To be sure, a war between Western European states is incomparably less probable today than in the days of trumpet-blowing, drum-beating nationalism. To the extent, however, that this integration was stimulated by a perception of a common danger, it may have contributed to polarization. Since the *dis*integration of the Communist bloc, brought about by the Sino-Soviet split, the dangers of another world war may have been attenuated. There is, to be sure, no way of weighing the local pacifying influence of regional integration against the increase of tensions brought about by reducing the number of centers of power and thus sharpening the rivalry among them. Whether the balance is positive or negative depends on the principal motives that have facilitated the integration, whether they stem from broadening the definition of "community" and thus can maintain the momentum of ever broader extension of the concept, or whether they stem from fear of a "common enemy".

Whatever be the results of integration on a scale larger than sets of individuals in direct contact with one another, such integration can be effected only with the help of ideological indoctrination. Identification with a fellow-citizen, or fellow-national, or fellow-X-ist, or fellow-man is different from that with one's mate, one's child, one's buddy, or one's neighbor. In the broader forms of integration, love takes on an abstract quality; cerebration takes precedence over affect. Indeed, the intellectualization of "love of humanity" may dull a person's sensitivities to human beings in the flesh. The less than adequate relations with family and friends of famous "lovers of humanity" are well known. Tolstoy, for one, was convinced that the only way to practice love was to do good *at this time in this particular situation to the person who happens to be at hand* without giving a thought to the broader consequences of one's actions. He dismissed as self-deluding or counter-productive all attempts to consciously structure society presumably for the purpose of improving relations among human beings.

In the days when the strongest ties of interdependence were between members of small communities bound by direct contacts, it may have made sense to epitomize love in the commandment "Love thy neighbor as thyself", where the meaning of "neighbor" was literal. To be sure, everyone is now everyone's neighbor in the sense of shrunken distances and all-pervasive nets of interdependence. But this change in the human condition can be appreciated only intellectually, not by immediate and direct experience.

The failure of world religions (by those I mean religions that emphasize the brotherhood of man and try to induce a corresponding affect) was, in my opinion, due to the fact that it is impossible to induce the affect of love for perfect strangers, for people with whom it is impossible to communicate because of language barriers, for people whose appearance is radically different from what one is used to and who for that reason usually seem unattractive, above all, for people whom one never saw and will never see.

What, then, remains? The only hope, it seems to me, is in raising the awareness of mutual interdependence of all human beings. And this awareness must transcend the interdependence based on exchange. For, given the present allocation of control over resources, exchange cannot be "fair" or balanced or profitable to all. Nor can it be adjusted by juggling prices of raw materials so as to give some of the countries of the hungry world a better break. Because some of the hungry countries have no resources to speak of. They have no wherewithal of exchange. True, they have no power either; so they could be left quietly to starve without much danger of a global revolt of the poor, the specter that has replaced the specter evoked by Marx and Engels in 1848. At any rate, aid to the hungry to forestall revolt would be simply an acceptance of the imperatives of the threat system. Aid to the hungry as a gesture of largesse is an extension of the exchange system: implicitly one puts the hungry under obligation, hence exacts from them a psychological tribute.

In a love system, a human being deserves consideration, assistance, and respect, not because of what he could do to you if denied these (as in a threat system) or for what he is able to give in return, be it only humble gratitude (as in an exchange system) but simply because he is an extension of self.

However, to argue this point on moral grounds is futile, for morality must be charged with affect, and one cannot love "everyone" in the sense of engaging one's affect. The argument is also weak on pragmatic grounds: it is not certain that letting tens of millions of Africans starve will have direct drastic consequences for the rest of the world. The argument can be made only on ideological grounds, but not in the usual way, that is, not by deriving the argument from an *a priori* formulated ideology, such as "the brotherhood of man" or something of this sort. By an argument on ideological ground I mean considering the ideological *consequences* of actions rather than their ideological antecedents. For instance, practicing threats and counter-threats, as in power diplomacy, *perpetuates* the ideology that accepts the threat system as a normal matrix of international relations. Practicing bookkeeping in all transactions *perpetuates* the ideology that accepts trade as the normal matrix of human relations. Similarly, "practicing love" is the only way of making the integrative system a serious competitor of the other two. It is essential to promote such competition, for although there are areas where an exchange system and even, perhaps, a threat system have their place, clearly the hegemony of the latter is fraught with danger, and the hegemony of the former would be tantamount to arrested development. To avoid such hegemony, the exchange system must be pressured out of some areas of human interactions, for example, where services are rendered that should be the birthright of every human being, such as succor in drastic need or medical help or education. It seems that the threat system must be forced out of most human relations, especially from international politics.

By "practicing love" I do not mean what revivalists mean. I mean engaging in an ideological and political struggle to promote actions and policies *incompatible* with either the threat system or the exchange system, in order to drive them from niches where they do not belong. I mean exposing the absurdities of Realpolitik in the light of a recognition that enemies are made, not given, and that their enmity is nurtured by threats. I mean exposing the superstitions and breaking the taboos imposed by the pieties of economics, where prosperity is identified with profits and salvation with solvency.

"Practicing love" means getting rid of the pernicious idea that discovering self is the same as differentiating oneself from others, that love and hate always come in complementary pairs. The problem, as I see it, is that of inducing integration in concentric circles, as it were, from self to family to community to a culture to humanity, inducing a realization that loyalty to one of these need not clash with loyalty to another. On the contrary, the loyalties on the different levels can and must reinforce one another.

For reasons already suggested, such a change of outlook, if it occurs, will not be the result of either a concerted effort of massive re-education (the proponents of the idea do not have the necessary resources or access to masses), nor of the emergence of a new world religion. If the change occurs, it will be in consequence of sobering, possibly traumatic experiences that will make it impossible to hold on to parochial beliefs, to give obeisance to bankrupt ideologies, or to render loyalties to disgraced elites. It will be in consequence of hard and long struggles. We can only hope, despite the dismaying lessons of history to the contrary, that the vision of a love system can guide these struggles without disintegrating in the process.

E.2.   A framework for the evaluation of arms proposals

THOMAS C. SCHELLING

This paper is an exploration of the different motives that can lead two countries to bargain about armaments. The purpose is to classify the alternative preferences about possession or nonpossession of weapons that the arms bargainers can have in mind, and to see what kinds of bargains are compatible with different preferences and what understandings and misunderstandings are likely.

I restrict the discussion to situations typically identified with arms control: the object is to reduce armament on the other side, and not, as in an alliance, to increase it. I discuss weapons that we prefer the other side not to have, and omit any weapons or systems of command and control that we might prefer they invest in for our joint safety. (And I assume that the alternative to their investment in a weapon is not just some other weapon that we like even less.) So I consider only weapons that each country prefers the other not to have.

To keep the analysis simple I assume that the choice is binary: to have it or not to have it. Some arms bargaining is in fact about all-or-none decisions, or decisions that are nearly so; ABM, biological weapons, weapons in orbit, MIRV, and many others have been approached as yes-no decisions. Other decisions are about quantities, numbers, sizes, distances, degrees and durations; but even for them, the special case of dichotomous choice can be illuminating if not directly applicable. Often in these cases the negotiation eventually leads to a binary choice to adopt or not to adopt some specified limit or reduction or increment.

1.   Alternative preference configurations

The variety of preferences arises from the fact that one side, while deprecating possession by the other side, can have any of several motivations about possessing the weapon itself.

One is that "our side" prefers *not* to have the system under any circumstances, simultaneously preferring that the other side not have it.

If our side has decided that ABM is a waste whether or not the other side has it, that hundred-megaton weapons or bombs in orbit involve too much risk or bad publicity whether or not the "other side" invests in such weapons, we have a *dominant negative* preference. By "dominant" I mean that *not* having the weapon is preferred *irrespective of whether the other side has it.*

A second possibility is that one side prefers to have the weapon whether or not the other side has it. The Soviets, to take an example, may prefer to have a FOBS if we do not have one and prefer to have it if we do. We may prefer to have heavy bombers if the Soviets do, and prefer to have them if the Soviets do not. Either side may feel that way about sea-based missiles. This is the case of a *dominant positive* preference, where "dominant" again means that having it is preferred *irrespective of whether the other side has it.* (The term "dominant" is used this way in conventional decision theory. I am tempted to use a term like "unconditionally preferred", but there are ambiguities that can be avoided by using conventional terminology.)

Now a third case. The weapon may be one that we are *not* motivated to acquire if the other side does *not*, but that we *would* invest in if the other side *did*. Although the logic was not always clear, it was often asserted during the 1960's that ABM was the kind of weapon that the United States could not afford to be without if the Soviets had it, although the United States might not want to put resources into it unless the Soviets did. Sometimes the basis of this motivation is military effectiveness and strategy: a "matching" weapon may be needed if the adversary has it, but not be worth having otherwise. Sometimes it is psychology and diplomacy: "our side" must not appear incapable of developing the weapon, too stingy to procure it, or plain inferior for lack of it if the other side has it. (Sometimes it is domestic behavior or politics: the arms bargainer believes that political and bureaucratic pressures will be irresistible if the other side embarks on the program, but can be contained if the other side does not.)

This third case is one in which there is no dominant preference but a *contingent* one, a preference conditional on what the other side does.[1]

2. *Illustrative matrices*

Each kind of preference can be depicted in a 2×2 matrix with a number in each of the four cells to denote the ranking of the outcome. Since each

---

[1] I omit the logically possible case that we want it if and only if "they" do not have it. It arises in other contexts but seldom in disarmament negotiations. See the Appendix for some discussion of neglected cases.

of the two countries can have the weapon or not have it, there are four outcomes: both have it, neither has it, we have it and they don't, they have it and we don't. I am supposing that each side knows which among the four outcomes it likes best, which least, which second, and which third.[2] (Sometimes it will not matter which is second and which third, or which third and which fourth, and "tied" rankings can take care of either order.) I have found it mnemonically easier to let higher numbers denote higher rank, and use 4, 3, 2 and 1 in that order to denote best, second best, third and last choices. Thus if one's most preferred outcome is that neither side have the system, the number 4 goes in the cell where the not-have row of the matrix intersects the not-have column.

Fig. 1 shows matrices corresponding to the three systems of preference for the country labeled "our side". The numbers have been inserted

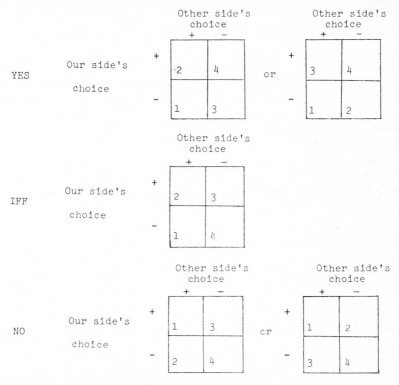

Fig. 1. Preference ranking.

[2]In other contexts this is often a perfunctory assumption. For national governments, especially the less centralized ones, it is at best an extreme simplification and often plain wrong.

in the lower left corners of the cells, to leave room for the other set of numbers—one number in each cell—for the "other side's" preferences.

 I refer to the two countries as two "sides"—"our side" and "other side"— to avoid ambiguous words like "enemies" or "partners". I call a dominant preference in favor of the system a YES preference, and a dominant preference not to have the system a NO preference; the contingent preference I label IFF—if-and-only-if the other side has it, too. The two rows of the matrix represent the choice of "our side" and the two columns the choice of the "other side". The number denoting the preference value of our side will be in the lower left-hand corner of the cell, the other side's in the upper right. (Matrices are easier to read if the two sets of numbers are staggered in that fashion.)

3. Two configurations of YES

There are two configurations of numbers consistent with the YES preference, and two for the NO preference. (There would be two for the IFF if I weren't omitting the weapon that we might want if and only if they did *not* have it. That possibility is considered in the Appendix.) The difference between the two NO preferences will usually not matter, but the difference between the two YES systems will. Note what the difference is: in both YES cases our side prefers to have the system if the other side does have it and also if the other side does not; but if the choice is between *both* having it and *both not* having it, in the first YES case, we prefer *both not*. In the second YES case we'd rather that both have it than have to do without it ourselves. Because that second case is stronger than a merely dominant preference, I hereby label it the YES! preference.[3]

Having identified the four preference rankings for our side, we have the same four for the other side. There is no logical reason why the two should have similar preferences for any given weapon, although symmetry will occasionally suggest that the attitude of one side toward a particular weapon ought not to be wholly different from the attitude of

[3]The two NO cases parallel the two YES cases: each NO case is a YES case with the rows interchanged. The YES! case is unconditionally wanting it, the NO! case (if we so label it) is unconditionally not wanting it. The YES case corresponds to, "We want it, but will do without if you do". The NO case is, "We don't want it, but we're willing to get it on condition you don't". Note that it is not, "We don't want it but will get it if you will". That case doesn't occur here because it corresponds to a weapon we want them to have and is accordingly omitted. The distinction between NO and NO! would be mainly of interest if the reverse of IFF—they want it if and only if we do *not* have it—occurred on the other side. Because that case is being omitted, the two NO cases are merged in the text. (In the interest of logical completeness, the reader can obtain that if-and-only-if-not case— IFFN—by interchanging rows in the IFF matrix.)

the other side. We thus have $4 \times 4 = 16$ permutations. Four of these are symmetrical, both sides having the same rank ordering of the outcomes vis-à-vis each other. In the other twelve cases, an IFF preference for our side will occur with, say, a NO preference for the other side; and, since any one of these asymmetrical combinations can be reversed, there are altogether sixteen different permutations and ten different combinations.

4. Sixteen cases

The sixteen permutations are in fig. 2. The four diagonal matrices are symmetrical: if we draw one of these four matrices from the point of view of the other side, reflecting the other side's choice in the two rows and our side's in the two columns, we get the identical matrix. The other matrices occur in pairs: the matrix corresponding to YES for us and NO for them has, from the other side's point of view, the configuration of the NO-YES matrix.

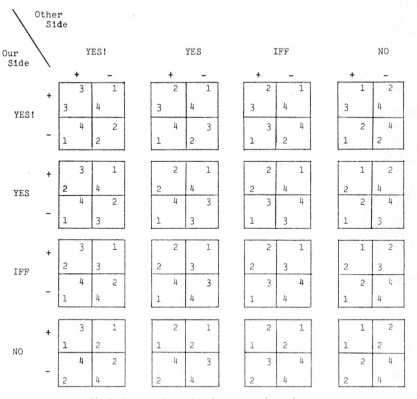

Fig. 2. Permutations of preference configurations.

5. Ranking only

In these matrices preferences are only "indexed", and not "measured" by the numbers. Strength of preference is not shown. If we want to depict a first choice strongly preferred over the second, a second choice barely preferred over the third, and a third moderately preferred over the last, we could impressionistically use numbers like 10, 4, 3 and 1 or, more extremely, 100, 10, 9 and 1. For some purposes that is necessary: sometimes it matters whether or not a preference between two outcomes is so weak as to be virtual indifference. In this paper we can get along with rank *orderings* and no cardinal quantities. (Evidently if we distinguished 4, 3, 2, 1 from 10, 3, 2, 1 we could end up with a dozen configurations for a single side and a gross of permutations to consider, although not all the permutations would be interestingly different.)[4]

6. A bargaining matrix: YES vs. YES

Begin with the combination of YES and YES, the second matrix on the diagonal from the upper left corner. This matrix is familar to students of bargaining and conflict (and because of its symmetry is generalizes to multi-party situations).[5] It has the following interesting characteristics.

First, each is *unilaterally* motivated to choose positively, whatever the other is expected to choose or has chosen. If they commit themselves to the weapon, we would elect to have the weapon; if they unilaterally promise not to have the weapon, we would welcome their promise but go ahead and get the weapon. But—if each of us makes that *independent* choice we both end up with a score of 2 instead of 3, with our second choice from the bottom rather than second from the top. Neither regrets his choice: had he chosen otherwise, he would have had the worst possible outcome, the other side having the system and himself not. If both should happen not to invest in the weapon, each has done "wrong", given what his preferences are, yet both are better off in terms of those very preferences than if both could change their minds!

This is the classic case in which something like "enforceable contract" can lead to a bargained result that is superior for both parties to what

[4]To avoid carrying along two sets of NO preferences and to avoid discriminating between them, they have been replaced by a 4-2-2-1 ordering in which the second and third ranks are both indexed by the number 2. Anyone who is uneasy about this suppressing of a possibly interesting distinction, or who is curious about the exhaustiveness of the classification altogether is invited to see the Appendix where the possible permutations are explored more completely.

[5]It is the matrix that, for historical reasons not worth going into, is known as "prisoner's dilemma".

they can achieve independently. Though each prefers to have the system, whether or not the other does, each has a *stronger* preference that *the other not have* it. Each gains more from the other's foregoing it than from his own having it. There is room for a "trade".

7. Trading with the enemy

Here, then, is the case in which "trading with the enemy" is a good bargain. If we can reach agreement to abstain from this weapon we both get 3 instead of 2. But this is an agreement that has to be enforced. If the agreement cannot be monitored, and if the internal consciences or legal systems will not coerce compliance, each will not only decline to keep his part of the bargain but will expect the other not to.

It is not the case that every weapon that gives a side some relative advantage but is merely costly and to no avail if both sides have it corresponds to this YES-YES matrix. A weapon that yields a relative superiority can still generate a NO preference if it makes more likely the outbreak of war or has other deplorable side effects. There are, furthermore, weapons that one could prefer to have on *both sides* rather than on neither side; "invulnerable retaliatory forces" to supplement vulnerable ones might appear jointly desirable. I hesitate to name examples of YES-YES weapons because any example will be evaluated by the reader and, if he evaluates the weapon differently from me, he may not find it a representation of the YES-YES matrix. But *suppose* that our side (whether or not you and I agree with this valuation) considers a fleet of warships in the Indian Ocean, or a forward-based missile system, or the deployment of a MIRV technology, worth having if the other side does not have it and perhaps even more worth having if the other side does have it, but nevertheless would consider any gains more than canceled out if both sides had it—no great relative advantage being achieved but some greater expense, some greater risk of war, some aggravation of diplomatic relations or some other undesirable consequence being entailed by joint possession of the weapon. Then we have the YES-YES situation and a basis for negotiated "exchange" if the result can be monitored and enforced.

8. Alternative agreements and understandings

An enforceable agreement is not the only kind of effective understanding that might be reached in this YES-YES case. Maybe one side can make a credible promise that it will abstain *if and only if* the other does. The second side then knows that its decision determines whether both have it or neither, and it can safely abstain. (A "credible promise" can be thought of as the deliberate incurring of some penalty on possessing the system if the other side does not, or on violating a promise, a penalty great enough to change the promising side's preference order from YES to IFF.)

A third way that restraint might come about is by each side's announcing that it will abstain as long as the other does. If both sides know each other's preferences and perceive that an enforceable agreement would be in their joint interest, they may perceive that a sufficient method of "enforcement" is simply each side's readiness to go ahead if the other does. Enforcement is by reciprocity. This requires that each be able to detect whether or not the other is proceeding with the weapon, and to detect it in time not to suffer by being a slow second.

9. Legislating IFF

An interesting kind of "credible promise" that might be available to the U.S. government would be a conditional legislative authorization. Suppose the Congress authorized procurement of a weapon system contingently—authorized appropriation of funds and procurement, with the authorization to take effect and the funds to be legally available only upon certification that the other side had unmistakably embarked on the program. (In earlier times the British Parliament legislated contingent automatic procurement authorizations for naval tonnage, thus signaling to the other side—France in the late nineteenth century—that British procurement would be determined by French procurement.)

10. Two qualifications about agreement

Before leaving this case of YES-YES, two observations should be made.

First, while a weapon characterized by YES preferences is a clear opportunity for reciprocated restraint, achieved with or without a formal enforceable agreement as long as the choices can be monitored, it is not true that both sides, even with full understanding of each other's preferences, ought always to be willing to agree on restraint. Since either side can deny the other something it wants—at the cost of denying the same thing to itself—it may perceive a bargaining advantage with respect to some *other* weapon in making agreement on this one contingent on that other one.

Second, neither side can be sure of the other's preferences. This YES configuration can occur without its being plain to both sides. Other preferences can obtain with one of the parties mistakenly thinking that the situation is YES-YES. The consequences of mistaken estimates will be looked at below.

11. Reciprocated IFF

A second configuration familiar in the study of bargaining is the symmetrical IFF matrix. This describes the weapon that each wants if and only if the other has it. It differs from the preceding case in that either side not merely is willing to forego it on condition the other do likewise, but has no incentive to obtain it unless the other does.

There are two outcomes that are "conditionally satisfactory". As long as neither has it, and neither has reason to expect the other to acquire it, neither is motivated to go ahead. If both have it, neither is willing to dismantle it unilaterally. But if either side confidently perceives the situation to be IFF-IFF, it can confidently abstain or dismantle in the knowledge that the other side will do likewise.

Neither expects the other to be secretly preparing to jump the gun and race to be the first to get the weapon: the other side doesn't want to be the only side to have it. This weapon is one that is valuable only in the role of "counter-capability" to the other's possession of the same weapon.

This is an easy case for arms control. It is necessary only for the two sides to *concert* with each other and to *reassure* each other. If both confidently perceive what the situation is there should be no problem. Of course, if each believes the other's preferences are in the YES! configuration, each may consider it a foregone conclusion that the other side will have the weapon and foresee no value in negotiating, and proceed with the weapon itself. (Without negotiating, they may never discover that they committed symmetrical errors in imputing wrong preferences to each other.)

Furthermore, it can be a tactical advantage to pretend that one's preferences are IFF when they are NO, if the other's preferences are YES: it offers some inducement for the other's restraint.

And, as when both had YES preferences, either side may consider it a bargaining advantage to threaten possession of the system, though its true preferences are IFF, to induce restraint on some *other* system that may be coupled with this one in negotiations.

Finally, as mentioned earlier, a YES configuration may be deliberately converted into an IFF decision, by formal legislative commitment to contingent procurement.

(I leave it to the reader to think about the likely behavior in an IFF-IFF configuration if there is absolutely no way for either side to monitor the other's possession.)

12. The NO-NO configuration

Ordinarily this would be a trivial case—a weapon that neither side wants, whether or not the other has it. There must be an infinity of ridiculous weapons that nobody is interested in having even if the other side is foolish enough to procure them. In isolation from other weapons, this is merely a logical category, empty of significance, that completes our matrix of permutations.

But in a wider context, as part of a logrolling package, one side might *pretend* that its preference was not NO but YES!; or it might, in aggressive bargaining, *threaten* to acquire the weapon despite its own preference not to have it. So the NO-NO case does not preclude bargaining.

13. The IFF-YES configuration

This situation, if clearly recognized, leads easily to the same result as IFF-IFF. It is equivalent to a YES-YES situation in which one has arranged a credible promise to abstain if the other does. The one with the YES preference knows that its own choice determines the outcome, between both having the system and both not. Since it prefers that both not, it can abstain.

Problems arise if the IFF motivation is misperceived, or if the YES is misperceived to be YES! by the IFF side. Misperception can lead both to believe that the inevitable outcome is both having it. The IFF then gets it, confirming the mistaken belief of the YES side. If the YES side believes that the IFF motive is YES!, it may not even initiate the bargaining that would be invited by a symmetrical YES situation.

And, again, either side may perceive a bargaining advantage in coupling this weapon with another, exploiting the threat value of declaring an intention to acquire this one, and pretending its motivation is YES!

A frustrating situation can occur if possession of the weapon cannot be monitored. As in the symmetrical YES case, the YES country would prefer to own this weapon even if the IFF country did not; if possession cannot be monitored, the IFF country must assume that the YES country will procure it. Expecting that, the IFF country procures it, too.

Thus with monitoring the combination of IFF and YES can be as benign as symmetrical IFF, without monitoring it can be as frustrating as symmetrical YES.

14. YES-NO

If motives are transparent and there is no coupling with any other negotiable weapon, the outcome in this case is that the YES country goes ahead and the NO country does not. But if the NO country can successfully *threaten* to acquire the weapon or *pretend* an IFF or YES motivation, it can induce the YES side to forego it.

Alternatively, if the NO country is unable to misrepresent its motives or to threaten credibly that it will procure the weapon, it can bring in another weapon for logrolling: it offers a concession on the other, or threatens refusal on the other, to induce the YES country to abstain on this one.

15. NO-IFF

This case does not differ significantly from NO-NO and nothing needs to be said.

16. The YES! configuration

Considered on its merits, the symmetrical YES! matrix is the trivial counterpart to the symmetrical NO matrix. There is no bargain that we'd be interested in, confined to this weapon alone. While each prefers the other not to have it, neither is willing to abstain merely to induce the other to.

Interest arises only if this weapon can be coupled with another. Thus among our sixteen permutations, seven preclude successful bargaining unless the weapon can be coupled with some other weapon or some other issue. The ramifications of this point are many.

First, it can appear a bargaining advantage to pretend one's motivation is YES! If coupling of two weapons were not possible, doing so would merely preclude agreement; but if one country's motivation is YES! on a particular weapon and the other's is YES on some other weapon the latter can refuse a bargain (or pretend a YES! motivation) on that second weapon in order to couple the two and overcome the first side's absolute preference for that first weapon.[6]

[6]With two weapons, a side can have one or the other, neither or both; for the two sides together there are 16 outcomes. To identify all the bargaining possibilities we would need the preference rankings of both sides among 16 outcomes, or 32 rank numbers. The 2×2

Second, the very possibility of a YES! preference can interfere with arms bargaining by being anticipated. It used to be commonly alleged that the Soviet Union had an attitude toward active defense that made no bargain on ABM possible: the Soviets would rather have ABM matched by ours than forego it on condition we do likewise. If that was a confident belief but a wrong one, and instead the situation was symmetrically YES (or IFF-YES or NO-YES), we could have missed an opportunity to bargain away ABM. If both sides are YES and believe each other to be YES!, discussion of the subject may seem so unpromising that the bargaining possibility is never discovered.

A third consequence of the YES! preference when the other side's is YES is a misunderstanding that spoils prospects for bargaining on other weapons. Suppose our preference is YES and we believe theirs is too, but theirs is really YES! Believing a bargain possible, we propose negotiation and are rebuffed; or we enter negotiation and discover that the other side insists on coupling this weapon with another that we believe irrelevant or inappropriate. We believe them to be holding out, jeopardizing a good bargain to get concessions on other issues. They may be quite unable to convince us that their preference is actually YES! and they are simply unprepared to forego the weapon merely on condition that we forego it. (We are unlikely to believe them if they tell us that, because that is precisely what they would tell us if indeed they were "just bargaining".)

17. Misperceptions

Before we leave these permutations, some further results of misperception are worth noticing. Suppose both sides are IFF but believe each other to be YES: neither believes his own abstention will induce the other to abstain, but both believe agreement may be possible if they negotiate. To avoid appearing NO, which might leave the other side (believed YES) free to obtain the weapon with impunity, one side may exaggerate its interest as YES. Though in principle agreement is possible, there is no guarantee that the negotiations succeed. Each may overstate

---

matrices for the two weapons separately contain 8 numbers each, or 16 in total. Because those numbers expressed only rank order and not magnitude, there is no way to operate arithmetically to derive the rank numbers for the 4×4 matrix. Even if we had used cardinal numbers to express strengths of preference, numerical operations would require that the two weapons be so independent of each other that the possession of either weapon on either side did not affect the preferences of either country for the other—not a likely situation if the weapons are important, and especially unlikely if they are "naturally coupled" in negotiation.

its case, get greedy, be inept, bog down in endless argument, or become domestically committed to the system. The negotiation having failed, each believes the other is going ahead, and so proceeds to get the weapon itself.[7]

Even NO configurations on both sides, if each believes the other to be YES, can lead to unnecessary negotiations to prohibit systems that neither side wants anyway. And if the negotiations fail, one or both may have got deluded into or committed to programs that, in the absence of bargaining, neither would have had any interest in.

18. Natural coupling, tactical coupling

Most of the foregoing discussion has looked at motivations, perceptions and tactics in relation to a single weapon—ABM, strategic bombers, sea-based missile systems, or MIRV for examples. Some of the discussion has referred to the coupling of two or more weapons or issues in a bargain.

There are several kinds of coupling worth distinguishing; and at the risk of proliferating terminology I have to introduce some terms to call attention to the distinction.

One is between "natural" coupling and "tactical". Natural coupling occurs when two weapons are complementary. For example, it may be proposed that a natural package is not an agreement forbidding ABM on both sides—there being nothing about the other side's ABM that makes us want ABM—but rather between *their* ABM and *our* offensive missiles. Or, we might argue that MIRV technology on our side is "naturally coupled" with ABM on their side. We may propose that if they proceed with ABM we shall double our missile force or MIRV our land-based missiles. We propose therefore to abstain from some *offensive* capability if they abstain from some *defensive* capability. We do this on grounds that we have an *IFF preference relation between our offensive capability and their defensive capability.*

Similarly, we might take the position that the "natural coupling" is between our sea-based system and their ASW.

---

[7]I consider it likely that each side was IFF on ABM but believed the other side to be YES, with a suspicion that it might be YES!, both believing that only a negotiated agreement could prevent ABM. Had the negotiations failed, both might have gone ahead with systems based on misperceptions—misperceptions that were apparently confirmed and aggravated by the negotiation itself. (Here is a case in which the fiction that the "U.S. Government" had a "preference" can only be shorthand for stating a retrospective prediction about the policies that might have emerged from a multitude of interests and positions in different parts of the executive and legislative branches.)

By "tactical coupling" I mean coupling, for bargaining purposes, two or more systems in which we and the other side have quite different interests. *They* may be concerned about forward-based bombers, *we* about ASW. The two have no natural relation. There is nothing about ASW that induces us to do anything about forward-based bombers. But there may not be a symmetrical agreement about forward-based systems that makes sense to both sides. And maybe we have nothing that quite corresponds to the particular ASW system that we deprecate on their side. So we propose—or they propose—that we restrain forward-based bombers and they restrain ASW.

This is what is usually called "packaging" or "logrolling". It is different from natural coupling. In natural coupling there is a YES or IFF relation between the one weapon on their side and the other one on our side. In the case of tactical coupling there is a weapon that concerns us that does not seem promising for separate agreement, and another that concerns them that also does not seem promising for separate agreement; by combining the two we may reach an agreeable pair of restraints.

19. Bargaining chips

The idea of a "bargaining chip" seems to be some weapon or plan or intention that one side has, that is of less concern to that side than to the other side and therefore is eligible to be traded away. To be "traded away" means to be yielded or abandoned on condition that the other side make some appropriate concession.

The term also is used to describe some project that a side merely *pretends* to be interested in, expecting a strong enough negative interest on the other side to make a trade possible.

Bargaining chips are not peculiar to arms bargaining, being familiar in tariff bargaining and other diplomatic bargaining and in fields like industrial relations. Because the term covers so wide an array of tactics, hardly any generalization can be offered about the wisdom or propriety of playing "bargaining chips".

But to identify the situations to which the term can apply, it is useful to notice several different intentions that a country can have for a weapon, some of which correspond to this notion of "bargaining chips".

(1) At one extreme is a weapon that a country is so interested in having that there is little likelihood it would bargain it away—a YES! interest. Of course, if the other side has a strong enough negative interest and is willing to make enough coupled concessions, almost anything is likely to be negotiable. Still, some weapon plans are not expected to be

part of any agreement or even to be discussed with a view to agreement. These will not be called "bargaining chips".

(2) A second category consists of projects a side is strongly interested in but considers within the realm of bargaining, the other side's negative interest possibly outweighing this side's positive interest. This kind of YES project is within the arena of bargaining and recognized as negotiable—not brought to the table just to be traded away, but nevertheless subject to negotiation. This, as I perceive the current usage, would usually not be called a "bargaining chip".

(3) The third category is YES projects that a country ordinarily would carry out but that are clearly of much more interest to the other side. These are the things that are "taken to market", or "brought to the bargaining table". There is nothing contrived or fictitious about them; they are genuine plans but they are recognized in advance as strong canditates for being traded away.

(4) Fourth are the "pure bargaining chips"—things that a country has no real interest in but make a difference to the other side. These are the things, NO or borderline, that one side could innocuously do, or do at slight cost, that pose a risk or nuisance to the other side. They are not bona fide intentions, but they are trading assets because they threaten the other side.

If these projects are of no value to the side that puts them forward, why does the other side have to make concessions to get them put aside? There are at least two reasons. One is that the side putting forward the bargaining chips may successfully *pretend* a strong interest. The second is that it may more brazenly *threaten* to carry out the project unless the other side pays a price. Depending on accepted standards of behavior, this mode of bargaining may or may not be characterized as "blackmail" or by some such term that identifies the motive and deprecates the tactic.

(5) Finally, a country may project a NO weapon that it would deplore acquiring, hoping that the other sufficiently deplores it to bargain for its elimination. The side putting it forward wants *both* to get something for abandoning the weapon *and* to preserve itself from having to acquire it. This case too, could be characterized by either pretense or blatant threat. Sometimes the ethical context of this tactic is judged according to whether it is employed cold-bloodedly for gain or instead is used to oppose—that is, to be bargained away against—something deemed improper that the other side proposes. (The threat to go through with a costly act of retaliation can be considered heroic or extortionate according to the way one judges the propriety of the other side's action that it is intended to deter.)

20. Absolute and contingent chips

In negotiating, a side can put forward a projected weapon expecting to trade it away but without linking it to some *particular* concession of the other side. Alternatively, it can put forward a contingent project with an IFF motivation—a project that will go forward if and only if the other side proceeds with a particular project of its own. This automatically links the bargaining chip with the particular exchange that is intended— with a matching project on the other side. If the United States pretends a strong interest in ABM believing the Soviets would pay some price in some currency to get the United States to abandon ABM, the proposal would be a bargaining chip of the general or absolute variety. But if the United States proposes ABM as a natural response to a Soviet ABM, or as a natural response to some Soviet offensive-weapon capability, implying not that we are YES toward ABM but IFF, with clear identification of what the IFF refers to on the other side, the project would be a "matched" or "contingent" bargaining chip.

Thus the contingent chip gets linked or coupled with some weapon on the other side. There may not need then to be any further bargaining. With the absolute bargaining chip the bargaining is essential—one pretends a YES or a YES! motivation and needs to be induced to abandon it by some concession on the other side. In the contingent case the chip is matched with something in particular, and if that something on the other side is abandoned, by reciprocal announcement or unilaterally, the result may be achieved without negotiation.

21. IFF and YES bargaining chips

A bargaining chip can be put forward in two quite different ways. Suppose the United States is only marginally interested in ABM or even reluctant, but resolved on a tactic of pretending an interest or incurring a commitment, subject to progress in SALT. At some stage the U.S. negotiators have to suggest that the ABM program is *negotiable* and *contingent*. (There may be a pretense that it is not, but a pretense merely designed to raise the bargaining price.) Inasmuch as there may be political and bureaucratic forces in favor of ABM as well as against it, the United States may be able to appear committed without having to pretend very hard.

Now there are two quite different commitments that the United States can appear to incur. One is to proceed with ABM if the Soviet Union does, and not otherwise. The second is to proceed with ABM unless *agreement* prohibiting ABM is reached with the Soviet Union. If successful, these two may come to the same thing; but the risks and procedures are different. If we commit ourselves, as a bargaining tactic, to match Soviet ABM there may be no need to reach formal agreement.

If instead we pretend a YES motive, we may commit ourselves to go forward unless an explicit agreement is reached. This tactic runs the risk that aborted negotiations leave us obliged, in consequence of a bluff, to go through with a program that we didn't want to go through with. But if the bargaining chip takes the IFF form, it is the other side's *behavior*, not the successful *negotiation*, that gets us off the hook.

22. Motivational context of bargaining chips

If the other side's motivation is known to be IFF we do not need the bargaining-chip tactic. We need only reassure them of our NO, and their IFF leads them to abstain. The "bargaining chip" is pertinent when the other side's motivation is believed to be YES.

If the bargaining-chip succeeds the results are fine, as far as this agreement is concerned. (We might in the longer run prefer not to establish too much precedent for playing with chips.) We fail if his motivation is YES!. In that case, if we bluffed an intent to proceed, we can be caught bluffing and back down or go ahead with a program we didn't want.

There is another danger. If we overplay our chip and pretend that our motivation is YES! to extract a high price, the other side may believe us! It may not even bother to bargain, and we end up committed to a program whose only purpose was to be traded away.

The risk of failure suggests that an IFF chip is safer than a YES or YES! chip. To become committed only on condition the other side proceed with some *action*, not committed in the absence of formal *agreement*, incurs less risk. A satisfactory result does not depend on a successful negotiation. If each side is IFF but thinks the other is YES, getting committed to a bargaining chip could mean that, if negotiations fail, both sides are committed to going ahead. If both sides are committed only to an IFF reaction, aborted negotiations can—may not, but can—leave both sides willing to wait and see.

23. Internal effect of bargaining chips

There are two different ways that bargaining chips are put forward. One is pretense, the other commitment. There are many ways a government can get committed to something it clearly would not care to do, even while it is evident that the commitment was incurred for bargaining purposes. A legal way to do this, mentioned earlier, is to get legislation that obliges the government, in certain contingencies, to do what it might not ordinarily wish to do (and to get Congress to go home for the fall season, leaving the Executive Branch with its hands tied). There are other ways.

Now, many kinds of bargaining entail enough privacy for a pretense to be plausible or a commitment not to appear rigged. But it is hard for a democratic government to pretend an interest in, say, ABM, for the benefit of a diplomatic audience abroad, without deceiving the domestic audience. A corporation or a divorce lawyer or a land speculator can try to deceive the other party; and the Soviet government usually needn't broadcast an embarrassing public contradiction of the position it takes in negotiations. But the U.S. government often cannot help it. Bargaining chips are probably ineffectual for a government that cannot bluff without telegraphing its bluff. It is anomalous that in the last few years the bargaining-chip idea became a subject of popular discussion precisely because the Executive Branch put forward positions that it explained at home to be "bargaining chips".

There is nothing tactically wrong as long as the government can become committed, whether or not its hyprocrisy is transparent. There is nothing tactically illogical in proposing to the home folks that one really wouldn't want ABM under any circumstances but needs to become committed to it. (If one can become convincingly committed.) But the pretence that typically makes bargaining chips so valuable is often unavailable to a government that must explain in a loud voice to a large audience that it didn't really mean what it said to its bargaining partner. And a democratic government risks losing some credibility at home—as the U.S. government probably did in making the argument so blatantly during SALT.

Precisely because the cold-blooded pretense is not easily available, a government may have to go through the motions of genuinely intending to go forward with the program, though part of the motive for the program was to generate a bargaining chip. The danger is that the government becomes genuinely committed, so committed that it forgets it didn't intend to go ahead, or so committed that it has to go ahead. It may become so committed that bargaining power within the government shifts in favor of those who want the weapon anyway. A government may believe it keeps the option of backing out of a commitment if the bargain doesn't come off, and discover that it lost the option.

24. The symmetry of bargaining-chip analysis

What has been said about "our side" and bargaining chips can usually be said about "the other side". The other side's interest in some weapon—a YES interest or an IFF interest—could be genuine, pretended, or contrived. (By "contrived" I mean that, without necessarily pretending a genuine interest, the other side adopts a *policy* of proceeding with a weapon if we do, or of proceeding in the absence of negotiated agreement, or of proceeding unless we abstain from some other weapon or negotiate an agreement about some other weapon.)

One difficulty in judging the other side's position with respect to some weapon is similar to the difficulty of knowing what our own side's position is. Within a government there are strong interests in favor of a weapon and strong interests opposed. Within a government there may be optimism about negotiation or pessimism. Within a government there may be a belief that the other side is already committed to procurement, so that an IFF motivation is a reason for proceeding with the weapon, not with negotiation. Within a government there may have been a tentative decision to proceed without full commitment, and no decisive determination yet of how strong the interest in the weapon is. To an observer not part of the government, there will be similar difficulties in judging the positions of both sides, although the USA and USSR clearly have governments that are different in their ability to pretend, to adopt conditional policies, to display or to disguise indecisiveness, to make up their own minds or to remain undecided, even to be incapable—when legislative as well as executive decisions are involved, or when allies have to be accommodated—of making up their minds or knowing what their own policies are.

25. Domestically-oriented "bargaining chips"

Bargaining chips can be used to influence *domestic* decisions. One way is to initiate development or procurement of a weapon on ostensible grounds that, even if in the end it should not be procured, it enhances our bargaining position. Then by confusion, commitment, or default the program gets to go forward unless the other side manages to "obstruct" it with an agreement. (Anyone who can sabotage the agreement can convert a bargaining position into a weapon program.)

Another tactic is the opposite. A government that has decided against a weapon in which there is popular interest, in the Congress or elsewhere, or which it has promoted in the past but has changed its mind about, may need an excuse to abandon the weapon. Converting it into a "bargaining chip" and reaching agreement can legitimize a decision that could not so readily be taken unconditionally.

Negotiation of the Non-Proliferation Treaty probably provided instances of both of these tactics abroad.

26. *An arms-control judgment on weapons*

The foregoing classification has at least a limited value, if only a limited value, in explaining or giving guidance on and clarifying the reasons why a person interested in sound strategy (including arms control) might favor or deplore a particular weapon program, or favor it only conditionally.

But this classification is abstract and somewhat uninformative because it does not relate either to the strategic characteristics of weapons, or to budgetary, diplomatic or domestic political considerations. It is not conclusive or comprehensive. Still, in clarifying and communicating one's attitude toward a weapon, even this classification can be useful.

People have opposed MIRV for Minuteman with a number of different motivational permutations. There are those who felt that MIRV was positively bad on military-strategic grounds or military-industrial grounds, whether or not the Soviets had MIRV, but who also believed that the Soviets were not going to have MIRV anyway—a NO-NO configuration. There were those who believed it was not only bad on military-strategic grounds but, worse, would induce the Russians to acquire it themselves although they wouldn't if we didn't—a NO-IFF configuration. There were people whose configuration was IFF-YES who believed we should declare a willingness to abstain as long as the Soviets did, and others who with the same IFF-YES configuration felt that we should choose negotiating a MIRV ban. There were those who felt our own position should be IFF but believed the Soviet position to be NO and felt it therefore a mistake to go forward; others felt it was IFF on both sides, and we would force the Soviets into it if we got it ourselves. Others have felt that our position was IFF but the Soviets' was YES, and we should make clear to the Russians that we would if they did, although it was not necessary to negotiate. Some undoubtedly felt that the Russian position was YES! and there was no possibility of negotiating a MIRV ban, while others agreed that the Soviet motivation was YES! and that MIRV could be successfully coupled with other weapons in a larger package. And so forth.

Evidently these are different views of what our own preference should be, what the Soviet preference is, and what the diplomatic prospects are. This classification does not explain on what grounds one arrives at a NO,

IFF or YES preference. What this classification does is to clarify the *arms-race considerations* in one's position toward a particular weapon. That is, it clarifies one's position on whether we unilaterally want the weapon, unilaterally don't want it, conditionally want it, think our acquisition will affect the other side, think an enforceable agreement might be negotiated, or think this weapon might usefully be coupled with another.

This classification will not much help clarify a position that is based primarily on broader diplomatic considerations or domestic political ones. When the time came to vote on ABM in the Senate, the issue may have been the war in Vietnam, the military-industrial complex, the Nixon Administration, executive-legislative relations, the size of the defense budget, or promises given and positions taken that constrained what one could say or favor or vote on. But to the extent that one rests his position on what is usually called the "arms race", on the interplay or interaction of development and procurement and deployment of strategic weapons on both sides, this classification is useful.

Appendix

Some readers may be troubled by a lack of symmetry in the two YES and NO configurations with a single IFF, uneasy about my collapsing the two NO configurations into a single compromise, curious about possible preference configurations that were neglected in this paper, or just interested in an exhaustive logical classification. In order to get on with some interesting cases I skipped the larger framework. This appendix is a long footnote to the first few pages.

There are altogether 24 different preference configurations for our side—for "having" or "not having" the system in question—if we confine ourselves to numbers like 4, 3, 2, and 1, thereby excluding ties and neglecting the sizes of intervals between "best" and "second best", etc. (There are $4 \times 3 \times 2 \times 1 = 24$ different ways that we can distribute these four numbers in the four cells of our 2×2 matrix.) There is a like number of configurations for the same four numbers for the other side. And any one of our configurations can be paired with any configuration for the other side, for a total of $24 \times 24 = 576$ different matrices. I repeat: this is a minimum number because it neglects any preference systems we might want to represent by numbers like 10, 6, 2, 1, or 3, 2, 1, 1.

These 576 matrices are all produced by Anatol Rapoport and Melvin Guyer in their article, 'A Taxonomy of 2×2 Games', *General Systems* (1966) 203–214. Because the author's abstract from the difference between "having" and "not having"—dealing only with unspecified dichotomous choices—they can avoid quadruplication and get along with a quarter of that number, or 144. And by eliminating the duplicate cases in which one side's preference is matched with a dissimilar preference for the other, they can cover every combination with 78 different matrices. (Twelve symmetrical cases occur in which one side's preference ranking is the mirror image of the other's. Sixty-six asymmetrical cases occur twice each; IFF-YES and YES-IFF, for example. Twice 66 is 132; adding the 12 makes 144.)

Of the 24 configurations for our side there are six in which we uniformly prefer them to have it—whatever "it" is—and six in which we prefer them not to have it, six in which we want them to have it if and only if we do and six in which we want them to have it if and only if we do not. There are likewise six for the other side in which they have a dominant preference for our not having it. So if we restrict attention to weapons that we always prefer each other not to have there are $6 \times 6 = 36$ pairs of preference rankings to consider.

Among the six apiece, one is the IFF case in which each prefers to have it if and only if the other does not. We can call it IFFN. It is obtained from the IFF matrix by interchanging the rows. Logically the IFFN case cannot be excluded. But it rarely corresponds to weapons, and I suppressed it, getting five rather than six matrices in fig. 1. That would have led to $5 \times 5 = 25$ matrices in fig. 2.

I then chose to neglect differences between the two NO configurations. In a longer paper I would have to resurrect the distinction. The longer paper might have to consider preferences as shown in the two matrices below. The other side has an IFFN configuration—a preference to have the weapon if and only if we do not. Depending on which of the two NO configurations we have, we may or may not see advantage in acquiring the weapon (visibly, irrevocably, and before the other side has it), inducing the other side to do without.

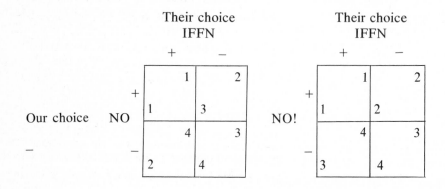

In either case, NO or NO!, the other side will acquire the weapon if we do not. With NO, if someone is to have it, we'd rather it be us. With NO! we'd rather let them go ahead and get it.

If we were dealing with bargaining situations other than those relating to weapons, the other form of the IFF configuration would undoubtedly be pertinent. There may be a number of contexts in which there is something that I would prefer to have only if you do not, and would prefer not to have if you do. It is hard to think of weapons that correspond to that preference. With a little imagination we can invent one. Consider any weapon such that if we both have it collision is inevitable and catastrophic. It is a positive advantage to have it as long as the other does not. I prefer you not to have it, whether or not I have it. If you do not, I can safely have it, and get an advantage; but if you have it I must avoid it to avoid collision. This situation meets my ground rule that we are discussing only weapons that I unconditionally prefer you not to have. It is the IFF case in reverse, that I labeled IFFN. If you are NO (but not NO!) you might preclusively acquire it to keep me from getting it.

By now it should be clear that two motivations led to my restricted set of matrices shown in fig. 2. One was the desire to stay within the realm of most familiar and plausible attitudes that a government could have toward its own possession of a weapon. This is a simplification that perforce neglects some interesting but unusual cases. The second was the desire to keep the number of matrices small enough to print legibility on a single page and capable of being quickly scanned and comprehended.

The paper was hardly a complete treatment even of the important cases included, so some screening out of possibly interesting matrices was probably excusable. But any reader who is attracted to the examination of more complex motivations, either through curiosity about logical possibilities or through an imaginative contemplation of less mundane weapon systems, will want a richer set of matrices to contemplate, and he has my encouragement.

E.3. A note on the joint use of GRIT and veto-incremax procedures

WALTER ISARD and PHYLLIS KANISS

1. Introduction

Despite the tremendous stimulation and provocation that we have received from Kenneth Boulding over the last decades, peace scientists as yet have not come up with superior, let alone workable, procedures for resolving conflicts—particularly conflicts of the prisoner's dilemma variety. (Here, independent maximizing behavior by the participants— each seeking short-run advantage over the other—leads to an inefficient solution; clearly participants stand to gain through cooperative decision-making.) One reason for this unhappy situation may be that perhaps each of us still remains too specialized in his scholarly pursuits and expertise to hit upon the right combination of elements that would characterize an effective and flexible cooperative procedure for situations of reality. This suggests the need for transdisciplinary efforts, so effectively propounded by Kenneth Boulding, and motivates the writing of this note.

Specifically, we wish to explore the possibility of joint use or synthesis of two approaches to the development of conflict-resolution procedures. The first approach draws upon the area of human communications, focusing on how parties to a conflict perceive each other's intentions and mutually create escalations and de-escalations of conflicts. From this perspective, Charles E. Osgood, a distinguished psychologist, has developed a procedure called Graduated and Reciprocated Initiatives in Tension-Reduction, or GRIT[1], which specifies how the intentions of the opposition may be shaped by certain initiatives calculated to reduce tensions. The second approach draws heavily upon game-theoretic, economic and regional science analysis, and is designed to have psychological appeal in terms of rationality. This procedure, developed

---

[1] See Charles E. Osgood, *An Alternative to War or Surrender*: *Perspective in Foreign Policy* and 'GRIT for MBER: A Proposal for Unfreezing Force-Level Postures in Europe', an unpublished paper. We draw very heavily upon the last item in section 2 of this note.

by the senior author[2], and referred to as the Veto-Incremax procedure, poses the conflict in rigorous mathematical form, and proceeds to specify steps by which participants may improve their positions through cooperation. We hope to show how these two approaches can be effectively synthesized to yield a still more flexible cooperative procedure—incorporating the strengths of both approaches while eliminating some of the weaknesses of each.

2. GRIT in a nutshell

The GRIT procedure represents an attempt to apply in international relations some of the principles of communications and learning that have been found to hold in interpersonal relations—where communication is more by deeds than words. GRIT essentially tries to establish a "learning process" between parties to a conflict, where what is learned is mutual understanding and trust.

Specifically, GRIT has been applied to situations in which both parties to a conflict have strong motives to disengage themselves, but in which negotiations have broken down and an unsatisfactory status quo have been frozen. For example, Osgood demonstrates how the GRIT procedure would be applied to the case of mutual and balanced force reductions in Europe, where both the United States and Soviet Union have strong motives for reducing tensions, but where negotiations have become deadlocked. Thus, there is a need to unfreeze the situation and create an atmosphere of mutual trust within which negotiations may proceed.

GRIT sets forward a strategy wherein one participant decides to take *unilateral initiatives to reduce tensions*, with the intention of propelling the opponent into *reciprocating*. Such steps are *necessarily graduated*, in order that security may be maintained throughout the process and that risk may remain within satisfactory limits. These small steps also have the advantage of not abruptly destabilizing the balance that may exist between two nations, or two blocs of nations, but rather of leading to a path of gradual change. The strength of GRIT therefore is that, unlike traditional negotiation, it substitutes *post*-commitment via reciprocation for *prior* commitment, thereby breaking the chains of mutual agreement-before-action and freeing both sides for taking the initiative.

Osgood specifies a number of rules for the application of GRIT, which ensure that national security can be maintained during the process, that

---

[2]See W. Isard, 'Veto-Incremax Procedure: Potential for Vietnam Conflict Resolution', *Papers*, Peace Science Society (International) X, (1968); and W. Isard, T. E. Smith *et al.*, *General Theory: Social, Political, Economic, and Regional* (MIT Press, Cambridge, Mass., 1969) Ch. 7, pp. 309–328.

the likelihood of reciprocation can be maximized, and that the genuineness of initiations and reciprocations can be evaluated. The rules (in the Soviet Union-U.S.A. context) consist of the following:

(1) Unilateral initiatives must not reduce our capacity to inflict unacceptable nuclear retaliation should we be attacked at that level.

(2) Unilateral initiatives must not cripple our capacity to meet conventional aggression with appropriately graded response using conventional weapons.

Rules one and two guarantee that if the opponent tries to take advantage of the initiative, we have the capacity to restore the status quo that existed before the process began.

(3) Unilateral initiatives must be graduated in risk according to the degree of reciprocation obtained from an opponent.

This rule represents the essential self-regulating feedback characteristic of GRIT: the relative risk remains roughly constant throughout the process.

(4) Unilateral initiatives should be diversified in nature, both as to sphere of action and as to geographical locus of application.

Thus, we may keep applying pressure upon an opponent to reciprocate and yet not weaken ourselves progressively in any one area.

(5) Unilateral initiatives must be designed and communicated so as to emphasize a sincere intent to reduce tensions.

(6) Unilateral initiatives should be publicly announced at some reasonable interval prior to their execution and identified as part of a deliberate policy of reducing tensions.

(7) Unilateral initiatives should include in their announcement explicit invitations to reciprocation in some form.

Rules 5, 6 and 7 are aimed not only in convincing the opponent of our intentions, but also in enlisting the pressures of world opinion on the side of continuing participation in the de-escalating of tensions.

(8) Unilateral initiatives that have been announced must be executed on schedule regardless of any prior commitments to reciprocate by the opponent.

(9) Unilateral initiatives should be continued over a considerable period, regardless of lack of reciprocation.

(10) Unilateral initiatives must be as unambiguous and as susceptible to verification as possible.

The procedure is thus designed to communicate to any opponent the following:

(1) If he tries to change an unsatisfactory existing status quo by force, we will firmly resist and restore the status quo.

(2) If he tries to change the status quo by means which reduce tensions, we will reward him by steps having similar intent.

(3) If he tries to take advantage of our conciliatory initiatives, we will shift immediately to firm and punishing resistance.

(4) If on the other hand, he reciprocates to our initiatives with steps of his own having similar intent, we will reward him with somewhat larger steps designed to reduce tensions.

It should be recognized that GRIT does not require that any "goodwill" already exist between the parties in conflict in order to succeed. What is required, rather, is sufficient self-interest on both sides, so that both parties recognize that it is to their advantage to move forward in the mutual de-escalation.

3. The basic elements of veto-incremax

The veto-incremax procedure has been designed for a conflict situation which may be viewed as a generalized version of the international conflict to which we have just alluded—a non-zero sum version of the prisoners' dilemma, in which independent maximizing behavior by participants leads to a solution less preferred by both than that which may be obtained through cooperation.

The prisoners' dilemma may be posed in the following form, using as an example the case of detente between two major powers. We conceive of the two nations as each having a set of alternatives, or an action space, from which they may choose an action; in the detente example, the action would be defined in terms of a continuum of equivalent military expenditures. Graphically, as in fig. 1, we measure along the vertical axis the action set of one player, using for simplicity one dimension only— i.e. expenditures stated in a standard currency unit, on some relevant weapon system, ranging from say 0–10 billion dollars. Along the horizontal axis, we measure the same for the other participant. The box connecting the two axes thus contains all the possible joint actions.

Associated with each participant is a (quasi-concave, ordinal) preference function for the outcomes associated with each joint action, where outcomes may be defined as perceived political-military position after discounting for military expenditures. The preference function for each nation is representable by a set of indifference curves on the joint action space, where, for a given nation, an indifference curve represents the locus of joint actions equally desired by that nation. In fig. 1, the indifference curves for nation Alpha are represented by the solid lines, for nation Beta, by the dashed lines. The numbers associated with the

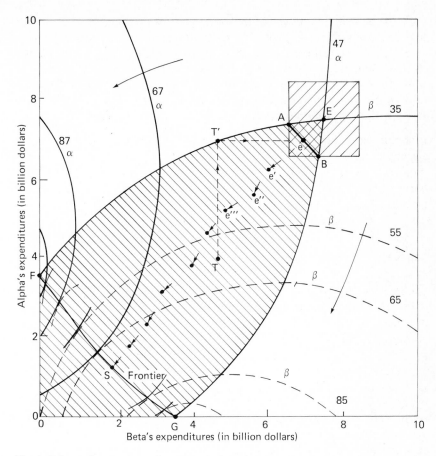

Fig. 1. Joint action space, preference orderings, improvement and commitment sets for nation α and nation β.

indifference curves are employed to indicate an ordering of preferences only; any other set of numbers which preserves the ordering can be used. Thus, the veto incremax procedure requires that participants state only their preferences among alternatives; no intercomparisons of utility are required. In fig. 1, Alpha's most preferred position can be seen to be point *F*, and Beta's most preferred position is point *G*.

Now, where each of the participants is motivated strictly to achieve the outcome that he most prefers, and where each of them behaves as a short-sighted Cournot maximizer, they will end up at the globally stable equilibrium point *E*, in the diagram. For if the participants are at some other point, say *T*, at some point in time, sooner or later one participant, say Alpha, though recognizing that eventually the other will react, senses that there will be a lag in this reaction and judges that he can achieve certain short-run gains through increasing his expenditures toward point T' and building up capability in the given weapon system. And Beta in time will react by increasing his expenditures. Ultimately they reach or come close to point E. We can see that E is an inefficient point, with both nations making relatively large expenditures on the weapon system, and both being on relatively low indifference curves. Clearly, both can improve their positions, or move to higher indifference curves, if they take part in a cooperative decision. What is required is a procedure which will take the participants to a joint action on the efficiency frontier (the line connecting F and G in the diagram and the tangency points of their indifference curves) where one nation can only reach a higher indifference curve at the expense of another nation's moving to a lower one.

The Veto-Incremax strategy was designed to provide a psychologically appealing procedure to reach such an efficient solution. It involves a maximization process taken over a series of small steps, eventually leading to a point on the efficiency frontier. The general properties of the veto-incremax procedure include the following:

1. Veto power: on any move the procedure allows each participant to exercise the veto power, which exercise commits participants only to the joint action in effect before the first move. This ensures that no participant will do worse than at the start. (Actually, in a more rigorous framework, the veto power is redundant, but it is retained for psychological reasons—i.e. the veto power may increase some participants' receptivity toward adopting a cooperative procedure.)

And, except when the veto power is exercised:

2. Objective achievement: The procedure ensures that the participants' objective will be achieved after a finite number of steps.

3. Pre-indeterminancy: The procedure allows each participant to ensure that for any number of initial steps, the joint proposals which may be reached cannot be determined uniquely by the other participant.

4. Guaranteed Improvement: The procedure ensures that no participant will ever be worse off on any move.

5. Limited Commitment: The procedure allows each participant to be as conservative and cautious as he desires with respect to the amount of change in proposed actions on any move; that is, within extreme limits, each participant is allowed to make as small a commitment as he desires.

The procedure consists of a series of moves in a step-by-step improvement process for each party. On each move, each participant is to make a proposal for a joint action. These proposals are however subject to the following rules:

Rule 1: In making any proposal for a joint action, each player shall not consider a joint action which would yield any participant an outcome less preferred than the joint proposal reached in the preceding move. On move one, this rule means that each participant's proposal for a joint action must lie within or on the boundary of the shaded area in fig. 1, enclosed by the indifference curves which course through the equilibrium point E.

Rule 2: On each move no player can propose a joint action which lies outside the commitment set. In fig. 1, the commitment set for the first move is the striped box centering on the equilibrium point. The commitment set is obtained by first identifying the maximum change along both the vertical and the horizontal axes which each participant is willing to allow on that move, and then by taking the least of these maximums first along the vertical and then along the horizontal.

We can imagine that in fig. 1, Alpha's proposal for a joint action will be A, located on its highest indifference curve within the commitment and improvement sets, and that, in similar fashion, Beta's proposed joint action will be B. Since these two proposals are not identical, the participants must adopt some compromise proposal, for instance the joint action e defined by the midpoint of the straight line connecting the proposed joint actions of the two participants (embodying a split-the-difference principle.) This joint action serves as the reference point for improvement during the second move. On move two, the participants identify another improvement set and define another commitment set, the commitments generally differing from the corresponding commitments made at the start of the first move. This process goes on through a series of compromise joint actions e', e'', e''',..., until some point s on the efficiency frontier is reached.

4. The synthesis

Now that we have presented both approaches, we can turn our attention to their synthesis. Specifically, we can show how the notion of unilateral initiatives can be incorporated into the veto-incremax procedure, and correspondingly how the veto-incremax procedure can be made part of the GRIT approach. In doing so, we will at the same time attempt some synthesis of the rich range of human communications and personality variables with those variables treated in mathematically rigorous decision-making models.

The veto-incremax procedure states little about the personalities that might be involved in a conflict situation, their drives, their hang-ups, their attitudes and the ways that they communicate with each other. It implicitly assumes that these variables are irrelevant, and further that there is a third party who has perfect rapport and communication with the two or more participants. But in reality none of this is so. We therefore must introduce some new variables in the veto-incremax approach.

Re personality types, one relevant continuum might run from highly aggressive to highly passive. Another continuum related to the first but different in important aspects, might run from a 100% leader to a 100% follower. These two continua allow a two-dimensional space defined by the four points: a highly-aggressive 100%-leader, a highly-aggressive 100%-follower, a passive 100%-leader, and a passive 100%-follower, although the passive 100%-leader and highly-aggressive 100%-follower types may be points which can only be approached but not reached in a two-dimensional characterization, because of possible contradiction. Other relevant continua might run from 100% optimistic to 100% pessimistic, from 100% secure to 100% insecure, from highly abstract to highly pragmatic. All these and other personality dimensions may be very important in any conflict situation.

In addition, a wide range of communication channels and surrounding environments may characterize a conflict situation. At the one extreme the environment may consist of those properties describable by an informal lunch get-together where conflicts though major are discussed in a casual manner and as secondary to the quality of the meal: there may be no ordering of individuals by rank or other characteristics, as in positions about a round table. At the other extreme the environment might comprise a highly formalistic spatial setting where positions are ordered by rank about a long rectangular table and where the meeting and discussion is confined solely to the conflict issue.

It is beyond the scope of this note to elaborate further on these important variables. We now want to demonstrate that there is the potential for including some of these variables in the veto-incremax procedure, and conversely that the mathematical formalism of an incremax procedure can be included in a human-communications situation basically describable in terms of some of the variables just discussed.

Let us begin by introducing the leader-follower continuum as a basic dimension in the veto-incremax procedure. Specifically let one of the participants be a unilateral action-taker and thereby be a leader; and let the other be a follower. Also, let us dispense with the third party who is implicit in the standard presentation of the veto-incremax procedure, and whose function is to bring together and guide the two or more participants in their moves. Further for the moment restrict the situation to a two-participant conflict, where perhaps mutual trust is low, and the traditional bargaining process seems to have broken down.

In being moved to take a unilateral initiative, the leader hopes his opponent will reciprocate to yield a joint action which is an improvement to both. If we adopt the rules set down by the incremax procedure, we can specify precisely certain features that the unilateral initiative should have. The initiative should first represent *guaranteed improvement* to the second participant as well as to the first. Thus, the leader considers only those joint actions which are in the improvement set. This requires, of course, that the leader have fairly complete knowledge of the preferences of the second party.

Next, the leader considers the extent of change that will be made by the initiative and the reciprocating action that it is hoped will occur. The leader knows that there is a maximum amount of change that the second party might undertake in any reciprocating action. Thus he sets the maximum for the second party as one possible limit for defining the commitment set. But he himself has his own security in mind in taking any initiative; specifically he wants to be in a position to be able to return to the initial stalemate position without jeopardizing his security—that is, to be able to restore the status quo. Therefore, he sets a maximum change in his unilateral initiative, which serves as another possible limit for the commitment set. By taking the minimum of both these, he is thus able to define a commitment set.

Next, the leader examines the intersection of the improvement set and the commitment set. Any point interior to this intersection is an improvement to both parties. In choosing a point within this area, the leader may define the joint action which he most prefers, the joint action which the second participant most prefers, and perhaps split the difference in identifying a point or a joint proposal for the achievement of which he takes a unilateral initiative. In terms of fig. 1, he chooses a level of expenditures corresponding to point *e* which is lower than his level corresponding to point *E*. He then hopes that his opponent will reciprocate by reducing his level of expenditures so as to be consistent with a joint action described by point *e*, inviting his opponent to do so because of the various desirable outcomes to the opponent. If the opponent does not reciprocate, he makes it clear to the opponent that he will go back to the stalemate position *E*. If the opponent does reciprocate, then he proceeds to the second move of the veto incremax procedure. First, he defines for the second move the improvement set and the limited-commitment set. Within the intersection of these two sets, he then defines the most-preferred joint actions (proposals). He then splits the difference between the most preferred joint actions to find that point to determine his unilateral action. Again he asks the opponent to reciprocate. And so the process continues à la GRIT.

Let us probe more deeply into possible action-reaction sequences by making explicit other personality variables. First the leader may be very perceptive of the series of positive actions and reactions that can be involved. After identifying the intersection of the two sets for the first round and the most-preferred joint actions of each participant, he may choose not to use a split-the-difference principle to determine the reference point for his unilateral initiative. He may judge it better to give his opponent somewhat more than half the difference at least on the first move. And he may suggest a joint action close to his opponent's most preferred joint action in order to start the process rolling and to build up confidence and trust.

Or suppose the party who takes unilateral initiative is a natural leader who likes to lead and derives much satisfaction from taking the first step, particularly if it leads to a series of actions and reactions which will be viewed by society as successful. Suppose it also turns out that the second party is an aggressive follower where his strategy is to let the other person take the first move, and then respond out of pure self interest to get as much as possible. Thus we have a situation where in fact the two participants might gain equal satisfaction or utility when a first unilateral initiative is followed by reciprocation after the leader has proposed a compromise wherein he yields more than 50% of the distance along the straight line connecting the most desired joint actions. For example he might yield 75% of the way, thereby requiring the aggressive follower to yield only 25%. (In more formal terms he may embed in his unilateral initiative a weighted average split-the-difference principle). Or if the follower is not only aggressive, but likes to demonstrate to the world that he always gets the better of the deal, the leader may be able to elicit reciprocation if he concedes only 51% of the distance. These types of personality mixes are however, not explicitly recognized and exploited in the standard veto-incremax statement.

Or consider two participants who might be almost identical in terms of aggressivity and other personality traits but who as political leaders represent distinctly different constituencies. One leader's constituents may be patient, willing to see much time transpire in order to reach the right kind of resolution. The other leader's constituency may be impatient for results and insist on demonstrated progress within a short time span. In all other respects, for example with regard to per capita income and know-how, the constituencies may be the same. In this situation we may easily imagine that the second leader may be the one to propose a unilateral initiative, but also be willing to undertake an initiative which involves a greater concession on his part.

Or suppose that the first participant is an aggressive imaginative leader and that the second is a normal unimaginative follower. The first must directly bear the time costs and the bother involved in planning and working out schemes. Though willing to do so, he may also insist that he be reimbursed for his trouble—reimbursed in that he is not motivated to take a unilateral initiative which would not involve the greater concession on the part of the follower if indeed the follower were to reciprocate.

On the other hand we can readily see where it wouldn't work to have the combination of an aggressive leader insisting on full reimbursement for his costs plus a 50% share, with an aggressive follower insisting upon more than 50%. We can imagine that the combination of two unimaginative aggressive followers would not work, or the combination of two aggressive leaders, each insisting on obtaining full credit for success.

Also, when we introduce bluffing and diverse dynamic elements, we can see for a wide range of cases of unilateral initiatives how there will be no sequence of actions and reactions. For example, imagine a unilateral initiative by a leader involving a concession which the second participant states is inadequate. The second participant, being perhaps an aggressive follower, may actually consider the concession reasonable, but may also feel that he can get more by bluffing. On the other hand the leader recognizes the possibility that the follower may be bluffing, but does not know whether in fact he is. Further, the leader does not know, should he make an additional concession in a first-round unilateral initiative, whether the follower might bluff still more and insist on still another augmentation of the concession. To avoid a series of subsequent concessions, and to be certain that he is not outwitted, the leader might decide that he must stick to his initial unilateral initiative. Thus we may have an unreciprocated initiative, and no resolution.

This particular case and numerous others where a unilateral initiative is not reciprocated, let alone advanced, suggest the introduction into the situation of a third party. This party should be one who is sensitive to the various psychological factors that are at play, who can identify differences in value systems that may exist, who can facilitate discussions and information-seeking activity, who can educate the participants as to the fundamental realities of the situation, and who is perceptive and particularly skilled in observing which dimensions of a problem are most important for each party. Thus he would be able to ask for large concessions from one party in areas of less importance to him but significant to the other. Such a third party is implicit in the veto-incremax procedure. His introduction suggests as a possibility the fusion of the veto-incremax procedure and the GRIT approach in an extended two-stage procedure. In this procedure, the participants might adopt the following rules:

Stage I Rules:

(1) The two parties come together at a fixed point in time, for purposes of socializing and for making unilateral proposals. The participants remain together for a set period of time, agreed upon at the start.

(2) If during the time period, one participant takes a unilateral initiative and it is reciprocated, then they are to continue to interact, through a series of rounds, until the conflict is in whole or large part resolved. Then *Stage II is ignored.*

(3) If neither of the participants takes a unilateral initiative during the time period, or if they achieve insufficient progress in one or more rounds of unilateral initiatives and reciprocation, then Stage II is begun.

(4) If both the participants simultaneously take unilateral initiatives, each insisting on the role of leader, and if no agreement can be reached on which initiative should be recognized, then Stage II is begun.

(5) If one participant takes a unilateral initiative which is not reciprocated, then Stage II is begun.

Stage II Rules:

(1) A sensitive perceptive mediator is called in to assist in the use of the veto-incremax procedure.

(2)–(3) The same as Rules 1 and 2 in section 3.

Concluding statement

We have presented some of the overlapping features of the GRIT and veto-incremax approaches. We have suggested certain ways in which these two approaches can be at least partially synthesized to apply to a broader range of conflict situations. Clearly, however, much more work must be done in introducing the *personality-mix* variables into a theoretic interdependent decision-making structure. Much more work needs to be done in developing effective definitions of concepts such as leader, aggressiveness, and pragmatism, and in developing relevant indexes of measurement. Then more significant progress should be attainable in formulating a wider range of more effective procedures for conflict resolution.

E.4.   A new arms age

MURRAY L. WEIDENBAUM

"Whatever the costs and benefits of the classical system of
national defense, however, it represents a system which is
no longer available to the developed world."
                                                Kenneth E. Boulding[1]

Since 1945, man has possessed the power to destroy human life on earth.
The reaction of many to that condition has been to dismiss summarily any
serious concern with the role of the military in society as defense of an evil
that should promptly be removed. In contrast, this paper is based on the
assumption that different groups of people, nations as well as other
institutions, will continue to be rivals for control over the wealth of the
world and power over its inhabitants.[2]

That rivalry may not always involve armed conflict, but the possibility
of settling disputes by force will remain. Thus, each society will continue
to take steps to insure its self-preservation. That may not necessarily
require arming to the teeth and it certainly does not require an agressive,
threatening stance in international relations. Yet, the need for national
armament is thus likely to continue on a substantial scale, although not
necessarily at the present level, for the predictable future.

That humane historian-philosopher, John Neff, may have provided the
most satisfactory explanation of the continued need to consider the
military establishment not as a temporary, unpleasant expedient, but in a
long-term framework. The following quotation is taken from the conclud-

---

[1]Kenneth E. Boulding, 'The World War Industry as an Economic Problem', in: Emile
Benoit and Kenneth E. Boulding (eds.), *Disarmament and the Economy* (Harper and Row,
New York, 1963) 15.
[2]This chapter draws upon materials in M. L. Weidenbaum, *The Economics of Peace-time
Defense* (Praeger, New York, 1974).

ing portion of his monumental study of war and progress:

Let us not hoodwink ourselves with notions of perpetual peace and the millennium. These only increase the danger of war, for they rest upon a misunderstanding of human nature. Men and women are not angels.[3]

1. The two superpowers

To begin with the obvious—which is often enough overlooked in discussions of the American "military-industrial complex"—there are two great military superpowers in the world today, the United States and the Soviet Union. Each is the kingpin in a major formal military alliance to which it provides "collective goods" in the form of military power, the United States in NATO and the Soviets in the Warsaw pact. Each is the power center of an even broader but looser alignment of nations—the United States in what we like to call, sometimes stretching our poetic license to the limit, the free world or the market-oriented economies; the Soviets among the communist nations or the controlled economies.

The two categories are quite subjective. Economic controls on the part of the United States or its allies are discounted as transient departures from a free economy, while reliance on profits and other capitalistic modes by the Soviet Union or its allies are dismissed as temporary experiments or aberrations. Nevertheless, the economic and political differences between the two groups of nations are substantial.

Numerous reasons are offered for the magnitude of military expenditures in the United States. Official explanations, of course, usually run in terms of responding to external stimuli—"the responsibility of leadership in the Free World", "protecting our citizens against external aggression", and so forth. In contrast, critics—Marxist and otherwise—often claim that this nation as well as other countries generally expand armed forces for internal reasons. These include responding to pressures from the military establishment and defense contractors, protecting and expanding American business interests overseas, and engaging in related imperialistic ventures.

A widely held hypothesis falls somewhere in between these two polar alternatives. In this third or intermediate view, the high levels of military outlays, in both the United States and the Soviet Union, are attributed primarily to the pattern of interaction between the two major world powers. Thus, the current arms race is seen as the result of mutual challenge and response between the two nations. Each has been in some measure responding to the other's military expenditures. While the

[3]John U. Neff, *War and Human Progress* (W. W. Norton, New York, 1963) 416.

United States has reacted to the Russian stimulus, it has perhaps unavoidably provoked USSR countermeasures that were, in turn, seen as demanding new American military activities to match them.[4]

This view is supported by an analysis of United States and USSR military expenditures during the 1950–62 time period. Almost half of the variation (48 percent) over time in one nation's defense spending could be explained by the other's.[5] These data provide some support for the view that either the two states are interacting or, at least, that one is responding very quickly to changes in the other's military outlays. Of course, other factors are obviously present (the unexplained 52 percent of the variation). Certainly, to a substantial extent the high and rising money outlays on armaments by the two super-powers reflect the revolution in military technology, which has given rise to such sophisticated and expensive items of military combat as ICBMs, space systems, and nuclear submarines.

The scale of physical resources used by a modern military establishment is so staggering that it is difficult to comprehend it. The U.S. Department of Defense owns $51 billion worth of land and buildings and $172 billion in supplies and equipment, mainly weapons. The holdings of individual corporations, however large and diversified, pale in comparison: Exxon reports ownership of $20 billion in land, plant, and equipment; General Motors reports $14 billion; and U.S. Steel a paltry $9 billion.[6]

2. The shifting strategic balance

Paradoxically, while the American society has been developing a more critical attitude toward its defense establishment, Russian military efforts have been accelerated. The armed forces of the Soviet Union are approaching those of the United States in many measures of military power. Reasonable opinions mainly differ only about whether the Soviets have caught up and surpassed, or are merely gaining on the United States.

Historical perspective is needed. In the 1950s, the United States developed the unprecedented power to devastate the heartland of any potential enemy. Compared to the Soviet Union, it was far ahead in all

[4]Bruce M. Russett, *What Price Vigilance?* (Yale University Press, New Haven, 1970) 7.
[5]Frederic L. Pryor, *Public Expenditures in Communist and Capitalist Nations* (Richard D. Irwin, Homewood, Ill., 1969) 113.
[6]U.S. House of Representatives, Committee on Government Operations, *Federal Real and Personal Property Inventory Report of the U.S. Government as of June 30, 1970* (U.S. Government Printing Office, Washington, 1971).

objective measures of such "strategic" power. Its stockpile of nuclear
weapons was many times larger than the Soviet's. It had more long-range
bombers and ICBMs with which to attack. It had more nuclear warheads
for those "carriers" to fire, and the accuracy of its weapons was superior.

In retrospect, the Cuban-missile confrontation in 1962 proved to be a
critical turning point in the relationship between American and Soviet
military power. Up to that time, Russia's strategic efforts mainly centered on defensive systems designed to reduce the damage from an
enemy attack. They consistently deployed more fighter aircraft, anti-
aircraft guns, and surface-to-air missiles than the United States.[7] In the
short run, the missile crisis yielded a victory for the United States, in that
the Russians under pressure removed their missiles from that key
location. But in the longer run, the results are proving to be quite
different.

After the 1962 crisis had passed, American strategic thinking began
giving greater emphasis to courses of action that would avoid such
confrontations in the future, with their accompanying possibility of
nuclear war with the Soviets. The buildup in the size of the American
ICBM and submarine-launched strategic forces slowed down noticeably
soon thereafter. It would have seemed reasonable to expect that the
Soviet leaders shared similar views, but they never gave any sign that
they were on the same intellectual wavelength. The basic Russian
reaction to the 1962 crisis was to plan to reduce or neutralize American
strategic superiority.[8]

The tale is told of the assignment of John J. McCloy by President John
F. Kennedy to assure that the Russians were keeping their promise to
remove their missiles from Cuba. In a meeting soon after, Soviet Deputy
Foreign Minister V. V. Kuznetsov told McCloy, "We will live up to this
agreement, but we will never be caught like that again".[9] At about that
time, the Soviet Union began a program of military development and
production that has been continuing full bore for over a decade now.

Unlike the case ten years ago, it is now very difficult to weigh in the
balance the relative military strengths of the USSR and the United
States. Fundamental differences in geopolitical positions, as well as the
great variety of weapon systems that each side possesses, complicate the
task of saying who is "ahead". Because there are so many factors
affecting a nation's strategic posture, no single way of assessing it is

[7]Edward Luttwak, *The Strategic Balance, 1972,* Washington Papers No. 3 (Library Press,
New York, 1972) 17–18.
[8]Walter D. Jacobs, 'Soviet Strategic Effectiveness', *Journal of International Affairs*, 20, No.
1 (1972) 69–71.
[9]Hugh Sidey, 'The Arms Race Hasn't Stopped', *Life*, (October 15, 1974) 4.

sufficient. Moreover, some observers believe that trying to balance off nuclear weapons of different sizes and characteristics, when a modest portion of either arsenal could wipe out the other nation, is an exercise which only perpetuates a madly expensive and essentially futile arms race. Nevertheless, some objective and useful measurements can be taken.

Let us compare the "strategic forces", those weapons that would be used in an all-out war to destroy the homeland of an enemy. The number of weapon carriers or "delivery" vehicles—air planes, missiles, and submarines—is clearly an important aspect of strategic force. The number of warheads that these vehicles can deliver to targets is another. The number of different targets that they can reach is still another. Finally, the effectiveness and the accuracy with which the warheads hit the intended targets are key factors.

At the present time, the United States no longer has an undisputed lead in all of these aspects of strategic power, although it clearly has retained its lead in some areas. It has more individual warheads, 5,700 to 2,500, and it is generally believed that they are more accurate, although generally smaller than the Russians'. Adding up the weight of the nuclear warheads that each side has at its disposal shows that the sheer poundage of the Soviet stockpile is greater, by about 2 to 1 (but a single nuclear weapon cannot destroy as large an area as several smaller weapons with the same total warhead weight).

In the total number of strategic "vehicles" capable of carrying nuclear bombs to a potential enemy, the Russians now possess a larger inventory of ICBMs (1,527 to 1,054) and the United States more submarine-launched ballistic missiles (656 to 628). But is an invulnerable submarine really equivalent to a single missile silo or a subsonic bomber? Is a faster-starting solid-fueled American Minuteman equal to a Soviet slow-to-start liquid-fueled ICBM? It is far easier to answer these questions with a simple "no", than to come up with a measure of equivalency.

A detailed examination of available information on the respective armed forces tends to be inconclusive. The United States leads in some categories, notably long-range bombers and tactical aircraft, and the Soviets in others, such as medium bombers and ICBMs, as well as numbers of tanks and size of armed forces. It is thus clear that the United States does not now possess that overwhelming strategic/nuclear power that it did five or ten years ago. An important shift in the relative balance between the two military superpowers has taken place during the last few years. The U.S.S.R. is now in a relatively stronger position vis-à-vis the armed strength of the United States than was the case in the early 1960's.

The fact that each of the two military superpowers possesses the power to exterminate the human race singlehandedly has created a certain commonality of outlook, a sort of interdependence keyed to the survival of both nations. Although they continue to compete, the nature of the conflict is seen as not permitting resolution by victory in the classical sense. The military forces of the two nations are relatively in balance, at least to the key extent that each is deterred from attacking the other for fear of unacceptable retaliation, and no third super state is likely to emerge.

3. Prospects for a lower U.S. military profile

The basic design of a nation's military establishment results from its evaluation of the external environment facing it and from the response it chooses to make. At the present time several factors point to a lower U.S. military profile in the coming decade than was the case in the preceding several decades. The potential external threats to the national security have not suddenly evaporated, but important changes have been occurring in the character of those threats.

During much of the period following World War II, the typical view in the United States was that the nation faced the threat of a unified communist bloc of nations dominated by the ideology and arms of the U.S.S.R. Gradually, differences arose among the communist nations, such as the emergence of a relatively independent Yugoslavia.

More recently the image of a monolithic Communist force has been shattered. Sharp rivalries have become visible among the communist nations, especially the growing antagonism between the Soviet Union and the Peoples Republic of China. The breakup of Communist Unity has relaxed some of their ideological inhibitions against dealing with the United States, and economic and political relationships have become more extensive.

Simultaneous with these political changes, the Soviet Union created a nuclear force comparable with that of the United States. This development had two related consequences. First, many in the United States viewed the time as ripe for serious consideration of formal limitations on armaments to prevent a spiraling arms race. Second, the growing military parity with the United States apparently relieved the Russians of at least some of their fears about the United States and permitted serious negotiations for the limitation of nuclear weapons and the first formal agreements in this area.

Particularly as a result of the Vietnam War, a new and more cautious appraisal is in the making of the military objectives which the United States can expect to achieve, particularly with conventional, non-nuclear forces. Simultaneously, there is greater appreciation of the relatively close but dangerously high level of balance between U.S. and U.S.S.R. nuclear capabilities.

This changing external environment hardly suggests an approaching general disarmament, and the difficulties being experienced in the second phase of the SALT talks attest to that. Neither does it inevitably lead to an acceleration of the arms race, particularly given the success of SALT. Rather, recent developments point to an undramatic intermediate position: a smaller overall military establishment in the United States in the 1970s than was characteristic of the 1960s, but far superior to the pre-Korean level—particularly if the Soviet Union adopts a similar attitude.

Perhaps more fundamentally, the nature of the challenges facing the American society is changing, and the change is toward greater complexity. The newer challenges are intensifying and show great potential of becoming as serious as any military threat. These relate to the basic stability of a modern society and the economic, social, ecological, and political strains which have become increasingly severe in the last several years. The tremendous increase in the destructiveness of modern weapons has, paradoxically, resulted in the decline of raw military power as an effective instrument of national policy. Because of their awesomeness, nuclear weapons are reserved for an apocalyptic situation and are not employed for traditional "sabre-rattling" purposes.

Although "cold war" may no longer correctly describe the political and military relationships between the major powers, there clearly still is a grim competition for position and influence. Future conflicts among nations are likely often to be resolved through means which are primarily non-military, such as economic and technological competition, and propaganda and maneuvering within the framework of the international political community. This is a difficult environment for the United States to learn to live in successfully, in part because the power relationships are changing. The assured availability of energy sources is becoming at times more critical than the precise number of ICBMs in place. Traditional military allies often become economic rivals.

The United States appears to be adjusting its sights to the fact that it no longer possesses the preponderance of military or economic or scientific power that it had in the earlier post-World War II period. No one nation is likely to achieve primacy across the entire spectrum of international competition. Along with other developed countries, the United States is going through the rather humbling but no doubt useful and necessary process of acknowledging the desirability of a more modest role in world affairs than it had grown accustomed to playing.

Internal pressures, to be sure, still exist to return the thrust of policy-making to the earlier formulation. But they are likely at the most to modify and not to reverse the new trend, which is better suited to the grim realities of the 1970's.

The United States has come a long way toward a more realistic understanding of the effective limits of its power. One of the memorable statements from the early 1960's was the portion of President John F. Kennedy's inaugural address that contained the phrase "we will pay any price and bear any burden". That piece of eloquence has not held up as a vital statement of national intentions. What seemed at the time to be a ringing affirmation of the national will turned out to be little more than melodramatic speechmaking.

More appropriate may be the words of the former British Chancellor of the Exchequer, Roy Jenkins: "The American tent will in the future not be quite so gloriously and uniquely sited on the very top of the highest hill ... but it will still have a very prominent and vital position in the future for large parts of the world."[10]

4. Concluding thought

We are still very much in an age of armaments, but it is a new arms age. The factors that contribute to or detract from a nation's security are numerous and varied. These factors include formal military strength in a very large and fundamental way. But, as Vietnam vividly demonstrates, a large and well-equipped military establishment does not suffice. National security comprises something that is both more and less than formal military strength—the will and morale of the people. A society that shows itself capable of promptly recognizing challenges, domestic and international, and taking the often painful action needed to meet them, goes a long way toward demonstrating its basic strength. A society that meets its own standards of equity and fairness to its citizens simultane-ously bolsters its overall security and attracts the necessary investments in arms to defend itself.

[10]Roy Jenkins, 'A Lesser Role for Uncle Sam, but Still a Vital One', *Saturday Review* (June 10, 1972) 12.

F.   The contributors

Robert U. Ayres, International Research and Technology Corporation, Arlington, Va., USA.

Emile Benoit, Professor, School of Business and International Affairs, Columbia University, New York, N.Y., USA.

Albert G. Hart, Professor of Economics, Columbia University, New York, N.Y., USA.

Janos Horvath, Professor of Economics, Butler University, Indianapolis, Ind., USA.

Walter Isard, Professor, Peace Science Department, and Regional Science Department, Wharton School of Finance and Commerce, University of Pennsylvania, Philadelphia, Pa., USA.

Phyllis Kaniss, Regional Science Program, Cornell University, Ithaca, N.Y., USA.

George Katona, Professor Emeritus, Institute for Social Research and Department of Economics, University of Michigan, Ann Arbor, Mich., USA.

Cynthia E. Kerman, 4200 Elsrode Ave., Baltimore, Md., USA.

Tapan Munroe, Associate Professor of Economics, University of the Pacific, Stockton, Calif., USA.

James N. Morgan, Professor of Economics, University of Michigan; and Program Director, Institute for Social Research, University of Michigan, Ann Arbor, Mich., USA.

Mancur Olson, Professor of Economics, University of Maryland, College Park, Md., USA.

Anita B. Pfaff, Wissenschaftlicher Rat and Professor of Economics, University of Augsburg; and Head, Center for the Study of the Grants Economy, in the International Institute for Empirical Social Economics, Augsburg, F.R. of Germany.

Martin Pfaff, Professor of Economics, University of Augsburg; and Director, International Institute for Empirical Social Economics, Augsburg, F.R. of Germany.

328   *The Contributors*

Anatol Rapoport, Professor, Department of Psychology, University of Toronto, Toronto, Canada.

Thomas C. Schelling, Professor, John Fitzgerald Kennedy School of Government, Harvard University, Cambridge, Mass., USA.

Robert A. Solo, Professor of Economics and Management, Michigan State University, East Lansing, Mich., USA.

Burkhard Strümpel, Associate Professor of Economics; and Program Director, Institute for Social Research, University of Michigan, Ann Arbor, Mich., USA.

Murray L. Weidenbaum, Professor of Economics, Washington University, St. Louis, Miss., USA.

G. Some notes on Kenneth E. Boulding

Institute of Behavioral Science, University of Colorado, Boulder, Colo.,
  USA
Born January 18, 1910
American citizenship granted, 1948

Earl of Sefton Scholarship at Liverpool Collegiate School, 1923–28
Open Major Scholarship in Natural Sciences at New College, Oxford,
  1928–32
B.A., 1st Class Honours, School of Philosophy, Politics, and Economics,
  Oxford, 1931, M.A., Oxford, 1939
Commonwealth Fellow at University of Chicago, 1932–34

Assistant, University of Edinburgh, 1934–37
Instructor, Colgate University, 1937–41
Economist, League of Nations Economic and Financial Section, Prince-
  ton, N.J., 1941–42
Professor of Economics, Fisk University, 1942–43
Professor of Economics, Iowa State College, 1943–46; 1947–49
Angus Professor of Political Economy and Chairman of Department,
  McGill University, Montreal, Quebec, 1946–47
Professor of Economics, University of Michigan, 1949–67
Co-Director, Center for Research on Conflict Resolution, University of
  Michigan, 1961–64; Research Director, 1964–65; Director, 1965–66
Professor of Economics, University of Colorado, 1968—
Director of the Program of Research on General Social and Economic
  Dynamics, Institute of Behavioral Science, University of Colorado,
  1967—

Fellow, Center for Advanced Study in Behavioral Sciences, Stanford,
  Calif., 1954–55
Visiting Professor, University College of the West Indies, Kingston,
  Jamaica, 1959–60

Danforth Visiting Professor, International Christian University, Tokyo, Japan, 1963–64

Visiting Professor of Economics, University of Colorado, 1967–68

Visiting Professor, University of Natal, Durban, South Africa, September 1970

Visiting Lecturer, Japanese Broadcasting Company, Tokyo, Japan, October 1970

Visiting Professor, University of Edinburgh, Edinburgh, Scotland, Oct–Nov 1972

John Bates Clark Medal, American Economic Association, 1949; Distinguished Fellow, 1969

American Council of Learned Societies Prize for Distinguished Scholarship in the Humanities, 1962

Fellow, American Academy of Arts and Sciences, 1958—

Fellow, American Philosophical Society, 1960—

Vice-President, American Economic Association, 1958; President, 1968

President, Society for General Systems Research, 1957–59

Vice-President and Chairman of Section K, American Association for the Advancement of Science, 1966–67

Vice-President, International Studies Association, 1969–70; President-elect, 1973–74

President, Peace Research Society (International), 1970

President, Association for the Study of the Grants Economy, 1970—

Married Elise Biorn-Hansen of Syracuse, N.Y., 1941. Children: John Russell, 1947; Mark David, 1949; Christine Ann, 1951; Philip Daniel, 1953; William Frederick, 1953.

Member, Religious Society of Friends (Quakers)

Publications

1932

Articles

The Place of the "Displacement Cost" Concept in Economic Theory. Economic Journal, 42, 165 (Mar 1932): 137–141.
The Possibilities of Socialism in Britain. Plan. (Exeter College, Oxford), *1, 4* (May 1932): 25–27.

1934

Article

The Application of the Pure Theory of Population Change to the Theory of Capital. Quart. Jour. Econ., 48 (Aug 1934): 645–666.

1935

Articles

A Note on the Consumption Function. Rev. Econ. Stud., 2, 2 (Feb 1935): 99–103.
The Theory of a Single Investment. Quart. Jour. Econ., 49, 3 (May 1935): 475–494.

1936

Articles

Professor Knight's Capital Theory: A Note in Reply. Quart. Jour. Econ., 50, 3 (May 1936): 524–531.
Time and Investment. Economica, NS 3, 10 (May 1936): 196–220.

Time and Investment: A Reply. Economica, NS 3, 12 (Nov 1936): 440–442.

1937

Review

Review of E. C. van Dorp, *A Simple Theory of Capital, Wages, and Profit or Loss.* Economic Journal 47, *187* (Sept 1937): 522–524.

1938

Articles and Pamphlet

An Experiment in Friendship. American Friend, 26, *26* (Dec 22, 1938): 541–542.
In Defence of the Supernatural. Friends Intelligencer, 95, *41* (Oct 1938): 677–678.
Making Education Religious. American Friend, 26, *20* (Sept 29, 1938): 408–409.
Paths of Glory: A New Way with War. (pamphlet) Glasgow: University Press, for the John Horniman Trust, 1938. 32 Pp.
Worship and Fellowship. Friends Intelligencer, 95, *35* (Aug 1938): 579–580.

1939

Articles

Equilibrium and Wealth: A Word of Encouragement to Economists. Canadian Jour. Econ. Pol. Science, 5, *1* (Feb 1939): 1–18.
In Praise of Maladjustment. Friends Intelligencer, 96, *32* (Aug 1939): 519–520.
A Pacifist View of History. Fellowship, 5, *3* (Mar 1939): 10–11.

Review

Quantitative Economics. Review of John R. Hicks, *Value and Capital, An Inquiry into Some Fundamental Principles of Economic Theory; and Henry Schultz, The Theory of Measurement of Demand.* Canadian Jour. Econ. Polit. Science, 5, *4* (Nov 1939): 521–528.

1940

Articles

In Praise of Selfishness. Friends Intelligencer, 97, 9 (Mar 1940): 131–132.
The Pacifism of All Sensible Men. Friends Intelligencer, 97, 50 (Dec 1940): 801.
A Service of National Importance. American Friend, 28, 25 (Dec 1940): 521–522.
Some Reflections on Stewardship. American Friend, NS 28, 22 (Oct 1940): 452–454.

1941

Article

The Economics of Reconstruction. American Friend, 29, 9 (Apr 24, 1941): 177–178.

Book

Economic Analysis. New York: Harper & Brothers, 1941. xviii + 809 pp. See also: 1948, 1955, 1966.

1942

Articles and Pamphlets

The Abolition of Membership. American Friend, 30, 17 (Aug 13, 1942): 350–351.
A Deepening Loyalty. Friend, 115, 26 (June 25, 1942): 467–468.
In Praise of Danger. Friend (London), 100, 2 (Jan 9, 1942): 9–10.
New Nations for Old. (Pendle Hill Pamphlet No. 17) Wallingford, Pa: Pendle Hill, 1942. 40 pp.
The Practice of the Love of God. (William Penn Lecture; pamphlet) Philadelphia: Religious Society of Friends, 1942, 31 pp.
Taxation in War Time: Some Implications for Friends. American Friend, 30, 8 (Apr 9, 1942): 152–167.
The Theory of the Firm in the Last Ten Years. American Economic Review, 32, 4 (Dec 1942): 791–802.
What is Loyalty? (reflections on "A Statement of Loyalty Issued by Members of the Society of Friends," Mar 28, 1918) *Friends Intelligencer,* 99, 27 (July 4, 1942): 425–426.

1943

Article

The Problem of the Country Meeting. Friends Intelligencer, 100, 46 (Nov 13, 1943): 748–749.

1944

Articles

Desirable Changes in the National Economy After the War. Journal of Farm Economics, 26, 1 (Feb 1944): 95–100.

The Incidence of a Profits Tax. American Economic Review, 34, 3 (Sept 1944): 567–572.

Is It the System or Is It You? Highbroad (Nov 1944): 14–17.

A Liquidity Preference Theory of Market Prices. Economica, NS 11, 42 (May 1944): 55–63.

Nationalism, Millennialism and the Quaker Witness. American Friend, 32, 20 (Oct 5, 1944): 397–398.

Personal and Political Peacemaking: Application of the Friends Peace Testimony. American Friend, 32, 17 (Aug 24, 1944): 347–348.

Review

Review of Robert A. Brady, Business as a System of Power. Journal of Land Public Utility Economics (Feb 1944): 85.

Verse

The Nayler Sonnets. Inward Light, 19 (Spring 1944): 4–13. Also published as: *There is A Spirit* (The Nayler Sonnets). New York: Fellowship Press, 1945. Pp. 26.

1945

Articles

The Concept of Economic Surplus. American Economic Review, 35, 5 (Dec. 1945): 851–869. Errata. *American Economic Review, 36, 3* (June 1946): 393.

The Consumption Concept in Economic Theory. American Economic Review, 35, 2 (May 1945): 1–14.

The Home as a House of Worship. Inward Light, 27 (Nov 1945): 6–8.

In Defense of Monopoly. Quarterly Journal of Economics, 59, 4 Aug

1945): 524–542. *Reply. Quarterly Journal of Economics, 60, 4* (Aug 1946): 619–621.

The Prayer of Magic and the Prayer of Love. Friends Intelligencer, 102, 15 (Apr 4, 1945): 235–236.

Times and Seasons: Friends Intelligencer, 102, 6 (Feb 10, 1945): 88.

Where is the Labor Movement Moving? Kiwanis Magazine, 30, 2 (Feb 1945): 11, 31–32.

Books:

Economics of Peace, New York: Prentice-Hall, 1945. Pp. ix + 277. French transl., Economie de Paix. Paris: Librairie de Medicis, 1946. Pp. 280.

German transl., *Friedenswirtschaft*. Bern, Switzerland: A. Francke A. G. Verlag. Pp. 350.

Spanish transl., *La Economia de la Paz*. Madrid: Revista de Occidente. Pp. 348.

Japanese transl., Tokyo: Kogaku Sha, 1949.

There is a Spirit (The Naylor Sonnets). New York: Fellowship Press, 1945. Pp. 26.

1946

Article

In Defense of Monopoly: Reply. See: Articles, 1945.

Reviews

Reply to Hayek. Review of Herman Finer, Road To Reaction. *Nation, 162, 1* (Jan 5, 1946): 22–23.

Standard American Protestantism. Review of Norman E. Nygaard, America Prays. American Friend, 34, 23 (Nov 14, 1946): 455.

1947

Articles

Economic Analysis and Agricultural Policy. (presentation at the Canadian Political Science Association meeting, Quebec, May 1947) *Canadian Journal of Economics and Political Science, 13, 3* (Aug 1947): 436–446.

The Inward Light. Canadian Friend, 44, 2 (July 1947: 5–6.

A Note on the Theory of the Black Market. Canadian Journal of Economics and Political Science, 13, 1 (Feb 1947): 115–118.

Review

Review of *Jobs and Markets* (Committee for Economic Development, Research Study). *Rev. Econ. Statis.*, *29* (1947): 52–54.

1948

Articles

Price Control in a Subsequent Deflation. *Rev. Econ. Statis.*, *30*, *1* (Feb 1948): 15–17.

World Economic Contacts and National Policies. In: *The World Community*, Quincy Wright, ed. Chicago: Univ. of Chicago Press, 1948, pp. 95–100; discussion, pp. 101–144.

(And others) *Does Large Scale Enterprise Lower Costs? Discussion.* Amer. Econ. Rev., *38*, *2* (May 1948): 165–171.

(The Net National Product Concept) Comment on Mr. Burk's Note. Amer. Econ. Rev., *38*, *5* (Dec 1948): 899.

Book

Economic Analysis. Revised edition. New York: Harper & Brothers, 1948. Pp. xxvi + 884.

Reviews

Samuelson's Foundations: The Role of Mathematics in Economics. *Review of Paul Samuelson, Foundations of Economic Analysis. Jour. Polit. Econ.*, *56*, *3* (June 1948): 187–199.

Professor Tarshis and the State of Economics. *Review of Lorie Tarshis, The Elements of Economics. Amer. Econ. Rev.*, *38*, *1* (Mar 1948): 92–102.

Review of *D. McCord Wright, The Economics of Disturbance. Rev. Econ. Statis.*, *30* (1948): 74.

1949

Articles

Collective Bargaining and Fiscal Policy. Industrial Relations Research Assn., *2* (Dec 1949): 52–68. Also in: Amer. Econ. Rev., *40*, *2* (May 1950): 306–320.

Is Economics Necessary? *Scientific Monthly*, *68*, *4* (Apr 1949): 235–240.

The Theory and Measurement of Price Expectations: Discussion (with others); Amer. Econ. Rev., *39*, *3* (May 1949): 167–168.

The Economic Consequences of Some Recent Anti-Trust Decisions: Discussion (with others). *Amer. Econ. Rev., 39, 3* (May 1949): 320–321.

Review

Review of Sumner H. Slichter, The American Economy: Its Problems and Prospects. Annals of the American Academy of Political and Social Science, 261 (Jan 1949): 201–202.

1950

Articles

Income or Welfare? Rev. Econ. Stud., 17 (1949–50): 77–86.
The Models for a Macroeconomic Theory of Distribution. In: *Economic Theory in Review.* Indiana Univ. Publications, Soc. Sci. Series No. 8 (1950): 66–95.
Our Lost Economic Gospel. Christian Century, 67 (1950): 970–972.
The Background and Structure of a Macroeconomic Theory in Distribution. In: *Economic Theory in Review,* (1950): 66–81.

Book

A Reconstruction of Economics. New York: John Wiley & Sons, 1950, Pp. xii + 311. Issued in Paperback, New York: Science Editions, 1962.

Pamphlet

Religious Perspectives of College Teaching in Economics. New Haven: Hazen Foundation, 1950. Pp. 24. *Reprinted* in: *Religious Perspectives of College Teaching,* Hoxie N. Fairchild, ed. New York: Ronald Press, 1952, pp. 360–383.

Review

Humane Economics. Review of Wilhelm Röpke, The Social Crisis of Our Time. Christian Century, 67, 44 (Nov 1, 1950): 1295.

1951

Articles

Asset Identities in Economic Models. In: *Studies in Income and Wealth,* Vol. 14 (papers from the Conference on Income and Wealth, Apr 1950). New York: National Bureau of Economic Research, (1951): 229–247.
Can We Control Inflation in a Garrison State? Social Action, 17, 3 (Mar 15, 1951): 3–24.

Comments. (on Professor Dr. Wolfgang F. Stolper, "The Economics of Peace") *Weltwirtschaftliches Archiv* (Keil, Germany), *66, 1* (1951): 146–147.

Defense and Opulence: The Ethics of International Economics. American Economic Review (Papers and Proceedings of the 63rd American Economic Association annual meeting, Chicago, Dec 1950), 41, 2 (May 1951): 210–220.

Wages as a Share in the National Income. In: *The Impact of the Union: Eight Economic Theorists Evaluate the Labor Union Movement,* D. McCord Wright, ed. (edited report of the Institute on the Structure of the Labor Market, American University, May 1950). New York: Harcourt Brace, 1951, pp. 123–148; discussion, pp. 149–167.

What About Christian Economics? American Friend, 39, 23 (Nov 8, 1951): 361.

Reviews

M. Allais' Theory of Interest. Review article of Maurice Allais, Économie et Intérêt. Journal of Political Economy, 59, 1 (Feb 1951): 69–73.

Democracy and Economic Challenge. Review of the 1950–51 William W. Cook Lectures on American Institutions. Michigan Alumnus Quarterly Review, 57, 18 (May 1951): 185–191.

Review of R. H. Coase, British Broadcasting. Jour. Higher Educ., 22 (1951): 110.

Review of I. M. D. Little, A Critique of Welfare Economics. Economica, 18, 70 (May 1951): 207–209.

Review of G. K. Zipf, Human Behavior and the Principle of Least Effort. Amer. Econ. Rev., 41, 3 (June 1951): 449–450.

1952

Articles

A Conceptual Framework for Social Science. Papers, Mich. Acad. of Sci., Arts, Letters, 37 (1952): 275–282.

Economics as a Social Science. In: *The Social Sciences at Mid-Century: Essays in Honor of Guy Stanton Ford,* Minneapolis: Univ. of Minnesota Press, 1952, pp. 70–83.

Implications for General Economics of More Realistic Theories of the Firm. Amer. Econ. Rev., 42, 2 (May 1952): 35–44.

Religious Foundations of Economic Progress. Harvard Bus. Rev. 30, 3 (May–June 1952): 33–40. Reprinted in: *Public Affairs* (Halifax, Canada), *14, 4* (Summer 1952): 1–9. Also reprinted in: *Business and Religion,* E.

S. Bursk, ed., New York: Harper Brothers, 1959, pp. 119–134.
Welfare Economics. In: *A Survey of Contemporary Economics, Vol. 2*,
B. Haley, ed. Homewood, Ill.: R. D. Irwin, 1952, pp. 1–34.
The Busted Thermostat (verse). *Mich. Bus. Rev.*, *4*, 6 (Nov 1952): 25–26.
The Great Revolution. Friends Intelligencer, *109*, *17* (Apr 1952): 231–232.

Book

Readings in Price Theory (W. G. Stigler and K. E. Boulding, eds.).
Homewood, Ill.: R. D. Irwin, 1952. Pp. x + 568.

Reviews

Discussion of papers by D. H. Brill, Ruth P. Mack, and K. Brunner and
H. M. Markowitz. *Econometrica 20* (July 1952): 497–498.
Review of Wesley Clair Mitchell, The Economic Scientist (Arthur F.
Burns, ed.). *Sci. Monthly, 75* (1952): 129–130.
*Review of William A. Paton, Shirtsleeve Economics. Mich. Alum. Quart.
Rev.*, (Summer 1952): 360.
Studies in Income and Wealth (Conference on Research in Income and
Wealth), Vol. XIII. *Econometrica 20* (Jan 1952): 107–108.
Review of Norbert Wiener, The Human Use of Human Beings: *Cyberne-
tics and Society. Econometrica 20* (Oct 1952): 702.

1953

Articles

Economic Issues in International Conflict. Kyklos, 2, 6 (1953): 97–115.
Economic Progress as a Goal in Economic Life. In: *Goals of Economic
Life*, Dudley Ward, ed. New York: Harper & Brothers, 1953, pp.
52–83.
*The Fruits of Progress and the Dynamics of Distribution. Amer. Econ.
Rev., 43, 2* (May 1953): 473–483.
The Quaker Approach in Economic Life. In: *The Quaker Approach*, John
Kavanaugh, ed. New York: G. P. Putnam's Sons, 1953, pp. 43–58.
I. *The Skills of the Economist*; II. *The Contribution of Economics to the
Understanding of the Firm:* (1) *Marginal Analysis*; III. (2) *The Theory
of Organization and Communications.* In: *Contemporary Economic
Problems.* Cleveland: Case Institute of Technology, 1953, pp. 1–40.
Toward a General Theory of Growth. Can. Jour. Econ. Pol. Sci., 19, 3
(Aug 1953): 326–340. Reprinted as S-350, Bobbs-Merrill Reprint Series
in the Social Sciences. Also *reprinted* in: *General Systems Yearbook,
1*, 1965, 66–75.

Book

The Organizational Revolution. New York: Harper & Brothers, 1953, Pp.
xxxiv + 286. *Paperback edition*: Chicago: Quadrangle Books, 1968. Pp.
xxxvi, 235. Japanese translation.

Reviews

*Economic Theory and Measurement. Review of Economic Theory and
Measurement, a Twenty Year Research Report*, 1932–1952, The Cowles
Commission. *Kyklos*: 2, 6 (1953): 149–152.
*Review of V. A. Damant, Religion and the Decline of Capitalism. Jour.
Relig. Thought, 10* (1953): 180–181.
Review of Benjamin Higgins, What Do Economists Know: *Jour. of
Bus.* 26 (Apr 1953): 139.
*Note on the Theory of Investment of the Firm. Review of Friedrich and
Vera Lutz, The Theory of Investment of the Firm. Kyklos*, 2, 6 (1953):
77–81.
Projection, Prediction, and Precariousness. *Review article of Gerald Colm,
The American Economy in 1960. Review of Econ. and Stat.*, 35, 4 (Nov
1953): 257–260.

1954

Articles

An Economist's View of the Manpower Concept. In: *Proceedings of a
Conference on the Utilization of Scientific and Professional Manpower.*
New York: Columbia Univ. Press. 1954, pp. 11–26. Discussion, pp.
26–33.
The Principle of Personal Responsibility. Rev. Soc. Economy, 12, 1 (Mar
1954): 1–8.
(Sales and Output Taxes) Comment. *Amer. Econ. Rev.*, 44, 1 (Mar 1954):
129.
Twenty-Five Theses on Peace and Trade. The Friend (Philadelphia, Pa.),
127 (1954): 290–292. Reprinted in: *the NUEA Discussion and Debate
Manual, Vol 2.* (1954–55): 155–158.
The Skills of the Economist (in Portugese): I. A arte do economista; II. As
aplicacôes da economia aos problemas de emprésa: a analise marginal;
III. As aplicacôes da economia ao estudo do comportamento humano
a teoria do comportamento econômico; IV. A aplicacâo da ciencia
econômica aos problemas de govêrno; V. Contribuicôes da ciência
econômica às outras ciências; VI. A ciência econômica e o futuro da
humanidade. *Revista Brasilerra de Economia*, (March 1954): 189.

Reviews

Reviews of Milton Friedman, *Essays in Positive Economics*. *Pol. Sci. Quart.*, 66 (1954): 132–133.

Review of Frank Grace, *The Concept of Property in Modern Christian Thought*. *Mich. Alum. Quart. Rev.* (May 1954): 272–273.

Review of Kenneth D. Roose, *The Economics of Recession and Revival*. *Annals Amer. Acad.* (Nov 1954): 178.

Projection, Prediction, and Precariousness: Correction and Apology. *Rev. Econ. Statis. 36, 2* (Feb 1954): 100.

1955

Articles

An Application of Population Analysis to the Automobile Population of the United States. *Kyklos, 2* (1955): 109–124.

Contributions of Economics to the Theory of Conflict. *Bull. of the Research Exchange on the Prevention of War, 3, 5* (May 1955): 485–502.

In Defense of Statics. Quart. Jour. Econ., 69, 4 (Nov 1955): 485–502.

The Malthusian Model as a General System. *Soc. and Econ. Stud., 4, 3* (Sept 1955): 195–205. Reprinted as: S-349 in the Bobbs-Merrill Reprint Series in the Social Sciences.

Notes on the Information Concept. Exploration (Toronto, Ont.), 6 (1955): 103–112.

Possible Conflicts Between Economic Stability and Economic Progress. *Farm Policy Forum 8* (1955): 30–36.

The Conservationist's Lament and the Technologist's Reply (verse). *Pop. Bull.* (Aug 1955): 70. Also in: *Man's Role in Changing the Face of the Earth*, Wm. L. Thomas, ed., Chicago: University of Chicago Press, 1956, p. 1087. Also in: *Industrial Water Engineering 3, 12* (Dec 1966): 33.

Parity, Charity, and Clarity: Ten Theses on Agricultural Policy. *Michigan Daily*, (Oct 16, 1955): 3.

Book

Economic Analysis. 3rd edition. New York: Harper & Brothers, 1955. Pp. xx + 905. Portuguese transl.: *Análise Econômica*. Rio de Janeiro: Editôra Fundo do Cultura. Vol. I, 364 pp; II, 384 pp.; III, 362 pp.; IV, 272 pp. (1961). Turkish transl.: *Iktisadi Tahlil*. Istanbul: Sermet Matbaasi (Istanbul Univ. Pub. No. 691), 1957. Pp. 472. Japanese translation, 1963. Burmese translation, 1962.

Reviews

Review of T. Haavelmo, A Study in the Theory of Economic Evolution.
Kyklos, Fasc. 1, (1955).
Review of Albert Lauterbach, Man, Motives, and Money. Social Order, 5
(1955): 135–136.
Review of P. Mendes-France and Gabriel Ardant, Economics and
Action. Christian Century, 72 (1955): 1024.
Review of Clarence B. Randall, Economics and Public Policy (Brookings
Institution), and a Foreign Economic Policy for the United States.
Christian Century, 72, (June 1955): 657–658.

1956

Articles

Economics and the Behavioral Sciences: A Desert Frontier? Diogenes, 15
(1956): 1–4.
Economics: The Taming of Mammon. In: *Frontiers of Knowledge in the*
Study of Man, Lynn White, Jr., ed. New York: Harper & Brothers,
1956, pp. 132–149.
Statement Before the Subcommittee of the Senate Committee on Foreign
Relations, U.S. Congress (on behalf of the Friends Committee on
National Legislation). In: *Control and Reductions of Armaments*
(Hearing of the Committee). Washington, D.C.: U.S. Government
Printing Office, 1956, Part 8, pp. 418–437.
Industrial Revolution and Urban Dominance: Discussion (with others) In:
Man's Role in Changing the Face of the Earth, William L. Thomas, Jr.,
ed. Chicago: University of Chicago Press, for the Wenner-Gren
Foundation for Anthropological Research and the National Science
Foundation, 1956: 434–448.
Limits of the Earth: Discussion. (with others) In: *Man's Role in*
Changing the Face of the Earth, William L. Thomas, Jr., ed. (1956):
1071–1087.
Changes in Physical Phenomena: Discussion (with others) In: *Man's Role*
in Changing the Face of the Earth, William L. Thomas, Jr., ed. (1956):
917–929.
Commentary. (Perspectives on Prosperity) Social Action, 22, 8 (Apr
1956): 15–16.
General Systems Theory: The Skeleton of Science. Management Science,
2, 3 (Apr 1956): 197–208. Also in: *General Systems* (Yrbk. of Soc. for
Gen. Syst. Res.) *Vol 1* (1956) pp. 11–17. Reprinted in: *Theories for*

Marketing Systems Analysis. Selected Readings. George Fisk and Donald F. Dixon, eds. New York: Harper & Row, 1967, pp. 4–10. Reprinted in: *Management Information, A Quantitative Accent.* Thomas H. Williams and Charles H. Griffin, eds. Homewood, Ill.: Richard D. Irwin, 1967. pp. 601–613. Reprinted in: *Communication for Managerial Control.* George Vardman and Carroll Halterman, eds. New York: John A. Wiley, 1967. Reprinted in: *Educational Data Processing: New Dimensions and Prospects.* Richard A. Kaimann and Robert W. Marker, eds. Boston: Houghton, Mifflin, 1967, pp. 6–15. Reprinted in: *Management Systems: A Book of Readings,* Peter P. Schoderbek, ed. New York: John Wiley & Sons, 1967, pp. 7–15.

Perspectives on Prosperity: Commentary. Social Action (Apr 1956): 15–16.

Some Contributions of Economics to the General Theory of Value. Philos. of Science, 23, 1 (Jan 1956): 1–14.

Structure and Stability: The Economics of the Next Adjustment. In: *Policies to Combat Depression,* Nat. Bur. Econ. Research, Princeton: Princeton Univ. Press, 1956, pp. 59–76.

Book

The Image: Knowledge in Life and Society. Ann Arbor: Univ. of Michigan Press, 1956. pp. 175. German transl., *Die Neuen Leitbilder.* Düsseldorf: Econ-Verlag GmbH, 1958. pp. 161. Paperback edition: Ann Arbor: Univ. of Michigan Press, 1961. pp. 184. Japanese transl., 1964.

Reviews

Review of J. T. Bonner, Cells and Societies. Amer. Anthropologist, 58, 1 (Feb 1956): 216.

Review of Neil W. Chamberlain, A General Theory of Economic Process. Soc. Order, 6 (1956): 128–130.

Review of Edward Duff, Ecumenical Social Thought. Soc. Order, 6 (1956): 392–397.

Review of C. Addison Hickman and Manford H. Kuhn, Individuals, Groups, and Economic Behavior. Southern Econ. Journal, 23, 2 (Oct 1956): 188–190.

Review of L. M. Lachmann, Capital and Its Structure. Amer. Econ. Rev., 46, 5 (Dec 1956): 988–989.

Review of G. Myrdal, An International Economy: Problems and Prospects. Christian Century, 73, 37 (Sept 1956): 1053–1054.

1957

Articles

Does the Absence of Monopoly Power in Agriculture Influence the Stability and Level of Farm Income? In: *Papers presented to the Subcommittee on Agricultural Policy of the Joint Economic Committee.* Government Ptg. Office, 1957, pp. 42–50.

Economic Theory: The Reconstruction Reconstructed. In: *Segments of the Economy — 1956*: A Symposium. Cleveland: Howard Allen, 1957, pp. 8–55.

A Look at the Corporation. The Lamp (Standard Oil of N.J.), 1957, pp. 6–7.

A New Look at Institutionalism. Amer. Econ. Rev., 47, 2 (May 1957): 1–12.

Organization and Conflict. Jour. Conflict Resolution, 1, 2 (June 1957): 122–134. Reprinted in: *American National Security: A Reader in Theory and Policy,* Morton Berkowitz and P. G. Bock, eds. New York: Free Press of Glencoe, 1965, pp. 327–336.

Some Contributions of Economics to Theology and Religion. Religious Education (Dec 1957): 446–450.

Some Reflections on Inflation and Economic Development. In: *Contribuĉoes à Análise do Desinvolvimento Econômico,* Rio de Janeiro: Instituto Brasilerro de Economia da Fundacão Getúlio Vargas, 1957, pp. 61–67.

Reviews

Review of Joe S. Bain, Barriers to New Competition: Their Character and Consequences in Manufacturing Industries. Admin. Sci. Quart., 2: 1 (June 1957): 116–118.

Review of J. M. Clark, Economic Institutions and Human Welfare. Amer. Econ. Rev., 47: 5 (Dec 1957): 1004–1005.

Review of Lester de Koster, All Ye That Labor; an Essay on Christianity, Communism and the Problem of Evil. The Reformed Journal, July–Aug 1957: 20.

The Parsonian Approach to Economics. Review of Talcott Parsons and Neil J. Smelser, Economy and Society. Kyklos, 3 (1957): 317–319.

1958

Articles

The Current State of Economics. Challenge (New York Univ.), *6: 10* (Aug–Sept 1958): 18–24.

Statement Before the Subcommittee on Agricultural Policy of the Joint Economic Committee, U.S. Congress. In: *Policy for Commercial Agriculture: Its Relation to Economic Growth and Stability* (Hearings of the Committee). Washington, D.C.: U.S. Government Printing Office, 1958, pp. 16–18.

Democracy and Organization. Challenge (New York Univ.) 6: 6 (Mar 1958): 13–17.

Evidences for an Administrative Science. Admin. Sci. Quart., 3: 1 (June 1958): 1–22. Reprinted in: *Administrative Control and Executive Action,* B. C. Lemke and J. D. Edwards, eds. Columbus, O.: Charles E. Merrill Books, 1961, pp. 118–123.

The Jungle of Hugeness. Saturday Review (Mar 1, 1958): 11–13. Reprinted in: *American Society in Action,* D. H. Riddle, ed. St. Louis: McGraw-Hill, 1965.

The Organization Man — Fact or Fancy? In: *The Emerging Environment of Industrial Relations.* E. Lansing: Michigan State Univ., 1958.

Religion and the Social Sciences. In: *Religion and the State University,* Erich A. Walter, ed. Ann Arbor, Mich.; Univ. of Michigan Press, 1958, pp. 136–155.

Secular Images of Man in the Social Sciences. Relig. Education, 53 (Mar–Apr 1958): 91–96. Reprinted in: *What is the Nature of Man?* Philadelphia: Christian Education Press, 1959, pl. 27–38.

The Sputnik Within. Liberation, 2: 10 (Jan 1958): 13–14.

Three Concepts of Disarmament. Amer. Friend (Feb 20, 1958): 53–54.

Universal, Policed Disarmament as the Only Stable System of National Defense. In: *Problems of United States Economic Development, Committee for Economic Development,* Jan 1958, pp. 361–367.

The Brandywine River Anthology (verse), *Mich. Bus. Rev.* (Mar 1958): 7–9.

T. R. (verse). *Lib. Cong. Jour. of Current Acquisitions,* 15 (May 1958): 100.

Books

Principles of Economic Policy. New York: Prentice-Hall, 1958. pp. vi + 440. Spanish transl.: Madrid: Aguilar, 1963. Pp. xxxvi + 427. Portuguese transl.: Sao Paulo, Brazil: Editora Mestre Jou, 1967. Pp. 483.

The Skills of the Economist. Cleveland, O.: Howard Allen, 1958. Pp. vi + 193. British edition: London: Hamish Hamilton, 1958. Pp. vi + 193. Japanese transl.: 1964. Canadian edition: Toronto: Clarke, Irwin & Co., 1958, Pp. vi + 193.

Reviews

Review of Thomas C. Cochran, The American Business System: A Historical Perspective. Bus. Hist. Rev., 32: 1 (Spring 1958): 116–119. (with John Kenneth Galbraith).

Review of Contribucoes à análise do desinvolvimento econômico. Amer. Econ. Rev., 48: 3 (June 1958): 462–463.

Theoretical Systems and Political Realities. Review of Morton A. Kaplan, System and Process in International Politics. Jour. Conflict Resol. 2: 4 (Dec 1958): 329–334.

Review of Erik Lundberg, Business Cycles and Economic Policy. Annals Amer. Acad. Pol. & Soc. Sci., 318 (July 1958): 179.

Review of James H. Meisel, The Myth of the Ruling Class: Gaetano Mosca and the "Elite". Mich. Alum. Quart. Rev., 65: 10 (Dec 6, 1958): 88–89.

Reviews of Wilbur Schramm, Responsibility in Mass Communication. Christian Century, 75 (Feb 26, 1958): 252.

1959

Articles

Foreword to T. R. Malthus, Population, the First Essay. Ann Arbor, Mich.: Ann Arbor Paperbacks, 1959, pp. v-xii.

The Knowledge of Value and the Value of Knowledge. In: *Ethics and the Social Sciences,* Leo R. Ward, ed. Notre Dame, Ind.: Notre Dame Univ. Press, 1959, pp. 25–42.

National Images and the International Systems. Jour. Conflict Resol., 3, 2 (June 1959) 120–131.

Organizing Growth. Challenge, 8, 3 (Dec 1959): 31–36.

Religious Foundations of Economic Progress. In: *Business and Religion,* Edward C. Bursk, ed. New York: Harper & Bros., 1959, pp. 119–134.

Symbols for Capitalism. Harvard Bus. Rev., 37, 1 (Jan–Feb 1959): 41–48. Reprinted in: *Readings in the Economics of Enterprise,* Ross Wilhelm, ed. Ann Arbor: Kirkcaldy Press, 1964.

Reviews

Review of Bernard Biet, Theories Contemporaines du Profit. Econometrica, 27, 2 (Apr 1959): 321.

Review of Arthur H. Cole, Business Enterprise in Its Social Setting. Admin. Sci. Quart. 4, 3 (Dec 1959): 361.

Review of F. E. Johnson and J. E. Ackerman, The Church as Employer, Money Raiser and Investor. Christian Century, 76, 47 (Nov 25, 1959): 1376–1377.

Review of John B. Rae, *American Automobile Manufacturers: The First Forty Years. Technology and Culture*, 1, 1 (Winter 1959): 104–105.

Review of J. K. Galbraith, *The Affluent Society*, Rev. Econ. and Stat., 41, 1 (Feb 1959): 81.

1960

Articles

Capital and Interest. Encyclopedia Britannica, Vol. IV (1960): 799–801. 1964 Ed., Vol. 4, 835–839.

The Costs of Independence: Notes on the Caribbean. Challenge, 9, 3 (Dec 1960): 14–18.

Decision-Making in the Modern World. In: *An Outline of Man's Knowledge of the Modern World*, Lyman Bryson, ed. New York: McGraw-Hill, 1960, pp. 424–442.

Disarmament (verse). *Fellowship*, 26, 17 (Sept 1, 1960): 24.

The Domestic Implications of Arms Control. Daedalus, 89, 4 (Fall 1960): 846–859. Digest in: *The Executive*, 4, 8 (Jan 1961): 24–26. Reprinted in: *Arms Control, Disarmament, and National Security*, Donald G. Brennan, ed. George Braziller, Inc., 1961: pp. 154–6, 158, 164. Reprinted as *"The Economics of Disarmament"* in: *American Government, Readings and Documents*, Peter H. Odegard, ed. New York: Harper & Row, 1964. pp. 576–582.

The Present Position of the Theory of the Firm. In: *Linear Programming and the Theory of the Firm*, K. E. Boulding and W. A. Spivey, eds. New York: Macmillan, 1960, pp. 1–17.

Scientific Nomenclature. Science, 131 (May 20, 1960): 874–876.

A Theory of the Small Society. Caribbean Quarterly, 6, 4 (1960): 258–269.

Violence and Revolution: Some Reflections on Cuba. Liberation 5, 2 (Apr 1960): 5–8. Excerpted in: *Current*, 3 (July 1960) as *The Fate of Agrarian Revolt*, pp. 36–37.

Standards for Our Economic System: Discussion. (with others) *American Economic Review*, 50, 2 (May 1960): 23–24.

Book

Linear Programming and the Theory of the Firm. K. E. Boulding and W. A. Spivey, eds. New York: Macmillan, 1960. French transl.: Paris: Dunod, 1964.

Reviews

Philosophy, Behavioral Science, and the Nature of Man. Review of Hannah Arendt, The Human Condition, and of Christian Bay, The Structure of Freedom. World Pol., 12, 2 (Jan 1960): 272–279.

Review of Edward S. Mason, ed., The Corporation in Modern Society.
Bus. Hist. Rev., 34, 4 (Winter 1960): 499–501.

Review of Reinhold Niebuhr, The Structure of Nations and Empires.
Review of Religious Research 1, 3 (Winter 1960): 122–124.

Review of Willard L. Thorp and Richard E. Quandt, The New Inflation.
Journal of the American Statistical Association, 55, 291 (Sept 1960):
616–617.

*Review of Overton H. Taylor, The Classical Liberalism, Marxism, and
the Twentieth Century. Amer. Econ. Rev., 50, 2* (Mar 1960): 168–169.

Review of Geoffrey Vickers, The Undirected Society. Jour. Pol. Econ., 68,
4 (Aug 1960): 419.

1961

Articles

Contemporary Economic Research. In: *Trends in Social Science,* Donald
P. Ray, ed. New York: Philosophical Library, 1961, pp. 9–26.

The Dynamics of Disarmament. Intercollegian, 78, 8 (May 1961): 10–14.

Economic Resources and World Peace. In: *The Challenge of the '60s
(Lecture-Seminary Series 1960–61*), Palo Alto, Calif.: Palo Alto Unified School District, 1961, pp. 27–35.

Our Attitude Toward Revolution. Think, 27 (June–Aug 1961): 27–29.

*Political Implications of General Systems Research. General Systems
Yearbook* (Ann Arbor, Mich.), 1961, pp. 1–7.

The Public Image of American Economic Institutions. In: *American
Perspectives,* Robert E. Spiller and Eric Larrabee, eds. Cambridge:
Harvard Univ. Press, 1961, pp. 117–133.

A Pure Theory of Conflict Applied to Organizations. In: *Conflict
Management in Organizations,* Ann Arbor, Mich.: *Foundation for
Research on Human Behavior,* 1961, pp. 43–51. Reprinted in: *The
Frontiers of Management Psychology,* George Fisk, ed. New York:
Harper & Row, 1964, pp. 41–49. Reprinted in: *Power and Conflict in
Organizations,* Robert L. Kahn and Elise Boulding, eds. New York:
Basic Books, 1964, pp. 136–145.

*Qu'est-ce que le progrès economique? Cahiers de l'Institute de Science
Economique Appliquée* (Paris), No. 110 (Feb 1961): 147–155.

Reflections on Poverty. In: *The Social Welfare Forum,* 1961 (*Nat.
Conf. on Soc. Welfare*), New York: Columbia Univ. Press, 1961, pp.
45–58.

Social Dynamics in West Indian Society. Soc. & Econ. Stud., 10, 1 (Mar
1961): 25–34.

Some Difficulties in the Concept of Economic Input. In: *Output, Input, and Productivity Measurement,* Princeton: Princeton Univ. Press, 1961, pp. 331–345.

The U.S. and Revolution. In: *The U.S. and Revolution: An Occasional Paper on the Free Society,* Santa Barbara, Calif.: Center for the Study of Democratic Institutions, 1961, pp. 4–7.

Where Do We Go from Here, if Anywhere? In: *Proceedings, 14th Nat'l Conf. on the Administration of Research,* University Park, Pa.: Penn. State Univ. Press, 1961, pp. 66–72.

Study of the Soviet Economy: Its Place in American Education. (discussion with others) In: *Study of the Soviet Economy,* Nicholas Spulber, ed. (Russian and East European Series, Vol. 25). Bloomington: Indiana University Publications, 1961, pp. 104–128.

Pamphlet

Economic Factors Bearing upon the Maintenance of Peace. Part I: *Perspective on the Economics of Peace.* New York: Institute for International Order, 1961. Pp. 38.

Reviews

Review of Raymond Aron, Introduction to the Philosophy of History. Christian Century, 78 (Aug 16, 1961): 981.

Review of Jean Fourastie, The Causes of Wealth. Technol. & Culture, 2, 3 (Summer 1961): 262–264.

Trying to Square the Circle. Review of Charles J. Hitch and Roland McKean, The Economics of Defense in the Nuclear Age. Bul. Atom. Sci. 17 (Mar 1961): 115–116.

Review of P. B. Medawar, The Future of Man: Predictions of a Biologist. Christian Century, 78, 20 (May 17, 1961): 623.

Review of Gunnar Myrdal, Beyond the Welfare State: Economic Planning and its International Implications. Admin. Sci. Quart., 6: 1 (June 1961): 107–109.

The Nightmare of Rationality. Review of T. C. Schelling, The Strategy of Conflict. Contemporary Psychology, 1961, 426, 426–427.

Review of Talcott Parsons, Structure and Process in Modern Societies. Psychiatry, 24, 3 (Aug 1961): 278–279.

Review of Dan Wilson, An Opening Way (Pendle Hill Pamphlet No. 113). *Quaker Life,* 2, 7 (July 1961): 189.

Verse

A Shelter for All. (Preamble to a Statement issued by the Friends National Conference on World Order, Richmond, Ind., Oct. 1961) *Friends Journal, 7, 23* (Dec 1, 1961): 489.

1962

Articles

Better R-E-D than Dead. New Republic, 147: 16 (Oct 20 1962): 15-16. Excerpted in: *Current, 32* (Dec 1962): 41-42.

Can We Afford a Warless World? Saturday Review (Oct 6 1962): 17-20. Reprinted as: *The Economic Implications of Warlessness* in: *A Warless World,* Arthur Larson, ed. New York: McGraw-Hill, 1962-63, pp. 59-74.

Economics and Accounting: The Uncongenial Twins. In: *Studies in Accounting Theory,* W. T. Baxter and Sidney Davidson, eds. London: Sweet and Maxwell, 1962, pp. 44-45. CPII pp. 219-232 RI.

The Ethical Perspective. In: *Ethical Implications of Rapid Economic Change in the U.S.A.* New York: National Council of Churches, 1962: 35-44. Revised and published as: *Christianity in a Changing Society. Concern* (Nov 15 1962): 4-22.

Ethics and Business: An Economist's View. In: *Ethics and Business, Three Lectures,* University Park, Pa.: Penn State Univ. Coll. of Bus. Admin., 1962, pp. 1-14.

An Interdisciplinary Honors Course in General Systems. Superior Student, 4 (Jan-Feb 1962): 31.

Is Peace Researchable? Continuous Learning, 1: 2 (Mar-Apr 1962): 63-69. Reprinted in: *Background, 6: 4* (Winter 1963): 70-77. Also in: *New Outlook 16: 8* (Sept 1963) 13-16.

Knowledge as a Commodity. In: *Series Studies in Social and Economic Sciences, Symposia Studies No. 11,* National Institute of Social and Behavioral Science, June 1962, pp. 1-6.

Notes on a Theory of Philanthropy. In: *Philanthropy and Public Policy,* Dickinson, ed. National Bureau of Economic Research, 1962, pp. 57-71.

The Peace Research Movement. Newsletter of the Council for Correspondence, N. D. (1962): 25-32. Reprinted in: *Alternatives to War and Violence,* Ten Dunn, ed. London: James Clarke and Co., 1963, pp. 40-50.

The Prevention of World War III. Virginia Quart. Rev. 38: 1 (Winter 1962): 1-12. Reprinted in: *An American Foreign Policy Reader,* Harry

H. Ransom, ed. New York: Thomas Y. Crowell, 1965, pp. 614–622. Also in: *Hacia una Tecnica de la Paz*, New York: *World Law Fund*, 1965, pp. 13–24. Also in: *The Strategy of World Order*, R. Falk and S. Mendlovitz, eds. Vol. 1, *Towards a Theory of War Prevention*, New York: *World Law Fund*, 1966, pp. 3–13. Also in: *Peace is Possible, a Reader for Laymen*, Elizabeth Jay Hollins, ed. New York: Grossman Publishers, 1966, pp. 82–89.

A Pure Theory of Death. In: *Behavioral Science and Civil Defense*, Geo. W. Baker and Leonard S. Cottrell, Jr., eds. (Nat'l Research Council Pub. # 997), Washington, D.C.: National Academy of Sciences, 1962, pp. 53–69.

The Relations of Economic, Political and Social Systems. Social and Economic Stud. 11: 4 (Dec 1962): 351–362.

Research and Development for the Emergent Nations. Ohio State University, *Conference on Economics of Research and Development.* Richard A. Tybout, ed., pp. 422–437, Comments, 438–472.

The Role of the Price Structure in Economic Development (with Pritam Singh). *Amer. Econ. Rev., 52: 2* (May 1962): 28–38.

Social Justice in Social Dynamics. In: *Social Justice*, Richard B. Brandt, ed. New York: Prentice-Hall (Spectrum S-38), 1962, pp. 73–92.

Some Reflections (verse). In: *The Church in a World That Won't Hold Still*, New York: National Council of Churches, 1962, p. 48.

Some Questions on the Measurement and Evaluation on Organization. In: *Ethics and Bigness: Scientific, Academic, Religious, and Military*, Harlan Cleveland and Harold D. Lasswell, eds. New York: Harper & Bros., 1962, pp. 385–395.

The University, Society and Arms Control. Journal of Conflict Resolution, 7, 3 (Sept 1963): 458–463; *Journal of Arms Control* (joint volume; Proceedings of the International Arms Control Symposium, Ann Arbor, Mich., Dec 1962), *1, 4* (Oct 1963): 552–557.

War as an Economic Institution. In: *The Causes of War. Final Report, 3rd Annual Seminar on International Affairs, Montreal*: Sir George Williams Univ., 1962, pp. 38–48.

Where Are We Going, If Anywhere? A Look at Post-Civilization. Human Organization, 21: 2 (Summer 1962): 162–167. Also in: *Practical Anthropology 11: 1* (Jan–Feb 1964): 14–24, 34. Also in: *Readings in Anthropology, 2nd Ed.*, J. D. Jennings, and E. A. Hoebel, eds. New York: McGraw-Hill, 1966, pp. 362–368. Condensed and retitled *After Civilization, What?* in *Bull. Atom. Sci. 18: 8* (Oct 1962): 2–6. Also in: *Voices, III, 2* (Spring 1963): 20–26. Also in: *1966 Amerika*, No. 121, *in Russian*, 32–34. Also in: *Health and the Community: Readings in the Philosophy & Sciences of Public Health*. N.Y.: Free Press, 1965, pp.

866–874. Alfred H. Katz and Jean Spencer Felton, eds. Condensed and retitled *Post-Civilization: In Liberation*, (Apr 1962): 22. Also in: *Seeds of Liberation*, Paul Goodman, ed. New York: George Braziller, Inc., 1965, pp. 12–23.

Book

Conflict and Defense. New York: Harper and Bros., 1962, Pp. ix + 343. Paperback Edition: New York: Harper and Row, 1963, Pp. ix + 349.

Reviews

Review of John Maurice Clark, Competition as a Dynamic Process. Annals Amer. Acad. Pol. & Soc. Sci., 343 (Sept 1962): 181–182.

Political Non-Science. Review of Marshall E. Dimock, The New American Political Economy, and of C. E. Ayres, Toward a Reasonable Society. Science, 136 (May 11, 1962): 509–510.

Review of George Caspar Homans, Social Behavior: Its Elementary Forms. Amer. Jour. Sociol., 67: 4 (Jan 1962): 458–461.

Pacifists, Too, Must Think. Review of Herman Kahn, Thinking About the Unthinkable. Fellowship, 28: 14 (Sept 1, 1962): 27–30.

Review of Gardiner C. Means, , Pricing Power and the Public Interest: A Study Based on Steel. Admin. Sci. Quart., 7, 2 (Sept 1962): 266–268.

Review of Fred L. Polak, The Image of the Future. Jour. Polit. Econ., 70: 2 (Apr 1962): 192–193.

Review of Kurt Samuelsson, Religion and Economic Action. Jour. Polit. Econ., 70: 4 (Aug 1962): 423–424.

Review of Allen M. Sievers, Revolution, Evolution and the Economic Order. Jour. of Finance (Sept 1962): 705–706. (17)

1963

Articles

Agricultural Organizations and Policies: A Personal Evaluation. In: *Farm Goals in Conflict, Ames, Iowa*: Iowa State University Press, 1963, pp. 156–166.

Arden House Poetry (verse). In: *Models of Markets*, Alfred R. Oxenfeldt, ed. New York and London: Columbia Univ. Press, 1963, pp. 369–371.

Comments on the Pope's Peace Encyclical. Continuum 1: 2 (Summer 1963): 214–217.

Conflict Management as a Key to Survival. Amer. Jour. of Orthopsychiatry, 33: 2 (Mar 1963): 230–231 (Abstract). Reprinted in: *Behavioral Science and Human Survival*. Milton Schwebel, ed. Palo Alto: *Science and Behavior Books*, 1965, pp. 103–111.

The Death of the City: A Frightened Look at Post-Civilization. In: *The Historian and the City*, Oscar Handlin and John Burchard, eds. Cambridge: M.I.T. Press, 1963, pp. 133–145. Abstracted in: *Ekistics 13: 75* (Jan 1962): 19–22.

The Future Corporation and Public Attitudes. In: *The Corporation and its Publics*, John W. Riley, Jr., ed. New York: John Wiley & Sons, 1963, pp. 159–175.

Hymn for Cold Warriors (verse). *Christian Century, 80: 16* (Apr 17 1963): 492.

The Misallocation of Intellectual Resources. Proceedings, Amer. Phil. Soc., 107: 2 (Apr 15, 1963): 117–120.

The Role of Law in the Learning of Peace. Amer. Soc. of Internatl. Law Proceedings, 1963, pp. 92–103.

The Society of Abundance. In: *The Church in a Society of Abundance*, Arthur E. Walmsley, ed. New York: The Seabury Press, 1963, pp. 9–27.

Towards a Pure Theory of Threat Systems. Amer. Econ. Rev., 53: 2 (May 1963): 424–434. Reprinted in: *American National Security: A Reader in Theory and Policy*, Morton Berkowitz and P. G. Bock, eds. New York: Free Press of Glencoe, 1965, pp. 337–343.

The Uses of Price Theory. In: *Models of Markets*, Alfred R. Oxenfeldt, ed. New York and London: Columbia Univ. Press, 1963, pp. 146–162.

The World War Industry as an Economic Problem. In: *Disarmament and the Economy*, Emile Benoit and Kenneth Boulding, eds. New York: Harper & Row, 1963, pp. 3–27.

Preface. (with Emile Benoit) In: *Disarmament and the Economy*, Emile Benoit and Kenneth Boulding, eds. New York: Harper & Row, 1963, pp. 7–10.

Book

Disarmament and the Economy, ed. with Emile Benoit. New York: Harper & Row, 1963. Pp. 310.

Reviews

Review of Milton Friedman, Capitalism and Freedom. Jour. of Bus. 36, 1 (Jan 1963): 120–121.

Two Recent Studies of Modern Society. Review of Sebastian de Graza, Of Time, Work, and Leisure, and Hugh Dalziel Duncan, Communication and the Social Order. Sci. Amer. (Jan 1963): 157–160.

The Knowledge Industry. Review of Fritz Machlup, The Production and Distribution of Knowledge in the United States. Challenge, 11: 8 (May 1963): 36–38.

Review of Victor Perlo, Militarism and Industry — Arms Profiteering in the Missile Age. Amer. Econ. Rev. 53: 4 (Sept 1963): 809–810.

Review of Joan Robinson, Economic Philosophy. Amer. Soc. Rev. 28: 4 (Aug 1963): 657–658.

Review of W. Lloyd Warner, The Corporation in the Emergent American Society. Am. Jour. Soc. 68: 6 (May 1963): 702.

Review of Quincy Wright, Wm. M. Evan and Morton Deutsch, eds. Preventing World War III: Some Proposals. Annals of the Amer. Acad. of Pol. and Soc. Sci., 348 (July 1963): 225–226.

1964

Articles

The Dimensions of Economic Freedom. Midway, 18 (Spring 1964): 70–75. Also in: *The Nation's Economic Objectives*, Edgar Edwards, ed. Chicago: Univ. of Chicago Press, 1964, pp. 107–122.

The Economist and the Engineer: Economic Dynamics of Water Resources Development. In: *Economics and Public Policy in Water Resource Development*, Stephen C. Smith and Emery N. Castle, eds. Ames, Iowa: Iowa State Univ. Press, 1964, pp. 82–92.

General Systems as a Point of View. In: *Views on General Systems Theory* (Proceedings of the 2nd Systems Symposium at Case Inst. of Tech.) Mihajlo D. Mesarovic, ed. New York: John Wiley & Sons, 1964, pp. 25–38.

Knowledge as an Economic Variable. The Economic Studies Quart., 14, 3 (June 1964): 1–6.

Market: Economic Theory. Encyclopedia Britannica, 1964, Vol. 14, pp. 913–914.

The Need for a Study on the Psychology of Disarmament. Our Generation Against Nuclear War, 3, 2 (Oct 1964): 39–41.

Needs and Opportunities in Peace Research and Peace Education. Our Generation Against Nuclear War, 3, 2 (Oct 1964): 22–25.

The Place of the Image in the Dynamics of Society. In: *Explorations in Social Change*, George K. Zollschan and Walter Hirsch, eds. Boston: Houghton-Mifflin and London: Routledge and Kegan Paul, 1964, pp. 5–16.

The Possibilities of Peace Research in Australia. Australian Outlook 18, 2 (Aug 1964): 165–169.

Toward a Theory of Peace. In: *International Conflict and Behavioral Science*, Roger Fisher, ed. New York: *Basic Books*, 1964, pp. 70–87.

Realism and Sentimentalism in the Student Movement. The ICU (Tokyo, Japan) 1963/64, 74–75.

Two Principles of Conflict. In: *Power and Conflict in Organizations,* Robert L. Kahn and Elise Boulding, eds. New York: Basic Books, 1964, pp. 75–76.

Why Did Gandhi Fail? In: *Gandhi — His Relevance for Our Times,* G. Ramachandran and T. K. Mahadevan, eds. Bombay: Bharatiya Vidya Bhavan, 1964, pp. 129–134.

Book

The Meaning of the Twentieth Century. New York: Harper & Row, 1964. Pp. xvi + 199. Paperback edition: N.Y.: Harper Colophon Books, 1965. Pp. 208. British Edition: Allen and Unwin, 1965. Mexican transl.: El Significado del Siglo XX: La Gran Transicion, trans. by Francisco Navarro R. Mexico: Uteha, 1966. No. 339–339a. Pp. 204. Portuguese Transl: O Significado do Seculo XX, trans. by Jayme F. Monteiro, Rio de Janeiro: Fundo Cultura, Mar. 1967. Pp. 121. Japanese transl: Japan: Iwanami Shoten, 1967. Pp. 189.

Pamphlet

The Evolutionary Potential of Quakerism. Wallingford, Pa.: Pendle Hill, 1964. Pp. 31.

Reviews

Review of Braybrooke and Lindblom, A Strategy of Decision: Policy Evaluation as a Social Process. Am. Sociol. Rev. (Dec 1964): 930–931.

Review Article: The Content of International Studies in College: A Review. Review of Haas & Whiting, Dynamics of Int. Rel.; McClelland, College Teaching of Int. Rel.; Morgenthau, *Politics Among Nations*; Organski, *World Politics*; Padelford & Lincoln, *The Dynamics of International Politics and Foreign Policy*; Schleicher, *International Relations*; Stoessinger, *The Might of Nations. Jour. of Conflict Res., 8, 1* (Mar 1964): 65–71.

Review of Alfred Kuhn, The Study of Society: a Unified Approach. The Accounting Review, 34, 2 (Apr 1964): 530–531.

Review of La Paix, Recueils de la Societé Jean Bodin. Comparative Studies in Society and History, 6, 2 (Jan 1964): 217–219.

Word Meanings in Economics. Review of Fritz Machlup, Essays on Economic Semantics (Miller, Fackler, and Davis, eds.), *Monthly Labor Rev. 87, 5* (May 1964): 577.

Review of Angus Maddison, Economic Growth in the West. Science, 146, 3648 (Nov 27, 1964): 1151–1152.

Review of Anatol Rapoport, Strategy and Conscience. Peace News
(London) 1480 (Nov 6, 1964): 8.

1965

Articles

America's Great Delusion. Labor Today, 4: 3 (June–July 1965): 21–23.
The Changing Framework of American Capitalism. Challenge, 14: 2
(Nov–Dec 1965): 39–42.
The Communication of Legitimacy. Channels (Western Michigan Univ.)
Spring 1965: 24–28.
The Concept of World Interest. In: *Economics and the Idea of Mankind*,
Bert F. Hoselitz, ed. New York and London: Columbia Univ. Press,
1965, pp. 41–62. Also in: *The Strategy of World Order*, Richard Falk
and Saul Mendlovitz, eds. Vol. 4, *Disarmament and Economic De-
velopment*, New York: *World Law Fund*, 1966, pp. 494–515.
The Difficult Art of Doing Good. Colorado Quart. (Univ. of Colo.), *13: 3*
(Winter 1965): 197–211.
Economics. In: *System Engineering Handbook*, Robert E. Machol, ed.
New York: McGraw-Hill, 1965, Chapter 35, pp. 35-1 to 35-8.
The Economics of Human Conflict. In: *The Nature of Human Conflict*,
Elton B. McNeil ed. Englewood Cliffs, N.J.: Prentice-Hall, 1965, pp.
172–191.
The Future of the Social Sciences. Science Journal, 1: 7 (Sept 1965): 3.
Great Society, or Grandiose? Washington Post, (Dec 5, 1965), p. E.3.
Reprinted in: *Concern, 8: 3* (Feb 15, 1966), pp. 4–5.
How Scientists Study "Getting Along". In: *Our Working World: Neigh-
bors at Work*, Teacher's Resource Unit, Chicago: Science Research
Associates, 1965.
*Statement Before the Subcommittee on Fiscal Policy of the Joint
Economic Committee, U.S. Congress.* In: *Fiscal Policy Issues of the
Coming Decade* (materials submitted to the committee) Washington,
D.C.: U.S. Government Printing Office, 1965, pp. 17–18.
*War as a Public Health Problem: Conflict Management as a Key to
Survival.* In: *Behavioral Science and Human Survival*, Milton
Schwebel, ed. Palo Alto, Calif.: Science and Behavioral Books, 1965,
pp. 103–110.
The Dilemma of Power and Legitimacy. In: *Power and Responsibility*,
Proceedings of the Institute of World Affairs, Vol. XL. Los Angeles:
University of Southern California, 1965, pp. 183–188.
Insight and Knowledge in the Development of Stable Peace. In: *No Time*

But This Present, Studies Preparatory to the Fourth World Conference of Friends 1967. Birmingham, England: Friends World Committee for Consultation, 1965, pp. 210–219.

Economic Libertarianism. In: *Conference on Savings and Residential Financing, 1965 Proceedings, Chicago: U.S. Savings and Loan League,* 1965, pp. 30–42; discussion pp. 42–57.

Looking Ahead to the Year 2000. Fellowship, 31: 5 (May 1965): 26–29.

The Menace of Methuselah: Possible Consequences of Increased Life Expectancy. Jour. of Washington Acad. of Sciences, 55: 7 (Oct 1965): 171–179.

Population and Poverty. The Correspondent, 35 (Autumn 1965): 38–40. Reprinted in: *Peace is Possible. A Reader for Laymen.* Elizabeth Jay Hollins, ed. New York: Grossman Publishers, 1966, pp. 49–53.

Reality Testing and Value Orientation in International Systems: The Role of Research. International Social Sci. Jour., 17: 3 (1965): 404–416; French trans., 432–445. Also in: *ISA Proceedings,* 1965, pp. 24–32.

Reflections on Protest. Bull. of Atom. Sci. 21: 8 (Oct 1965): 18–20. Reprinted in: *Social Education 30: 1* (Jan 1966): 28–30, 33. Reprinted in (in part): *Teach-Ins: U.S.A., Reports, Opinions, Documents,* Louis Menashe and Ronald Radosh, eds. New York: Praeger Paperbacks, 1967, pp. 281–285. Reprinted as *"What the First "Teach-In" Taught Me"* in: *Dissent, 13: 1* (Jan–Feb 1966): 10–15. Reprinted as *Towards a Theory of Protest* in: *ETC. 24, 1* (Mar 1967): 49–58.

Social Sciences. In: *The Great Ideas Today,* R. M. Hutchins and M. J. Adler, eds. Chicago: *Encyclopedia Britannica,* 1965, pp. 254–285.

War as an Investment: The Strange Case of Japan (with Alan Gleason). *Peace Research Society (International), Papers,* Vol. III, 1965, Walter Isard and J. Wolpert, eds. Philadelphia, pp. 1–17.

Reviews

Review of David T. Bazelon, The Paper Economy. Admin. Sci. Quart. 9: 4 (Mar 1965): 450–451.

Review of Karl De Schweinitz, Jr., Industrialization and Democracy. Amer. Econ. Rev. 15: 1 (Mar 1965): 181–182.

Is Economics Obsolescent: Review of Adolph Lowe, On Economic Knowledge. Sci. Amer., 212: 5 (May 1965): 139–143.

The Medium and the Message. Review of Marshall McLuhan, The Gutenberg Galaxy, and Understanding Media. Can. Jour. of Econ. and Pol. Sci. 31: 2 (May 1965): 268–273.

Scabbard or Sword? Review of Walter Millis, An End To Arms, and *Thomas S. Power with Albert A. Arnhym, Design for Survival. Book Week,* May 2, 1965, pp. 15, 17.

1966

Articles

The Concept of Need for Health Services. Milbank Memorial Fund Quarterly 44: 4, Part 2 (Oct 1966): 202–225.

Conflict Management as a Learning Process. In: *Conflict in Society,* Anthony de Reuck and Julie Knight, eds. London: J. & A. Churchill, 1966, pp. 236–248; discussion, pp. 249–258.

The Dilemma of Power and Legitimacy. In: *Power and Responsibility, Proceedings of the Institute of World Affairs* (Dec 1964), Los Angeles: Univ. of S. California, 1965, pp. 183–188.

Economics and Ecology. In: *Future Environments in North America.* Being the record of a Conference convened by the Conservation Foundation in April, 1965, at Airlie House, Warrenton, Virginia, F. Fraser Darling and John P. Milton, eds. Garden City N.Y.: The Natural History Press, 1966, pp. 225–234, with a summary by the author; pp. 217–219.

The Economics of Knowledge and the Knowledge of Economics. Am. Econ. Rev. 16: 2 (May 1966): 1–13. (Richard T. Ely Lecture, 1965.)

The Economics of the Coming Space-Ship Earth. In: *Environmental Quality in a Growing Economy,* Essays from the Sixth RFF Forum, Henry Jarrett, ed. Baltimore, Md.: Johns Hopkins Press for Resources for the Future, Inc., 1966, pp. 3–14.

The Ethics of Rational Decision. Management Science, 12: 6 (Feb 1966), B-161–B-169.

Expecting the Unexpected: The Uncertain Future of Knowledge and Technology. In: *Prospective Changes in Society by 1980 Including Some Implications for Education. Reports Prepared for the First Area Conference. Designing Education for the Future. An Eight-State Project.* Denver, Colorado, July, 1966, Edgar L. Morphet and Charles O. Ryan, eds. pp. 199–215. Reprinted in: *The Education Digest, XXXIII, 3* (Nov 1966): 7–11; (Retitled: *The Uncertain Future of Knowledge and Technology.*)

The Feather River Anthology (verse). *Industrial Water Engineering 3, 12* (Dec 1966) 32–33.

Impressions of the World Conference on Church and Society (Geneva, July, 1966), *Quaker Life, Ser. VII, 9* (Sept 1966): 287–289.

Is Scarcity Dead? The Public Interest 5 (Fall 1966): 36–44.

The Knowledge Boom. Challenge 14, 6 (July–Aug 1966): 5–7.

Notes on the Politics of Peace. Bull. Atomic Sci. 22, 7 (Sept 1966): 30–32.

The Parameters of Politics. Edmund J. James Lecture on Government, April 21, 1966. *Univ. of Illinois Bull. 63, 139* (July 15, 1966): 1–21.

Arms Limitation and Integrative Activity as Elements in the Establishment of Stable Peace. Peace Research Society (International) Papers (Vienna Conference, 1966), Vol. VI (1966): 1–10.

Towards the Development of a Security Community in Europe. Proceedings of the Sixteenth Pugwash Conference on Science and World Affairs, Sopot, Poland, Vol. V (Sept 1966): 122–130.

The Peculiar Economics of Water Supply. Chemistry 39, 9 (Sept 1966): 20–21.

A Profile of the American Economy. Washington, D.C., USA. *America, 10, 120* (1966): 10–13 (in Russian); *America, 15, 93* (1966): 8–11 (in Polish).

Quakerism in the World of the Future. Friends Journal 12, 2 (Jan 15, 1966): 29–31.

The Role of the Museum in the Propagation of Developed Images. Technology and Culture VII, 1 (Winter, 1966): 64–66.

Summary of Papers given at the American Psychiatric Association in New York May 3, 1965 (verse). *Bull. Menninger Clinic 30, 5* (Sept 1966): 313–314.

Verifiability of Economics Images. In: *The Structure of Economic Science,* Sherman Krupp, ed. Englewood Cliffs, N.J.: Prentice-Hall, 1966, pp. 129—141.

The Wisdom of Man and the Wisdom of God. In: *Human Values on the Spaceship Earth,* New York: *Council Press (National Council of the Churches of Christ),* 1966, pp. 1–33.

Books

Economic Analysis, 4th Ed. 2 volumes. New York: Harper and Row, 1966.
Translations: Spanish, Japanese.

The Impact of the Social Sciences. New Brunswick, N.J.: Rutgers University Press, 1966. Pp. vi + 117.

Pamphlet

The Political Consequences of the Social Sciences. Lecture delivered before the First Annual Political Awards Dinner, December 6, 1965. Kalamazoo: Michigan Center for Education in Politics, Western Michigan University, 1966. Pp. 13.

Reviews

Review of James S. Coleman, Introduction to Mathematical Sociology. Am. Soc. Rev. 31, 1 (Feb 1966): 131–32.

Review of Fred Charles Iklé, How Nations Negotiate. Am. Jour. Soc. 71, 5 (Mar 1966): 601.

Review of Oskar Lange, Wholes and Parts: A General Theory of System Behavior, Econometrica 34, 2 (Apr 1966): 510.

Review of Robert K. Merton, On the Shoulders of Giants; a Shandean Postscript. Am. Soc. Rev. 31, 1 (Feb 1966): 104–5.

Review of Kalman J. Cohen and Richard M. Cyert, Theory of the Firm: Resource Allocation in a Market Economy. Econometrica, 34, 4 (Oct 1966): 902–903.

Knowledge vs. Wisdom in the Relations Between Scientists and the Government: review of Don K. Price, The Scientific Estate. Sci. Amer. 214, 4 (April 1966): 131–134.

Space, Technology, and Society: From Puff-Puff to Whoosh. Review of Bruce Mazlish, ed. *The Railroad and the Space Program: An Exploration in Historical Analogy, Science, 151, 3713* (Feb 25, 1966): 979.

Review of Anatol Rapoport and Albert Chammah, Prisoner's Dilemma: A Study in Conflict and Cooperation. Michigan Daily, Feb 2, 1966, p. 4. Also in: *Michigan Quarterly Review 6, 2* (Spring 1967): 142–144.

Review of Barbara Ward, Space Ship Earth, Fellowship 32, 9 (Sept 1966): 29.

Review of E. G. West, Education and the State: A Study in Political Economy, Univ. of Chicago Law Review 33, 3 (Spring 1966): 615–618.

1967

Articles

Arms Limitation and Integrative Activity as Elements in the Establishment of Stable Peace. In: *Peace Research Society; Papers, VI,* Vienna Conference 1966.

The Basis of Value Judgements in Economics, In: *Human Values and Economic Policy,* Sidney Hook, ed. Proceedings of the Eighth Annual New York Univ. Institute of Philosophy, Washington Square, New York, May 13–14, 1966. New York: *New York Univ. Press,* 1967: 55–72.

The Boundaries of Social Policy. Social Work 12, 1 (Jan 1967): 3–11.

Dare We Take the Social Sciences Seriously? American Behavioral Scientist, 10, 10 (July 1967): 12–16. Also in: *American Psychologist, 22, 11* (Nov 1967):

An Economist Looks at the Future of Sociology. et al., 1, 2 (Winter 1967): 1–6; comment by Talcott Parsons, 6–7.

Evolution and Revolution in the Developmental Process. In: *Social*

Change and Economic Growth (Annual Meeting of Directors of Development Training and Research Institutes, Bergen, Norway, July 11–15, 1966). Paris: Development Centre of the Organization for Economic Co-operation and Development, 1967: 19–29.

Human Resources Development as a Learning Process. Farm Policy Forum 19, 2 1966–67: 27–35. Also in: *Human Resources Development,* Edward B. Jakubauskas and C. Phillip Baumel, eds. Ames, Iowa: Iowa State Univ. Press, 1967: 46–55.

The Impact of the Draft on the Legitimacy of the National State. Chapter in: *The Draft, A Handbook of Facts and Alternatives,* Sol Tax, ed. Chicago: *The Univ. of Chicago Press,* 1967: 191–196.

Is There a General Theory of Conflict? Industrial Conflict and Race Conflict (Proceedings of the 1967 Annual Spring Meeting, Detroit, Mich., May 5–6, 1967): 4–12.

The Learning and Reality-Testing Process in the International System. Journal of International Affairs 30, 1 (1967): 1–15.

The Learning Process in the Dynamics of Total Societies. In: *The Study of Total Societies,* Samuel Z. Klausner, ed. Garden City, N.Y.: Doubleday & Co., Anchor Books, 1967: 98–113.

The Legitimacy of Economics, West. Econ. Jour. V, 4 (Sept 1967): 299–307.

The Old Agricultural Lag (verse). In: *No Easy Harvest,* Max Millikan and David Hapgood, Mass. Institute of Tech., 1967, p. xii.

The Price System and the Price of the Great Society. In: *The Future of Economic Policy,* Myron H. Ross, ed. Lectures given at Western Mich. Univ., Winter Semester, 1966. Ann Arbor: Bureau of Business Research, Graduate School of Business Administration. The University of Michigan, 1967. *Michigan Business Papers,* No. 44, 57–73.

The Prospects of Economic Abundance. In: *The Control of Environment: A discussion at the Nobel Conference,* Gustafus Adolphus College, 1966. John D. Roslansky, ed. Amsterdam: North-Holland Publishing Company, 1967: 39–57.

The Role of the War Industry in International Conflict. Jour. of Soc. Issues 23, 1 (Jan 1967): 47–61.

Technology and the Integrative System. In: *Today's Changing Society, A Challenge to Individual Identity.* Clarence C. Walter, ed. New York: Institute of Life Insurance, 1967: 57–73.

The "Two Cultures", In: *Technology in Western Civilization,* Vol. II. Melvin Kransberg and Carroll W. Pursell, Jr., eds. New York: *Oxford Univ. Press,* 1967: 686–695.

The University and Tommorrow's Civilization: Its Role in the Develop-

ment of a World Community. Jour. of Higher Educ. XXXVIII, 9 (Dec 1967): 477–483. Also (Retitled *The Role of the University in the Development of a World Community*) *Higher Education in Tomorrow's World*, Algo D. Henderson, ed. Ann Arbor, Michigan: *The Univ. of Mich. Press*, 1968. Pp. 135–141.

Pamphlet

The Mayer-Boulding Dialogue on Peace Research. Wallingford, Pa.: *Pendle Hill Pamphlet 153, 1967.* Pp. 30.

Reviews

Review of Raymond A. Bauer, ed., *Social Indicators. Science 155, 3762* (Feb 3 1967): 550–551.

The Scientific-Military Industrial Complex, Review of John Kenneth Galbraith, The New Industrial State and H. L. Nieburg, In the Name of Science. The Virginia Quarterly Review 43, 4 (Autumn 1967): 672–679.

Review of Philip Green, Deadly Logic: The Theory of Nuclear Deterrence. Dissent 14, 4 (July–Aug 1967): 496–498.

Review of Carl G. Gustavson, The Institutional Drive. Technology and Culture.

Review of Robert L. Heilbroner, The Limits of American Capitalism. The New York Review of Books 7, 12 (Jan 12, 1967): 29–31.

Review of John Jewkes, Public and Private Enterprise. The Lindsay Memorial Lectures, given at the University of Keele, 1964. *Science 155, 3766* (Mar 3, 1967): 1095.

Am I a Man or a Mouse—or Both: Review of Konrad Lorenz, On Aggression; and Robert Ardrey, The Territorial Imperative: A Personal Inquiry into the Animal Origins of Property and Nations. War/Peace Report 7, 3 (Mar 1967): 14–17.

Review of Ben B. Seligman, Most Notorious Victory: Man in an Age of Automation. N.Y. Times Book Review. Jan 1, 1967, p. 25.

Review of G. L. S. Shackle, A Scheme of Economic Theory. The Jour. of Bus. 40, 1 (Jan 1967): 102.

Review of Robert Solo, Economic Organizations and Social Systems. Science 157, (Sept 8 1967): 1158–1159.

Review of Lester B. Lave, Technological Change: Its Conception and Measurement. American Journal of Sociology, 72, 5 (Mar 1967): 563.

Milking the Sacred Cow. Review of John Kenneth Galbraith, The New Industrial State. Book Week, July 18, 1967, pp. 2, 12.

1968

Articles

Accomplishments and Prospects of the Peace Research Movement. Arms Control and Disarmament. Vol 1, 1968, 43–58.

America's Economy: The Qualified Uproarious Success. In: *America Now*, John G. Kirk, ed., New York: Athenum, 1968, 143–161.

Business and Economic Systems. In: *Positive Feedback*, John H. Milsum, ed., Toronto: Pergamon Press, 1968, 101–117.

The City as an Element in the International System. Daedalus, 97, 4 (Fall 1968), 1111–1123.

A Data-Collecting Network for the Sociosphere. Impact of Science on Society XVIII, 2 (April/June 1968), 97–101.

Reflection of the Election—An Interview with Kenneth Boulding. Town and Country Review (Boulder, Colo.), Nov 14, 1968, pp. 4, 6.

Is Ugliness the Price of Prosperity? In: *Seminar on Environmental Arts and Sciences: Summary of Proceedings.* (held in Aspen, Colo., Aug 1968) Boulder, Colo.: Thorne Ecological Foundation, 1968.

The Legitimation of the Market. (C. Woody Thompson Memorial Lecture, Midwest Economics Association annual meeting, Chicago, Apr 1967) *Nebraska Journal of Economics and Business, 7, 1* (Spring 1968): 3–14.

Man's Choice: Creative Development or Revolution. In: *The United States in a Revolutionary World—Occasional Papers*, Robert H. Simmons, ed. Pasadena, Calif.: American Friends Service Committee, 1968, pp. 1–7.

The Dynamics of Society. Bell Telephone Magazine 47, 3 (May/June 1968), 4–7.

The Economics and Financing of Technology in Education: Some Observations. In: *Planning for Effective Utilization of Technology in Education*, Edgar L. Morphet and David L. Jesser, eds. Denver: *Designing Education for the Future*, 1968, 367–372.

Education for the Spaceship Earth. Social Education XXXII, 7 (Nov 1968), 648–652. Also in: *An Examination of Objectives, Needs and Priorities in International Education in U.S. Secondary and Elementary Schools.* Washington, D.C.: U.S. Dept. of HEW, Office of Education, Bureau of Research, July 1969, 316–323.

Ethical Dilemmas in Religion and Nationalism. New York: Ethical Culture Publications, American Ethical Union, 1968. Reprinted in: *ETC XXVII, 1* (Mar 1970), 27–24.

Grants Versus Exchange in the Support of Education. In: *Federal Programs for the Development of Human Resources, a Compendium of*

Papers, Vol. 1, Washington, D.C.: U.S. Government Printing Office, 1968, 232–238.

Greatness as a Pathology of the National Image. In: *U.S. Foreign Policy: Responsibilities of a Superpower in International Politics.* Champaign, Illinois: Univ. of Illinois, Extension in International Affairs, September 1968, 35–42.

A Historical Note from the President. American Economic Review 58, 5 (Dec 1968), 1509–1510.

The Legitimation of the Market. Nebraska Journal of Economics and Business 7, 1 (Spring 1968), 3–14.

Machines, Men and Religion. Friends Journal 14, 24 (Dec 15, 1968), 643–644.

The Many Failures of Success. Saturday Review (Nov 23, 1968), 29–31.

The "National" Importance of Human Capital. In: *The Brain Drain,* Walter Adams, ed. New York: Macmillan Company, 1968, 109–119.

A Peace Movement in Search of a Party. War/Peace Report 8, 1 (Jan 1968), 12–13.

Preface to a Special Issue. Journal of Conflict Resolution 12, 4 (Dec 1968), 409–411.

Requirements for a Social Systems Analysis of the Dynamics of the World War Industry. Peace Research Society (International), Papers, IX, 1968, 1–8.

Revolution and Development. In: *Changing Perspectives of Man,* Ben Rothblatt, ed. Chicago: University of Chicago Press, 1968, 207–226.

Statement (on Learning, Teaching, Education, and Development) In: *1968 Coloradan,* Vol. 70. Boulder: Associated Students of the University of Colorado, 1968, p. 166.

Town and Country Interviews Dr. Kenneth Boulding. Town and Country Review (Boulder, Colo.), Apr 11, 1968, pp. 1, 11, 13–14; Apr 18, 1968, pp. 8, 11–12.

The Role of Economics in the Establishment of Stable Peace. Economisch-Statistische Berichten (Rotterdam, Netherlands) 53e jrg., 2639 (Apr 10, 1968), 332–334.

The Specialist with a Universal Mind. Management Science 14, 12 (Aug 1968), B-647–B-653.

The University as an Economic and Social Unit. In: *Colleges & Universities as Agents of Social Change,* W. John Minter and Ian M. Thompson, eds. Boulder, Colorado: Western Interstate Commission for Higher Education, 1968, 75–87; Wednesday Night Colloquium discussion, 89–128.

Values, Technology, and Divine Legitimation. In: *Science, Philosophy, Religion,* Lt. Gerald P. McCarthy, ed. Kirtland Air Force Base, New Mexico: Air Force Weapons Laboratory, 1968, 4–16.

What Can We Know and Teach about Social Systems? Social Science Education Consortium Newsletter, University of Colorado, No. 5 (June 1968), 1–5. Also in: *Social Science in the Schools,* Irving Morrissett and W. W. Stevens, Jr., eds. New York: Holt, Rinehart and Winston, 1971, 140–161.

Book

Beyond Economics: Essays on Society, Religion, and Ethics. Ann Arbor, Michigan: University of Michigan Press, 1968. Pp. 302. Ann Arbor Paperback, 1970. Nominated for a National Book Award, 1970.

Monograph

The Effects of Military Expenditure upon the Economic Growth of Japan (edited with Norman Sun). Tokyo, Japan: International Christian University, 1968.

Pamphlets

Friends and Social Change. Philadelphia, Pa.: Friends General Conference of the Religious Society of Friends, 1968. Pp. 4.

Profile of the American Economy. Washington, D.C.: United States Information Agency, 1968. Pp. 4.

Reviews

Review of Général d'Armée André Beaufre, Deterrence and Strategy. Political Science Quarterly 83, 1 (Mar 1968), 109–111.

Review of C. E. Black, The Dynamics of Modernization: A Study in Comparative History. History and Theory 7, 1 (1968), 83–90.

Review of David Easton, A Systems Analysis of Political Life. Behavioral Science 13, 2 (Mar 1968), 147–149.

"Prognostics": A Guide to Present Action. Review of Herman Kahn and Anthony J. Wiener, The Year 2000: A Framework for Speculation on the Next Thirty-Three Years. Saturday Review LI, 6 (Feb 10, 1968), 36–37.

In the Money. Review of Ferdinand Lundberg, The Rich and the Super-Rich, and Ben B. Seligman, Permanent Poverty: An American Syndrome. The New York Review of Books 11, 4 (Sept 12, 1968), 40–42.

Asia: Soft States and Hard Facts. Review of Gunnar Myrdal, Asian Drama: An Inquiry into the Poverty of Nations. The New Republic 158, 18 (May 4, 1968), 25–28.

Review of Report from Iron Mountain on the Possibilities and Desirability of Peace. Trans-action 5, 3 (Jan–Feb 1968), 16.

Review of Gordon Tullock, The Organization of Inquiry. Journal of Economic Issues 2, 2 (June 1968), 259–261.

Observations Unlimited. Review of Eliot Janeway, The Economics of Crisis: War, Politics, and the Dollar. New York Times Book Review, 73, 3 (Jan 21, 1968): 24.

1969

Articles

David Fand's "Keynesian Monetary Theories, Stabilization Policy, and the Recent Inflation" A Comment. Journal of Money, Credit and Banking 1, 3 (Aug 1969), 588–589.

Economic Education: The Stepchild Too is Father of the Man. Journal of Economic Education 1, 1 (Fall 1969), 7–11.

Economics as a Moral Science (Presidential Address, American Economic Association, December 29, 1968). *American Economic Review 59, 1* (Mar 1969), 1–12.

Education and the Economic Process. In: *The Alternative of Radicalism: Radical and Conservative Possibilities for Teaching the Teachers of America's Young Children* (Report of the 5th Nat'l Conference, US. Office of Education Tri-University Project in Elementary Education, New Orleans, January 1969), Thomas R. Holland and Catherine M. Lee, eds. 1969, 72–82.

The Effects of the War Industry. In: *National Priorities* (Testimony before the Subcommittee on Economy in Government of the Joint Economic Committee, Congress of the United States, 6/4/69). Washington, D.C.: Public Affairs Press, 1969, 135–139. Excerpted in: *American Militarism 1970,* Erwin Knoll and Judith Nies McFadden, eds. New York: The Viking Press, 1969, 89–95.

Failures and Success of Economics. Think 35, 3 (May/June 1969), 2–6. Reprinted in: *The Congressional Record,* July 9, 1969, E5743-E5745.

The Fifth Meaning of Love: Notes on Christian Ethics and Social Policy. Lutheran World (July 1969), 219–229. Also in: *Lutherische Rundschau 19, 3* (July 1969), 281–295, entitled *"Die fünfte Deutung des Wortes Liebe—Gedanken über christliche Ethik und soziale Planung".*

The Formation of Values as a Process in Human Learning. In: *Transportation and Community Values.* Washington, D.C.: Highway Research Board, *Special Report 105,* 1969, 31–38; discussion, 39–45.

The Grants Economy. Michigan Academician (Papers of the Michigan Academy of Science, Arts and Letters) 1, 1 and 2 (Winter 1969), 3–11.

Heretic Among Economists. Interview with Kenneth Boulding by Lewis Beman. Business Week, Jan 4, 1969, 80–82.

The Interplay of Technology: The Emerging Superculture. In: *Values and*

the Future, Impact of Technological Change on American Values, Kurt
Baier and N. Rescher, eds. New York: The Free Press, 1969, 336–350.

A Memorandum on the Facilitation of Behavioral Thinking: Four Modest
Proposals for Highly Advanced Study (with Richard Christie). The
Subterranean Sociology Newsletter IV, 1 (Oct 1969), 5–8.

Modern Man and Ancient Testimonies. Quaker Religious Thought XI, 1
(Summer 1969), 3–14.

The Need for a University of the Building Industry. American Institute of
Architects Journal 51, 5 (May 1969), 79–90.

Preventing Schismogenesis. Comments on "Protest or Conform: Some
Social Psychological Perspectives on Legitimacy" by Richard Flacks.
Journal of Applied Behavioral Sciences 5, 2 (1969), 151–153.

Public Choice and the Grants Economy: The Intersecting Set. Public
Choice, VII (Fall 1969), 1–2.

Research for Peace. Science Journal (England) 5A, 4 (Oct 1969), 53–59.

The Role of Exemplars in the Learning of Community. World Studies
Education Service Bulleting (London). No. 10 (Jan 1969), 15–16.

Some Unsolved Problems in Economic Education. In: Five Levels of
Incompetence (Report of the 1969 Grove Park Institute), Thomas
Vogt, ed. Washington, D.C.: CONPASS, 1971, 37–50.

Stability in International Systems: The Role of Disarmament and De-
velopment. In: International Security Systems: Concepts and Models of
World Order, Richard B. Gray, ed. Itasca, Illinois: F. E. Peacock
Publishers, 1969, 193–210.

The Task of the Teacher in the Social Sciences. In: The Quest for
Relevance: Effective College Teaching; Vol. III, The Social Sciences.
Washington, D.C.: U.S. Dept of HEW (Mar 1969), 3–24.

Technology and the Changing Social Order. In: The Urban-Industrial
Frontier: Essays on Social Trends and Institutional Goals in Modern
Communities, David Popenoe, ed. New Brunswick, N.J.: Rutgers
University Press, 1969, 126–140.

Statement Before the Subcommittee on Economy in Government of the
Joint Economic Committee, U.S. Congress. In: The Military Budget and
National Economic Priorities (Hearings of the Committee). Washing-
ton, D.C.: U.S. Government Printing Office, 1969, Part I, pp. 137–141.

Research for Peace. Science Journal (London), 5A, 4 (Oct 1969): 53–58.

Die Zukunft als Möglichkeit und Design (The Future as Chance and
Design: in German; Bauwelt 50 (Berlin), 60 (Dec 15, 1969): 1807–1811.

The Threat System. In: The Cost of Conflict, John A. Copp, ed. Ann
Arbor, Michigan: Bureau of Business Research (Michigan Business
Papers, Number 51), 1969, 3–17.

What Don't We Know that Hurts Us! In: Selected Readings in Economic

Education. Roman F. Warmke and G. Draayer, eds. Athens, Ohio: Ohio Council on Economic Education, College of Bus. Admin. Ohio University, 1969, 3–17.

Pamphlets

The Role of the Church in the Making of Community and Identity. Greeley, Colorado: First Congregational Church, 1969. (Ethan Allen Cross Memorial Lecture Series).

The Role of Legitimacy in the Dynamics of Society. University Park, Pa: Center for Research of the College of Bus. Admin., Penn. State Univ., 1969. Pp. 13. (Graduate School Lecture Series, 1967)

Reviews

Growth and Grace: Incompatible? Review of Alfred Balk, The Religion Business; Nino Lo Bello, The Vatican Empire: Arthur Herzog, The Church Trap: D. B. Robertson, Should Churches Be Taxed? Saturday Review (Feb 8, 1969), 27–28.

Economics Imperialism. Review of David Braybrooke and Charles E. Lindblom, A Strategy of Decision; Mancur Olson, Jr., The Logic of Collective Action; Bruce M. Russett (ed.), *Economic Theories of International Politics. Behavioral Science 14,* 6 (Nov 1969), 496–500.

A Forecast by Scientists. Review of Nigel Calder, ed., *War: The Anthropology of Armed Conflict and Aggression. Comparative Studies in Society and History 11, 1* (Jan 1969), 109–111.

Case Study in Non-Decision. Review of Congressman Richard D. McCarthy, The Ultimate Folly: War by Pestilence, Asphyxiation and Defoliation. The New Republic 161, 22 (Nov 29, 1969), 24–25.

Tragic Nonsense. Review of Herbert Marcuse, An Essay on Liberation. The New Republic 160, 12 (Mar 29, 1969), 28, 30.

Review of J. E. Meade, The Growing Economy. Journal of Economic Literature 7, 4 (Dec 1969), 1161–1162.

Review of Arthur E. Morgan, Observations. Religious Humanism 3, 2 (Spring 1969), 92.

Review of Kenneth Schneider, Destiny of Change: How Relevant is Man in the Age of Development? Administrative Science Quarterly, 14, 2 (June 1969), 318.

Review of Philip Sporn, Technology, Engineering, and Economics; and Sheldon Novick, The Careless Atom. Science 165, 3892 (Aug 1, 1969), 483–484.

Review of Morton Fried, Marvin Harris and Robert Murphy, eds., War: The Anthropology of Armed Conflict and Aggression. Comparative Studies in Society and History, 11, 1 (Jan 1969): 109–111.

Dialogue with a Marxist. Review of David Horowitz, Empire and Revolution: A Radical Interpretation of Contemporary History. Book World (Chicago Tribune), *3, 31* (Aug 3, 1969): 6.

Verse

The Ditchley Bank Anthology. Michigan Business Review 21, 2 (Mar 1969), 17–19. Also in: *Journal of Money, Credit, and Banking 1, 3* (Aug 1969), 354, 462, 507, 555, 624, 681, entitled *"Ditchley Park Anthology; Minutes in Verse."*

X Cantos. Michigan Quarterly Review 8, 1 (Review 1969), 29–31. Reprinted in: *The Actuary (Newsletter of the Society of Actuaries) 4, 3* (Mar 1970), 6; *4, 4* (Apr 1970), 6; *4, 7* (Sept 1970), 5.

1970

Articles

The Balance of Peace. Peace Research Society (International), Papers, XIII, 1970, 59–65.

Can We Curb Inflation Without Recession? If So, How? The Denver Post, February 15, 1970.

Can There Be a National Policy for Stable Peace? AAUW Journal 63 (May 1970), 172–174.

The Challenge of the Great Transition. The Mainichi Newspapers (Tokyo) (Mar 3, 1970), 9.

The Crisis of the Universities. The Colorado Quarterly 19 (Autumn 1970), 120–129.

The Deadly Industry: War and the International System. Introduction to Peace and the War Industry, K. E. Boulding, ed. Chicago: Aldine Publishing Company, 1970, 1–12.

Factors Affecting the Future Demand for Education. In: *Economic Factors Affecting the Financing of Education,* Roe L. Johns *et al.,* eds. Gainesville, Florida: National Educational Finance Project, Vol. 2, 1970, 1–27.

The Family Segment of the National Economy. Journal of Home Economics 62 (Sept 1970), 447–454.

Fragmentation, Isolation, Conflict. In: *Twenty-Five Years: 1945–1970,* G. Kerry Smith, ed. Washington, D.C.: American Association for Higher Education, 1970, 254–267.

Fun and Games with the Gross National Product — The Role of Misleading Indicators in Social Policy. In: *The Environmental Crisis,* Harold W. Helfrich, Jr., ed. New Haven: Yale University Press, 1970, 157–170.

Fundamental Considerations. In: *Perspectives on Campus Tensions,*
David C. Nichols, ed. Washington, D.C.: American Council on Education, 1970, 3–17.

*The Impact of the Defense Industry on The Structure of the American
Economy.* In: *Adjustments of the U.S. Economy to Reductions in
Military Spending,* Bernard Udis, ed., Dec 1970, pp. 399–433. Also in:
The Economic Consequences of Reduced Military Spending, Bernard
Udis, ed. Lexington, Mass.: D. C. Heath, 1973, pp. 225–252.

Social Systems Analysis and the Study of International Conflict. In:
Problems of Modern Strategy. London: Chatto and Windus, for The
Institute for Strategic Studies, 1970, pp. 77–91.

Some Hesitant Reflections on the Political Future. In: *1970 Coloradan,*
Vol. 72. Boulder: Associated Students of the University of Colorado,
1970, pp. 204–205.

*Statement Before the Select Subcommittee on Education of the House
Committee on Education and Labor, U.S. Congress.* In: *Environmental
Quality Education Act of 1970* (Hearings of the Committee). Washing-
ton, D.C.: U.S. Government Printing Office, 1970, pp. 597–605.

The Future as Chance and Design. Published in German as *"Die Zukunft
als Möglickheit."* In: *Bauwelt 50* (15 Dec, 1969), 1807–1811.

Gaps Between Developed and Developing Nations. In: *Toward Century
21: Technology, Society, and Human Values,* C. S. Wallia, ed. New
York: Basic Books, 1970, 125–134.

Is Economics Culture-Bound? American Economic Review 60, (May
1970), 406–411.

The Knowledge Explosion. In: *To Nuture Humaneness: Commitment for
the '70's.* Mary-Margaret Scobey and Grace Graham, eds. Washington,
D.C.: Association for Supervision and Curriculum Development,
National Education Association, 1970, 86–92.

A Look at National Priorities. Current History 59 (Aug 1970), 65–72.

A New Ethos for a New Era. In: *Canada and the United States in the
World of the Seventies,* R. H. Wagenberg, ed. Windsor, Ontario: Simon
& Schuster, Inc., copyright Univ. of Windsor Press, 1970, 93–98.

No Second Chance for Man. The Progressive 34 (Apr 1970), 40–43.
Reprinted in: *The Crisis of Survival.* Glenview, Illinois: Scott, Fores-
man and Company, 1970, 160–171.

The Philosophy of Peace Research (*Proceedings of the International
Peace Research Association Third Conference 1969*); *Vol.* 1,
Philosophy of Peace Research. Assen, Netherlands: Van Gorcum &
Company, 1970, 5–19.

The Real World of the Seventies and Beyond. In: *Training a Ministry in
the Seventies for a World of the Seventies and Beyond.* New York:
Association for Clinical Pastoral Education, 1970, 10–22.

The Role of the Undergraduate College in Social Change. Perspectives 1 (Feb 1970), 17–20.

The Scientific Revelation. Bulletin of the Atomic Scientists XXVI (Sept 1970), 13–18. Excerpted and entitled *"The End is in Sight for Galloping Science", Washington Post,* Sept 6, 1970.

Testimony on behalf of H. R. 14753, a Bill to Authorize the United States Commissioner of Education to establish educational programs to encourage understanding of policies and support of activities designed to enhance environmental quality and maintain ecological balance. In: *Environmental Quality Education Act of* 1970. Washington, D.C.: U.S. Government Printing Office, 1970, 597–605.

What Is the GNP Worth? In: *Earth-Day-The Beginning.* New York: Arno Press, Bantam Books, 1970, 143–144.

Books

Economics as a Science. McGraw-Hill Book Company, 1970. Pp. 161. McGraw-Hill Paperback, 1970.

Peace and the War Industry (Edited and with an introduction by K. E. Boulding). Aldine Publishing Company (TRANS-action Book 11), 1970. Pp. 159.

A Primer on Social Dynamics. The Free Press, 1970, Pp. 153. Free Press Paperback, 1970.

The Prospering of Truth (The Swarthmore Lecture 1970, London Yearly Meeting, Aug 1970). London: Friends Home Service Committee, 1970. Pp. 51.

Pamphlet

War Industry and the American Economy. (Third Annual William Carlyle Furnas Memorial Lecture, Northern Illinois University, Nov 1969). De Kalb, Illinois: Dept. of Economics, Northern Ill. Univ., 1970. Pp. 18.

Reviews

The Politics of Knowledge. Review of Peter F. Drucker, The Age of Discontinuity: Guidelines to Our Changing Society. TRANS-action, 7, 6 (Apr 1970), 81–82.

Review of William R. Ewald, Jr., ed., Environment and Policy: The Next Fifty Years. American Journal of Sociology 75, 5 (Mar 1970), 878–880.

Review of John Hicks, A Theory of Economic History. American Journal of Agriculture Economics (Nov 1970), 619–620.

Review of Warren F. Ilchman and Norman Thomas Uphoff, The Political

Economy of Change. American Political Science Review 64, 2 (June 1970), 603–604.

Review of Nathan Leites and Charles Wolf, Jr., Rebellion and Authority; An Analytic Essay on Insurgent Conflicts. A RAND Corporation Research Study. The Annals (Nov 1970), 184–185.

Time as a Commodity. Review of Staffan B. Linder, The Harried Leisure Class. The New Republic 162, 8 (Feb 21, 1970), 27–28.

Tantalizing Questions. Review of Margaret Mead, Culture and Commitment, A Study of the Generation Gap. The Virginia Quarterly Review 46, 2 (Spring 1970), 339–341.

Tools on a Grand Scale. Review of Emmanuel G. Mesthene, Technological Change, Its Impact on Man and Society. Science 168, 3938 (19 June, 1970), 1442.

When Cost Push Comes to Shove. Review of Arthur M. Okun, The Political Economy of Prosperity. TRANS-action 7, 11 (Sept 1970), 64–68.

1971

Articles

After Samuelson, Who Needs Adam Smith? History of Political Economy 3, 2 (Fall 1971), 225–237.

The American Economy After Vietnam. In: *After Vietnam: The Future of American Foreign Policy,* Robert W. Gregg and C. Kegley, Jr., eds. Garden City, New York: Anchor Books, Doubleday & Company, 1971, 307–323.

Discussion of Allen V. Kneese's, "Environmental Pollution: Economics and Policy." American Economic Review 61, 2 (May 1971), 167–169.

The Dodo Didn't Make It: Survival and Betterment. Bulletin of the Atomic Scientists XXVII, 5 (May 1971), 19–22.

Environment and Economics. In: *Environment; Resources, Pollution and Society,* William W. Murdoch, ed. Stamford, Connecticut: Sinauer Associates, Inc., 1971, 359–367.

The Impact of the Defense Industry on the Structure of the American Economy. In: *Adjustments of the U.S. Economy to Reductions in Military Spending,* Bernard Udis. ed. Prepared for the United States Arms Control and Disarmament Agency ACDA/E-156 (Dec 1970), 399–433.

Knowledge as a Road to Peace. Bulletin of the Peace Studies Institute (Manchester College, Indiana), Aug 1971, 1–4.

The Legitimacy of Central Banks. In: *Reappraisal of the Federal Reserve Discount Mechanism, Vol. 2.* Washington, D.C.: Board of Governors of the Federal Reserve System (Dec 1971), 1–13.

The Meaning of Human Betterment. Nebraska Journal of Economics and Business 10, 2 (Spring 1971), 3–12.

The Misallocation of Intellectual Resources in Economics. In: *The Use and Abuse of Social Science,* Irving L. Horowitz, ed. New York: E. P. Dutton, Inc. for TRANS-action Books, 1971, 34–51.

The Need for Reform of National Income Statistics. American Statistical Association Proceedings of the Social Statistics Section, 1970. Washington, D.C.: American Statistical Association, 1971, 94–97.

People Eyeing 21st Century as Age When Mankind Matures. The Japan Times (Tokyo), Jan 1, 1971, 6.

The Pursuit of Happiness and the Value of the Human Being. The Japan Economic Journal (Tokyo), Jan 1, 1971, Supplement No. 2, 39 (in Japanese).

Unprofitable Empire, Britain and India 1880–1947, A Critique of the Hobson–Lenin Thesis on Imperialism (with Tapan Mukerjee). Peace Research Society (International), Papers, XVI, 1971, 1–21.

An Epitaph: The Center for Research on Conflict Resolution, 1959–1971. Journal of Conflict Resolution, 15, 3 (Sept 1971): 279–280.

Letter on "Happiness." (in Japanese) *Sankei Shimbun Newspaper* (Tokyo), Jan. 1, 1971, p. 27.

Toward a Modest Society: The End of Growth and Grandeur. In: *Economic Perspectives of Boulding and Samuelson,* Durham: Whittemore School of Business and Economics, University of New Hampshire, 1971, pp. 7–20; reply, pp. 21–22.

A World-Famous "Economist-Philosopher" Gives His Views on Religion, Radicalism, the Hippies and More.(interview) *Seikyo Times* (Tokyo), *113* (Jan 1971): 31–32, 37–38.

What do Economic Indicators Indicate? Quality in the GNP. In: *Economics of Pollution* (The Charles C. Moskowitz Lectures, 1971). New York: New York University Press, 1971, 33–80.

Where Does Development Lead? Carnets de l'enfance (Assignment Children). Paris: UNICEF 13 (Jan–March 1971), 48–57.

Books

The Collected Papers of Kenneth E. Boulding, Volumes I and II. Edited by Fred R. Glahe. Boulder, Colorado: Colorado Associated University Press, 1971.

Pamphlet

Toward the Year 2000. Social Science Education Consortium (Boulder, Colorado), Publication # 132, Monograph Series, 1971. Pp. 14.

Reviews

Living with Violence. Review of Hannah Arendt, On Violence, and E. V. Walter, Terror and Resistance: A Study of Political Violence. War/Peace Report 11, 6 (June–July 1971), 17–18.

Review of Gottfried Dietze, Youth, University, and Democracy; Also D. Henderson, The Innovative Spirit; and Lewis B. Mayhew, Arrogance on Campus. AAUP Bulletin 57, 2 (June 1971), 296–297.

Review of E. J. Hobsbawm, Industry and Empire, An Economic History of Britain Since 1750. History and Theory 10, 1 (1971), 147–149.

Review of John R. Platt, Perception and Change: Projections for Survival. Michigan Quarterly Review X, 4 (Fall 1971), 195–197.

Review of Joan Robinson, Economic Heresies: Some Old-Fashioned Questions in Economic Theory. Business Week (May 22, 1971), 12.

The Intellectual Framework of Bad Political Advice. Review of W. W. Rostow, Politics and the Stages of Growth. The Virginia Quarterly Review 47, 4 (Autumn 1971), 602–607.

1972

Articles

Economics and General Systems. In: *The Relevance of General Systems Theory*, Ervin Laslo, ed. New York: George Braziller, 1972, 77–92.

Economics as a Not Very Biological Science. In: *Challenging Biological Problems: Directions Toward Their Solution*, John A. Behnke, ed. New York: Oxford University Press, 1972, 357–375.

Future Directions. (with Martin Pfaff) In: *Redistribution to the Rich and the Poor: The Grants Economics of Income Distribution*, Kenneth Boulding and Martin Pfaff, eds. (Grants Economics Series). Belmont, Calif.: Wadsworth, 1972, pp. 387–390.

Introduction. In: *Economic Imperialism: A Book of Readings*, Kenneth Boulding and Tapan Mukerjee, eds. Ann Arbor: University of Michigan Press, 1972, pp. ix–xviii.

Japan Should Produce "Things" With Value Rather Than a "Strong Yen." (interview in Japanese) Nikkei Business (Tokyo), Dec 25, 1972, pp. 63–65.

The Future of Personal Responsibility. American Behavioral Scientist 15, 3 (Jan/Feb 1972), 329–359.

Grants Economics: A Simple Introduction (with Martin Pfaff and J. Horvath). The American Economist XVI, 1 (Spring 1972), 19–28.

The Grants Economy and the Development Gap (with Martin Pfaff). In: *The Gap Between Rich and Poor Nations*, Gustav Ranis, ed. London: Macmillan Press, 1972, 143–163.

The Household as Achilles' Heel. Journal of Consumer Affairs 6, 2 (Winter 1972), 110–119.

Human Betterment and the Quality of Life. In: *Human Behavior in Economic Affairs: Essays in Honor of George Katona*, Burkhard Strumpel et al., eds. Amsterdam: Elsevier Scientific Publishing Company, 1972, 455–470.

Interview with K. E. Boulding. In: *Philosophers of the Earth, by Anne Chisholm*. New York: E. P. Dutton & Company, 1972, 25–38.

Introduction to Analysis of the Problem of War (Garland Edition) by Clyde Eagleton. New York: Garland Publishing, 1972, 5–7.

The Liberal Arts Amid a Culture in Crisis. Liberal Education LVIII, 1 (Mar 1972), 5–17.

Man as a Commodity. In: *Human Resources and Economic Welfare: Essays in Honor of Eli Ginzberg*, Ivar Berg, ed. New York: Columbia University Press, 1972, 35–49.

New Goals for Society? In: *Energy, Economic Growth, and the Environment*, Sam H. Schurr, ed. Baltimore: Johns Hopkins University Press for Resources for the Future, 1972, 139–151.

The Role of the Social Sciences in the Control of Technology. In: *Technology and Man's Future*, Albert H. Teich, ed. New York: St. Martin's Press, 1972, 263–274.

The Schooling Industry as a Possibly Pathological Section of the American Economy. Review of Educational Research 42, 1 (Apr 1972), 129–143.

The Three Faces of Power. In: *50 Years of War Resistance: What Now?* London: War Resisters' International, 1972, 18–21.

Toward a Theory for the Study of Community. In: *Issues in Community Organization*, Lawrence Witmer, ed. Chicago: Center for the Scientific Study of Religion, 1972, 23–31.

Toward the Development of a Cultural Economics. Social Science Quarterly 53, 2 (Sept 1972), 267–284.

Toward a Pure Theory of Foundations. Non-Profit Report 5, 3 (March 1972), 1–22.

Towards a Twenty-First Century Politics. Colorado Quarterly XX, 3 (Winter 1972), 309–319.

The Weapon as an Element in the Social System. In: *The Future of the International Strategic System*, Richard N. Rosecrance, ed., San Francisco: Chandler Publishing Company, 1972.

Books

The Appraisal of Change (in Japanese). Tokyo: Japan Broadcast Publishing Company (Nippon Hoso Shuppan Kyokai), 1972. Pp. 176.

Economic Imperialism (edited with Tapan Mukerjee). Ann Arbor: University of Michigan Press, 1972. Pp. 338.

Redistribution to the Rich and the Poor: The Grants Economics of Income Distribution (edited with Martin Pfaff). Belmont, California: Wadsworth Publishing Company, 1972. Pp. 390.

Reviews

Review of Martin Bronfenbrenner, *Income Distribution Theory. Journal of Economic Issues* (Sept 1972), 123–128.

The Wolf of Rome. Review of Jay W. Forrester, *World Dynamics. Business and Society 2* (Summer 1972), 106–109.

Search for Time's Arrow. Review of Nicholas Georgescu-Roegen, *The Entropy Law and the Economic Process. Science 175, 4026* (Mar 10, 1972), 1099–1100.

The Gospel of St. Malthus. Review of Garrett Hardin, *Exploring New Ethics for Survival: The Voyage of the Spaceship Beagle. The New Republic 167, 9* (Sept 9, 1972), 22–25.

Review of Michael Hudson, *Super Imperialism: The Economic Strategy of American Empire. Book World* (The Washington Post) *VII, 53* (Dec 31, 1972), 7, 13.

Review of Fred Iklé, *Every War Must End. Political Science Quarterly 87, 4* (Dec 1972), 705–707.

Yes, the Wolf is Real. Review of Dennis and Donella Meadows et al., *The Limits to Growth. The New Republic 166, 18* (Apr 29, 1972), 27–28.

Review of Bruce Russett, *What Price Vigilance? The Burdens of National Defense. American Political Science Review, 66, 1* (Mar 1972): 217.

Verse

A Ballad of Ecological Awareness. In: *The Careless Technology: Ecology and International Development.* M. Taghi Farvar and John P. Milton, eds. Garden City, N.Y.: The Natural History Press, 1972, 3, 157, 371, 669, 793, 955.

History Press, for the Conservation Foundation and the Center for the Biology of Natural Systems, Washington University, 1972, pp. 3, 157, 371, 669, 793, 955.

New Goals for Society? In: *Energy, Economic Growth, and the Environment,* Sam H. Schurr, ed., Baltimore: Johns Hopkins University Press, for Resources for the Future, 1972, p. 139.

1973

Articles and Monograph

Aristocrats Have Always Been Sons of Bitches. (interview) *Psychology Today, 6, 8* (Jan 1973): 60–64, 67–68, 70, 86–87.

ASGE—In Retrospect and Prospect. Association for the Study of the Grants Economy Newsletter, 5 (Dec 5, 1973): 2–3.

Can There Be a Growth Policy? In: *Man and His Environment: The Vail Experience* (Summary of the 3rd Vail Symposium, Aug. 1973). Vail, Colo.: The Printery, for the Town of Vail, 1973, p. 19.

The Challenge of Change. (Lecture 10 in "America and the Future of Man" Course by Newspaper) Distributed by Copley News Service for the Regents of the University of California in all major newspapers in the U.S., Dec 6, 1973.

Communication of the Integrative Network. In: *Communication: Ethical and Moral Issues,* Lee Thayer, ed., New York: Gordon and Breach, 1973, pp. 201–213.

Economic Theory of Natural Liberty. In: *Dictionary of the History of Ideas,* Vol. II, Philip P. Wiener, ed.-in-chief. New York: Charles Scribner's Sons, 1973, pp. 61–71.

The Economics of Ecology. In: *Final Conference Report for the National Conference on Managing the Environment.* Washington, D.C.: Office of Research and Development, U.S. Environmental Protection Agency, 1973, pp. 11–13 to 11–17.

The Economics of Energy. Annals of the American Academy of Political and Social Science, 410 (Nov 1973): 120–126.

Equality and Conflict. Annals of the American Academy of Political and Social Science, 409 (Sept 1973): 1–8.

Foreword. In: *Image and Environment: Cognitive Mapping and Spatial Behavior,* Roger M. Downs and David Stea, eds. Chicago: Aldine, 1973, pp. 7–9.

Foreword. In: *The People: Growth and Survival,* by Gerhard Hirschfeld. Chicago: Aldine, for the Council for the Study of Mankind, 1973, pp. xiii–xvi.

Foreword. In: *The Image of the Future,* by Fred Polak, translated from the Dutch and abridged by Elise Boulding. San Francisco and Amsterdam: Jossey Bass/Elsevier, 1973, pp. 5–6.

General Systems as an Integrating Force in the Social Sciences. In: *University Through Diversity: A Festschrift for Ludwig von Bertalanffy,* Vol. II, William Gray and Nicholas D. Rizzo, eds. New York: Gordon & Breach, 1973, pp. 951–967.

Intersects: The Peculiar Organizations. In: *Challenge to Leadership: Managing in a Changing World* (A Conference Board Study). New York: Free Press, for the Conference Board, 1973, pp. 179–201.

Introduction. In: *Poverty and Progress: An Ecological Perspective on Economic Development,* by Richard G. Wilkinson. New York: Praeger, 1973, pp. 13–20.

Looking Ahead. Interview: Kenneth E. Boulding. In: *Economics '73–74': Text.* Guilford, Conn.: Dushkin, 1973, pp. 10–11.

Love, Fear and the Economist. (interview) *Challenge,* 16, 3 (July–Aug 1973): 32–39.

Organization Theory as a Bridge Between Socialist and Capitalist Societies. Journal of Management Studies, 10, 1 (Feb 1973): 1–7.

Role Prejudice as an Economic Problem. American Economic Review, 63, 5 (Dec 1973): 1049–1053.

The Shadow of the Stationary State. Daedalus, 102, 4 (Fall 1973): 89–101.

Social Dynamics. In: *Summer School in Peace Research: Grindstone Island 1973.* Dundas, Ont.: Canadian Peace Research Institute, Nov 1973, p. 26.

Social Risk, Political Uncertainty, and the Legitimacy of Private Profit. In: *Risk and Regulated Firms,* R. Hayden Howard, ed. East Lansing: Michigan State University Graduate School of Business Administration, 1973, pp. 82–93.

System Analysis and Its Use in the Classroom. (with Alfred Kuhn and Lawrence Senesh; SSEC Monograph Series, Publication No. 157) Boulder, Colo.: Social Science Education Consortium, 1973. Pp. 58.

A Theory of Prediction Applied to the Future of Economic Growth. In: *International Symposium "New Problems of Advanced Societies".* Tokyo: Japan Economic Research Institute, 1973, pp. 53–61.

Books

Kenneth E. Boulding Collected Papers, Vol. III: *Political Economy,* Larry D. Singell, ed. Boulder: Colorado Associated University Press, 1973, ix + 614 pp.

The Economy of Love and Fear: A Preface to Grants Economics. (Grants Economic Series) Belmont, Calif.: Wadsworth, 1973. Pp. 116.

Peace and the War Industry. 2nd edition. (edited, and with a revised introduction; Transaction/Society Book Series—11) New Brunswick, N.J.: Transaction Books, 1973. Pp. 213.

Transfers in an Urbanized Economy (edited with Martin and Anita Pfaff; Grants Economics Series) Belmont, Calif.: Wadsworth, 1973. Pp. 376.

Book Reviews

Multiply and Replenish: Alternative Perspectives on Population. Review of Howard M. Bahr, Bruce A. Chadwick, and Darwin L. Thomas, eds., Population Resources and the Future Non-Malthusian Perspectives. Dialogue: A Journal of Mormon Thought, 8, 3/4 (1973): 159–163.

Global Economics: A Failure So Far. Review of Jagdish N. Bhagwati, ed., Economics and World Order: From the 1970's to the 1990's. War/Peace Report, 12, 5 (July–Aug 1973): 30–31.

Review of William Breit and Roger L. Ransom, The Academic Scribblers: American Economists in Collision. Journal of Political Economy, 81, 4 (July–Aug 1973): 1041–1042.

Review of Lester R. Brown, World Without Borders. International Development Review, 15, 2 (1973): 30.

Zoom, Gloom, Doom and Room. Review of H. S. D. Cole et al., eds., Models of Doom: A Critique of the Limits to Growth; Ralph E. Lapp, The Logarithmic Century: Charting Future Shock; and John Maddox, The Doomsday Syndrome. New Republic, 169, 6 (Aug 11, 1973): 25–27.

Review of Edgar S. Dunn, Jr., Economic and Social Development: A Process of Social Learning. Urban Studies (Glasgow), 10, 1 (Feb 1973): 105–106.

Big Families Do Pay. Review of Bernard James, The Death of Progress; Mahmood Mamdani, The Myth of Population Control: Family, Caste, and Class in an Indian Village; and Herbert N. Woodward, The Human Dilemma. New Republic, 168, 9 (Mar 3, 1973): 22–23.

Review of Richard A. Peterson, The Industrial Order and Social Policy. Administrative Science Quarterly, 18, 4 (Dec 1973): 555–556.

Review of John Rawls, A Theory of Justice. Journal of Economic Issues, 7, 4 (Dec 1973): 667–673.

Review of G. L. S. Shackle, Epistemics & Economics: A Critique of Economic Doctrines. Journal of Economic Literature, 11, 4 (Dec 1973): 1373–1374.

Verse

COPRED, A Prophecy. Peace and Change, 1, 2 (Spring 1973): 60.

Reflections. In: Final Conference Report for the National Conference on Managing the Environment. Washington, D.C.: Office of Research and Development, U.S. Environmental Protection Agency, 1973, p. 3.

1974

Articles

Bottleneck Economics. Technology Review, 76, 6 (May 1974): 16–17.

The Doubtful Future (Addison L. Roache Lecture, Indiana University-Purdue University, Indianapolis, March 18, 1974). *The Review* (Alumni Association of the College of Arts and Sciences, Graduate School, Indiana University, Bloomington, Ind.), 16, 4 (Summer 1974): 27–37.

ECON is a Four-Letter Word. In: *Increasing Understanding of Public Problems and Policies—1973* (based on presentations at the 23rd National Public Policy Conference, planned by the National Public Policy Education Committee, Gull Lake, Brainerd, Minn., Sept 17–21, 1973). Chicago, Ill.: Farm Foundation, 1974, pp. 137–146.

Ethics of Growth. Technology Review, 76, 4 (Feb 1974): 10, 83.

Foreword. In: *Creative Tension: The Life and Thought of Kenneth Boulding*, by Cynthia Kerman. Ann Arbor: University of Michigan Press, 1974, pp. 6–8.

Foreword. In: *The Logic of Social Systems*, by Alfred Kuhn. San Francisco: Jossey–Bass, 1974.

Future Education Pattern at MSC. (letter to the editor) *The Denver Post*, Sept 14, 1974, p. 8.

Imagining Failure, Successfully. Technology Review, 76, 7 (June 1974): 8.

Introducing Freshmen to the Social System. (with Elise Boulding) *American Economic Review* (Papers and Proceedings of the 86th Annual Meeting of the American Economic Association, New York, Dec. 28–30, 1973), *64, 2* (May 1974): 414–419.

Kenneth E. Boulding. (interview) In: *On Growth: The Crisis of Exploding Population and Resource Depletion*, Willem L. Oltmans, ed., New York: G.P. Putnam's Sons/Capricorn Books, 1974, pp. 437–441.

The Learning of Peace (presidential address delivered at the International Studies Association Annual Meeting, St. Louis, Mar 20, 1974). *International Studies Notes, 1, 2* (Summer 1974): 1–8.

Plains of Science, Summits of Passion. Technology Review, 77, 2 (Dec 1974): 6.

Pricing in the Energy Crisis. Technology Review, 76, 5 (Mar/Apr 1974): 8.

A Program for Justice Research (Paper presented at the plenary session of the International Peace Research Association Fifth General Conference, Varanasi, India, Jan 3–8, 1974). *Bulletin of Peace Proposals, 5* (1974): 64–72.

The Quality of Life and Economic Affluence. In: *Environmental Spectrum: Social and Economic Views on the Quality of Life*, Ronald O.

Clarke and Peter List, eds., (Papers presented at the Symposium on Economic Growth and the Quality of Life, Oregon State University, Corvallis, May 10–11, 1973). New York: D. Van Nostrand, 1974, pp. 82–95.

Reflections on Planning: The Value of Uncertainty. Technology Review, 77, 1 (Oct/Nov 1974): 8.

The Social System and the Energy Crisis. Science (Special issue on Energy), *184, 4134* (Apr 19, 1974): 255–257.

The Theory of Human Betterment. Technology Review, 76, 8 (July/Aug. 1974): 8, 63.

Universities, University Knowledge, and the Human Future. Lux Mundi (Seoul, Korea), *3, 2* (Feb 1974): 9–12.

What Went Wrong, If Anything, Since Copernicus? (Paper presented at the American Association for the Advancement of Science Symposium on Science, Development and Human Values, Mexico City, (July 2–3, 1973). *Bulletin of the Atomic Scientists, 30, 1* (Jan 1974): 17–23. Also available on tape in the "Speaking of Science," Conversations With Outstanding Scientists series, Vol. III. American Association for the Advancement of Science, 1973.

The World as an Economic Region. In: *Regional Economic Policy; Proceedings of a Conference* (held in Minneapolis, Nov 2, 1973). Minneapolis: Federal Reserve Bank of Minneapolis, June 1974, pp. 27–34.

Book

Kenneth E. Boulding Collected Papers, Vol. IV: *Toward a General Social Science,* Larry D. Singell, ed., Boulder: Colorado Associated University Press, 1974. viii + 623 pp.

Reviews

Review of Daniel Bell, The Coming of Post-Industrial Society, A Venture in Social Forecasting. Journal of Economic Issues, 8, 4 (Dec 1974): 952–953.

Defense Spending: Burden or Boon? Review of Emile Benoit, Defense and Economic Growth in Developing Countries. War/Peace Report, 13, 1 (June 1974): 19–21.

Review of Bernard Brodie, War & Politics. Friends Journal, 20, 3 (Feb 1, 1974): 77–78.

Review of Wilson Clark, Energy For Survival: The Alternative to Extinction. Smithsonian, 5, 7 (Oct 1974): 130.

Review of Alexander Eckstein, ed., Comparison of Economic Systems:

Theoretical and Methodological Approaches. Political Science Quar-terly, 89, 1 (Mar 1974): 236–238.

Minus the Spark. Review of John Kenneth Galbraith, Economics & the Public Purpose. Monthly Labor Review, 97, 10 (Oct 1974): 80–81.

Review of Gene Sharp, The Politics of Non-Violence; and *R. S. Samp-son, The Discovery of Peace. Armed Forces and Society, 1, 1* (Fall 1974): 139–144.

Review of Ben Whitaker, The Philanthropoids: Foundations and Society. The Chronicle of Higher Education, 9, 2 (Sept 30, 1974): 10.

H.   *Index of names*

I. Subject Index

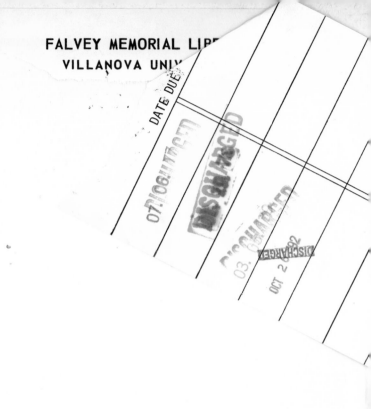